Different and Distinctive but Nevertheless Baptist

A History of Northminster Baptist Church (1967–2017)

MERCER UNIVERSITY

MERCER UNIVERSITY PRESS

Endowed by

TOM WATSON BROWN

and

THE WATSON-BROWN FOUNDATION, INC.

Different and Distinctive but Nevertheless Baptist

A HISTORY OF NORTHMINSTER BAPTIST CHURCH (1967–2017)

C. Douglas Weaver & Aaron Douglas Weaver

MERCER UNIVERSITY PRESS | *Macon, Georgia*
2018

MUP / H957

Published by Mercer University Press
1501 Mercer University Drive
Macon, Georgia 31207

9 8 7 6 5 4 3 2 1

Books published by Mercer University Press are printed on acid-free paper that meets the requirements of the American National Standard for Information Sciences—Permanence of Paper for Printed Library Materials.

Printed and bound in the United States.

This book is set in AdobeCaslon

ISBN 978-0-88146-680-5
Cataloging-in-Publication Data is available from the Library of Congress

To the "Founding Five" and to Northminster's Family of Faith
Past, Present, and Future

The James N. Griffith Series in Baptist Studies

This series on Baptist life and thought explores and investigates Baptist history, offers analyses of Baptist theologies, provides studies in hymnody, and examines the role of Baptists in societies and cultures around the world. The series also includes classics of Baptist literature, letters, diaries, and other writings. For a complete list of titles in the series, visit www.mupress.org and visit the series page.

—C. Douglas Weaver, Series Editor

Contents

Acknowledgments

Local church history is important. What great thinkers have written and what denominational bodies have declared in resolutions and organizational ministries are important, but "lived religion" at the ground level provides a fuller picture of the story of the Christian faith. The story of Northminster Baptist Church, Jackson, Mississippi, is one of those narratives that richly adds to our understanding of how faith has been lived in a particular setting. Northminster has had notable lay involvement and significant pulpit ministry. The congregation has focused on worship within its walls, ecumenical relationships with other churches, and extensive ministry to the local community of Jackson. The story of Northminster is a story worth telling.

A viable local church history depends on the quantity and quality of local church records. Many churches have unrecoverable gaps in their stories because of the absence of good records. Such a dilemma is not the case with Northminster; the congregation has maintained a rich, even remarkable, amount of "primary source" documents. Writing a thorough church history was possible because of the care and attention given to the preservation of the church's material. Indeed, Northminster has a keen sense of appreciation for its fifty-year heritage as a community of faith. Beyond the written material, church members preserved oral interviews from its past, and during the process of writing of this history, volunteered in the collection of additional oral interviews.

Special thanks are due to many people in the process of writing this history. Barbara Webb, the congregation's longtime church clerk, has rightly been honored by the congregation for her stellar work as the one most responsible for preserving Northminster's historical material. Beyond her preservation efforts, Barbara was an email away with answers to questions, large and small. Kelley Williams Sr. was equally important for his role as liaison to our work on Northminster's history. Like Barbara Webb, he was a treasure chest of information, and his interest in recording and sharing the church's legacy was second to none.

Working with Chuck Poole has been a joy, and observing him do ministry makes it easy to see why he has had such a profound positive impact on the identity of Northminster Baptist Church. Other members of the congregation helped us along the way and appreciated our efforts. The congregation's passionate participation in a year-long series of events commemorating their fiftieth anniversary was inspiring.

Many thanks to our families: Pat (Doug's wife), Alexis (Aaron's wife), and Oliver and Miriam (Aaron's children). We wrote this history from Atlanta, Georgia (Aaron), and Waco, Texas (Doug), and shared endless emails, many phone calls and several visits to Jackson throughout the process. Coauthoring a book as a father-son team was an experience we found immensely enjoyable!

We also wish to thank Marc Jolley and Mercer University Press for supporting this project.

Special thanks to Malcolm Foley, PhD student in church history at Baylor University, for assistance in compiling the index.

Doug and Aaron Weaver, Summer 2018

Preface

Church histories are usually written long after the deaths of those who made the history or observed it in the making. The idea of a fifty-year history of Northminster Baptist Church began to germinate in 2011 when the history committee started looking into a project to digitize the church's records and archives. We recognized the treasure-trove of information that Barbara Webb had collected, organized, and preserved as church clerk dating back to Northminster's days as a mission. We thought, "Let's use it to write a fifty-year history while Barbara, who documented it, and many of those who made it are still around."

We were amazed at Barbara's memory and ability to find needles in the haystack. We joked that she was a searchable database with a lifetime warranty. But what to do when the warranty expired? Or, if there were a fire or tornado or other disaster that destroyed the haystack?

The deacons approved our recommendations for projects to digitize the archives, to write a fifty-year history, and to fund both from designated gifts. The historical paper records have been digitized, and other records have been stored offsite in a secure, climate-controlled, and disaster-hardened facility. Northminster's treasure is now in the vault. New records are scanned and added to the database and storage cache.

While Northminster has no members who are church historians, our congregation does have a longtime friend who is—Dr. Walter "Buddy" Shurden, minister at large at Mercer University in Macon, Georgia. Buddy knows Northminster from serving as an occasional guest preacher over the years, and his brother, Bob, served as interim pastor following the tenure of Dudley Wilson. We asked Buddy for advice and here is part of his reply: "Your church's history is important not only to you and your members but to the entire Baptist community. Your church has had a distinctive history, image, and role in Baptist life. You have had some of the most visible Baptist ministers among white Baptists of the South. You deserve and should demand a quality history.

"You should secure a professional historian to write the history. I would recommend that you secure a church historian who knows the story of Baptists in America, especially in the South.

"Your local church history should be interpretive and set within the context of American religion, Mississippi History, and Baptist history. Appendixes could include lists of pastors, deacons, chairs of deacons, presidents of women organizations."

Dr. Shurden offered additional suggestions, including recommendations for authors and a publisher. We thanked him for his help, took his recommendation, and engaged Dr. Doug Weaver and his son, Dr. Aaron Weaver, to write this fifty-year history of our church. We also contracted with Mercer University Press to serve as the publisher.

Doug is professor of religion at Baylor University and author of two local church histories, *Every Town Needs a Downtown Church: A History of First Baptist Church, Gainesville, Florida* (2000) and *Second to None: A History of Second-Ponce de Leon Baptist Church, Atlanta, Georgia* (2004). He is the author of *In Search of the New Testament Church: The Baptist Story* (2008), co-editor of *The Acts of the Apostles: Four Centuries of Baptist Interpretation* (2009), editor of a new edition of E. Y. Mullins's *The Axioms of Religion* (2010), co-editor of *Exploring Christian Heritage: A Reader in History and Theology* (2012), among others. He is currently working on *Baptists and the Holy Spirit* (2018).

Aaron is communications director for the Cooperative Baptist Fellowship in Atlanta, Georgia, where he is the editor of *fellowship!* magazine. A prolific writer and Baptist historian like his father, Aaron received his Ph.D. in religion and politics at Baylor University with a dissertation focused on the environmental views and advocacy of Baptists. Aaron is the author of *James M. Dunn and Soul Freedom* (2011) and editor of *CBF at 25: Stories of the Cooperative Baptist Fellowship* (2016), and *A Baptist Vision of Religious Liberty and Faithful Politics: The Writings of James M. Dunn* (2018).

We asked the Weavers to capture Northminster's distinctive values, norms, beliefs, customs, and missions and ministries that are important to its members and that differentiate it from other Baptist churches. We asked them to place events at Northminster in the context of wider events and issues in the local community, state, and nation as well as the wider communities of Baptists and other faiths.

The Weavers have followed Dr. Shurden's suggestions and met our requests. We are grateful for their efforts, which took more than two years, and the manuscript they produced. The Weavers reviewed our digital and paper archives, listened to recordings, and viewed video interviews with members.

They spoke with more than forty current and former members, pastors, and staff.

Initially, we considered publishing and presenting the book at the fiftieth anniversary celebration on May 7, 2017. We decided to wait, however, to allow for this historic event to be covered by the Weavers too.

During fall 2016, we began preparing for the celebration with a series of Adult Studies programs on Northminster's history, which concluded in April 2017. Programs included the church covenant (Chuck Poole); visual arts (Amy Williams, Gwen Anderson, Jeanne and Steve Cook); music (Richard Joiner); recollections by founders and charter members (John Palmer, Leland Speed, Barbara Webb, Jean Williams, Donna Barksdale); hymns and the liturgical year (Tim Coker); growing up at Northminster (Gray Jackson, Dudley Wooley, Kelley Williams Jr.); lessons from being a deacon (Mike Peters, John Purvis, Stewart Boone); and former pastors' sermons (Suzanne Boone, Mike Peters, Cathy Davis, Tim Coker, Eddie Mahaffey).

Dr. Shurden presented "The Reformation and Northminster—500 and 50" at Northminster's Winter Lecture Series. The theme for the Northminster Winter Women's Retreat was special.

We thank all who prepared us for the celebration and offer special thanks to the celebration committee, whose commitment, planning, and attention to details made it a success: Cheryl Allen, Bill Boone, Tricia Boyd, Kirk Sims, Harry Vickery, and Amy Williams (*ex officio*).

One of the highlights of the celebration was the return of former pastors John Thomason, Roger Paynter, and Brian Brewer (and his wife, Amy, and daughter, Brittany). The panel discussion with the former pastors and Dudley Wilson (who participated via telephone) and the audience interaction afterwards were the highlights of the weekend.

We also thank Dudley for his participation by phone and regret he was not able to be present in person. I am grateful to Dudley for our many phone conversations about Northminster's early days and his 1969 "Crisis at Christmas" sermon, which I presented as one of the Adult Studies sessions.

Thanks also to Emily Benzenhafer and Kay Sullivan for the fiftieth anniversary commemorative stoles they made and Emily presented to the former pastors. Thanks to Anne Guidry and Amy Williams, who were responsible for the bronze plaques featuring the benedictions of all the former pastors, which were highlighted during the panel discussion.

Thanks to Jann Puckett and Gray Jackson for their review and comments on the Weavers' manuscript and to other members of the history committee: Paul Buckley, Anne Guidry, Jo Ann Ratliff, Charlotte Robinson, and Philip Taff.

And finally, a special thanks to Barbara Webb. Dr. Shurden's first question when I asked him about writing Northminster's history was, "What kind of records do you have?" I told him about our archives digitization project and asked Barbara to send him an index and some samples.

Here is his reply:

> As a historian, I am AMAZED and GRATIFIED for the rich, specific, and inspiring nature of these PRIMARY documents. These are treasures, ABSOLUTE TREASURES. You have materials here that most Baptist churches would die for!

Thanks, Barbara, for our wonderful records. Thanks for your responses and participation during this process, the information provided to the Weavers, and your careful review and commentaries. Thank you for your selfless service to Northminster for more than fifty years. You are truly a Servant Leader.

—Kelley Williams Sr.
Chair, History Committee
November 20, 2017

Abbreviations

(used in footnotes)
N Bulletin—church worship service bulletin
N Bylaws—church bylaws documents
N Deacons—deacons' minutes
N History—church-written historical summaries
N Minutes—church business-meeting minutes
N News—church newsletter, *Northminster News*
N Steering Committee Minutes—steering committee formed during Northminster's origins

**All materials cited in the footnotes that relate directly to the history of Northminster Baptist Church (e.g., all of the minutes and documents cited above, brochures, pamphlets, fliers, letters, transcriptions of oral interviews by David Stricklin) are located in the digital archives of the church. The archives are a private church collection owned by the congregation of Northminster Baptist Church. The authors were given complete access to all of the materials and are used by permission in this book. Emails cited are in the possession of the authors.

**Footnotes follow the guidelines of Mercer University Press. Church documents are cited by title and date. Pagination of some of the church documents is not included because of the nature of unpublished material. Several audios cited from fall 2016 to spring 2017 came from the congregation's yearlong celebration of their fiftieth anniversary. The Adult Studies Ministries sponsored the Sunday evening sessions. The audios are also in the church digital archives.

An article titled "New Mission Begins" from the May 11, 1967 edition of the *Baptist Record*, the newspaper of the Mississippi Baptist Convention, highlighted the formation of the Northeast Jackson Baptist Mission and featured its five-member Steering Committee. From left to right: Rubel Phillips, John Palmer, Leland Speed and Bob Guyton. The committee's fifth member, Atley Kitchings, was not present when the photo was taken.

Northminster began in May 1967 as the Northeast Jackson Baptist Mission. It met in the Hinds Baptist Association Building on Lakeland Drive. Five months later, the mission relocated to the vacant Jewish Synagogue on Woodrow Wilson Avenue (pictured). The new church held services at the synagogue, courtesy of the Beth Israel Congregation, until September 1968 when Beth Israel received permission from the Mississippi Supreme Court to lease the land to Standard Oil Company, at which point the old sanctuary was demolished. *Photo Credit: Institute for Southern Jewish Life courtesy of Amy Finkelberg.*

From May to October 1967 retired minister Harvey Whaley served as Interim Pastor of Northeast Jackson Baptist Mission. Whaley was instrumental in establishing an emphasis on reverent, formal worship. He wore a pulpit robe to the congregation's first worship service and introduced the processional and the recessional "as appropriate and orderly ways to begin and conclude a worship service—symbolic of the pilgrimage of people of God through the centuries, singing as they go." Whaley's enduring legacy is seen in the congregation's frequent remembrance of his defining motto: "We agree to differ. We resolve to love. We unite to serve."

Dudley Wilson was the first full-time pastor of Northminster Baptist Church (1967–1975). He helped create a standard of preaching excellence that characterized the congregation's fifty-year history. Wilson developed strong ecumenical ties with the local Jackson community and strengthened the bond with Beth Israel and Rabbi Perry Nussbaum. As a young pastor with a young family, the congregation considered Wilson a good fit for a growing, young church filled with young adults. As Northminster's first pastor, Wilson answered the call to "share with us this venture of faith."

Northminster pastor Dudley Wilson (top left) and eighty Northminster children pictured at the groundbreaking service for the church's permanent home on Ridgewood Road. On October 3, 1971, after worship at the Mississippi School for the Blind, the congregation gathered at its new property for a special service, where Wilson operated a bulldozer and led a litany asking God to "use . . . this structure as an instrument to produce living signs of Thy presence and meaning in the world." Thirty-five years later, thirty-six sons and daughters of the children pictured in this photo celebrated the groundbreaking for Northminster's education building and columbarium.

John Claypool (1977–1981) was a preeminent pulpiteer and prolific writer with a national following (mailing list of 2,000-plus for written and taped sermons). He was considered one of the best, if not the best, Southern Baptist preachers of his era. Claypool led Northminster in its efforts to be a teaching church, and he was an advocate for racial equality and other social concerns throughout his ministry.

The watercolor of Northminster's church building was created by member Thomas Cochran. Tom Biggs, the architect, incorporated ideas from "town hall" meetings with the congregation into his design. Beloved member Roger Stribling Jr. suggested clear windows so that passersby could look in to see what the different kind of Baptists at Northminster were doing and perhaps might be curious enough to join them in worship. The name "Northminster" was also an idea from a 1967 town hall meeting—suggested by member Trenton Shelton. Construction of Northminster's church building was completed in three stages: sanctuary (1973), Great Hall (1988) and balcony addition to the sanctuary (2002).

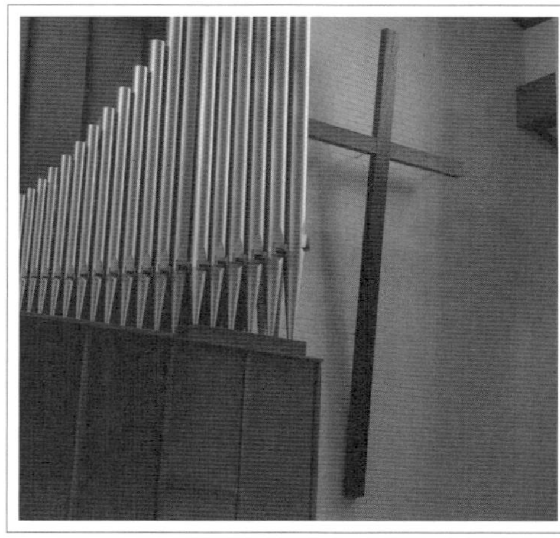

In 1986, Northminster member Steve Cook designed a logo for the church which combined the two most prominent features of the sanctuary: the cross in the chancel (pictured top right) and the transept window (pictured bottom). The logo (pictured top left) was intended to reflect the nature and purpose of Northminster, with the cross serving as a reminder of the congregation's Christ-centered life and the transept window as a symbol of the congregation's openness. This simple but elegant logo is often drawn by children (and some adults, too!).

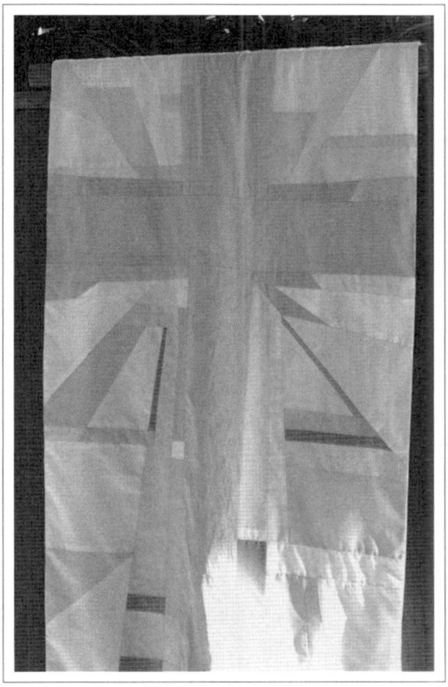

The Easter banner (pictured top left) is one of five processional banners used to signal the beginning of worship. Northminster member Cavett Taff (deceased) created the Easter banner as well as banners for Advent (pictured top right), Christmas and Lent at the request of the Worship Committee. These banners were inspired by various seasonal images on the church's worship bulletins. Northminster members Gwen Anderson and Amy Williams created the church's Pentecost banner (pictured bottom left).

In 1990, Northminster started a new tradition during Holy Week, the "flowering of the cross." A cross draped in black is placed out in front of the church on Maundy Thursday where it remains bare as a reminder of Christ's suffering until Easter morning when families transform it into a symbol of new life, decorating the cross with flowers.

Above, the Lenten Cross was first draped in a purple shroud in 1989 after three years of discussions by the Worship and Music Committee about making the liturgical year more intentional through visual elements. Northminster member Jeanne Cook, who chaired the committee, believed the rich purple wool fabric to be most appropriate for the season. Northminster members Linda and Trenton Shelton donated the hand-crafted cross to the church in 1980.

Below, the Log Cross is placed above the baptismal pool during Lent. This cross was a gift from Northminster member Charles Guest, who designed and built it. On Easter Sunday lilies provided by members surround the cross in memory/honor of loved ones.

Billy Trotter (pictured) served as Northminster's organist for forty years (1977–2017). He was named Organist Emeritus upon his retirement in June 2017. Trotter's signature pieces included "Jesus is Nailed to the Cross" by Dupré and "Toccata" by Widor. Trotter often played the Widor piece as a recessional. Many worshipers would not leave the sanctuary until after he finished and showed their appreciation with applause.

An Allen Organ was installed when the Northminster sanctuary was completed in 1973. The magnificent Austin Pipe Organ was a gift of the Stribling and Puckett families and many other church members in memory of Roger Stribling Jr., who died tragically in an airplane crash in 1975. The initial installation was finished in 1980, and a dedication service was held on March 22, 1981. Pipes to complete the original design were added in 2007 in memory of Mattie Lou Stribling.

Tim Coker conducts the Northminster choir as Billy Trotter plays the organ during worship on March 13, 2016. Since the first service on May 7, 1967, music has been central to the worship-focused identity of Northminster. Coker described the centrality of music during a special service in 2007 to dedicate additions to the organ: "Music at Northminster is selected to reflect the same timeless and permanent quality that characterizes the other elements of the worship service. The choir and organ together lead and encourage the congregation to participate in the act of worship. God calls us to make a joyful noise."

Above, Northminster celebrated a groundbreaking service for its education building and columbarium on April 23, 2006 with a church dinner on the grounds. From left to right: Jim Eley (architect), Stewart Boone, Lucian Harvey (builder), Susan Pratt and Brian Brewer (pastor).

Below, Northminster children pose with pastor Brian Brewer at the groundbreaking service for the education building and columbarium. From left to right: Jonathan Boone, Logan Scott, Zach Watson, Jon-Sanders Watson, Conner Watson, Graham Eklund, Robert Crisler, Rose Daniels, Brittany Brewer, Mary Hannah Smith, Sam Boone, Jake Williams, Clay Wooley, Zach Williams, John Wooley, Davis Bourne, Benjamin Smith and Tori Wilson.

Northminster has enjoyed a vibrant ministry for children since its inception thanks to strong lay leadership. In 1970, Phyllis Eddins directed the church's first summer Vacation Bible School and Jean Williams began the Children's Choir. The portfolio of children's activities has continued to expand over the years.

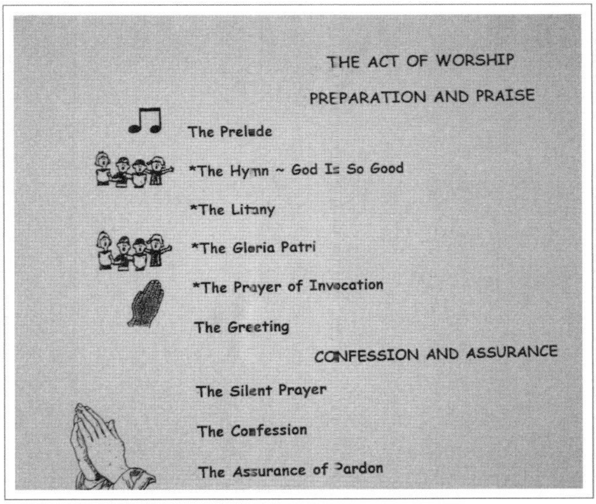

Northminster children participate in "Children's Church" in the church chapel, which was first opened and used on March 31, 1997 thanks to a generous gift from the Lucian Harvey family. The chapel was designed as a place of prayer, worship, reflection and devotion and is also used for families at funerals and brides at weddings. Preschoolers use the chapel as a way of learning what to expect when they begin attending regular worship services with their parents. Prior to its conversion to a chapel, the space was used for office and storage purposes. The Northminster chapel was dedicated during a special litany and prayer of consecration on June 21, 1998

Chuck Poole (1997–2003, 2007-present) is unique among pastors at Northminster because he was the pastor, left to work for a nonprofit ministry, and then returned. Poole encouraged the congregation to engage the local community—the innovative Wider Net initiative is a product of this encouragement and discipleship. Poole is noted for his poetic preaching style in which he focuses on careful speech and compassionate care. His ministry is captured in the words, "Jesus had long arms that reached over walls across hard lines and around weary souls . . . everyone is embraced, welcomed, and received by the long armed love of God."

Above, Northminster began a formal ministry partnership in 1972 with Operation Shoestring, an ecumenical ministry serving low-income families in Jackson and offering a variety of social services. During the summer of 2001 as part of the Wider Net initiative, Northminster members began providing breakfast and devotionals for summer camps in the Mid-City neighborhood at Operation Shoestring.

Below, from 2001-2017, members such as Beverly Lawrence (pictured) have served more than 14,000 breakfasts and led nearly 200 devotionals. The partnership with Operation Shoestring runs deep with Northminster youth serving as summer interns and members leading art classes and tutoring students.

COLTS
21

89

COLTS
46

The Wider Net initiative led to church members forming deep and meaningful relationships with families and children from the Mid-City/Georgetown neighborhood. In 2007, Northminster's Steve Carmody (opposite page, top) and Kelley Williams Jr. (opposite page, middle) coached the Georgetown Colts alongside friends Titus Snell and Kenny Groves from Mt. Wade Baptist Church, an African-American congregation in Georgetown. Abandoned duplexes adjacent to Mt. Wade Baptist were torn down to create a practice field. The Colts played in a Jackson city league at Smith-Wills stadium. For many of the kids, it was their first experience with organized athletics. One player from the 2007 Colts, Jamaal Clayborn, would play collegiate football. Clayborn was a two-year starter for Mississippi State University and earned a degree in Environmental Science.

In 1989, a partnership was birthed between Northminster and Habitat for Humanity to build homes for low-income families. This partnership was taken to a new level in 2000 when the Special Missions Project Committee selected Habitat as a ministry for the new Wider Net initiative in the Mid-City/Georgetown neighborhood. Northminster would fulfill its initial three-year commitment to build six homes and purchase fourteen additional lots. In 2006, the congregation joined alongside other faith communities in support of Habitat's New Neighbor program to build ten houses for families displaced by Hurricane Katrina and Hurricane Rita. To date, Northminster and its interfaith partners have helped build ninety-two Habitat homes, representing a $10 million investment resulting in lower crime, higher home values and a significantly strengthened community.

In 2011, Northminster member Jim Johnston, a recently retired gastroenterologist, went with his Sunday School class (taught by Mary Foose) to see the Habitat houses that the church had helped to build on Wood Street in the Mid-City community. During the visit, Johnson observed the derelict homes and abandoned lots on the other side of the street and was inspired to take on the problem of neighborhood blight. Johnston started Revitalize Mississippi, which cleared and restored 200 abandoned lots in 2016, and he became a vocal advocate for those who reside in the neighborhood to acquire, maintain and build homes on the lots.

Northminster senior pastor Chuck Poole (back center), associate pastor Jill Barnes Buckley (front center) and church member John Palmer Jr. (deceased, back left) pictured with participants of the Wood Street Bible Class. The class began in 2002 for senior adults in the Mid-City neighborhood as part of the Wider Net initiative. Poole led this Thursday morning class at the Mid-City Community Center on Wood Street, also affectionately known as the "Yellow Church." Poole has said that the Bible Study group illustrates the two-way street of need in the transformative relationship between the Northminster congregation and the Mid-City/Georgetown community. Fifteen years later, in 2017, the weekly class continued to meet—praying, thinking, studying, learning and growing together while loving one another.

Northminster ordained member Courtney Allen (left) to the gospel ministry on July 31, 2011 with pastor Chuck Poole (right) leading the service. Allen, a "child of the church," graduated from the School of Divinity at Wake Forest University and in May 2015 was called as senior pastor of Grace Baptist Church in Richmond, Virginia. During its first 50 years, Northminster ordained eight ministers, including six women.

E4

MAY THESE BELLS BECKON US TO WORSHIP,
CALL US TO CELEBRATION,
ENABLE OUR GRIEVING,
AND REMIND US OF THE ETERNAL
IN THE MIDST OF THE TEMPORAL.

✝

IN GRATITUDE FOR
THE COMMUNITY OF FAITH THAT IS
NORTHMINSTER BAPTIST CHURCH
A.D. 1991

A4

BE NOT AFRAID!

Luke 1:30

✝

IF GOD SPEAKS TO YOU IN
THE RINGING OF THE BELLS,
"TAKE OFF YOUR SHOES FOR
THE PLACE ON WHICH YOU
STAND IS HOLY,"

Exodus 3:5

A.D. 1995

G4

TO THE GLORY OF GOD
PATER, FILIUS, SPIRITUS SANCTUS
TRES IN UNUS.

✝

NORTHMINSTER BAPTIST CHURCH
A.D. 1991

C4

THESE BELLS GIVEN BY
MR. AND MRS. LUCIAN A. HARVEY, JR.
IN HONOR OF THEIR PARENTS WHO GAVE THEM LIFE,
THEIR CHILDREN WHO GIVE THEM LIFE AND
THEIR GRANDCHILDREN WHO ADD JOY TO LIFE.

✝

NORTHMINSTER BAPTIST CHURCH
A.D. 1991

F4

LOVE MAKES US ONE.

Phil. 2:2

✝

BY THE GOODNESS OF GOD
YOU WERE BORN INTO THIS WORLD;
BY THE GRACE OF GOD
YOU HAVE BEEN KEPT
ALL THE DAY LONG,
EVEN UNTIL THIS HOUR.

JRC IV

A.D. 1995

NORTHMINSTER BAPTIST CHURCH

In 1990, Northminster received a generous donation from the Lucian Harvey family for the purpose of purchasing and installing three cast bells for the church's bell tower. The three bells—C4, E4, and G4 made by Paccard in France and appropriate for ringing as a call to worship, marriages, funerals and times of celebration—were selected by a special committee and installed. "May these bells beckon us to worship, call us to celebration, enable our grieving and remind us of the eternal in the midst of the temporal," the inscription on Bell E4 reads. The inscribed bells were dedicated on May 12, 1991. Three years later, Northminster accepted another generous gift from the Lucian Harvey family to commission and install two more bells for the church's carillon, completing the ensemble.

Three of Northminster's former pastors were able to attend the congregation's 50th anniversary celebration, May 5–7, 2017. The former pastors were given special stoles for their pulpit robes as they helped lead in Sunday worship. After leaving the pastorate at Northminster, each beloved pastor continued a fruitful ministerial career. From left to right: Brian Brewer (2005–2007) departed Northminster to teach historical theology at G. W. Truett Theological Seminary at Baylor University in Waco, Texas. Roger Paynter (1989–1996) left to serve as senior minister of First Baptist Church in Austin, Texas, from 1996 until his retirement in 2014. John Thomason (1983–1989) ministered in several Methodist parishes, most recently at Woodbury United Methodist Church in Woodbury, Connecticut. *Photos from 50th anniversary celebration courtesy of Christina Boteler.*

To begin the 50th anniversary weekend, a panel discussion featuring former pastors was held Saturday afternoon on May 6, 2017 in the Northminster sanctuary. Kelley Williams Sr. (right) moderated the conversation with former pastors John Thomason (left), Roger Paynter (center), Brian Brewer (second from right) and Dudley Wilson (participated via phone - not pictured).

Bob Guyton (left) and his wife Kathy (right) are welcomed by Suzanne Boone (center) during the anniversary weekend's conversation with living former pastors. Guyton, one of the "Founding Five," was chair of the Steering Committee of the Northeast Jackson Baptist Mission.

Following the 50th anniversary worship service, the Northminster congregation enjoyed dinner on the grounds and a time of remembrance in the Great Hall where an open microphone allowed former and current members to share what Northminster meant to them.

During the time of remembrance, John Thomason (pictured) and other former pastors shared memories as did several charter members who were in attendance—including John Palmer and Leland Speed.

Above, the 50th anniversary celebration was a time of fun and fellowship for the Northminster family. Pictured from left to right Marty Hitt Kelly, Becky Starling, Cathy Davis, Roger Paynter (former pastor), and Annette Hitt.

Below, Northminster pastor Chuck Poole (left) shares a laugh with former pastor Brian Brewer and family.

James and Rosie Jefferson (pictured center) smile alongside the security, catering and custodial staff at the 50th anniversary celebration. The Jeffersons received a rousing round of applause during the banquet for their dedicated service to Northminster over the past 35 years.

Chapter 1

Beginnings
"Well, are we gonna just keep talking or we gonna do something?"[1]

The traditional narrative of the founding of Northminster Baptist Church recalls a "happenstance meeting" on a downtown street corner—Amite and Lamar streets—in Jackson, Mississippi in 1966. Leland Speed, John Palmer, and Bob Guyton, all members of First Baptist Church in downtown Jackson, found themselves on the street corner in conversation about starting a new Baptist church in northeast Jackson. Rubel Phillips joined them. They had discussed the possibility of a new Baptist congregation at various times before, but this time, a decision was made to really investigate the possibility.

In later reflections, Leland Speed said the "happenstance" meeting was a regular occurence. A typical day for the young business professionals often included a 10:00 A.M. coffee break at a little café called Doctor Gus'. Discussion—or complaining about their experiences at First Baptist Church—did occur, and then continued on the street as they returned to work. Standing outside the entrance to their building (Deposit Guaranty Bank), Bob Guyton said, "Well, are we gonna just keep talking or we gonna do something?" "The decision was made right there," Speed recalled. A meeting was held the next day at Guyton's office with Atley Kitchings joining them. So began the "founding fathers" of Northminster Baptist Church.[2]

"Fathers" does not denote seasoned veterans of church life; they were a youthful group, with the oldest being just forty-one. Bob Guyton was the leader among friends, and his aggressive "front-wheel drive" leadership style made things happen. According to Rubel Phillips, Guyton "pulled us until we were over-worked and then he thought of another project."[3] The group relied on Speed's father, Leland "Pappy" Speed, who was mayor of Jackson

[1] From Founding Five to Northeast Jackson Baptist Mission

[2] Leland Speed, interview by Aaron Weaver, February 23, 2016, 2.

[3] Rubel Phillips, "Reflections on Northeast Jackson Baptist Mission," (n.d.).

in the 1940s, for wise counsel and financial assistance in the early days. The founding fathers planning a church is certainly filled with the watchful eyes of young, educated business professionals—movers and shakers, no doubt. At the same time, Bob Guyton later reflected, they recognized their dream was a daunting task, but believed "it was done because it was God's will and we were carrying out God's will."[4]

Decisions from this initial organizational meeting proved visionary and revealed the group's intentions. The five men affirmed that it was their "desire for more personal involvement" in church life. They were committed to staying Baptist but wanted something unique, or as Phillips recalled, "distinctive, but orthodox; different, but nevertheless Baptist."[5] A meeting was held with Fred Tarpley, the director of missions of the Hinds County Baptist Association, who supported the creation of a mission. Then, a meeting of ten people was held January 19, 1967—the first specific date available in church records regarding the church's origins—at the Allstate Insurance Company. The small group voted to continue pursuing the possibility of a mission and elected the "founding" group of five—Guyton, Speed, Palmer, Kitchings, and Phillips—as a Steering Committee with Guyton as chair of the group.[6]

The Steering Committee had an informational meeting on January 31, 1967, about the possibility of forming a new Baptist mission. A week earlier they had circulated a handout—developed with the assistance of Fred Tarpley of the association—of general information about the possible formation of a Baptist mission in Northeast Jackson. The area between Eastover and Northside Drive did not have a Baptist church. Demographics revealed that in the next five years Northeast Jackson would grow from 1,840 residences (7,500 people) to 2,400 residences (9,600 people). Around 40 percent of the residents were estimated to be active or inactive Baptists.

---

[4] Bob Guyton, "Northminster Celebration" (Northminster Baptist Church 25th celebration, May 16, 1992).

[5] "Northminster Baptist Church: The Beginning—1967," (n.d.); Phillips, "Reflections on Northeast Jackson Baptist Mission."

[6] Phillips, "Reflections on Northeast Jackson Baptist Mission." Phillips recalled several families involved in these early meetings beyond the Steering Committee. They included Homer and Jane Best, Ross and Betty Bass, Byron and Jamie Speed, John and Dot Kitchings, Jaime and Mary Ann Miller, and Eddie and Maxine Guillot.

Other denominations were filling the gap, and some Baptists, particularly younger ones, were leaving the fold, according to the flier. The conclusion was clear: Northeast Jackson was ripe for a new Baptist church.[7]

The informational session highlighted the reasons that a new mission was justified: opportunities for active participation and leadership, new approaches to religious training (couples' classes rather than all-male or all-female classes), and association with a "young, dynamic, aggressive, progressive congregation." And, certainly for those Baptists attending churches farther away like First Baptist in downtown Jackson, an opportunity to attend church closer to home and for children to be in Sunday school with those in their neighborhood was a goal.[8]

Ten families made a commitment to a mission at the January 31 meeting—the number that Tarpley said they needed to move forward. Planning thus continued with other meetings. Barbara Webb remembers attending an information session. Webb related that she had not gone to church from the age of sixteen to thirty-two, having had bad experiences with churches obsessed with success by numbers. She and her husband liked what they heard about the vision for a new church at the meeting—the emphasis on numbers was missing and the importance of reverent worship was highlighted. They committed and became part of the charter group of families.[9]

In addition to a second informational meeting, the Steering Committee continued to seek cooperation with other Baptists in the area and visited pastors to solicit understanding and support. The committee knew that to be accepted by other Baptists in Jackson they needed the cooperation, even the sponsorship of local Baptists such as Broadmoor Baptist Church and Woodland Hills Baptist Church as well as the Hinds County Baptist Association. Members of the Steering Committee met with pastors of Broadmoor and Woodland Hills and the Missions Committee of the association to solicit support and gave their assurance of commitment to Scripture and to Baptist practices.

---

[7] N Steering Committee Minutes 1 24 67; N History 5 3 87.

[8] N Steering Committee Minutes 1 31 67, which includes the document "Informational Meeting."

[9] Anne Guidry and Amy Williams, *Echoes of Grace: Northminster Baptist Church PrimeTimers Devotion Book* (Jackson, MS: Northminster Baptist Church, 2015) 98.

The goal was to get thirty families and receive approval from the missions committee of the association to move forward with its formation. Success came quickly, and on February 28, 1967, the Hinds County Baptist Association, following the lead of Tarpley's indispensable support, gave approval of mission status for the thirty-four families who had made the pledge. Having reached this stage of affirmation, the steering committee created several committees to help develop an organization. For example, John Palmer led the finance work, Leland Speed led the site committee, and Atley Kitchings chaired an organization committee that worked to create a Sunday school.[10]

The Steering Committee knew that they especially needed the affirmation and cooperation of their own home church, First Baptist Church, Jackson. Early in the organizational process, the steering committee met with Douglas Hudgins, pastor of First Baptist Church. Hudgins was a powerhouse in Mississippi Baptist life and was known in the larger work of the Southern Baptist Convention.[11] In his reflections about the church's origins, Rubel Phillips suggested that Hudgins had significant misgivings that at least five of his younger families were making plans to leave First Baptist Church. By their own admission, the group of young Baptists had not been as involved as they might have been at First Baptist. One of their motivations—to have more opportunities for leadership—implied that the younger Baptists at First Baptist were frustrated at having to "pay their dues" before substantive leadership opportunities were forthcoming at the highly structured "establishment" downtown "first" church. As Bob Guyton later reflected, "It was a time of change...young men and women, together, were impatient for advancement and leadership, yet couldn't get through the old guards in too many institutions."[12] Other later reflections of the founding story paraphrased the motivation as a part of the congregation's commit-

---

[10] N Steering Committee Minutes 1 31 67, "Informational Meeting"; "Northminster Baptist Church: The Beginning—1967"; N History 3 15 67; Phillips, "Reflections on Northeast Jackson Baptist Mission".

[11] Richard Aubrey McLemore and Nannie Pitts McLemore, *The History of First Baptist Church of Jackson, Mississippi* (Jackson, MS: Hederman Brothers, 1976) 281. Hudgins was president of the Mississippi Baptist Convention in 1961; in 1969, he resigned from First Baptist Church, Jackson, to become executive director of the Mississippi Baptist Convention.

[12] Guyton, "Northminster Celebration".

ment to more comprehensive lay renewal and lay leadership: "Well, where we have been, we were not able to be in leadership, and we never knew what was going on.... By the time we knew about it, the action had been taken."[13]

Another potential problem was that these young Baptists were talking of forming a "progressive" church of some sort. It is no surprise, then, that Hudgins questioned the Steering Committee about their doctrinal commitments. First Baptist Church wanted to know if the mission would be dedicated to "New Testament Baptist doctrine" and to "uncompromising Baptist doctrine."[14] Most of the founders had never been questioned so directly about their beliefs, and Guyton remembered that he was "scared to death" being confronted by the "very powerful" demeanor of Hudgins. Rubel Phillips came to the rescue, however. Called the one "member of the establishment by virtue of the fact that he was a deacon" of First Baptist (who had already run for governor in the state of Mississippi), Phillips immediately answered Hudgins, "Yes, sir. I believe in all of that and I'm sure my associates do also."[15] Hudgins thus gave his approval, and in April 1967, First Baptist Church approved a recommendation to co-sponsor the mission congregation.[16]

Early records do not refer to the congregation defining itself as "progressive" or as a "different" church in terms of openness to all races. Early members and attendees were white; it was Jackson in the 1960s. But the context of race certainly was a reason that some were attracted to the new mission. Douglas Hudgins, pastor of First Baptist Church—dubbed "the single most powerful religious institution in Mississippi during the civil rights years,"[17]—attempted for the most part to be apolitical and focus on personal faith rather than applying the gospel to social issues. He thought the gospel message was distracted when directed away from concerns of individual salvation, and issues of civil rights were, he contended, not religious matters. However, Hudgins had opposed—like most white Mississippians—the groundbreaking 1954 Supreme Court decision, *Brown v. Board of Edu-*

[13] Mary Hendrick, interview by David Stricklin, March 1, 1992, 6.

[14] N History 3 15 67; Statement of First Baptist Church, Jackson.

[15] Ibid.

[16] N History 3 15 67; Phillips, "Reflections on Northeast Jackson Baptist Mission."

[17] Charles Marsh, *God's Long Summer: Stories of Faith and Civil Rights* (Princeton, NJ: Princeton University Press, 1997) 89.

cation, which mandated desegregation and outlawed "separate but equal" public facilities.[18] In the 1960s, Hudgins's resistance to making civil rights a gospel issue resulted in his refusal to speak out against violence toward civil rights workers and African Americans, but the fact that his congregation was home to highly influential segregationists like Governor Ross Barnett and other prominent figures like the Hedermans, owners of the Jackson newspaper, *The Clarion-Ledger*, a strong critic of civil rights, was surely another factor that contributed to an atmosphere of silence.[19] In 1963, the year after the forced desegregation of the University of Mississippi with the admission of James Meredith, Hudgins and First Baptist Church resisted a visit of students from the African-American institution Tougaloo College. First Baptist Church passed a policy to prohibit African Americans from worshiping at the church.[20]

While attitudes about civil rights issues varied widely among the original members of Northminster, apparently one reason for the dissatisfaction with First Baptist Church was that church's decision to exclude African Americans from its worship services.[21] Several charter members of North-

---

[18] Randall Balmer, *Encyclopedia of Evangelicalism* (Waco, TX: Baylor University Press, 2004) 346; Marsh, *God's Long Summer*, 99–112; John Dittmer, *Local People: The Struggle for Civil Rights in Mississippi* (Chicago: University of Illinois Press, 1994) 62–63.

[19] Randy J. Sparks, *Religion in Mississippi* (Jackson: University Press of Mississippi for the Mississippi Historical Society, 2001) 229. Sparks noted that the Hederman family supported the white supremacist Citizens' Council and gave it media access. The Citizens' Council pressured white ministers who supported civil rights (Marsh, *God's Long Summer*, 89–90). Theologian Charles Marsh's view of Hudgins's ministry in the context of race is blunt: "Douglas Hudgins was the premier theologian of the closed society. He articulated in his sermons, Bible studies, and occasional writings, and embodied in his church leadership, an austere piety that remained impervious to the sufferings of black people, as well as to the repressive tactics of the guardians of (racial) orthodoxy, many of whom were lodged in his own congregation."

[20] Marsh, *God's Long Summer*, 100–101; McLemore and McLemore, *The History of First Baptist Church of Jackson, Mississippi*, 262.

[21] McLemore and McLemore, *The History of First Baptist Church of Jackson, Mississippi*, 296. In 1973, First Baptist said it re-affirmed its commitment to having people from all races worship at the church—excluding "any persons or organized groups who come for the purpose of demonstrating, who seek to disrupt, or who seek publicity," 296. In this 1973 declaration, First Baptist Church gave a similar

minster recalled that they wanted a church that was open to anyone who wanted to attend. They did not want to have their children worship in an environment where exclusion characterized worship.[22] Donna Sones (Barksdale) was a part of a group of Mississippi College students who started attending the church because they wanted to find a more inclusive place on racial issues—and still be Baptist.[23] Ruby Bradley was another young woman who came to the church in its early days because of its call for open dialogue regarding race. Jim and Mary Hendrick also came to Northminster because of racial segregation at their local Baptist church.[24] The mission was certainly not formed because of civil rights—some church members opposed the massive changes of the 1960s—but openness in Northminster's original DNA pointed in the direction of open dialogue rather than exclusion.

The Interim Period of Harvey Whaley

The congregation's first weekend of activity was Friday through Sunday, May 5–7, 1967. On Friday and Saturday evenings, worship workshops were held with the first worship service on Sunday morning at the Hinds County Baptist Association chapel on Lakeland Drive. Karen Gilfoy was the choir director and Jonathan Sweat the organist. Hymn books, a pulpit, pulpit chairs, a communion table, and offering plates were given by First Baptist Church.[25] Eighty-one people attended Sunday school with eighty-six in worship; an offering of $600 was collected. According to Sweat, the electronic organ was so tiny he could barely play it—wrong notes and a professional musician did not mix![26]

Dr. Harvey T. Whaley was the workshop leader and guest preacher. Whaley brought experience to the young band of Baptists. He had pastored

---

justification as they did for their 1963 decision—people at that time "sought to use this church for purposes other than worship." See p. 309–311.

[22] Speed, interview, 4.

[23] As a single college student, her name was Donna Kennedy (Donna Sones, interview by David Stricklin, February 29, 1992, 2, 4; Rubel Phillips, interview by David Stricklin, March 1, 1992, 7). Phillips said that a commitment to an open church was a consensus from the outset (Elizabeth Dean, interview by David Stricklin, February 29, 1992, 3).

[24] Hendrick, interview, 2–5.

[25] Phillips, interview, 5; N Bulletin 5 7 67.

[26] Jonathan Sweat, interview by David Stricklin, February 29, 1992, 3.

Southern Baptist churches in New Orleans; Beaumont, Texas; and Raleigh, North Carolina, and was in May 1967 semi-retired but serving as the interim pastor at Northbridge Baptist Church in Charleston, South Carolina.[27] Charter members John and Dot Kitchings had been members of the progressive St. Charles Avenue Baptist Church, New Orleans, where Whaley had pastored. Bob Guyton thought Whaley, who was more than seventy years old, had "the youngest and brightest spiritual mind of anyone I've ever seen."[28]

Whaley left a formative imprint on the fledging congregation when he led a reverent, liturgically oriented worship hour that stood (intentionally, no doubt) in stark contrast to a more typical Southern Baptist worship service. Attendees were asked in the bulletin to bow in prayer as they entered the "sanctuary." The service began with a processional of choir and pastor to the front of the sanctuary. An American flag and Christian flag were brought into the little chapel and placed at the front by youth—more typical Baptist elements at the time. A focus on praise and adoration, which included a responsive reading, was followed by a shift to confession and intercession. Silent meditation and a congregational recitation of the Lord's Prayer were practiced. Formal hymns, as opposed to old-fashioned revivalistic gospel tunes, were sung during the service, and in subsequent bulletins a "great hymn" would be featured with a description of its theological meaning.[29]

The worship hour, in good Baptist and Protestant fashion, featured a sermon. After the sermon, a recessional hymn was sung rather than a traditional evangelistic invitation hymn. The bulletin invited worshipers to sign a charter membership book at the entrance of the sanctuary right after the service (and throughout that first summer, a member of the Membership Committee was available after the service to answer questions about joining the congregation).[30] The worship service was very different from what many were used to, but they liked its sense of reverence. Dudley Wilson, the church's first permanent pastor, and subsequent pastors, later maintained the basic structure of worship. No doubt, however, that some were still

[27] N News 4 21 67; Phillips, "Reflections on Northeast Jackson Baptist Mission."

[28] Guyton, "Northminster Celebration."

[29] N Bulletin 9 3 67.

[30] N Bulletin 5 7 67; N Bulletin 8 27 67.

grappling to take it all in that first Sunday, as one observer later quipped, "The first service was really kind of, 'Okay, what's coming next, incense?'"[31]

Whaley also led the first worship service in his clerical-academic robe. The robe caught everyone's eye, even though he had told the Steering Committee beforehand that he was going to wear it. The Steering Committee actually discussed Whaley's robe in its meeting after the first worship service. They liked it and declared that they wanted to continue the practice in subsequent worship services—which Whaley did.[32] Whaley's use of the robe (and the other more liturgical elements) sent a message to the congregation about the seriousness of the worship experience and its new non-traditional possibilities for a group of Southern Baptists. As Whaley suggested, the "spirit of worship seeks to recover the riches of the historical Christian church."[33] Later reflections also asserted that the liturgical innovations were part of a desire to reclaim the focus on lay participation in the worship service instead of the more typical practice of "spectatorship."[34]

Church members were also struck by the motto gleaned from Whaley's first sermon and subsequently owned it as their own self-defining confession: "If we could not agree to differ, we have no freedom. If we do not resolve to love, we have no Christianity. If we do not unite to serve, the Kingdom of God and the world suffer."[35] Or put succinctly, "We agree to differ. We resolve to love. We unite to serve."[36] With exhortations about the priority of reverent worship from both Harvey Whaley and then L. D. Johnson later that summer and fall, one of Northminster's defining characteristics was being molded from the outset of the church's history.

The emerging mission made additional organizational decisions during these first days. All male members were asked to serve as ushers. An initial fundraising drive netted $2,500. During its second week (the second week of May 1967), the mission was officially named Northeast Jackson Baptist

---

[31] Speed, interview, 8.

[32] N Steering Committee Minutes 5 8 67; Kelley Williams Sr., interview by David Stricklin, February 29, 1992, 5.

[33] N Bulletin 10 15 67.

[34] N History 5 1 77.

[35] Jan Purvis, "Reflections on Becoming Church," (February 24, 1991).

[36] N Bulletin 7 9 67; N Bulletin 10 22 67; J. Kelley Williams Sr., "Northminster History: Traditions, Norms, Values, and Stones," (February 13, 2005); "Northminster Baptist Church: The Beginning—1967."

Mission. The Steering Committee thought it best to postpone any decision about a permanent name until they knew where they would be located. Leaving no stone unturned to be cooperative and do things with proper business-like protocol, the Steering Committee also met with the association's Executive Committee to review the details of the first week and to provide other updates. Whaley was also immediately named interim pastor—though the church remarkably was already looking for a full-time pastor—and he began the interim on July 2, 1967.[37] That Sunday, the congregation's worship included a celebration of American independence with a responsive "liturgy for Americans."[38]

Attendance during the beginning months averaged about eighty. In August 1967, seventy-six people made up the membership. Despite business-like planning, growing pains were evident on occasion. The service of June 6, for example, spurred the Steering Committee—which was meeting every Monday to discuss the prior day's worship—to examine details like making sure bulletins were available prior to the worship hour and developing more effective ways of recognizing and welcoming visitors.[39] One of the most significant aspects of the early years was the Monday evening discussion groups where participants discussed their dreams for the new mission. Whaley assisted reflection about theological identity. The meetings were lauded for their focus on the congregation's foundational commitment to lay participation. "We are a people's church," was an early and consistent refrain.[40]

Sunday school was another area of intentional focus on lay participation, and in some novel ways. In the early days, classes were not structured in typical Southern Baptist fashion—no "graded" classes according to age and gender were created—another element of the "different" way that the congregation developed its identity.[41] Barbara Webb recalled that she went to the Baptist bookstore to look at curriculum materials, but kept telling the

---

[37] N Deacons 5 1 67; N Steering Committee Minutes 5 8 67; N Steering Committee Minutes 5 12 67.

[38] N Bulletin 8 2 67.

[39] N News 6 7 67; N News 8 7 67; N Steering Committee Minutes 6 5 67; Guyton, "Northminster Celebration."

[40] Dean, interview, 5; Jan Purvis, interview by David Stricklin, February 29, 1992, 3; Hendrick, interview, 6.

[41] Jann Puckett, interview by Aaron Weaver, February 22, 2016, 3.

store employee that her group was not interested in the materials she was being shown. The clerk asked, "Are you sure this is a Baptist church?"[42] Webb ended up with educational materials from five different denominations, a sure sign of the fledgling congregation's distinctive spirit.

Sunday school attendees also had never attended co-ed Sunday school classes before and found the experience a broadening of their Christian pilgrimage. In addition, the classes were also arenas of sometimes intense participation. Jean Williams recalled that everyone in the class engaged in discussion and the conversation was serious and deep: "Most of the people were raising questions and saying things that I was shocked that they would say in a Sunday school class, in a formal setting like that.... I had never been in a situation that I felt like people were free to say what they really thought and to question theology. It was done and it was accepted and people learned from it."[43]

Church records in the early days indicate financial commitment was forthcoming—the $600 raised at the first service and the $2,500 initial fundraising drive. Founding members knew they needed significant financial commitments, and those who were business professionals with some means knew this meant giving more than they had in their previous church involvement. According to Bob Guyton, the Steering Committee developed an ambitious agenda; that is, they took the small list of involved families and assigned a specific amount to ask from each. Guyton commented, "One of the members who was known for being conservative and tight with his money was absolutely shocked at the amount we asked him for—but he gave it—and so did every other member of our church."[44]

Staff

The staff of the mission—volunteer and paid—began to take shape quickly. The first week of May, Barbara Webb was named church secretary and amazingly was still keeping church records in 2017. Karen Gilfoy served as choir director at the mission's first service and then volunteered as director of music, but by September 1967, the church voted to pay her for her

[42] Barbara Webb, cited in Adult Studies Evening Sessions audio, "Laying the Foundation (Charter Members)," March 26, 2017.

[43] Jean Williams, interview by David Stricklin, February 29, 1992, 4.

[44] Guyton, "Northminster Celebration."

work. Nevertheless, Gilfoy resigned because of the demands of school, and Lester Reeves, chair of music at Hinds Junior College, succeeded her. In late May, James Furlow, a member of the music faculty of Hinds Junior College, was offered the position of organist ($35 a week) after Jonathan Sweat played the first two weeks before leaving for Michigan for school (Sweat was to be given the option of becoming the organist when he returned to Jackson that fall, but Furlow became permanent).[45]

Search for a Site

Worshiping in the little chapel of the Hinds County Baptist Association was no doubt cramped quarters for worshipers used to larger, well-appointed facilities. Nevertheless, the original site brought warm memories in later years of a developing communal identity. Jane Best's gratitude was exuberant; she said that she had two special places of worship in her Christian pilgrimage: the National Cathedral in Washington, D.C., and the little chapel on Lakeland Drive.[46]

Still, the Site Committee worked tirelessly to find temporary facilities for worship and a place for a permanent home. They were already looking for a permanent site in May, the mission's birth month, while acknowledging that they would need increased membership and significant budget pledges to move forward. John Palmer told the Steering Committee that the congregation had budget pledges of $24,000 but would need $60,000 before a building program should be initiated.[47] Limitations did not stop mission leaders from dreaming, however. In June, while on Pulpit Committee business, Atley Kitchings and Rubel Phillips visited with the staff of Mountain Brook Baptist Church, located in a wealthy section of Birmingham, Alabama. They saw the church as a model for their future church—about 1,000 to 1,500 members, which started with a chapel and Sunday school rooms, then an education building, before building a beautiful sanctuary.[48]

---

[45] N Steering Committee Minutes 5 29 67; N Steering Committee Minutes 8 25 67; N Steering Committee Minutes 9 11 67; N Steering Committee Minutes 9 25 67; N Bulletin 9 24 67.

[46] Jane Best, interview by David Stricklin, February 29, 1992, 3.

[47] N Steering Committee Minutes 5 29 67; N Steering Committee Minutes 6 5 67; N News 6 7 67. The new Beth Temple Israel was built on Old Canton Road.

[48] N Steering Committee Minutes 6 5 67.

While appreciative of the space provided for worship by the association, the Site Committee began looking immediately for different facilities. Both Millsaps College and Belhaven College were discussed in an early June meeting. By September, other sites were being considered: St. Andrew's Day School, Millsaps Christian Center, and the vacant Jewish Synagogue on Woodrow Wilson. Beth Israel was their choice, and the mission moved into the old Jewish worship center with its first service at this site on October 22, 1967.[49]

The move to the old synagogue revealed the talents of the young business professionals. Leland Speed, chair of the Site Committee, knew a member of the Jewish congregation, Maurice Joseph, who was also in the real estate business and was marketing the property. In the wheeling and dealing for the site, Joseph graciously offered the property rent free, rebuffing Speed's offer of rent. Joseph, however, said that he would need a thirty days' notice if he needed the property vacated. Speed remembered that he told his friend, "Maurice, there ain't no way we can get out in thirty days, come on now, get real," and was able to extend the thirty days' notice up to ninety days.[50] After several months of feeling displaced, the Northeast Jackson Baptist Mission had its first real sense of having a stable home at Beth Israel.[51]

At least for a while, some early participants questioned whether they should even have a permanent church building. Kelley Williams Sr. remembered that he traveled to Houston, Texas, and met with members of a church there that intentionally had no building. Given the definition of church centered on people—the body of Christ—rather than being a building, the congregation raised the question, "Should financial resources be put into significant construction or be used for ministry purposes?"[52]

Nevertheless, the push toward a permanent site for the congregation developed rapidly. Planning involved negotiations with various businesses and homeowners during summer 1967. Extensive discussions with Pop Primos, a Greek restaurateur, for five acres at the corner of Ridgewood

---

[49] Ibid.; N Steering Committee Minutes 9 11 67; N Steering Committee Minutes 10 6 67.

[50] Speed, interview, 4.

[51] "Northminster Baptist Church: The Beginning—1967."

[52] Williams, interview, 6.

Road and Meadowbrook Road failed and was a real disappointment because he had initially agreed to sell.[53] Property on Lakeland Drive was considered before the committee shifted focus to property on Eastover Drive and Ridgewood Road, which eventually became the congregation's permanent location. Two homes needed to be purchased, however. The committee was excited at its meeting in late August 1967 when it was reported a Dr. Snyder was willing to sell—thus making the prized property available.[54]

The Influence of L. D. Johnson

Historical reflections since the congregation's formation all highlight the pivotal, profound importance of reading and interacting with L. D. Johnson, chaplain of Furman University (South Carolina), in the early development of the church's identity. Beginning on July 17, 1967, a Monday evening discussion group began meeting regularly. Its first topic—which turned out to be an eight-week study—was an examination of Johnson's forty-nine-page essay, "Southern Baptists in the Seventies," where he evaluated the current state of Southern Baptist ministry and made prognostications about the future and ways to address various issues. Then, at the urging of the study group, Johnson visited the church on Saturday, September 16, to discuss his paper and preach the next day.[55]

The document certainly exhibited several progressive features and ministry concepts that actually developed in the church's life. For example, Johnson noted that ecumenism was growing, and denominational colleges would experience crisis. Theological education must be open and forward-looking. He touted historical-critical reading of Scripture: "Insistence upon the literal meaning of all of the Bible is no longer a tenable position among people who are educated."[56] Tracking social trends, Johnson said secularism

[53] N Steering Committee Minutes 6 27 67; N Steering Committee Minutes 7 5 67. Leland Speed said the failed sale with Pop Primos was a "real kick in the stomach" (Speed, interview, 6).

[54] N Steering Committee Minutes 7 5 67; N Steering Committee Minutes 8 7 67; N Steering Committee Minutes 8 25 67; N Steering Committee Minutes 9 29 67.

[55] N Bulletin 7 16 67; N News 7 20 67; N News 9 12 67; N Bulletin 9 17 67; "Northminster Baptist Church: The Beginning—1967."

[56] L. D. Johnson, "Southern Baptists in the Seventies" (Northminster Baptist Church, 1967) 24.

would increase and metropolitan areas would continue to explode in population. In words common decades later, Johnson said that "the world of the 70s will be more than it is today a post-Christian world."[57]

Johnson told the youthful charter members of the mission that they were among the group he believed most responsible for providing leadership in the Southern Baptist Convention in the next decade. He suggested several ways they could help remake the SBC, which included more ecumenical openness as Southern Baptists seemed "afraid to hear what other people have to say." He advocated a re-examination of current success symbols for the life of faith, a commitment to a "converted church membership," and church renewal through intensive Bible study in small lay-led groups in order to make "Bible study the serious business of the church."[58] Johnson further declared that the church must have a social mission (race was included in his remarks, but not emphasized) and must give priority to the enrichment of worship. Authentic worship was characterized by corporate worship with a vertical focus directed to God. Hymns, for example, needed to cease being subjectively oriented with attention on the singer and be re-oriented with attention toward the divine.[59]

It is no wonder that Johnson's role in the church's formation has been highlighted. His "state of the church" address reads like a blueprint for much of the congregation's emerging identity, especially the focus on lay leadership, an active membership, the priority of corporate worship that still paid attention to social concerns, and ecumenical openness. Charter members point to Johnson's influence regarding its progressive open baptismal policy that would be formulated later—though the document does not deal with "open baptism" specifically. His ideas certainly resonated with some of the early goals of church members. He provided direction and influenced significantly the articulation and crafting of an identity about what it could mean to be Southern Baptist yet different; traditional, but progressive and cutting edge.[60]

---

[57] Ibid., 23.

[58] Ibid., 29, 39.

[59] Ibid., 42.

[60] Purvis, "Reflections on Becoming Church"; Williams, "Northminster History"; Speed, interview, 5; "Northminster Baptist Church: The Beginning—1967."

Search for a Pastor

The young congregation wasted no time in organizing a Pulpit Committee, chaired by Rubel Phillips, and giving concentrated attention to bringing in a full-time pastor as soon as possible. Before May had passed to June 1967, the committee had already made some visits to prospective pastors, and they were determined to consider only "top quality candidates."[61] The process was a bit harder and longer than they (unrealistically) hoped as they admitted that they had a "tough assignment," and some members were already "saddle weary" from traveling. In addition, the Steering Committee believed that they had to present an attractive financial package to attract a top-flight pastor. In June, for example, the committee visited Dr. Lamar Jackson and Dudley Wilson, both in Birmingham, Alabama. Jackson was not interested in the position, but recommended Wilson. Visits were also made to other prospects like Dr. John McClanahan (Arkansas) and Dr. Edwin Young (North Carolina). At the beginning of August, the Pulpit Committee reported that they had considered twenty pastoral candidates, heard thirteen of them, and had a short list of three.[62] Rubel Phillips recalled that the committee received seventy recommendations and reviewed biographical and background information on fifty-three candidates.[63]

The Pulpit Committee needed a pastor that would take on the task of helping to build a new mission into a church. Church members wanted someone who would be compatible with the defining focus on dignified, solemn worship. An educated congregation, comprising many young business professionals, "wanted it to be elevated above a little bit of what we had been brought up in." At least for some, that meant thoughtful, reflective preaching in contrast to hellfire and brimstone approaches.[64]

On August 8, 1967, the wait was over. The Pulpit Committee recommended Dudley Wilson of Fairfield Baptist Church in Birmingham, Alabama, to come preach in view of a call to the pastorate. Wilson, a young

---

[61] N Steering Committee Minutes 5 29 67. The Pulpit Committee consisted of Rubel Phillips, chair; Ross Bass; Lynn Camper; Kathy Guyton; John Kitchings; Al Meena; Pat McMullan Jr.; Jamie Speed; and O. B. Wooley.

[62] N Steering Committee Minutes 6 5 67; N News 6 7 67; N Steering Committee Minutes 6 27 67; N Steering Committee Minutes 7 5 67; N News 8 7 67.

[63] Phillips, "Reflections on Northeast Jackson Baptist Mission."

[64] Phillips, interview, 9.

pastor of thirty-seven years old, was a graduate of Samford University and Southern Baptist Theological Seminary and had served two other churches in Alabama (First Baptist Churches of Aliceville and Guin) before Fairfield. Wilson hesitated—not accepting at first the invitation to preach—but he later agreed and preached at the mission on September 3. Wilson's name was recommended to the congregation in its business session on September 24, but they were told he had not yet accepted. The financial package was $18,000 per year, with four weeks of vacation and a two-month sabbatical leave every fourth year (with some Steering Committee members realizing that help with a housing purchase would soon be needed).[65]

While Wilson was hesitant or deliberative—no doubt because he would be leaving an established congregation for a mission start without facilities—the Pulpit Committee was persistent. Atley Kitchings, John Kitchings, and Al Meena personally delivered the invitation to Wilson in Birmingham the day after the church's vote to extend the call. Wilson promised a decision by October 1; the Steering Committee noted in their October 6 minutes that he accepted. Finally, the mission had the pastor they wanted. Wilson's first Sunday was October 29, 1967. Then, on November 5 Wilson was installed in a service at Beth Israel synagogue, a visible symbol itself of the unique origins of the Northeast Jackson Baptist Mission.[66]

Wilson came excited to this new evolving venture. He was certainly told that he was being gifted with a group of committed movers and shakers, or even committed malcontents. In humorous fashion, Leland Speed remembers his father's first conversation with Wilson at the service at Beth Israel to introduce the new pastor. The elder Speed said to Wilson, "Well, young man, I hope you're strong." Wilson replied, "Well I'll do my best. I'm young." As soon as the Speeds were where Wilson could not hear them, the younger Speed said to his father, "Why did you say that?" The elder Speed sarcastically replied, "Because he's got half the malcontents in Northeast Jackson in here and he's going to be tested." The younger Speed pushed back a bit and said, "What do you mean *malcontents*?" And the elder Speed summed up what an older generation most likely was thinking, even if they

---

[65] N Steering Committee Minutes 7 28 67; N Steering Committee Minutes 8 7 67; N Minutes 9 24 67; N Bulletin 9 3 67.

[66] N Steering Committee Minutes 9 25 67; N News 9 25 67; N Steering Committee Minutes 10 6 67.

were supportive of the mission: "If you weren't a bunch of malcontents, you'd have stayed where you were."[67]

The Early Years: Reflections

Harvey Whaley's last Sunday with the congregation was on October 22, 1967, the first Sunday that the congregation used the facilities of Beth Israel. A year later, Catrina Parrott Whaley, Harvey Whaley's spouse, wrote an open letter to the mission from their home in Deland, Florida. She reminisced that the congregation had "started as a group of persons serious about religion and eager to call forth a new quality of spiritual life." She commended their focus on children and was grateful that they had an "experience of deep devotion together."[68]

Kelley Williams Sr. later reflected that the congregation of the early years was "a diverse group with strong, frequently conflicting views on social, political, and cultural issues and the church's role in society." Or in more vivid language, "Many of us were malcontents or rebels with causes—but different causes. We challenged each other." Nevertheless, the group of strong personalities ended up with "servant leaders" with important responsibilities in a church with a focus on laity.[69] The journey of a "different but nevertheless Baptist" church had begun.

---

[67] Speed, interview, 4–5.

[68] N Steering Committee Minutes 5 14 67; Catrina Parrott Whaley to mission, in N History 8 2 68.

[69] Williams, "Northminster History."

Chapter 2

The "Wilderness Experience" Without a Home, Developing a Church Identity, and the Ministry of Dudley Wilson

Constitution of the Church

The business meeting of the Northeast Jackson Baptist Mission on December 10, 1967, was surely a moment of satisfaction for the congregation. Members had been anxious to be declared a full-fledged church—not just a mission—since its infant days during the summer.[1] The Hinds County Baptist Association had told the Steering Committee in October, in light of the membership numbers and progress on finding sites for worship, that they were entitled to church status. In retrospect, progress from mission status to constituted church was quite rapid.

At this business session in December, a resolution was approved to incorporate as a nonprofit corporation. Other key components to transitioning from mission to church occurred. The name Northminster Baptist Church was formally approved along with a church covenant and a plan for a three-year rotation among the Board of Deacons. Members of the Steering Committee became part of the original group of deacons and assumed leadership roles: Rubel Phillips, chair; Bob Guyton, vice chair and chair-elect; Leland Speed, secretary; and John Palmer, treasurer. Thus, on December 17, 1967, Northminster Baptist Church was officially constituted. Both Fred Tarpley, director of missions of the Hinds County Baptist Association, and Arthur Rutledge, executive secretary of the Home Mission Board of the Southern Baptist Convention, attended.[2]

The Charter Membership Roll, which had been evolving through the mission's early existence, now had thirty-six families and 133 people (forty-

---

[1] N Steering Committee Minutes 7 5 67.

[2] N Minutes 12 10 67; N Steering Committee Minutes 10 11 67; N Deacons 12 5 67; N Deacons 12 21 67.

six couples, four single parents, seven single adults, and thirty children).[3] According to church records at First Baptist Church, Jackson, fifty-three of its members were given letters of membership transfer to become charter members at Northminster.[4] Several others came from Broadmoor Baptist Church. The church membership had numerous successful business professionals, so the church has always been known as a wealthy congregation. The church attracted others, however, and some remembered that they took their time committing to the new church because they wanted to see that their gifts—which were not material—would contribute to the church's identity. They gladly affirmed that the church was a place for people with different gifts.[5]

Two facets of the church's founding constitution were especially notable. Church members had discussed several names (e.g., Ridgewood Baptist, Northeast Baptist, Meadow Brook Baptist) and provided input to a Naming Committee, chaired by Dr. Jim Hendrick. Charter member Trenton Shelton offered the name Northminster. Members were intrigued by the name, its history, meaning, and that it did not include an "i" in the middle of the word (similar to Westminster Abbey, London). As no one had ever heard of such a name for a Baptist church, its uniqueness seemed to fit the congregation's visionary identity.[6] Jane Best later recalled that the name was chosen because of the congregation's desire to minister to the needs of "north"-east Jackson.[7]

The inclusion of a church covenant was also foundational to the church's identity. Wilson wrote the covenant, which was approved by the congregation, and it was read at subsequent significant events throughout the church's history:

---

[3] J. Kelley Williams Sr., "Northminster History: Traditions, Norms, Values, and Stones," (February 13, 2005).

[4] Richard Aubrey McLemore and Nannie Pitts McLemore, *The History of First Baptist Church of Jackson, Mississippi* (Jackson, MS: Hederman Brothers, 1976) 278–79.

[5] Suzanne Boone, interview by Aaron Weaver, February 22, 2016, 2.

[6] Bob Guyton, "Northminster Celebration" (Northminster Baptist Church 25th Celebration, May 16, 1992). Rubel Phillips, interview by David Stricklin, March 1, 1992, 12.

[7] Jane Best, interview by David Stricklin, February 29, 1992, 4; Leland Speed concurred (Leland Speed, interview by Aaron Weaver, February 23, 2016, 9).

Believing that it is in response to the call of Jesus Christ that we have given ourselves to Him as the Lord and Savior of our lives, we publicly acknowledge Him as the Head of the Church and as the true pattern for life and all of life's relationships.

So it is now that we covenant with Him and with one another to live together in love as He has commanded, to feel and to demonstrate genuine concern for one another, to exercise a watch-care over each other as He does with all of us.

Understanding that it is a shared life to which we have been called, and knowing that to live involves happiness and disappointment, success and failure, fulfillment and emptiness, pleasure and suffering, we covenant to share the joys and the sorrows, to bear together the burdens, to pray sensitively for one another, to affirm in the spirit of Christ that we are our brother's keeper.

Believing that the gathered community is one of great meaning, we commit ourselves to participation in the regular assemblies of the church, in its ministries of worship, instruction, and service. We intend by the corporate sharing of our lives with God through His Son to build a witness of faith, love, understanding, and strength that shall be an eloquent testimony of His presence in the world.

Realizing that it was to the world of human need that our Lord came, that it was for the world of people that He gave Himself, and that it is in the world that we find ourselves called to be His servants, we dedicate our lives to ministering in the world, ever alert to the voice of human need wherever the cry may be heard.

Aware that as bearers of His name we personally embrace His Lordship, we shall strive in all of our ways and relationships, in our families, the church and the wider community, to honor and serve Him. Committed to serving, we gladly enter into the larger fellowship of the Christian community, especially into the Hinds County Association, the Mississippi Baptist Convention, the Southern Bap-

> tist Convention and the Baptist World Alliance, as we seek cooperatively to serve Christ in our world.
>
> Sharing a personal commitment to Jesus Christ and a deep concern for the world, and bound by the bonds of love and understanding, we seek to allow the church to be instrumental in accomplishing God's purpose in the world.[8]

The covenant document was a clear indication that the charter members wanted personal commitment to faith in Jesus Christ and a commitment to communal witness that included ecumenical sensitivity. The church would be a faith community that provided watch care and accountability between members. Or to use the language of the church's broader vision, Northminster members committed to each other to be a church of worship, education, service, and cooperation. While the final draft was written by Wilson, the covenant was based on the "studied conviction that the congregation has insisted upon lay involvement."[9]

Development of a Long-Range Plan

In January 1969, Bob Guyton suggested that the young church needed an overall evaluation of its ministries. An Evaluation Committee was created and after a six-week study presented the congregation's first long-range plan—the first of several in the church's history—in September. The plan's details were typical of a group growing and maturing as an organization.[10] The committee considered worship as the church's strongest ministry, and thus did not suggest any changes. They recommended that a religious education committee be established and a library started to help lay teachers. They recognized the pastor needed part-time help in the area of religious education. They asked for a fellowship after vesper services and a monthly covered dish rather than a mid-week service. They thought informational meetings would be helpful after the suppers—an attempt to get the laity in-

---

[8] The church covenant is found in various church documents. For example, N Bulletin 12 17 67 and N Bulletin 2 15 74. The current 2017 covenant is listed in the appendix.

[9] Jan Purvis, "Reflections on Becoming Church," February 24, 1991.

[10] N Deacons 1 8 69; N News 9 22 69.

volved in the life of the church. No doubt, they concluded, a permanent church home would enhance the congregation's ministries.[11]

Charter Membership... Open Baptism

People who joined the Northeast Jackson Baptist Mission became charter members of Northminster Baptist Church. A charter membership roll was placed at the front of the sanctuary, and a member of a Membership Committee was available at the "invitation" to assist interested persons in signing.[12] In January 1968, the church discussed revisions to the traditional method of becoming a church member. In addition to the typical method of requesting membership at the end of the worship hour, the deacons proposed that a prospective member could meet with the pastor privately to discuss membership. Formal membership to the church, in either case, would be granted only after the candidate completed a six-week new-member orientation process led by the pastor, Dudley Wilson. The congregation approved both methods of seeking membership—public and private—but balked initially on the required six-week orientation process before passing it a week later.[13] Wilson was pleased with the move toward an orientation program in which prospective members would learn about the church's covenant, its ministries, and some Christian history—because it would "indicate that church membership is a serious relationship, not to be taken lightly."[14]

These methods of affirming church membership revealed that the congregation was keenly interested in commitment and participation. They were not, however, interested in hard sells or pressured evangelism, traits often associated with revivalistic Baptist life. Jonathan Sweat remembered that people who wanted to join the church could do so quietly during the time of meditation. As Sweat uniquely phrased it, "They didn't want anyone to join the church who couldn't read" and follow the order of worship.[15] Ac-

---

[11] N Long Range Plans 1969, dated 9 8 69 from Committee to the Deacons.

[12] N Steering Committee Minutes 5 29 67; N Steering Committee Minutes 8 25 67.

[13] N Minutes 1 28 68; N Minutes 2 4 68.

[14] N Minutes 1 31 68. Includes letter from Dudley Wilson to the congregation.

[15] Jonathan Sweat, interview by David Stricklin, February 29, 1992, 15.

cording to Bill Boone, Northminster "represented a little bit of a sanctuary, in this was a place you could come and we weren't going to put a lot of pressure on you." To use the language of Baptist evangelism, Suzanne Boone said, "We don't sing forty verses of 'Just as I Am.'"[16] Dudley Wilson's recollections affirm this approach. He recalled that in his deliberations with the Pulpit Committee, he was told that the congregation did not want typical pressured invitations for their children. Wilson said that the invitation during his tenure at Northminster was regarded as "a meditative moment for persons to make decisions whether public or private" without emotional pressure; it was "one facet of the worship service, compatible with all of the preceding elements. It was the conclusion not the climax of the worship service."[17] Professions of faith of children were hoped for of course, but as part of a larger context of family and church instruction, mentoring, and nurture. In Southern Baptist experience, this intentional connection between membership and discipleship was ahead of its time.

On December 24, 1967, the first Sunday after the congregation was constituted as a church, Wilson implemented this "meditative moment," which he called a "responsive meditation," right after the sermon and before the recessional hymn in the order of worship. The church bulletin included a different prayer each week to facilitate quiet meditation. Throughout his tenure as pastor, worship included this meditation though the description of it in the church bulletin evolved. For almost four years, the bulletin stated, "The Responsive Meditation is to be a quiet time during which the meaning of the service may be pondered by each worshiper. A person may wish to use this time to trust his life to Christ. Another may wish to join this fellowship by transfer. Every worshiper may meditate upon the service and its personal meaning." In 1974, the responsive meditation focused even less on evangelism and more on Christian maturity: "The Responsive Meditation is a time of invitation to Christian discipleship and church membership, as well as a period in which each person may reflect on the worship experience and its personal meaning."[18]

---

[16] B. Boone and S. Boone, interview (2016), 20.

[17] Dudley Wilson, email to Kelley Williams Sr., February 22, 2016.

[18] N Bulletin 12 24 67; N Bulletin 8 23 70; N Bulletin 3 17 74. In 1975, the Responsive Meditation was altered to "The Responsive Meditation is an invitation to church membership and to deeper commitment" (see N Bulletin 3 30 75).

There were, of course, professions of faith and baptisms with the use of the responsive meditation. Ironically, Wilson's son, Jeff, was the first profession of faith (December 24, 1967) during his pastorate at Northminster.[19] Since the congregation had no permanent facility with a baptistery, early baptisms were held at Broadmoor Baptist Church.[20] On March 31, 1968, eight people were baptized: Al Meena, Jackie Meena, Carmen Besterman, Linda Dean, Lex Phillips, John Speed, Mark Webb, and Jeff Wilson.[21]

Developing a theology of baptism was a matter of prime importance to the congregation. Church members have recalled that L. D. Johnson's influential views on open baptism—evidently shared with charter members during his visit in summer 1967—led the church to move in a progressively ecumenical direction regarding the church's baptismal policies. Significant changes to membership policies were made in 1973. The congregation revised their baptismal policy to "open baptism," that is, accepting as members those who had been baptized as infants in other denominations. On February 18, 1973, a Sunday evening forum was held to discuss potential changes. The existing membership policy was reviewed with its four traditional Southern Baptist methods of a believer becoming a member: transfer of letter from another Baptist church, profession of faith accompanied by believer's baptism by immersion, statement of former membership in a Baptist church, and transfer from another denomination with believer's baptism by immersion. While these methods were to be maintained, a recommendation was passed that allowed for a fifth category: "Christians from other denominations who wish to become members of Northminster without being rebaptized." While this opened membership to Christians who had been baptized as infants in other denominations, Northminster included the following clarifying comment:

> (Until members received under this procedure are recognized by the Hinds County Baptist Association and the Mississippi Baptist Convention, they will not be eligible for election as messengers to association meetings or state conventions. Also, in the event of transfer to an-

---

[19] Wilson, email.

[20] Elizabeth Dean, interview by Aaron Weaver, February 22, 2016, 8.

[21] N Bulletin 4 7 68. A second baptismal service was held on September 8, 1968.

other Baptist church, their letter of transfer will state that they were accepted without baptism by immersion).[22]

No doubt unique for a Southern Baptist church, the baptismal policy was not controversial.[23] With a baptismal theology in hand, the church had its first parent-child dedication service in May 1974.[24]

In light of the baptismal policy, the congregation's existing open communion policy—observance of the Lord's Supper open to all Christians—was maintained. However, a motion to strictly enforce the church's covenant affirmation of active and accountable membership was controversial and defeated. The motion recommended that members who had neither contributed financially nor attended services be contacted and asked to resume participation; members who failed to do so would be placed in an inactive file. The motion was seen by some as a logical interpretation of the expectations of accountability to the church covenant, but others no doubt viewed the covenant in less binding terms. Tension between siding with "law or grace" has often flared in the life of the church. Said another way, in the "free church" context of voluntary church membership, tension between uncoerced faith and covenant-membership accountability has not been rare in the history of Christian discipleship. Forging an inclusive path forward, the congregation followed the recommendation of Kelley Williams Sr. to defeat the measure.[25]

The bylaw revisions of 1973 that highlighted the change in baptismal policy also re-affirmed the church's commitment to its foundational ministries in four areas: worship, education, service, and cooperation. For the latter, they asserted: "The Church seeks a spirit of ecumenism in efforts to cooperate with other fellowships in meeting the needs of the community."[26]

Staff

The church worked tirelessly with Dudley Wilson to provide him the type of support he would get at an established, well-to-do church. From the outset, they paid his dues for a clergy membership at the country club in

[22] N Minutes 2 25 73; N Bylaws 2 25 73.
[23] Barbara Webb, interview by Aaron Weaver, February 23, 2016, 3.
[24] N Bulletin 4 21 74.
[25] N Minutes 2 25 73
[26] N Bylaws 2 25 73.

Jackson.[27] It took a year and a half, but they set up a full benefits package (e.g., life insurance, retirement). Wilson was also encouraged to begin working on a doctor of ministry degree from San Francisco Theological Seminary while pastor.[28]

The church was not financially ready in its infancy to hire additional full-time staff. The staff included several part-time members, however, during Wilson's pastorate. Leslie Reeves served as music director from October 15, 1967, to April 8, 1968, and then Karen Gilfoy returned in June as permanent choir director (in 1973 the church staff listing reverted to calling her "choirmistress"). Phil Stanberry served as minister of Christian education beginning in February 1975—fulfilling a strong desire of the church to put some focus on religious education.[29] He was an instructor in religious education at Mississippi College in nearby Clinton. Youth directors, usually employed in the summers, were college students. They included Robin Nichols, Mississippi College (1971); Sam Prestridge, Mississippi College (1972); Lindsey Gunn, University of Mississippi (1972); Dan Jones, then current member and third-year medical student (1973); and Ed Richardson, Mississippi College (1975).[30]

Deacons

The original board of deacons included the church's "founding five" plus O. B. Wooley and Wirt Yerger. Rubel Phillips was already ordained as a deacon, and the others were ordained at the church's first deacon ordination service on December 31, 1967, two weeks after the congregation was constituted a church.[31] In 1969, a three-year deacon rotation plan was implemented. The process had a self-perpetuating function, or an intentional

[27] N Steering Committee Minutes 10 23 67.

[28] N Deacons 6 11 69; N News 6 1 72.

[29] N Bulletin 10 15 67; N Bulletin 4 8 68; N Bulletin 6 9 68; N Bulletin 11 1 73.

[30] The year 1974 has no newsletters. N News 2 18 71; N News 5 25 72; N News 5 16 73; N News 2 26 75; N News 4 30 75; N Deacons 5 9 72; N Deacons 2 21 74; N Bulletin 2 28 71; N Bulletin 6 11 72; N Bulletin 8 3 72; N Bulletin 6 3 73; N Bulletin 6 15 75. No summer youth minister was hired in 1974. Nell and Ed Wall of the Youth Committee were especially active in leadership (see N Bulletin 10 13 74).

[31] N Bulletin 12 24 67.

goal of continuity. The three rotating off the board became three members of the five-member committee to recommend the next group of deacons. Noteworthy, however, was that the other two members of this Deacon Nominating Committee that first year were women (Elaine Rainey and Hilda Calhoun). The congregation voted on the ballot provided by the committee.[32]

In 1970, the deacons developed a type of family ministry plan, popular in Southern Baptist churches, with the intent of dividing the church families for visitation purposes. Deacons worked on another program in 1972 with the goal that deacons would visit church families at least twice a year. Deacon minutes certainly reveal a sense of care for family outreach throughout the Wilson era. At the same time, while the church was developing an identity with focus on lay involvement, implementation or defining it was not always clear and consistent. For example, in fall 1970, Wilson told the deacons he wanted them and other laity to assist in worship by doing the call to worship and leading responsive readings. However, the deacons agreed only to think about it and two months later told Wilson they still were not ready to commit to it.[33]

Bylaw changes in 1973 shifted even greater responsibility to lay involvement in the deacon process. Church members were to recommend names for deacon election, and then a nominating committee would select the candidates for a congregational election. In July 1975, the congregation voted to revise the number of deacons from a fixed nine to having three deacons per every 100 members. The move set the stage for the election of a woman deacon—a story told below—in just a few months.[34]

Church Sites

On October 15, 1967, the congregation approved the move to the Jewish synagogue, Temple Beth Israel, and established a home base. The property had been vacant for a while and needed some immediate work. Elizabeth Taylor remembered that church members worked every night of the week before the first service, trying to get the space ready for worship.

---

[32] N Deacons 9 15 69.

[33] N Deacons 10 8 70; N Deacons 12 9 70; N Deacons 4 11 72; N Deacons 9 20 73; N Deacons 1 24 74.

[34] N Bylaws 2 25 73; N Bylaws 7 13 75; N News 7 16 75.

Leather seats were split wide open with stuffing coming out of the open seams, but the cushions (there were no pews) were patched and even painted! Other repairs were made in the early days. Classrooms were remodeled. One father purchased carpet for a nursery because he did not want his baby to crawl on a "dirty floor."[35] Rabbi Nussbaum, the leader of the Jewish community in Jackson, visited and noticed the gas heaters were producing a heavy gas odor and needed to be fixed. By November, Bill Pope had installed a new heating system.[36] Nussbaum also extended a welcome through humor applicable to Baptists. When he first met Wilson at the synagogue, the rabbi said, "Okay, go up there and open those doors (at the front of the sanctuary), I want to see if you can put a tub in there."[37]

With a permanent pastor and a stable place to worship, the congregation grew. As the earliest members recalled, they started to see faces that they did not recognize.[38] Many regarded worshiping at the synagogue as a powerful experience; seeing the symbols of the Jewish tradition (e.g., chandeliers adorned in Hebrew writing) expanded horizons for people of typical Baptist/Christian backgrounds.[39]

By May 1968, Northminster knew that the stay at the old Temple Beth Israel facility could be temporary, and the congregation stayed less than a year. The Mississippi Supreme Court ruled that the Jewish congregation could lease the land to Standard Oil Company, which meant the old sanctuary would be demolished.[40] Consequently, the Beth Israel Congregation asked Northminster Baptist Church to vacate the property by September 1, 1968. Northminster members were grateful for their stay, however, and gave their Jewish friends $1,400 to purchase a sign for their property as a gift of their gratitude.[41] The sign still stood in 2017.

Several sites were considered for the church's next temporary home: Millsaps College, Belhaven College, and the University of Mississippi Nurs-

---

[35] Elizabeth Taylor, interview by David Stricklin, February 20, 1992, 4.

[36] N Minutes 10 15 67; N Steering Committee Minutes 10 23 67; N Steering Committee Minutes 11 27 67.

[37] Speed, interview, 5.

[38] Phillips, interview, 12.

[39] Suzanne Boone, interview by David Stricklin, March 1, 1992, 3.

[40] N Deacons 5 8 68; N Minutes 6 2 68.

[41] N Deacons 6 12 68; N Deacons 9 11 68; N Minutes 8 18 68; N Bulletin 9 1 68.

ing School. The best choice, the congregation decided, was the Mississippi School for the Blind on Highway 55 North at the corner of Eastover Drive. The school had a 300-seat auditorium. No rent or maintenance was required except paying $2,300 to air-condition the auditorium. The verbal arrangement was for a two-year stay, and the first service was held on September 8, 1968.[42]

According to church records, the time spent at the Mississippi School for the Blind went well. There were a few hitches as time went on. In March 1970, the school's superintendent, R. C. Benton, sent Dudley Wilson a letter with a bill requesting $4,206.20 for janitorial services for the year March 21, 1969, to March 19, 1970. Benton wrote candidly, "There seems to be a need for this type service or to have someone assigned to the building on Wednesday evenings. There is no one to turn off the lights, empty trash cans, clean up the food, and put the furniture back in place. All of these things create a great deal of confusion on Thursday morning.... We shall appreciate your attention in this matter."[43] Later that year in November, the school requested that the building not be used for any activities during the week that involved children. It is no surprise, then, that the deacons occasionally discussed the possibility of moving to a new location—for example, the former Mormon church on I-55 North. Most of their attention, however, was directed toward the construction of their own permanent church facilities.[44]

The time at the School of the Blind has been interpreted warmly, though frankly, in subsequent years. Despite the occasional glitches, Donna Kennedy (Barksdale) remembered that the congregation had to leave all of the chairs "exactly as [they were] when we went in on Sunday" because the movement of the furniture would create obstacles for the visually impaired children who would be there on Mondays. Kennedy suggested that because "we had to go and come as though we hadn't been there, the spirit of the church left with the people when they left the building." In other words, Northminster members were learning what it meant to be church as a living

[42] N Deacons 7 10 68; N Deacons 9 11 68; N Deacons 6 11 69; N Deacons 8 13 69; N News 9 5 68; N Minutes 8 18 68.

[43] N News 3 20 70.

[44] N Deacons 8 12 70; N Deacons 11 11 70.

body of Christ rather than as an institution or a building.[45] Kennedy was also struck by the congregation's willingness to speak to relevant issues. Teaching a youth Sunday school class, Mary James Dean and Leland Speed told the young people that day's lesson was about the rich young ruler in the Bible. Dean asked Speed to speak from the point of view of the rich, young ruler. "Well! That certainly got our attention," Kennedy remembered. "Of course, he spoke eloquently and well but the strongest point in my mind was.... This place [Northminster] speaks to the reality of the day."[46]

Youth had fond memories of playing hide and seek on the second floor—"a scary place" remembered Dudley Wooley—or finding their way to the school's gym and skating rink, especially if they were late for a church activity. But like Kennedy, Kelley Williams Jr. remembered the time after worship when the group had to put furniture back in its exact place as a time of learning to be a community of faith to those around them.[47]

The more common metaphor for understanding the four-year stay at the School for the Blind has been to describe it, in biblical terms, as a "wilderness experience" or a "wandering" before settling into a permanent church structure. While there were new faces, others left because of a lack of a church facility. It was seen as a time of "testing" or as a "winnowing experience" with the "hardcore Northminsters" remaining.[48] Still members persevered, and at times with good-natured commitment. Karen Gilfoy sometimes had a challenge getting men to participate in choir. When the choir was down to about five female voices, Gilfoy playfully referred to the choir as the "vestal virgins."[49] On another occasion, the ceiling unexpectedly began to leak during worship. Roger Stribling Jr. found two buckets and placed them on the floor to catch the water. The sound from the leak hitting the

[45] Donna Sones, interview by David Stricklin, February 29, 1992, 5. Kennedy was Sones's maiden name.

[46] Donna (Kennedy) Barksdale, letter read at "Laying the Foundation (Charter Members)," Adult Studies Evening Session, March 26, 2017.

[47] Dudley Wooley and Kelley Williams Jr., cited in audio "Growing Up at Northminster," Adult Studies Evening Session, April 2, 2017.

[48] Jan Purvis, interview by David Stricklin, February 29, 1992, 5; Speed, interview, 3; Kelley Williams Sr., interview by Aaron Weaver, February 23, 2016, 3.

[49] Speed, interview, 8.

buckets was impossible to miss, and Gilfoy quipped to the choir, "Roger Stribling has never lived in a house with a leak in his life."[50]

There was progress in acquiring a permanent site on which to build a new church as early as October 1967. The church approved a recommendation from Leland Speed and the Site Committee to purchase six and a half acres at the northwest corner of Eastover Drive and Ridgewood Road. Options to purchase several lots, plus two houses, had been obtained for $185,000. The sale was not without difficulty, however. Some homeowners in the area objected to the presence of a church next to their property and insisted upon some building restrictions before they were willing to cooperate. Good news prevailed in late January 1968 when it was announced that the prized property had been secured. Of the two houses acquired, Miller and Snyder, the latter was pegged to be the parsonage.[51]

When the congregation approved its first formal budget in October 1967, the total budget of $100,000 had $50,000 for operating expenses and $50,000 for debt service. The congregation affirmed borrowing up to $100,000 to finance the $25,000 down payment on the new property with $70,000 to cover equity payments when mortgages were due on the two houses. The deacons immediately set up a Building Committee in March 1968 and planning continued.[52]

In a business session in early March 1969, the deacons and Finance Committee informed the congregation that with a debt of $165,000, it was necessary to retire that large amount at a more rapid rate than the $50,000 in the annual budget. If not, they would not make adequate progress toward financing the construction of the new church. Bob Guyton's recommendation to have a $100,000 capital funds drive that month, to be paid by the end of September, was approved, with Homer Best to chair the effort. Within a week, the church reported that 87 percent had been pledged and by the end of the month, they had easily oversubscribed the goal with pledges of $108,330.[53]

---

[50] Story told by Suzanne Boone, cited in "Laying the Foundation (Charter members)."

[51] N Minutes 10 15 67; N Steering Committee Minutes 10 23 67; N Steering Committee Minutes 11 13 67; N Minutes 1 28 68; N Deacons 5 8 68.

[52] N Minutes 10 15 67; N Deacons 3 20 68.

[53] N Deacons 1 8 69; N Minutes 3 2 69; N News 4 17 69.

In March 1970, the church approved Biggs, Weir & Chastain to be the architects.[54] Six months later a building model was on display for the congregation to see, and the Building Committee expressed hope—too optimistically—that the new church home would be completed by the end of 1971. In December, finance chair Rubel Phillips called the upcoming year 1971 a crucial year in the financial life of the church and urged members to subscribe the church budget so that building plans would proceed without hitches, hopefully as soon as February 1. Final architectural plans, however, were not approved until August. On September 1, 1971, the congregation approved Byrd Construction to build the church, at a cost not to exceed $480,000. The building loan was approved for $500,000 for twenty years at 8 percent annual interest.[55]

Besides the celebratory significance of the church's first service in May 1967, the groundbreaking service for the permanent church home was easily a close second in terms of importance in the congregation's early history. On October 3, 1971, after worship at the Mississippi School for the Blind, the congregation gathered at its new property on Ridgewood Road for a groundbreaking service. Dudley Wilson operated a bulldozer as part of the groundbreaking ceremony. Attendees reported a warm memory of Roger Stribling, who would later lose his life in a tragic accident. According to the story, "Stribling was happy as a Stribling-Puckett Caterpillar tractor went to work, and he passed out 'Cat' hats to the crowd."[56] In addition to the festive elements of the groundbreaking, Wilson reminded the congregation in a litany, addressed to God and read responsively, about the penultimate importance of structures: "Keep us from the temptation to give a building ultimate meaning, which we reserve for Thee.... Remind us that we intend no monuments to Thee in wood, brick and steel, and lead us to the use of this structure as an instrument to produce living signs of Thy presence and meaning in the world."[57]

Having worked out a covenant document with the neighborhood, the church began construction. The church promised not to purchase more

[54] N Deacons 3 20 68; N Minutes 2 22 70; N Deacons 2 18 70.

[55] N Minutes 11 22 70; N News 12 17 70; N Deacons 7 29 71; N Minutes 8 1 71; N Deacons 9 5 71; N Minutes 9 12 71.

[56] N News 4 30 75.

[57] N Bulletin 10 3 71.

property in the Hazelvern subdivision nor have any access to Pinewood Drive. Once neighbors were assured that the church would not build on the rear of the property adjacent to their homes, they agreed to lift restrictions that non-residential construction in that area was unallowable until 1975. The congregation was relieved; they had waited long enough.[58]

As construction progressed, the congregation was confronted with purchasing various worship fixtures, and budget concerns were natural given fears about escalating building costs. In December 1972, an Allen Electronic Organ was purchased for $8,600. In May 1973, when the Music Committee asked for $950 for a piano for the choir room, however, the deacons recommended that efforts should concentrate on getting a piano as a gift or as a loan from someone. The deacons also hoped someone would give a piano to the youth Sunday school as well rather than the church having to find money for another purchase. Finances were a concern as pledges of about $19,000 were still outstanding and the deacons doubted they would ever receive it all. (Through the years, members graciously responded to the call for pianos. S. H. "Mac" and Ann McDonnieal gave a Steinway for use in the choir room and on special occasions in the sanctuary. For the activities in the Great Hall, O. B. and Easie Wooley gave a Kimball that belonged to O. B.'s mother. For the Sunday school area, Trenton and Linda Shelton gave an antique piano that had belonged to Linda's mother.)[59]

The long-sought-after permanent church home was soon a reality. Deacons reported in March 1973 that they hoped the new facilities would be ready by May 6. It took a few more weeks of patience, but the first service in the new building was held on May 27, 1973.[60]

The church held a special dedication of its new sanctuary, with seats for about 400 worshipers, and educational space, on February 24, 1974.[61] Dot Kitchings was chair of the Dedication Committee. Owen Cooper, layperson from Yazoo City and president of the Southern Baptist Convention, was the guest speaker. As the congregation would do at subsequent special dedications, they read the church covenant in the service. The special bulletin included a brief history of the church and listed the charter members. The

---

[58] N Deacons 10 6 71; N Minutes 10 6 71.
[59] N Deacons 12 5 72; N Deacons 5 17 73; N Deacons 6 28 73.
[60] N Deacons 3 15 73.
[61] N Bulletin 2 24 74.

bulletin also gave clear evidence that the church was investing significant theological meaning in the sanctuary's architecture. Wilson wrote that the "dynamic architecture" "creates an inspiring ambience for contemplation, worship, and the education ministry of the church." The liturgical setting was true to the roots of the congregation's dream of being "different." Wilson explained,

> The sanctuary embodies a traditional basilica design with a broad nave flanked by colonnaded side aisles. The center aisle leads directly to the communion table which symbolizes the shared life of the church. In the light-filled transept, the pulpit, baptistery, and distinctive planter on the left balance the lectern, organ and choir area on the right. The divided chancel is an historical arrangement which allow church ceremonies to be conducted from the lectern; the word of God is proclaimed from the pulpit which is raised to give symbolic priority to this part of the worship service. The choir area is placed on a level with the pews to symbolize that all are a part of the worshipping church family.[62]

Subsequent reflections about the style of the church building reaffirmed its theological significance for church members and reiterated Wilson's original explanation. Open-ended pews symbolized the openness of the church to all comers. Clear windows, rather than stained glass windows, meant that the congregation was open to the outside world—and that the world could see what the congregation was doing. (Roger Stribling Jr. first suggested the clear windows so that "people could look in to see what those different kind of Baptists were doing and perhaps might be curious enough to join them in worship.") Having the choir and lectern on the same level as the church meant that all who were present were equal participants in the worship service, but the raised pulpit gave priority to the proclamation of the gospel message. When an organ was installed in 1981, its pipes were seen as a witness to God as Trinity.[63]

In 2005, Kelley Williams Sr. offered historical reflections about the process of constructing the church facility. The "wilderness experience" without a permanent home was characterized by both positive and negative membership shifts. Membership grew (267 additions) but also changed (72

[62] N Bulletin 2 15 74.

[63] S. Boone, interview (2016), 2. Leland Speed told the story of Roger Stribling's suggestion (Speed, interview, 7).

losses). The congregation was extremely proud of its building, but the experience, Williams Sr. concluded, "led us to grow closer as church family and to realize that the church is not a building."[64]

Ministry of Stewardship

Beyond issues of building construction and debt reduction, the church's first formal budget (October 1967) also revealed decisions regarding missions and other ministry emphases. An amount of $7,600 was set aside for missions: $5,000 for the Southern Baptist Convention's giving mechanism, the Cooperative Program; $600 for the Hinds County Baptist Association; and $2,000 dollars for local missions. These figures indicated that the congregation would not follow the SBC plea to give at least 10 percent (a tithe) of the budget to the Cooperative Program. Despite the financial standing of many members, deacons' minutes and church newsletters frequently made appeals regarding increased giving. The church newsletter often asked members to tithe.[65] The church used a pledge card program to subscribe the budget. Pledges usually came in, though later than the deacons wished. Pleas from the deacons often sounded urgent, reminding members to fulfill their pledges because not all families were contributing. Growing organizational pains also included episodes where financial reports were not being turned in—once for five straight months in 1969–1970—to the deacons.[66]

As budgets grew, so did financial health and expenditures. For example, the church's financial planners were ecstatic at the outset of 1972, announcing 1971 was the first year in the church's brief history that gifts exceeded the budget ($3,443 over the $105,000 budget). The 1972 budget rose to $110,000; the amount for missions remained stable. The budget was actually oversubscribed. The almost sacred Southern Baptist mission offer-

---

[64] Williams, "Northminster History."

[65] N News 2 26 75; Barbara Webb, email to Doug Weaver, June 22, 2017. Newsletters were sent out sporadically for several years; a formal, regularly published church newsletter began in February 1975, under the leadership of Mary Hendrick, and a nine-member committee that she chaired. In the early years, much of the church news was delivered in the form of simple letters from Dudley Wilson to the congregation.

[66] N Steering Committee Minutes 10 15 67; N Steering Committee Minutes 11 27 67; N Deacons 11 20 68; N News 8 29 69; N Deacons 12 17 69; N Deacons 3 11 70; N News 10 16 68; N News 4 10 70.

ings, Lottie Moon Christmas Offering for Foreign Missions and the Annie Armstrong Home Missions Offering, were observed in these early years.[67]

Financial matters were not always smooth. John Kitchings reported to the church in June 1973 that with the expenses of constructing a new church facility, their tradition of being a "year-end giving congregation" was a luxury they could no longer afford.[68] The budget needed monthly attention. What the deacons agreed *not* to tell the congregation was a discovery made that spring: a church bookkeeper had embezzled $10,767.79 from the congregation's funds. Six months later the financial books were still in disarray, out of balance, and out of date. Finally, a new bookkeeper was hired to get the financial records in order.[69] In August 1973, the building loan was raised an additional $60,000 to $560,000. The 1974 budget grew again ($146,744.68) and reconfigured the missions allocation. There was $5,000 for the Cooperative Program, still $2,000 for local missions and $600 for the association, but now $1,000 for a Gulf Shores ministry.[70]

The strain of the building project was obvious to budget watchers, even in a church with noted wealth. The first payment on the building loan occurred on March 1, 1974. In 1975, the congregation heard repeated messages about near budget crises; 1974 budget receipts were only 80 percent of the operating budget, and pledges at the outset of 1975 were badly running behind. Income was exceeding expenses by $2,000 a month.[71] During summer 1975, just before he resigned in September, Dudley Wilson said it had been a very good summer except for finances. The congregation borrowed money to cover operating expenses, but the financial anxiety was not long-term. By

[67] N Deacons 11 30 71; N News 1 21 72.

[68] N News 6 5 73; N Deacons 7 25 73.

[69] N Deacons 2 5 73; N Deacons 3 15 73; N Deacons 4 12 73; N Deacons 5 17 73; N Deacons 6 28 73. At this June 28 meeting, Leland Speed said the embezzlement incident had been reviewed and recorded in the deacons' minutes and that was enough disclosure (N Deacons 12 20 73; N Deacons 1 22 74; N Deacons 1 3 74). Barbara Webb volunteered in 1974 to bring order to the financial records, and the 1974 audit showed the records consistently improved and maintained on a current basis. See N News 2 26 75.

[70] N Minutes 8 26 73.

[71] N Deacons 1 3 74; N Deacons 5 22 75; N News 2 26 75.

fall, even though the pastor had left, giving was no longer a matter of serious concern.[72]

Ministry of Worship

Dudley Wilson had an easygoing manner that proved important in a young congregation. At the same time, he brought the dignified worship leadership that the congregation desired. His style, however, was different from his interim predecessor, Harvey Whaley. Wilson did not wear a robe, and unlike most liturgically oriented ministers, he only used note cards and did not write out his sermons.[73] Church members, however, loved Wilson's pulpit delivery and said he prayed "beautiful prayers."[74] Benedictions were short, but beloved, such as the one delivered at his last worship service at Northminster in 1975: "Loving Father, Thou hast blessed our coming in; bless Thou now, we pray Thee, our going out. Amen."[75]

Wilson's approach to ministry attracted various types of congregants. Bobbie and Robert (Dub) King joined while Wilson was pastor because he fulfilled the church's founding focus on a "free pulpit." Donette Lee recalled that she divorced during Wilson's ministry, and he made her feel accepted: "Divorced people were not segregated or made to feel half instead of whole."[76] Dudley Wooley recalled that when Roger Stribling Jr. died in an airplane accident, Wilson became emotional during the memorial service and could not speak. The incident, Wooley said, revealed to him how much the church members loved each other.[77]

An early expression of the congregation's ecumenical development of liturgical worship was the observance of days associated with the Christian calendar. A few progressive Southern Baptist churches observed such days in the 1960s and 1970s, but most eschewed the "high church" tradition in wor-

---

[72] N News 8 27 75; N Deacons 8 24 75; N Deacons 1 18 78. The deacons' minutes of January 18 note that the operating loan had been paid off.

[73] Barbara Webb, email to Aaron Weaver, February 25, 2016; Phillips, interview, 6.

[74] Jean Williams, interview by David Stricklin, February 29, 1992, 9.

[75] Dudley Wilson, email to Kelley Williams Sr., June 18, 2014.

[76] Anne Guidry and Amy Williams, *Echoes of Grace: Northminster Baptist Church PrimeTimers Devotion Book* (Jackson, MS: Northminster Baptist Church, 2015) 59, 62.

[77] Dudley Wooley, "Growing Up at Northminster."

ship.[78] There was no immediate implementation of the entire cycle of the Christian liturgical calendar, but a candlelight Christmas Eve service was begun in 1967. Then at Easter 1968, a whole week of "pre-Easter" services was held, highlighted by a Maundy Thursday Lord's Supper observance. The church was then open for prayer on Good Friday. Wilson did not ask the church to observe the forty days of Lent prior to Easter, but he did introduce the topic in the church bulletin and suggested that the congregation use the six weeks as a time of personal preparation for Easter. The Easter season worship experience also included the use of purple antependia hanging on the lectern and the pulpit.[79] These special services continued in subsequent years.[80] A thoroughgoing use of the language of the Christian calendar became commonplace as early as December 1968 with an Advent celebration. Subsequently, the liturgical seasons of Epiphany, Lent, Holy Week, Eastertide, Pentecost, and Kingdomtide defined worship at Northminster Baptist Church.[81]

The use of paraments as visual elements in liturgical worship was explained in a May 1975 newsletter: "Northminster uses five basic colors on its choir stoles, the Bible bookmark on the lectern, the pulpit hanging, and on the communion table as a runner." Three months later, the church newsletter expressed great appreciation to Beth Israel for a gift of gold and red paraments.[82] The paraments—engraved with Psalm 133:1, "How good and how pleasant it is for Brothers to dwell together in unity"—the church bulletin noted, were a symbol of the bond of unity with the Jewish congregation.[83] Wilson also frequently referenced Northminster's emphasis on litur-

[78] First Baptist Church, Gainesville, Florida, began having "pre-Easter" services in 1960. See C. Douglas Weaver, *Every Town Needs a Downtown Church: A History of First Baptist Church, Gainesville, Florida* (Brentwood, TN: Southern Baptist Historical Society, 2000) 113. On the other hand, Second-Ponce de Leon Baptist Church, Atlanta, Georgia, began celebrating Advent in 1987. See C. Douglas Weaver, *Second to None: A History of Second-Ponce de Leon Baptist Church* (Brentwood, TN: Baptist History and Heritage Society, 2004) 173.

[79] N Bulletin 12 10 67; N Bulletin 3 3 68; N Bulletin 4 7 68.

[80] N News 4 4 68; N News 4 12 73; N Deacons 12 17 69; N Deacons 3 11 70; N Deacons 12 17 69.

[81] N Bulletin 12 1 68; N Bulletin 3 22 70; N Bulletin 1 16 72; N Bulletin 4 30 72; N Bulletin 11 1 73.

[82] N News 5 28 75; N News 8 20 75.

[83] N Bulletin 8 77 75.

gical silence. Some of his last newsletter reflections about worship revolved about the necessity of quiet time for contemplation prior to the service. Even muted conversation in the sanctuary was inappropriate, Wilson wrote.[84]

While the congregation focused on reverential worship, in 1975 Northminster's children performed a musical, a typical Southern Baptist children's ministry activity. Twenty-three children from third to sixth grades sang *Hey God, Listen!*[85] Since the congregation had intentionally not set up a rigorous structure of programs in the early days, often new ministries (or older ones at other churches) would get started upon the initiative of the laity. For example, Jean Williams, who had taught music in public schools, initiated the children's music ministry. It was Williams's way of plugging into the church's evolving lay ministry portrait. She continued in the children's music ministry for thirteen years.[86]

During the Wilson years, the congregation grappled with the most effective means of developing fellowship and community. The Monday evening discussion group, so pivotal in the church's early months, was moved to Sunday nights. Topics still revealed the attendees' openness to progressive ideas. For example, they studied the sermons of their contemporary, Carlyle Marney, liberal-minded Baptist gadfly and minister, as well as the early twentieth-century document "Why I Am a Baptist," by the "father" of the Social Gospel movement, American Baptist leader Walter Rauschenbusch.[87] The topic of abortion was addressed. In spring 1968, Wilson led a Pastor's Forum that discussed the Sunday sermon of that morning, and he led a Baptist history class. Vespers after the discussion group was offered as a nod toward the more traditional Southern Baptist Sunday evening worship. Dot Kitchings of the Worship Committee thought these moves helped the church maintain a family feeling. In summer 1968, however, the church suspended Sunday evening activities and resumed the services in October, a practice that continued in subsequent years. In an era when most Southern Baptists geared up youth activities in the summer, the Northminster ap-

[84] N News 3 26 75; N News 7 2 75.
[85] N News 4 16 75; N Bulletin 5 11 75.
[86] Williams, interview, 11.
[87] N Bulletin 10 8 67; N Bulletin 6 2 68.

proach reflected the mobility and frequent travel habits of the congregation.[88]

Similar to how the children's music ministry began, Vacation Bible School was also birthed as a lay ministry effort. Jean Williams, whose son was of preschool age, wanted him to have the experience of VBS. After discussing the idea with other women, Williams told Phyllis Eddins that she would assist if Eddins would lead the summer program. Other mothers were recruited to join the effort.[89] The result was the church's first Vacation Bible School for children in 1970 with Phyllis Eddins as director. Results were encouraging: 108 enrolled, with an average attendance of 102. Nevertheless, the church tinkered with scheduling VBS because of summer family schedules and even tried having the sessions on five successive Mondays during summer 1975.[90]

Serious religious education—something more than just Southern Baptist Convention-based literature study—was important to the Northminster congregation. In April 1970, popular Mississippi College religious education professor Dr. Phil McCarty led a four-week consultation on "How to Study the Bible." Later that year, Foy Valentine of the SBC Christian Life Commission led an adult retreat. McCarty returned—with a teaching style the church described as "provocative"—to lead the January Bible study, a SBC calendar event, in 1971.[91] The church frequently recruited local college professors, especially from Mississippi College and Millsaps College, as leaders of the Sunday evening discussion group.[92] Issues surrounding worship and study also had down-to-earth practical elements as well. The deacons discussed moving Sunday school from 9:30 a.m. to 9:15 a.m. because of tardy

[88] N News 2 15 68; N Minutes 3 24 68; N News 4 4 68; N Minutes 5 29 68; N Deacons 5 14 69; N Minutes 6 2 68; N News 10 2 69; N Bulletin 10 6 68. Abortion, neither pro nor con, is mentioned in N Bulletin 1 17 71.

[89] Williams, interview, 11; Guidry and Williams, *Echoes of Grace*, 102.

[90] N Deacons 7 8 70; N News 5 28 75.

[91] N News 4 7 70; N News 12 28 71. In 1971, Norman Rodgers of the Church Training Department of the Mississippi Baptist Convention consulted with the church as an educational consultant (see N News 10 12 71).

[92] Lewis Nobles, president of Mississippi College, led the adult discussion group on Sunday evening on the "Role of Baptists in Christian Education" (N News 10 21 71). George Boyd, English chair at Millsaps College, led a six-week study on religious poetry of the seventeenth century (N News 2 8 72).

attendees to worship. Coffee breaks for fellowship also caused tardy worshipers![93]

Women in Leadership and Ministry

During its early years, Northminster's decision making—like in other Southern Baptist settings—was normally male-dominated. Deacons were all male. In a 1968 letter revealing the sign of Baptist times, Wilson, at the suggestion of the Finance Committee, invited the men of the church to a meeting to be fully informed regarding the financial matters of the congregation.[94] Women did find places of leadership during the Wilson years, however. In 1973, for example, Jan Purvis was director of Sunday school, and Dot Kitchings taught a co-ed adults class along with her husband, John.[95]

In typical Southern Baptist fashion, Northminster women were involved in mission groups. The formation of a Woman's Missionary Union, the women's auxiliary of the SBC, however, did not occur in the first year of the church's existence. In June 1968, Elizabeth Dean was elected to serve as the first president of the women's group. By September 1968, gatherings were held at Covenant Presbyterian Church or as prayer groups in homes.[96] The first meeting held at Covenant was called a "W.M.S.," for Woman's Missionary Society.[97] A regularly functioning W.M.S. (an old-fashioned interchangeable term with W.M.U.) was apparent by December when a week of prayer for foreign missions and the Southern Baptist Lottie Moon Christmas offering were observed. Girls in Action, a missions group for teenage girls, was also formed.[98]

During the Wilson years, church bulletins revealed a vibrant ministry among the women's missions group and used the designations W.M.S., W.M.U., and Northminster Women interchangeably to describe them.[99] In 1971, for example, Dot Kitchings was president of the WMU, and the An-

---

[93] N Deacons 5 13 70; N News 6 5 70; N News 6 9 72.
[94] N News 6 20 68.
[95] N Minutes 9 16 73.
[96] Dean, interview, 2; Best, interview, 4.
[97] N Bulletin 6 9 68; N Bulletin 9 15 68; N Bulletin 9 29 68.
[98] N Bulletin 12 1 68; N Bulletin 12 22 68; N Bulletin 11 1 70.
[99] N News 6 29 70; N Bulletin 11 8 70; N Bulletin 12 7 70; N Bulletin 1 3 71.

nie Armstrong and Lottie Moon offerings, the major mission offerings of the WMU in support of SBC mission efforts, were promoted that year and again in later years.[100] The next year the WMU participated in some mission/social ministry projects such as sewing disposable pads for the American Cancer Society.[101] By 1974 to 1975, the women's group had settled on just one name, Northminster Women. A slow shift from specifically Southern Baptist WMU emphases was evident (offerings to Lottie Moon and Annie Armstrong had never been large) In 1974, the church had an "Advent Week of Prayer" with a special offering for foreign missions, but no mention was made in church materials of Lottie Moon (if there was a Baptist "saint," a name freely and frequently invoked, it was Lottie's). In 1975, in addition to the traditional women's group meetings during the day (for women who did not work outside the home) a "Ladies Night Group" for working women was also formed.[102]

In 1973, the move toward having women deacons evidently began. That September, the Deacon Nominating Committee, tasked with bringing six names to the floor for election, nominated all males, as had been the church's practice. However, for the first time, three women—Suzanne Grogan, Dot Kitchings, and Jan Purvis—were nominated from the floor. The church was apparently not ready yet for the inclusive shift because three men won the election. Significantly, in 1974, the church received a ballot with five men and one woman, Suzanne Grogan. Again, however, only men were elected.[103] The church newsletter had a "sounding board" column in which people could make suggestions; one such article in March 1975 revealed that someone in the congregation wanted more women in a variety of visible church positions. "If women are available to be nominated for position of deacon in our church," the comment read, "why not add some women to the Usher Committee to assist with the bulletins, seating, and taking up the collection?"[104]

---

[100] N News 10 12 71; N News 1 21 72; N Deacons 1 22 74; N Bulletin 1 2 72; N Bulletin 4 1 73.

[101] N News 5 9 72.

[102] N News 5 28 75; N News 7 2 75; N Bulletin 5 5 74; N Bulletin 12 1 74.

[103] N Minutes 9 16 73; N Minutes 9 29 74.

[104] N News 3 26 75.

The best opportunity for a woman to be elected as a deacon seemed to present itself in 1975 when the church modified its bylaws regarding the size of the Board of Deacons. In July, just two months before Dudley Wilson resigned, the congregation voted to adjust the number of deacons from a fixed nine to three deacons per every 100 members. Such a move made sense as the congregation grew—more deacons were needed to do the work. The specific bylaw change gave general guidelines for deacons and did not mention male or female eligibility. However, the church newsletter indicated that the new bylaw's use of "deacon" meant the deacon could be a man or a woman—a significant, explicit statement for the congregation. No interpretive commentary was offered in the newsletter or the deacons' minutes about the progressive shift.[105]

With the bylaw change, the election of a woman deacon seemed to be the logical and expected step. The number of deacons increased to twelve from the previous nine for the election of deacons in September. With three new deacon slots and three deacons having rotated off the board, the congregation voted for six new deacons. Of the twelve candidates presented, however, Jan Purvis, president of Northminster Women, was the only woman. Given the push for women deacons for two consecutive years, without success, the appearance of only one woman on the ballot seems ironic unless it functioned as a strategic effort to focus on one candidate. In the end, Jan Purvis was elected the first woman deacon in Northminster's history. She was fifty-one years old, older than deacons had typically been in the brief history of the church. With the modifications to the size of the deacon board, four new deacons received three-year service terms, one received a two-year term, and one a one-year term. Purvis received the one-year term.

Church records make no explanation of the brevity of her service time. Purvis explained later that the new deacons drew straws and she simply came up the "loser." Outsiders could have wondered if she ended up with the "short end of the stick" because she was a woman. Later reflection contended that such speculation missed the point; that is, Purvis's election was not because she was a woman. Purvis later related that the decision to ordain her was not controversial—that while a commitment to women in ministry was "not written down in our DNA," it "was really there" in the congrega-

[105] N Bylaws 7 13 75; N News 7 16 75.

tion's foundational identity.[106] In an era where the election of a woman deacon would have been controversial at most Southern Baptist churches, Northminster members said the election of Purvis was simply the right thing to do because she was such a stellar leader.[107] Dudley Wilson recalled that he did not apply any kind of pressure to get Purvis nominated or elected because she was a woman. His recollection that there was no visible show of elation at her election (no more than would be shown for the election of any good leader)[108] is, in retrospect, a remarkable story on its own. Northminster was a "different" church testifying of its being cutting edge in a different manner.

Purvis's election perhaps was made easy because her leadership qualities were widely acknowledged; nevertheless, her election triggered a long tradition of women deacons at the church. The actual hour of the election, however, was clouded by the resignation of their pastor. Dudley Wilson read his letter of resignation to the church while the votes for the election were being counted. At his last Sunday evening service on September 21, 1975, Wilson led the ordination service of Jan Purvis and Trenton Shelton.[109]

Ministry of Cooperation: Southern Baptist Convention and Ecumenism

In the late 1960s, internal conflict festering in the Southern Baptist Convention was still a few years away from bubbling over at the local level. During his pastorate, Wilson spoke in favor of what he (and observers of Baptist history) declared to be a key historic Baptist principle: local church autonomy. After attending an annual meeting of the SBC, he said, "Despite some default and occasional infringement by denominational agencies, the autonomy of the church is still central in Southern Baptist life."[110] Wilson was the Mississippi representative to the Christian Life Commission of the SBC (elected June 1974), helped train candidates for the SBC Journeyman

---

[106] Purvis, interview, 12.

[107] Speed, interview, 10.

[108] Dudley Wilson, email to Doug Weaver, March 13, 2016.

[109] N Bylaws 9 7 75; N Minutes 9 7 75; Purvis, interview, 9, 10, 12; Purvis, "Reflections on Becoming Church"; N News 9 17 75; N Bulletin 9 21 75. Deacons' minutes never mention the issue of women deacons. Even when Jan Purvis and another (male) deacon are ordained, Purvis is not mentioned by name. See N Deacons 8 21 75 and N Deacons 9 11 75.

[110] N News 6 4 75.

program (a two-year foreign missions experience), and was a member of the Mississippi Religious Liberty Conference—a topic of importance to Baptists.[111] A few other Northminster members were actively involved in Southern Baptist life. Some attended meetings of the SBC's Christian Life Commission. In Mississippi Baptist life, for example, George Purvis was elected a vice president of the board of the Mississippi Baptist Convention in 1968.[112]

Ecumenical relations with neighboring Protestant churches began in the early years of Northminster's existence. Advertisements of ecumenical opportunities were often included in church bulletins. Immediately after Wilson's arrival in Jackson, for example, a meeting of the Jackson Interfaith Fellowship, held at the new Temple Beth Israel, was publicized. Thanksgiving gatherings, sponsored by the Jackson Clergy Alliance, were also advertised. In February 1968, women of the church were invited to attend World Day of Prayer services at St. Paul's Episcopal and Central United Methodist churches. An invitation to attend a meeting of the ecumenical group, Church Women United, first appeared in 1971; involvement in the organization increased extensively during the ministry of John Claypool.[113]

In August 1968, a joint worship service was held with Covenant Presbyterian Church, with additional services in subsequent years.[114] Some church members were involved in interracial civil rights activity and there met Monsignor Bernard Law, vice general from the Catholic diocese of Natchez-Jackson—who later became a well-known, controversial cardinal in Boston, Massachusetts. Law spoke at Northminster's Sunday evening discussion group in May 1971.[115] The congregation participated in other cooperative endeavors. For example, in 1972, the Youth Committee worked with, and received consultation from, those who worked with the youth of Fondren Presbyterian Church.

Dudley Wilson was very active in ecumenical ministry. He participated in the ordination of Catholic Bishop Joseph Howze, auxiliary bishop of the

---

[111] N Bulletin 6 9 74; N Bulletin 7 7 74.

[112] N Bulletin 12 1 68.

[113] N Bulletin 10 9 67; N Bulletin 2 18 68; N Bulletin 11 24 68; N Bulletin 5 2 71; N Bulletin 11 21 71.

[114] N Bulletin 8 12 69; N News 10 22 69; N News 8 14 70.

[115] N Bulletin 5 23 71; Purvis, interview, 13.

Natchez-Jackson diocese. In 1973, he served on the program of the Lay School of Religion, an ecumenical project of St. Andrew's Episcopal School (where two of his children attended).[116] He was also the speaker at the 1975 World Day of Prayer of the local chapter of Church Women United.[117]

Some observers have been critical of how religious traditions responded to the anti-Semitism present in Jackson and in Mississippi in general in the 1960s. Journalist Jack Nelson told the story of the Ku Klux Klan's bombing of Beth Israel on September 18, 1967, and then the bombing of Rabbi Nussbaum's home later on November 21. Nelson noted that Baptist groups did not denounce the bombings with any kind of public or official condemnation. In particular, Nussbaum was upset that the leading Baptist of Jackson, Douglas Hudgins of First Baptist Church, did not denounce the bombing on his televised worship service even though the rabbi had asked him to address it. One member of Northminster, Ken Dean, had been particularly active in cooperative work with the Anti-Defamation League, and it was Dean who, after the explosion awoke him during the night, called the regional director of the ADL to notify him of the attack on the synagogue. Nussbaum had worked with Dean closely and even hosted an interracial meeting at the synagogue that Dean organized (the event was controversial even in the Jewish community, many of whom were segregationists unlike Nussbaum). The individual relationship between Dean and Nussbaum, however, apparently encountered some frustration along the way.[118] In the heat of the bombing of his home, Nussbaum told Dean, "You're a white Christian—a Baptist, the worst kind for Jews. You've got a responsibility for what happened too. It's the Sunday-school lessons from the New Testament in Baptist churches that lead people to commit such terrible acts."[119]

---

[116] N Deacons 6 6 72; N News 3 13 73.

[117] N News 9 10 75.

[118] Jack Nelson, *Terror in the Night: The Klan's Campaign Against the Jews* (Jackson: University Press of Mississippi, 1996) 43–50, 60, 67, 71–73. Nussbaum, a Canadian, had previously worked in northern synagogues. In Jackson, he moved from a cautious public position on race (as many in his congregation were segregationists) to more open progressive stances. He left Jackson in 1973.

[119] http://archives.livedtheology.org/nodereference/thickbox/2157/thickbox_reference_full?width=700&height=500.

Northminster did not make any official statement about the bombings, though other personal acts of condolences were offered.[120] Dudley Wilson remembered hearing the explosion at Nussbaum's house—they lived just a few blocks apart—and going there to check on the rabbi. The Baptist pastor was standing by the Jewish rabbi when the police arrived to check on the explosion. Wilson remembered that the church expressed dismay at the attack in their worship following the tragedy. Thirteen days after the KKK attack on Nussbaum's residence, Northminster received a thank you note. "We shall always be grateful for your words of comfort when our lives were endangered on November 21, 1967," Nussbaum wrote. "We pray with you, especially at this season so important for all peoples of Faith, that the day will soon dawn when dreams of Peace, Liberty, and Human Dignity will be fulfilled, and men, women, and children everywhere will not need to live in fear of their fellows."[121]

At a later date, Wilson, who had an ongoing collegial relationship with Nussbaum, delivered a sermon for a National Brotherhood Week service at St. Andrew's Cathedral. Nussbaum heard the sermon, titled "The Reality of Brotherhood," and then asked Wilson to deliver it as a guest speaker at the synagogue for a Sabbath-eve service.[122] In 1971, Rabbi Nussbaum also spoke to the Sunday evening discussion group at Northminster.[123] Perhaps the most revealing indicator of the Jewish-Christian relations that developed out of the Wilson pastorate occurred in 1977 when Wilson returned to Jackson to officiate the wedding of Al Binder, a member of the Jewish congregation and a Jackson-based lawyer, and Nancy Geno, who was visiting Northminster and joined the church later that year. Binder and Wilson had become friends during the latter's ministry at Northminster. The wedding was not at

---

[120] There is no mention of the bombings in any church newsletter, church bulletin, or deacons' minutes.

[121] Kelley Williams Sr., "Adult Studies Evening Session, Comments on Dudley Wilson's sermon, 'Crisis at Christmas,'" (delivered December 10, 1969, Northminster Baptist Church)," October 2, 2016.

[122] "Northminster's Wilson to Talk at Beth Israel," *Northside Sun*, March 18, 1971; Dudley Wilson, email to Doug Weaver, March 13, 2016.

[123] N Bulletin 4 18 71.

the church or the synagogue, but members of both congregations attended.[124]

The decision to call the old Beth Israel facility Northminster's first stable worship home was a pivotal sign that the developing Baptist congregation would express an open, ecumenical, even interfaith, witness. As Donna Sones (Barksdale) noted as she considered attending the church as a college student, "We knew that if a Baptist church was meeting at the synagogue that they had to take a slightly different view of things."[125]

Outreach Ministries: Sports, Missionaries

Church recreation characterized most Baptist churches of the late 1960s and early 1970s. Northminster was no different, fielding youth basketball teams and a men's softball team. A bit unique for a church was a focus on tennis tournaments among members, but church members enjoyed that Wilson participated (and was good).[126] Youth ministry at the church included recreation activities, and some of those were adventurous. No doubt it is easier to remember later with a smile how pool players knocked holes in the walls of the recreation room with their pool sticks during their youthful participation.[127]

The church had some members who were involved in international missions. In 1969, A. B. and Kathy Short were appointed to serve at Hong Kong Baptist College as part of the two-year Southern Baptist Journeyman program. In 1972, Bob Coggins served as a medical missionary at Sandblast Island. The church gave him $150 in support. Lydia and Dan Jones did summer missions in Massachusetts for the SBC's Home Mission Board.[128]

Lay Leadership

From the outset, the congregation said that the church needed to be characterized by active lay involvement in ministry and congregational deci-

---

[124] Kelley Williams Sr., "Adult Studies, Comments on Dudley Wilson's sermon, 'Crisis at Christmas.'" Binder did not join the church (Barbara Webb, email to Kelley Williams Sr., October 20, 2016).

[125] Sones, interview, 4.

[126] N News 5 19 69; N News 12 15 71; Speed, interview, 5.

[127] N Deacons 7 18 74.

[128] N News 5 19 69; N News 6 1 72; N Deacons 6 6 72.

sions. In theological terms, church members wanted to embody Baptist DNA of congregational polity and the priesthood of all believers. Northminster developed an extensive list of committees—another Baptist practice of the mid-twentieth century—as an expression of congregational participation. It was no surprise, then, that members occasionally asked probing questions to make sure their commitments were being implemented. For example, in a September 1968 business meeting, Jaime Miller asked if the $2,000 budgeted for local missions would be spent at the discretion of the Missions Committee or if issues involving disbursement of funds would be discussed by the entire congregation and approved. If a particular missions issue was the context for Miller's question, church records were silent. Whatever the case, Miller was assured that the congregation would approve all monetary decisions from the committee with the exception that the pastor was given discretion to use some of the budgeted funds for individuals in need.[129] Throughout the Wilson years, a focus on voluntary lay service was emphasized. "Voluntary service is the foundation of the serving church," Wilson affirmed.[130] In later years, church members stressed that a lack of staff was not a reason for a lack of ministry: "the members did church."[131]

Social Ministry and Race Relations

The congregation had a keen sense for social ministry from the early days. Both men and women were active leaders on the Missions Committee. In spring 1969 the Missions Committee urged the church to participate in a clothing drive being promoted by the junior high students. The committee also funded small scholarships for a YMCA camp and for students from Mississippi College to do summer missions in Colorado.[132] Jan Purvis recalled that her first missions activity was transporting African-American children from an auxiliary branch of the YMCA to the downtown YMCA so they could go swimming.[133]

The Missions Committee report of 1969, for example, revealed an ambitious agenda: a visit to the Bethlehem Center (a "colored daycare center

[129] N Minutes 9 29 68.
[130] N News 5 14 75.
[131] Williams, "Northminster History."
[132] N News 3 18 69; N News 5 27 69.
[133] Purvis, interview, 11.

for young people"), interest in Operation Shoestring (developing a drug fund for needy individuals at a local pharmacy with the help of Dr. Julius Ratliff), more clothing drives, and implementation of a survey to identify church members willing to volunteer for various projects.[134]

Diversity in a congregation can often be seen through differences in political opinions and participation in public life. At times, political concerns were kept out of the doors of the church, at other times they were not. Various politically active, high-profile figures were members of the congregation in its earliest days. Ken Dean was an ordained Baptist minister who, as director of the Mississippi Council on Human Relations, took strong pro-integrationist positions in the public arena. He was considered, even for a civil rights worker, too radical by some because he worked with SNCC (Student Nonviolent Coordinating Committee), which played a major role in the sit-ins, freedom rides, and voter registration efforts in the early civil rights movement and would evolve to focus more on Black Power in the late 1960s.[135] On the other hand, Rubel Phillips, one of the congregation's founding five, had affirmed segregation of public life (e.g., opposing the desegregation of the University of Mississippi as most white Mississippians did at the time), became a Republican in the early 1960s, and ran for governor of Mississippi twice (1963, 1967). Wirt Yerger Jr., the founding chairman of the Mississippi Republican Party and ardent states' rights champion, was also a charter member of the church before leaving in 1973.[136]

Consequently, one area of controversy involving local missions was the issue of race, or ministry in the context of Jackson's ongoing civil rights tensions. Mississippi historians note that Lutherans and Episcopalians generally had open-door policies toward African Americans, but Presbyterians, Methodists, and Baptists usually resisted church integration—the more typical response in Mississippi.[137] Church records at Northminster Baptist

---

[134] N News 10 6 69.

[135] Nelson, *Terror in the Night*, 214. Nelson said that Dean talked to both the SNCC and to Klan sympathizers, so his civil rights work seemed suspicious to people with different viewpoints. At the same time, Nelson found Dean a reliable source for his work.

[136] Barbara Webb, email to Doug Weaver March 11, 2016; Speed, interview, 5.

[137] Randy J. Sparks, *Religion in Mississippi* (Jackson: University Press of Mississippi for the Mississippi Historical Society, 2001) 244.

Church are mostly silent on the role of race in the church. Dudley Wilson recalled that from the outset of his negotiations with the Pulpit Committee about becoming the church's pastor, he stated that the church had to be open to all; enforced segregation of worship could not be tolerated. Wilson said that there was some resistance to such a policy from church members. There was never a written policy as such.[138]

Interviews with charter members do reveal tensions at the church—again, membership comprised both civil rights activists and others not so inclined. The Sunday school hour, structured for intensive lay participation, was the place in church life where race (and other issues like war and peace) were discussed, and at times, rancorously, according to church memory. As Kelley Williams Sr. noted, "we literally in the early days had members on the political left who were civil rights workers and members of the political right who were Ku Klux Klan sympathizers. It was a very charged environment. We had Sunday school classes where people would get up and leave sometimes in tears, sometimes in anger." Williams Sr. suggested that one of the goals of the new member orientation program that Wilson led was to "let the people know what they were getting into."[139] Leland Speed also remembered Sunday school as a place where "thinking people, people you enjoy associating with, or butting heads with...could express a diversity of opinion." In his colorful manner, Speed said the discussions needed his perspective because there were some "real Bolsheviks" present. In later reflections, Speed noted that the congregation "prided ourselves on this diversity of opinion," yet he noted that "the heat got too heavy for some people."[140]

The Sunday evening discussion group evidently also discussed racial issues on occasion. In a church bulletin advertisement—that had no subsequent follow-up in any church document—the congregation was invited to watch *A Time for Burning*, a documentary about a Lutheran minister who attempted to persuade his all-white congregation to reach out to African-American Lutherans in the city. Northminster's church bulletin noted that the movie was about "a church experiencing tensions over social change."[141]

---

[138] Dudley Wilson, email to Doug Weaver, March 13, 2016.
[139] Kelley Williams Sr., interview by David Stricklin, February 29, 1992, 9.
[140] Speed, interview, 5; B. Boone, interview (2016), 24.
[141] N Bulletin 8 4 68.

Dudley Wilson was personally involved in a multitude of ministries to improve race relations and civic life in general. During his ministry, he moderated two televised public affairs programs, *In These Days* and *Interrobang*. He was involved in the "The Assortment," "an interracial group that worked to bring some stability to the community in the early days of racial crisis." Wilson was also a member of the Community Service Association, the local antipoverty agency; a member of the Alcohol Services Program; and president of the Downtown YMCA. Wilson was the only white Baptist member of the Jackson Clergy Alliance, the first interfaith, interdenominational, and interracial clergy group in the city (founded by Rabbi Nussbaum among others), and he served as its first president when it merged with two other groups to become the Jackson Ministerial Alliance.[142]

One of the church families heavily involved in civil rights work who desired for the church's ministries to anchor some social ministries around racial concerns was Dr. Jim and Mary Hendrick. The family's journey to Northminster reflects the congregation's openness to a diversity of views. The Hendricks were both heavily involved at Calvary Baptist Church, Jackson, with Dr. Hendrick having been the chair of deacons, but the church's membership strongly resisted any progress regarding civil rights for African Americans. Mary said that she and her husband were "converted" during the civil rights struggle. Mary related how her daughter, off at college, told her parents she could not return to their home church. Consequently, the Hendricks were drawn to the openness at Northminster. They became involved in the Monday evening discussion groups in summer 1967, even before committing to the church as members, and were extremely pleased with the attraction to the progressive, ecumenical Baptist future as being outlined by L. D. Johnson in those formative discussions.

The Hendricks, like Wilson, were involved in many interracial community activist programs, but the question of how to navigate that participation within church life was an ever-present issue, according to Mary Hendrick. In later reflections, she said that "race has caused trouble from the very first" in the life of the congregation but acknowledged progress had

[142] N News 9 10 75. First reference to the television program *In These Days* was N Bulletin 9 22 68.

been made in later decades. No doubt, the reflections were conditioned by memories of two key events in the 1960s that involved disappointment.[143]

The first notice in church records about anything pertaining to racial issues involved Jim Hendrick asking the deacons in November 1969 to recommend to the congregation a resolution supporting Mississippi College's decision to sign a letter of compliance regarding desegregation laws. The leading Baptist college in the state, MC had no official ties to the church, of course, but had many informal connections to the congregation (the school has a Leland Speed [Sr.] Library, and several of the more progressive professors and students were members of the congregation). Through the 1950s and 1960s, the school's administration had been strongly opposed to desegregation of its student population, so much so that Mississippi historian Randy Sparks has described the school as the "segregationist citadel" of the state.[144] For example, popular president Dotson McGinnis Nelson (1932–1957; the current administration building at MC is named Nelson Hall) wrote a pro-segregationist tract, *Conflicting Views on Segregation*, which was published by the Association of Citizens' Councils. The deacons at Northminster thoroughly discussed Hendrick's motion about Mississippi College—deacon minutes say that each deacon present spoke—but in the end, no one seconded the motion and thus no vote was taken. Attitudes toward civil rights and Baptist affiliated colleges were no doubt conflicted.[145]

The question of the integration of Jackson public schools is never mentioned in church records, but Dudley Wilson addressed the topic from the pulpit in the midst of unrest in the city. The Fifth Circuit Court in New Orleans decreed on December 1, 1969, that desegregation of the schools would occur in fall 1970, but many in Jackson were taken aback when the United States Supreme Court on December 9 ordered schools to desegregate immediately. Jackson's newspaper, the *Clarion Ledger*, announced to its readers in its December 10 edition that the integration would begin just a few weeks later in January 1970. The three-year-old Northminster congregation, with its growing body of young families, had ninety-three children, with forty-four under the age of three. Wilson had four children in the public schools, two in junior high, and two in elementary school. With emo-

[143] Mary Hendrick, interview by David Stricklin, March 1, 1992, 3–4, 10.
[144] Sparks, *Religion in Mississippi*, 230.
[145] N Deacons 11 19 69.

tions running high in Jackson, Wilson preached a sermon on December 14 titled "Crisis at Christmas."

Wilson told the congregation that he decided to address the public-school issue because of the "fear and anxiety" and "emotional stress" present in the city with the impending societal changes. In an era when some whites responded to desegregation laws by creating their own private schools (sometimes unaccredited private church schools), and many lashed out with visceral emotional anger at all branches of the government, Wilson urged his congregants to be faithful, law-abiding citizens as Christians are called to do, according to Romans 13 (the primary biblical passage cited for Christian citizenship). They did not have to like the ruling of the Supreme Court regarding desegregation, but they should obey it as the law of the land. Wilson cautioned against fear and said that panic could adversely complicate the tense situation. In his most progressive assertions, Wilson reminded the congregation that American society was not guiltless when it came to white and black relations. As the Jews paid for the sins of their fathers (Exod 20:5), the current problem was traceable back to the sin of slavery. He noted,

> The tenor of the New Testament teaching for the life of the Christian is one of letting loose of one's self in the way of the Christ. Part of today's problem is that we have really never done this. We have gained and protected our prosperity and privilege. We have cared little about how it has been with Blacks or with the poor. It has not mattered that the educational standards for their schools were poor, that facilities until this decade were pitiful. We made it, one way or another, and we expected them to do likewise. The problem this poses for Christians is that it is neither a Christian attitude nor a Christian way of looking at the world.[146]

Wilson exhorted his hearers to ask, "How can I help my neighbor?" and to do what was best for the common good. He suggested that parents not shield their children from the preparation and experiences of living in the "real world." Wilson concluded with a plea to support public school education as part of the practice of Christian citizenship because "public school

---

[146] Dudley Wilson, "Crisis at Christmas" (delivered December 10, 1969), in *Northminster: Reflections on Past Voices for Future Service* (Jackson: Northminster Baptist Church, 2016) 5.

education has the dimension of being a laboratory in which the young participate and learn how it is in the world."[147]

Church members responded to the desegregation mandate differently. Some, like Wilson, ultimately had mixed responses. Wilson's two oldest children (Cindy and Jeff) remained and graduated from the integrated public school. The two youngest children (Beth and Frances) started in public schools but were soon placed in St. Andrew's, a private school. Dudley and his wife, Inez, decided that the public-school setting for their youngest children, who had expressed fear in their new public school, was not a safe learning environment. Some other Northminster parents followed a similar path.[148]

Another issue involving race soon created havoc in the Board of Deacons and revealed how the issue of race caused tension in churches and their ministries even when charity and benevolence were involved. In January 1971, the Missions Committee recommended giving $1,000 of the $2,000 allotment for local missions to a daycare center being established at an African-American church, Mt. Helm Baptist Church, at 300 East Church Street. This project was sponsored and arranged by the Jackson Urban League—Jim Hendrick was its president, and its motto was "equal life chances and equal life results for Blacks and other low income families"—and would be financed with local (25 percent) and federal (75 percent) funds.[149]

A fundraising letter for the daycare center sent out by the Urban League, however, brought consternation from some church members. When asking for funds, the letter indicated that Northminster had already voted to give $1,000 for the project.[150] The May 1971 meeting of the deacons began with discussion about the letter. Some church members complained that the letter implied that the church had voted to make a direct contribution to the Jackson Urban League. After considerable deliberation, Homer Best, seconded by John Kitchings, made a motion to send a letter to church mem-

---

[147] Ibid., 12.

[148] Kelley Williams Sr., "Adult Studies, Comments on Dudley Wilson's sermon, 'Crisis at Christmas.'"

[149] N Deacons 1 20 71; N Minutes 1 31 71.

[150] Jackson Urban League fundraising letter (general, not addressed to church), February 9, 1971.

bers to clarify the situation, in other words, that Northminster was supportive of the creation of the daycare center but had not given any direct support to the Jackson Urban League. A separate letter would be sent to the Urban League expressing disapproval of the use of the church's name in a fundraising campaign for the League (rather than just the daycare center) and the League was instructed not to use the name of the church in any future communications.[151] When Jack Dean, chair of the deacons, wrote the congregation, he explained the Missions Committee support of the daycare center. According to Dean, the Missions Committee had previously (in 1968) looked into Northminster developing a ministry for children of low-income families but had decided the church did not have the resources to fund it.[152]

The situation still had not resolved ruffled feelings. In June 1971, Hendrick met with the deacons about the issue, feeling he had been misrepresented. He suggested that the $1,000 church contribution be resubmitted to the congregation for review. However, George Purvis moved that no reconsideration be undertaken, and his motion was unanimously carried.[153] Twenty-five years later, Mary Hendrick noted that the church eventually accomplished some good things involving race relations. However, she remembered the Urban League story as "one of the deep sorrows of our lives" and a "devastating experience."[154] Negotiating racial justice was no doubt a challenge, even at churches that had repudiated the segregationist exclusions going on at other churches in Jackson.

The first recognition at Northminster of the Southern Baptist-sponsored Race Relations Sunday occurred in February 1972. No observance was held during worship—that came during the ministry of John Claypool. The church bulletin noted, "Throughout the Southern Baptist Convention, today is designated Race Relations Sunday, a day on which we remember not only the universal appeal of Christ but also the application of Christian faith to relationships."[155] Issues of race at Northminster were open to dialogue and heated debate, unlike the exclusionary atmosphere that characterized explicitly segregationist churches in the region, but certainly

---

[151] N Deacons 5 17 71.
[152] Jack Dean to church members, 5 20 71.
[153] N Deacons 6 21 71.
[154] Hendrick, interview, 14.
[155] N Bulletin 2 3 72.

social tensions were rarely missing at Northminster in this era of rapid social change.

The church was involved in a variety of social ministries in the early 1970s. The church televised services in 1973–1974.[156] Other ministries were more social-service oriented. In 1972, for example, $500 was given to a Youth Crisis Center (church member A. B. Short was the director), and $500 to a hospital in the Philippines (where Billy Jernberg had served as a summer missionary). In 1973, the Missions Committee promoted a hot lunch program for the elderly of rural Hinds County.[157] Adults and youth worked with a significant initiative in social ministry at the Good Samaritan Center. In 1974, $2,000 was allotted to the center on North Farish Street, and Missions Committee chair Suzanne Grogan joined their board.[158]

Another significant social ministry during the early years was support of Operation Shoestring, an ecumenical ministry located in and serving the inner city of Jackson and working primarily with the urban poor, both black and white. The ministry focused on a variety of social services: tutoring, crisis intervention, preschool for twenty children, a counseling referral service, medical services (providing inoculation and maternity services), and a thrift shop. The church newsletter gave significant space to explaining Operation Shoestring as an ecumenical ministry effort that would maximize the church's local missions emphasis and its ecumenical participation. The ministry would also provide hands-on opportunities for members to gain expertise "in working with and for Jacksonians of classes and races different from their own." Prior to June 1972, there had been some involvement in the ministry. In June, however, the church decided to support the agency more formally with a gift of $500. The Missions Committee also recommended that up to five church members do an internship at the ministry.[159] In 1975, the church was still heavily involved in the work of Operation Shoestring, especially its medical work, which had been a key component from the outset. The congregation allotted $600 for support of the weekly volunteer medical clinic—paying the drug bill for cases requiring special prescriptions

[156] N Minutes 11 11 73; N Deacons 3 37 74.

[157] N News 6 1 72; N Deacons 6 6 72; N Minutes 11 11 73.

[158] N Minutes 4 7 74. Northminster was one of nine cooperating churches supporting the Good Samaritan ministry (see N Bulletin 10 27 74).

[159] N Minutes 6 11 72; N News 6 9 72; N News 6 27 72.

not available from drug samples donated to the clinic—after having given $603 in the last year.[160]

Dudley Wilson's Resignation

Dudley Wilson resigned on September 7, 1975, to become the pastor of Calder Baptist Church, Beaumont, Texas. His last Sunday was September 21. The sermon was a tribute of thanksgiving to the congregation. They had been his partner in the gospel; the relationship was not pastor to people but they were friends, he said. Wilson warmly remembered the church's call to him to be the pastor in the same vein as they said, "Come and share with us this venture of faith." Wilson concluded the sermon with an illustration about Ara Parseghian, the legendary Notre Dame football coach who had recently resigned. To a crowd at a Notre Dame basketball game who had cheered him wildly then sat hushed as he addressed them, Parseghian said, "These have been the greatest years of my life and now I leave, but I will always be Notre Dame." Wilson's last sermonic words were, "I will always be Northminster."[161]

Dudley Wilson returned to preach at the church several times. The church newsletter included plaudits for Wilson's ministry. He was applauded for taking an "unorganized group" and helping instill in them a sense of family, particularly notable when there was early bickering over the church's developing identity. Wilson was praised for setting a standard of excellence (and brevity) in the pulpit for subsequent pastors, and for establishing the congregation as a strong Southern Baptist church "while allowing us to be innovative and creative." Wilson commented that the most significant gift the church gave him was "the people of Northminster have accepted me as a person who is the minister."[162]

---

[160] N News 3 26 75.

[161] Dudley Wilson, "Sermon," Northminster Baptist Church, September 21, 1975.

[162] N News 9 10 75; Williams, "Northminster History." Even at his third anniversary as pastor, Wilson was praised for creating a sense of the church as family (see N Bulletin 10 25 70).

Chapter 3

On the Map: Church Growth and the Ministry of John Claypool

The Interim between Dudley Wilson and John Claypool

Staff: Interim Pastors and Guest Preachers. Supply preachers during fall 1975 included Bradley Pope, director of the Baptist Student Union at Mississippi College; Robert Shurden, professor of New Testament at MC; Foy Valentine, executive director of the Christian Life Commission of the Southern Baptist Convention; and Carlyle Marney, a well-known progressive Baptist pastor. Shurden became the interim pastor on November 9, 1975.[1] The Pulpit Committee announced in the spring that it was doing "intense work," but they were not yet ready to present a candidate.[2] Shurden—who later reflected that his interim at Northminster was "one of the best experiences of my life…the congregation's commitment to quality brought the very best out of anyone"[3]—announced he was not going to carry the interim pastorate into fall 1976. Consequently, the congregation, now a year without a regular pastor, felt they needed a new interim who would assume full-time pastoral responsibilities. Seasoned pastor Dr. Lewis Rhodes became interim in September 1976. He had preached at the church twice that summer as well as during the church's earliest days when worship was conducted at the Mississippi School for the Blind (two daughters were members of Northminster). Rhodes had been pastor of Daniel Memorial Baptist Church in Jackson but most recently had retired from Broadway Baptist Church in Knoxville, Tennessee.[4]

---

[1] N Minutes 11 2 75.

[2] N News 4 14 76.

[3] Robert Shurden, correspondence with Doug Weaver, March 23, 2016. Students at Mississippi College considered Shurden a powerful preacher and teacher. Doug Weaver took several classes with Shurden and considered him the best professor at MC.

[4] N News 7 21 76; N Deacons 8 8 76.

Lay Leadership. The emphasis on lay leadership was evident in the interim era. The congregation said it wanted to be involved in the approval of the interim pastor; the process should not just be left in the hands of key leaders. At the same time, the deacons rejected a motion in one of their meetings that deacons and their spouses "assume worship service duties" to check lighting and other arrangements and to assist the supply pastor in welcoming members.[5] A definition of lay leadership was not uniform but evolving.

Ministry of Education and Service. The Wilson years prepared Northminster to grapple with some theologically progressive traits. In September 1975, the church newsletter asked, "Is there a generation gap between what you were taught about Christian doctrines as a child and what you would like to incorporate into your creative adult life?" For example, the Sunday evening discussion group looked at the doctrine of creation in a six-week study and used professors from Mississippi College and Millsaps College as resource facilitators. One session was on biological theories of the origin of life, and another compared creation myths in ancient cultures (Babylonian, Sumerian, African, Indian, and Chinese) with the biblical account of creation. The group also read the writings of German theologian Helmut Thielicke, not the easy reading usually found in traditional church training sessions.[6]

Throughout the interim era, ministries continued. The vibrant ministry for children, the Children's Choir, performed the musical *A Rhyme, a Riddle, a Song* by well-known Baptist musician, Buryl Red.[7] The language of Advent permeated Christmas worship. One aspect of the Christmas celebration that became common in Baptist circles, even for those that did not give great focus to Advent, was the use of the Chrismon tree to enhance the visual imagery of the season. In terms of social ministry, the church paid $391.32 for the purchase of medicine for Operation Shoestring where church members Jim Hendrick and Sam Walters provided staff leadership. Allen Harris, a student from Ole Miss, was hired as summer youth director.

[5] N News 10 1 75; N Deacons 9 25 75.
[6] N News 10 1 75.
[7] N News 5 12 76.

United States Congressman Thad Cochran joined the church in February 1976.[8]

Ministry of Stewardship. Financial difficulties that concerned the congregation continued for a while during the interim period. In October 1975, S.H. McDonnieal Jr., chair of the deacons, reported to the congregation that $3,200 in bills could not be paid at the end of the last month and a mortgage payment of approximately $5,100 was due with no money to cover it. Consequently, the church would have to borrow money to meet the obligations. With fewer personnel expenses, however, debt issues eventually subsided, and by January 1976 the $7,500 borrowed for operational expenses had been repaid.[9]

Women in Leadership and Ministry. Women had long provided leadership in missions in Southern Baptist life. During the interim period, Northminster continued to observe a week of prayer for foreign missions and took up collections for both the Lottie Moon Christmas Offering (international or "foreign" missions) and the Annie Armstrong Offering (domestic or "home" missions).[10]

In 1976, the recognition of women in positions of official leadership expanded further. The Deacon Nominating Committee of six included three women: Jan Purvis, Dot O'Brien, and Jerri Harvey. The ballots for the deacon election in August had ten names, including two women, Jerri Harvey and Donette Lee. Two additional names, one of which was Margaret Phillips, were added to the ballot from the floor. Five deacons were elected, including one woman, Jerri Harvey. The Committee on Committees also had women representatives. The committee, which had ongoing members like the chair of deacons, the incoming chair, and the president of Northminster Women, also elected Jerri Harvey as one of its three at-large members.[11]

---

[8] N News 2 11 76; N News 2 18 76; N Deacons 5 16 76; N News 10 19 76.
[9] N News 10 8 75; N News 1 14 76.
[10] N News 11 5 75; N News 3 10 76.
[11] N News 7 13 76; N Minutes 8 22 76.

The Calling of Dr. John Claypool

Though Northminster was not a long-established church, the congregation was determined to get the best pastor available in Baptist life. "If it were Billy Graham, so be it. We would persuade him to come here" was the attitude of the search committee. Kelley Williams Sr., pulpit search chair, recalled, "We were not deterred by reality and by the limitations of our situation, so when we got ready for number two (after Graham), we just went about that the same way. Who's the best pulpitarian in the convention? John Claypool. Well, we'd get John Claypool."[12]

Robert Shurden, interim pastor, remembered the focus on Claypool in similar terms. Shurden recalled offering the names of several prospective pastors to the Pulpit Committee. Included in his list was John Claypool, his friend and former mentor in preaching at Southern Baptist Theological Seminary. Shurden cautioned, practically withdrawing the suggestion when he concluded, "But you will never get him to leave Texas to come to Mississippi, and you probably cannot afford him." Shurden related that a "bright and insightful member of the search committee" said, "That is the person we want." When Claypool was called as pastor, Shurden was impressed and "learned anew never to tell Northminsters what they 'cannot' do."[13]

Kelley Williams Sr. revealed how timing and circumstance aided the congregation's ability to call Claypool: "John is just fantastic in the pulpit but not overly enamored of the administrative work.... As far as administration and running the staff of thirty or forty people, that gets to be a chore. It's not fun. It turned out that we called John at a time when he had just about had it up to here with the big church staff and all of those demands and complications and distractions." "Deliberate calculated strategies" on both sides—church and pastor—were part of the call process, Williams Sr. acknowledged, but the church no doubt believed that John Claypool had a divine call to be the new pastor of Northminster Baptist Church.[14]

In late August 1976, Williams Sr. reported that progress was being made in the search for a pastor. He offered details about the search, acknowledging that some time was intentionally allotted for healing after the

---

[12] Kelley Williams Sr., interview by David Stricklin, February 29, 1992, 10.
[13] Robert Shurden, correspondence.
[14] Williams, interview, 10.

loss of the church's first pastor. Since January, however, the Pulpit Committee—composed of Williams Sr., S. H. McDonnieal, Jan Purvis, Rubel Phillips, Jim Ratliff, Denise Hester, Nancy McDaniel, Zach Taylor, and Lucian Harvey Jr. (who had just replaced Sunday school superintendent Earl Eddins, who had moved out of state), had looked at more than fifty candidates and had conducted in-depth conversations with eight men from five different states. As of August, "several active prospects" were being considered.[15] No doubt the lengthy duration of being without a pastor was challenging to a still-youthful congregation. Suzanne Boone remembered that "it just seemed so long." She recalled that July 4th felt like the low point. The country was celebrating and the church was struggling. "I don't think I can hang on much longer," she told her husband, Bill. "The joy is gone. There just doesn't seem to be the same spirit here." His response was one of acknowledgement yet perseverance. Prayer and reflection were absolutely necessary, he said, "We can't give up now."[16]

The long process was soon over, however. A letter extending a call to become pastor of Northminster Baptist Church was sent on September 8, 1976, to prominent Baptist pastor John Claypool. Claypool was currently at Broadway Baptist Church, Fort Worth, Texas (and before that, Crescent Hill Baptist Church, Louisville, Kentucky) a church populated with many professors, staff, and students from Southwestern Baptist Theological Seminary. There was no "trial sermon"—the typical Baptist method of inviting a prospective pastor to preach to the church in view of the call—but Claypool had been a guest preacher at the church in July.

The search committee's letter to Claypool discussed the congregation's identity and ministry intentions.[17] Couching its vision for Claypool in terms of Northminster's focus on laity, the letter declared, "As Pastor you will be our spiritual leader. You will not practice our religion for us but will help and enable us as we search together for understanding and growth in faith." The letter also emphasized Northminster's desire to focus on the spiritual nurture of their children. Summarizing prior negotiations, the letter outlined three promises, all which reflected the reputation and pulpit prominence of the prospective pastor. First, Northminster would as soon as possible add a

---

[15] N Minutes 8 22 76.

[16] Suzanne Boone, interview by Aaron Weaver, February 22, 2016, 11.

[17] N News 6 29 76.

full-time associate pastor (as an intern probably). Second, the church would arrange to continue a ministry of sermon distribution, both written and taped sermons, that Claypool had at his previous churches. Third, the letter noted a significantly increased benefits package in light of Claypool's expected scholarly pursuits. Four weeks of vacation and five weeks for church-related activities like continuing education would be provided, as well as a sabbatical of twelve weeks every third year in lieu of the nine weeks of vacation and leave.[18]

Claypool accepted the church's offer with arrangements that he would begin in December 1976. He spent the month of November as a research fellow at Yale Divinity School (his son, Rowan, was a student at Yale). Claypool told Northminster that his goal was to spend time reading the Scriptures and studying "contemplation, meditation and the whole range of Christian spirituality." The church had one opportunity to see Claypool before he began his pastoral duties when he gave a keynote address at the Mississippi Baptist Convention on November 17, which was held at First Baptist Church, Jackson.[19]

The Assessment of Interim Pastor Lewis Rhodes

While the congregation awaited the arrival of John Claypool, Lewis Rhodes completed his interim pastoral duties. In October 1976, Rhodes wrote a remarkably straightforward column in the church newsletter of his "mid-term impressions." He offered positive, yet challenging words. He affirmed that the "Northminster experience was needed for this city. It meets some of the needs of some people. It probably will meet more people at points of their needs." Rhodes noted there was significant talent in the church, and he affirmed the focus on worship as a key to congregational identity. The church was "an alternative to 'sect' type worship." Without departing from the best of the Baptist tradition, some of the best of the Christian tradition is used. Rhodes complimented the church for having a vision of hope and for working to move beyond negative criticisms of its emerging vision. Still, the "embryonic vision" was "unclear and undefined as yet," and the "positive ingredients of the vision have not emerged in bold relief." Finally, Rhodes completed his assessment with a word about the

[18] N Minutes 9 8 76.
[19] N News 9 22 76; N News 11 9 76.

church's ministries. He praised Northminster for its "authentic gestures" of ministry to the larger society but said how the congregation decided to show concern for the world was part of the "unwritten agenda" of their future.[20]

Just as Rhodes had written a midterm assessment of his short interim ministry at Northminster, he offered another remarkable final three months' assessment in the last column he wrote for the church newsletter at the end of November. The column was again a straightforward reflection piece, written by someone who cared for the church but with a bluntness rarely read in church documents. The recently retired pastor was certainly willing to say it like he saw it. He affirmed his earlier impressions made six weeks earlier and added more positive comments, but he was even more challenging and pointed than in his original list. Rhodes commented,

> 1. The wedding of John Claypool and Northminster was honorable and the covenant was made in good faith. Living together should make of it a good marriage.
> 2. There is a bit too much seriousness about being and doing church to suit me (that may indict me and compliment you). A healthy sense of humor about yourself could work for your salvation. Coming of age brings with it the capacity to laugh *at* and *with* oneself.
> 3. An adequate balance between staff direction and lay direction has not evolved as yet.
> 4. There is expressed concern about the image of the church, particularly, how Southern Baptists view Northminster. You have to decide how mortgaged you wish to be to a denomination.
> 5. Northminster is an all-white church.
> 6. Northminster is a male-controlled church.
> 7. Northminster is overwhelmingly of one economic class.
> 8. I hear the "golden oldie" playing from time to time: We want the type (if not content) of religious education for our children that we had. There is a residue of "gimme that old time religion."
> 9. There is a desire to remain small yet to have programs that come only with larger numbers.
> 10. Can you be saved from institutionalism? Institutionalism is giving priority to saving the institution, believes it serves a useful pur-

[20] N News 10 19 76.

pose by its mere existence, assuming its being born gives it the right to live on and on, a mindset that turns to saving the church, rather than putting the church to the service of persons.[21]

Some of Rhodes's reflections were addressed in explicit ways. For example, the role of women in the congregation's leadership structure was beginning to expand, and the question of the relationship to Southern Baptists would also soon heat up. The issue of race found its way even more into the church's newsletter during the next few years. Other issues were, it seems, a matter of debate. One thing was certain: the congregation was pleased to have John Claypool coming. The church approved a budget of $195,412 and was ready to grow.[22]

The Claypool Years

Staff. Some staff transitions occurred as Claypool began his ministry. James Furlow, who had been the church organist since the third Sunday of the church's history, resigned in December 1976. Billy Trotter, a professor at Mississippi College, assumed organist duties in January 1977. The next month MC professor, Phil Stanberry, resigned his part-time work in religious education but remained an active church member.[23]

Part of the church's negotiations with Claypool before he arrived was the hiring of an associate minister or intern. In January 1977, he announced that Owen Henderson, a December graduate of Southwestern Baptist Theological Seminary, was a candidate to be the church's first "pastoral intern." Claypool was pleased, suggesting the two-year internship would make Northminster a "teaching church." The position would certainly place the congregation on the cutting edge of theological education (and for Southern Baptists, ahead of their time) where service in a local church became the final stage of a minister's professional training before assuming a more permanent position. The intern would assume the duties of an associate pastor though the initial work was with youth and young adults.[24] Henderson stayed until September 1, 1978, when he left to begin a clinical pastoral care

[21] N News 11 30 76.
[22] N News 11 30 76.
[23] N News 2 3 77.
[24] N News 1 19 77; N Minutes 1 23 77.

program. The congregation appreciated the positive impact Henderson made in youth work.[25]

After Henderson's departure, the church, especially the deacons, decided to hire a full-time staff member to address the congregation's desire for a more vibrant, extensive educational program. After discussion, and an amendment proposed by Jann James during a church business meeting, the new position was "associate minister" rather than "associate minister of education."[26] Also, a student intern from Mississippi College would work with youth and be supervised by the new associate minister.[27] Charlie Johnson, who later became a well-known Baptist pastor in Texas, was named the student intern during fall 1978.[28] Johnson served as an intern for a year and became the first person to be "licensed" as a gospel minister by Northminster Baptist Church. After Johnson graduated from Mississippi College and moved to Pontotoc, Mississippi, Claypool preached his ordination sermon. Claypool cited Johnson's internship as another excellent exhibit of Northminster as a "teaching church."[29] In later reflections, Johnson said that Northminster and Claypool were "unbelievably affirming of me" and "the internship benefitted me more than the church." Johnson was certainly grateful, noting that Claypool became his mentor while he was at Northminster and continued in that role for the next thirty years.[30]

In August 1978, Henry Grady Guest was called as associate minister. He was a Mississippi native and attended William Carey College and Southern Baptist Theological Seminary. He had a progressive or "cutting edge" résumé, with leadership training at Church of the Savior in Washington, D.C.—a church known for its focus on communal spirituality and socially progressive positions. Guest had also been a minister of religious education at a predominantly African-American congregation in Lexington, Kentucky, and did education and youth ministry in Wiggins, Mississippi, where he developed an extensive summer day camp for the whole communi-

[25] N News 8 16 78.

[26] N News 5 4 78; N Minutes 6 4 78.

[27] N News 5 4 78; N Minutes 6 4 78.

[28] N News 9 20 78.

[29] N News 5 16 79; N News 9 23 80.

[30] Charlie Johnson, telephone interview with Doug Weaver, March 30, 2016. Johnson and Weaver first knew each other as classmates at Mississippi College.

ty. Guest's background foreshadowed the type of ministry he attempted to offer at Northminster.[31]

Given the church's decision to call Guest as associate minister rather than give him a title that restricted his work to education, Claypool spoke highly of Guest's openness and flexibility. When Claypool was to be absent one Sunday soon after Guest's arrival, the pastor informed the congregation that Guest would be preaching and reminded them that, though Guest was an associate, he was "an authentic minister of the whole church."[32] Guest offered various educational programs, in particular, academic studies of the Bible on Sunday evenings that would give the congregation the type of Christian education they said they wanted—studies that moved beyond the more elementary biblical training often associated with Sunday school.

Guest was working out his ministerial identity during his experience at Northminster. He eschewed the more traditional language of "shepherd" to denote the expected ministerial leadership style and opted for the nonconventional (and controversial) term "shaman"—as one who desires to lead him/her into a peculiar devotion to things of the spirit. "It means I don't spend eight hours a day sitting behind a desk which sometimes raises the difficulty of justifying the use of time by traditional, business-oriented standards," Guest elaborated. "Many mornings I stay at home to study. Occasionally I take a day off to play." Guest sometimes complained about doing the mundane facets of a job and was asked if he was unhappy at Northminster. His reply was revealing—"I have my moments"—but he also knew his dissatisfaction was due to his "quest toward omnipotence."[33] By November 1979, Guest's identity pilgrimage, played out in the church's newsletter, neared a climax. He said, "Gone is my passion for converting Catholics, Jews, and other heathen, and in its place has come a new passion for being creatively engaged with the poorest, most oppressed parts of the human family." Guest advocated daily time, silence, and contemplative prayer with Scripture meditation—all emphases of the Church of the Savior, which had profoundly influenced him.[34]

---

[31] N Minutes 8 13 78.

[32] N News 10 5 78.

[33] N News 9 5 79; N News 9 12 79; N News 9 19 79.

[34] N News 11 7 79.

Guest offered a ministry of progressive (no doubt most said *radical*) social advocacy. Beginning in January 1979, Guest used the church newsletter to attack what he believed was the immoral nuclear arms race that engulfed American foreign policy.[35] Several months later, he advocated for a nuclear freeze, saying, "Nuclear terror is appropriate to a Godless philosophy." In October 1979, he preached a sermon, "Freeing Pharaoh," where he identified Pharaoh in the Moses story as comparable to the United States government, which oppressed and exploited the poor. In his strongest message offered at the outset of 1980, only weeks after ninety people, including sixty-six Americans who had been taken captive on November 4, 1979, in the Iran hostage crisis, Guest declared that the Ayatollah Khomeini could be used as "a metaphor for at least one level of our own national existence. Like a mirror, he reflects that insanely violent side of us holding the world hostage by a threat to commit mass murder via nuclear war."[36] In contrast to Guest's confrontational political statements, John Claypool criticized Khomeini in a sermon as an example of the dangers of oversimplifying complexities into absolutized single issues. Claypool's more measured sermonic reflections never compared the terrorism of Iran to American nuclear power.[37]

In January 1980, after sixteen months at Northminster, Hank Guest resigned his position with the stated intent to plant a church called Ecclesia in Jackson to be patterned after the Church of the Savior. Upon Guest's resignation, Claypool said he and Guest had been talking about his dream of a church plant for almost a year. Guest and Claypool offered a joint sermon on January 27 to demonstrate, according to Claypool, how Guest's "vision grows out of Northminster's original dream to be an innovative and an alternative expression of the Body of Christ here in Jackson."[38] In the sermon, Guest said he wanted to be a servant to the poor since God identifies most with the weak and the poor. Claypool said Guest's alternative community was not a "negative splitting but a positive enlargement of opportunity."[39]

---

[35] N News 1 24 79.

[36] N News 9 26 79; N News 10 17 79; N News 1 2 80.

[37] John Claypool, "Simplicity, Complexity and Our Present Crisis," sermon, Northminster Baptist Church, January 6, 1980.

[38] N News 1 23 80.

[39] John Claypool and Hank Guest, "Hello and Goodbye," a (shared) sermon, Northminster Baptist Church, January 27, 1980.

To support Guest's transition, the church provided him ninety days of salary. Remarkably gracious, the church newsletter allowed Guest to promote his new church, inviting members to meet and explore the new venture in a meeting at the home of A. B. and Janie Short (the only other members committed to joining Guest at that time). No other announcement about Guest's new venture appeared in future Northminster publications, however. While Claypool's words about Guest were indeed gracious, the church newsletter was never used by subsequent ministers in the way that Guest did.[40] Guest stayed in Jackson for a year before leaving to be a part of the Church of the Savior, which he often promoted. The Guest saga no doubt had conflicted elements for the congregation.

Northminster had its first female ministerial staff members during the Claypool years. In May 1979, Karen Overstreet was named summer youth director, but she then stayed on as regular staff.[41] Adults who were youth during Overstreet's ministry had good, humorous memories of her work. Kelley Williams Jr. said that when Overstreet was pregnant, she had the youth play a game, "guess my diameter." Dudley Wooley remembered a youth trip to the beach when they smelled a strong burning smell coming from Overstreet's station wagon. The emergency brake had been left on and the brakes were ruined.[42]

After Hank Guest resigned, the congregation again reassessed its staff needs and reiterated that the "faithing" of the congregation's children was a theological priority. Ed Wall, deacon chair, said that Pat Travis, the current church secretary, was easily recognized by the congregation as the right person to join the ministerial staff. Travis was a graduate of Mississippi College and Southern Baptist Theological Seminary and was already known as a resource person for children and youth ministry conferences in larger Baptist circles.[43] Consequently, in March 1980, Travis was called as minister of Christian education, rather than associate minister, with a focus on education and family life enrichment.[44] Her husband, James Travis, was chaplain

[40] N Minutes 2 10 80; N News 2 13 80.

[41] N Deacons 5 27 79; N Deacons 3 16 80.

[42] Kelley Williams Jr. and Dudley Wooley, cited from audio, "Growing Up at Northminster," Adult Studies Sunday Evening Session, April 2, 2017.

[43] N Minutes 3 24 80.

[44] N News 3 5 80; N Minutes 3 30 80.

and director of Pastoral Services at the University Medical Center in Jackson. When Claypool took a sabbatical during summer 1980, James Travis was hired to provide temporary pastoral service consultation to the congregation.[45] Barbara Webb continued as church clerk during the Claypool years. Her work was described as similar to the human heart—"rarely visible but utterly crucial!"[46]

Polity: Bylaws

Just a few months after Claypool began his pastorate, Northminster extensively revised its bylaws. The congregation reaffirmed a statement promoting both open communion as their approach to the Lord's Supper and open baptism (acceptance of infant baptism for a transfer of membership from a denomination that practiced it). Also re-affirmed were the congregation's defining four-prong ministry goals of worship, education, service, and cooperation.[47] Other bylaws also revealed significant markers about the congregation's self-identity. The historic Baptist principle of local church autonomy (i.e., the congregation was under the control of no other ecclesiastical organization) was affirmed as were cooperative affiliations with the Hinds-Madison Baptist Association, the Mississippi Baptist Convention, and the Southern Baptist Convention.[48]

The bylaws also elaborated on the nature and functions of deacons. In addition to deacons being referred to as "persons" rather than men, the primary function or identity of deacons was reoriented. In the church's original bylaws, deacons were tasked with handling the business and financial affairs of the church. They were, in typical Southern Baptist fashion, a "*board* of deacons." In the revised bylaws, the deacons still had these responsibilities, and they recommended the church's budget. However, an explicit declaration of the importance of congregational polity that preserved lay leadership was highlighted. While the deacons recommended the church budget, "It is recognized that the Board of Deacons shall in all matters be subject to the direction of the congregation." The bylaws, moreover, significantly shifted the focus of deacon work to ministry. Revisions indicated that, in line with

[45] N Deacons 4 27 80.
[46] N News 7 12 78.
[47] N Bylaws 6 27 77; N Minutes 6 26 77.
[48] N Bylaws 6 27 77.

New Testament practice, deacons were "servants of the church" and were "to serve with the Pastor and staff in performing pastoral ministries, in proclaiming the gospel to believers and non-believers."[49] In subsequent years, deacons were active in servant/pastoral type functions, but continued to be a business-like, decision-making Board of Deacons as well.[50]

Church Facilities

In January 1979, per request of the deacons, George Purvis moderated a meeting about church facilities and how they related to meeting the needs of ministry. Claypool suggested the church needed a place where more physical interaction was possible. He noted how Northminster's original vision had designs for a Great Hall, a Common Room, and more educational space. However, Claypool said that any decision about facilities should not rely on his or any clergy perspective Leland Speed then explained how the original architectural layout had been pruned because of financial realities: parking, then a music building, then offices and classrooms, and most painfully, a fellowship hall, were all scrapped because of costs.

Other members then spoke in favor of adding facilities. Suzanne Boone emphasized the need for a building to assist with outreach to the community. Dick Barnes was bluntly provocative, noting he had previously attended a church with a gym but it had not really aided ministry. "I really don't know whether God cares if we build buildings," Barnes declared. If they built a new facility, he would vote for it, but he wanted the church to protect its priorities to community ministry rather than just having a building for "our white Anglo-Saxon Protestant folks." The discussion forum ended with a motion for the Building Committee to bring a report to the church by May 1979.[51]

Over the next several months, additional facilities became a necessity. Classroom space was desperately needed, and the church purchased a porta-

---

[49] Ibid.

[50] N Deacons 1 28 12. In a historical overview of the deacons, John Purvis noted that in 1981 the deacons voted to have the vice chair of deacons automatically ascend to chair the next year. For many years the vice chair of deacons also served as the chair of the Finance Committee. Purvis added that deacon ordination services were held on Sunday evenings until 1979, at which time they were moved to Sunday mornings.

[51] N Minutes 1 28 79.

ble building to relieve overcrowding. Attendance was booming in worship with visitors especially coming to hear Claypool preach. Adding a balcony in the sanctuary was considered but scuttled due to a lack of designated pledges.[52]

Ministry of Worship

John Claypool was known for the quality of worship in services he led and the reverence that accompanied that worship—a hallmark of Northminster from its birth. Church members, however, remember a very personable Claypool. He was not an elitist superstar who looked down on people. Mike Peters, in his twenties, loved playing racquetball with Claypool. Peters recalled that after his first match with his pastor, he went home and said, "This is great; the preacher's just like me. He cusses. He's competitive. He wants to win that point. He'd hit me if that meant him winning the point."[53] Charlie Johnson, college intern at the time, also remembered Claypool's lighthearted side. As choir director, Karen Gilfoy, passionately attended to all of the minute details of an Advent service, Claypool whispered to Johnson, "This is turning out to feel like a damn Cecil B. DeMille production."[54]

Claypool's racquetball and humor notwithstanding, his focus on worship was his calling. Claypool articulated a theology of worship and liturgical expression to the congregation that nurtured its identity and quest to be a community of serious, educated worshipers. He also offered a focus on worship that fostered Northminster's quest for an ecumenical identity. The language of the Christian calendar—Advent, Lent, Holy Week—continued to be commonplace in worship at Northminster. The use of Chrismons at Christmas was also continued providing visual Christian imagery to the season. In 1977, Lillian Kimbrough gave a living pine to the church in memory of Kerry Kimbrough for use in the Chrismon celebration. On Christmas day, after the worship service, the tree was planted on church grounds. The Chrismon ministry continued, and for the next four years Elizabeth Taylor led the effort (as well as the sermon tape ministry).[55] During the Claypool

[52] N Deacons 10 21 79; N Minutes 8 24 80; N Deacons 3 15 81; Jane Best, interview by David Stricklin, February 29, 1992, 7.

[53] Mike Peters, interview by Aaron Weaver, February 22, 2016, 14.

[54] Johnson, telephone interview.

[55] N News 12 1 77; N News 12 2 80.

years, the children's music ministry continued its practice—under the leadership of Jean Williams and Donette Lee—of performing children's musicals such as *SAM*, a folk musical (the story of the Good Samaritan), *Jonah's Tale of a Whale*, and Ken Medema's *The Story-Tellin' Man*.[56] The use of youth as acolytes in the worship hour was begun during Claypool's ministry.[57]

Given that the Pulpit Committee told Claypool that they were concerned about the spiritual nurture of their children, it is no surprise that he offered a theology of children and baptism in his initial months. In June 1977, Claypool presented a view of baptism that took conversion seriously in the life of children but added a focus on spiritual growth not often found among the more revivalistic Southern Baptist churches of the day. Claypool's theology of conversion also made age distinctions not often heard in typical Baptist evangelism. When a child around nine years old initiated conversation about conversion, Claypool suggested, the child should be taken seriously. Claypool said that he told children that conversion was just "the beginning and not the end of the Christian process." Still, the conversion experience was important because "one must begin somewhere, and the definite feeling that God loves them and has sent Jesus to be the 'the Way, the Truth, and the Life' for them is a legitimate basis for setting out in His followship."[58]

Claypool's theology of baptism for youth ages twelve and older was more typical of Southern Baptists, yet he still emphasized a spiritual process. He said that with twelve-year-olds the church is justified in taking the initiative about sharing the need for conversion. As Dudley Wilson before him, Claypool cautioned that he did not believe in manipulation or undue pressure. Claypool also questioned having a pastor's class that so "routinize(s) the process…(it) automatically deposits them into the Baptistery."[59]

Claypool continued the Northminster practice of having a Parent-Child Dedication service during congregational worship. In addition, he

---

[56] N News 12 14 76; N News 5 19 77; N News 5 11 78; N News 12 2 80; N Bulletin 5 24 77; N Bulletin 5 20 79.

[57] N Bulletin 12 4 77.

[58] N News 6 30 77. Other Baptists were reflecting on a theology of children at this time. See William L. Hendricks, *A Theology of Children* (Nashville: Baptist Sunday School Board, 1980).

[59] N News 6 30 77.

offered a separate personal service of Child Dedication after the worship hour. However, this was not a service of infant baptism. He commented: "We Baptists do not baptize infants for reasons that in my judgment are valid."[60]

Claypool was developing a sacramental theology that was most likely one step in his personal journey toward ministry in the Episcopal Church after he left Northminster. While he never wrote a pastoral admonition for church members to engage in extensive contemplation or the spiritual discipline of solitude, Claypool did undertake a personal six-day silent retreat—the longest one of his ministry he said—at the Laity Lodge retreat center in the Hill Country of Texas during summer 1979.[61]

The congregation was exhorted to incorporate a sacramental perspective toward its two primary worship ordinances: baptism and the Lord's Supper. Claypool spoke of the two as "the traditioning process" and referenced the Lord's Supper as "Holy Communion," which was "nourishment for the journey" of the Christian life. He did not employ the language of "Eucharist" while at Northminster, but the congregation was urged to move away from understanding baptism and the Lord's Supper as simply acts of "observing"—again the dominant Southern Baptist view—and to adopt the more Catholic mode of speaking of "celebrating," which seeks to recover "authentic celebration in relation to spiritual realities."[62]

By the third year of his ministry, August 1979, Claypool wrote in his weekly newsletter column that he preferred the word "sacraments" to the more typical Southern Baptist word, "ordinances." Fleshing out further his preference for celebration rather than observance, Claypool opined that "there is more to these rituals than obeying rote commands." "They are gracious gifts as well—pointing to the coming of new life and the continued sustenance that our Lord provides," Claypool wrote. "This sense of gift makes the verb 'observe' too remote and stand-offish for me. Celebrate suggests that one plunges into the middle of things."[63] The practice of Holy Communion was, of course, "open communion," not a closed communion that prohibited participation of members of other churches or to only those

[60] N News 7 14 77.
[61] N News 6 27 79.
[62] N News 5 19 77; N News 11 8 78.
[63] N News 8 15 79.

Christians who had received believer's baptism by immersion. "This table belongs to our Lord, not to this church or any particular denomination," Claypool affirmed. "Thus, if you belong to Him, all of this belongs to you."[64]

Claypool also articulated a theology of preaching that was compatible with the congregation's focus on laity. He commented that a sermon should not be the last word "handed down" dogmatically from the preacher, but "the first word" to "stimulate ongoing conversation and growth of insight." Citing Jewish theologian Martin Buber—famous for speaking of relationship with God as I-Thou (subject to subject) rather than I-It (subject to object)—Claypool wrote that preaching was "dialogical" and relational. He told the congregation that he listened carefully to the things church members said and to the questions they asked and then developed sermons to be "an appropriate response to these realities." Consequently, Claypool occasionally had a series of Sunday evening forums—as Dudley Wilson had done—where the congregation could gather to talk about the sermons heard in the morning worship hour. He hoped that "out of it should come a greater awareness of the diversity that is the genius of Northminster."[65] Claypool's first forum series occurred almost immediately, in January 1977, with others in subsequent years.[66] To the congregation, he embodied what Donette Lee later reflected about the legacy of preachers at Northminster: they had strong preaching gifts and did not speak down to the people.[67]

The focus on active, visible lay participation was also evident in Claypool's approach to the invitation to join the church at the end of the worship service. During the formative years at Northminster, the altar call with people responding to a verbal invitation was not emphasized. Claypool, however, believed that an oral invitation was needed as part of worship. Jonathan Sweat recalled that Claypool "did it in his own beautiful manner. Certainly not pleading for anyone to come." Active, visible lay participation in the

[64] N News 2 17 81.

[65] N News 1 5 77.

[66] N News 1 7 78; N News 1 6 81.

[67] Carolyn Sloss Ratliff, comp., *Life is Gift: Remembrances of John Rowan Claypool IV* (Birmingham: St. Luke's Episcopal Church, 2015) 62.

public decision-making process to follow Christ, Claypool thought, could be achieved without sacrificing the dignity of worship.[68]

To provide space for the invitation, a new section was added to the order of worship in the church bulletin: "Commitment," followed by a written invitation, and then "A Time for Response." The written invitation stated: "Northminster is an open fellowship that wants to give its gifts of life and ministry to others. If you would like to explore what it would mean to join this covenant community, please indicate this to the minister or express this desire by coming forward at this point of the service."[69] Covenant language meant that joining the church was individual and communal.

The Northminster congregation had to share Claypool's preaching with the wider Christian world. He was known, even before coming to the church, as one of America's best preachers, not simply one of the best Baptist pulpiteers. As negotiated with the Pulpit Committee, the church immediately installed a recording system and began a ministry of distributing tapes of the sermons as Claypool's previous churches had done. For example, the church newsletter advertised two sermons each per three-dollar tape.[70] Early on, Elizabeth Taylor mailed cassettes to sixty subscribers each month. Barbara Webb handled the printed sermon ministry and mailed around 2,000 sermons to a worldwide audience.[71]

No doubt Claypool's preaching was compelling. Visitors came to Northminster just to hear him preach. Guy Parker reflected that the first time he heard Claypool preach, the experience moved him to tears. The preaching even made an impact on the church's youth that was felt later in life, according to Leigh Pollard (later Farrell). As church seeds scattered, Farrell, whose family joined Northminster while she was a high school junior, later joined the Episcopal Church in Birmingham, Alabama, where Claypool ministered in the 1990s.[72]

---

[68] Jonathan Sweat, interview by David Stricklin, February 29, 1992, 8.

[69] N Bulletin 1 16 77; N Bulletin 2 13 77.

[70] N News 1 26 77 (and others); Ratliff, *Life is Gift*, 25. Prior to Broadway Baptist Church, Fort Worth, which published Claypool's sermons, Crescent Hill Baptist Church published the sermons as well.

[71] Barbara Webb, email to Aaron Weaver, February 25, 2016; N Bulletin 3 20 77.

[72] Ratliff, *Life is Gift*, 88, 139.

Claypool's preaching travels took him to other churches (Baptist and non-Baptist), pastors' schools, retreat centers, and to academic settings such as Yale and Princeton.[73] Claypool's most prestigious invitation came when he was asked to give the Lyman Beecher Lectures on Preaching (created in 1872 and the oldest continuing lectureship of its sort in the country, Claypool said) at Yale Divinity School in February 1979. Claypool was only the third Southern Baptist lecturer (the others were John A. Broadus, 1889; and Edwin M. Poteat, 1940, a brother of Northminster member Isabelle Turner). Claypool expressed gratitude to the church for allowing him to devote serious time to such academic endeavors. Being pastor in a large congregation, Claypool admitted, would make such teaching activity hardly possible.[74] The congregation showed their enthusiasm for Claypool's prestigious honor when George Purvis presented him a personalized leather carrying case as a gift from the church. Claypool was particularly touched by the letters TWBD and TWBS, which were embossed in gold on the case. The acronyms stood for "Thy Will Be Done" and "Thy Word Be Spoken," and reflected Claypool's practice to put these initials on the final draft of his written sermons.[75]

Ministry of Worship: The Organ

One of the defining elements of Northminster's worship was the focus on music. The organ took a central role in this identity in 1980. In November 1978, it was announced that Mr. and Mrs. Roger Stribling Sr. offered funds to the church for an organ as a memorial gift in remembrance of their son, Roger Stribling Jr. The younger Stribling, who died in an airplane accident in 1975, had been a deacon and Sunday school teacher and had been extensively involved in the development of the church's property and landscaping; a garden in his memory was created on the northern portion of the church grounds.

---

[73] Claypool spoke at the following conferences and lectured at the various schools: Chowan [NC] Religious Emphasis Week, N News 3 24 77; Pastor's School at University of Richmond, at Pastor's Institute at St. Olaf's College in Minneapolis at Laity Lodge in Hill Country, Texas, N News 7 21 77; Claypool at Princeton University, N News 7 5 78; Ridgecrest [NC] SBC National Retreat Center, N News 8 16 78; Yale University, N News 11 7 79.

[74] N News 2 7 79.

[75] N News 2 21 79.

The deacons accepted the gracious gift from the Striblings with the understanding that an organ would conform to the needs and design of the church as determined by an ad hoc organ committee. The committee was chaired by Dr. Jonathan Sweat, professor of music at Millsaps College, and included Linda Shelton, Alan Perry, Nancy McDaniel, Sherry Greener, Bill Pharr, Lucian Harvey Jr., Karen Gilfoy, and Billy Trotter (Gilfoy and Trotter as *ex officio*). The organ was first used the Sunday before Christmas 1980 and was formally dedicated on March 22, 1981. Special recitalist for the service of dedication was Marilyn Mason, university organist at the University of Michigan.[76] In a sermon giving thanks for the "Great Organ," Claypool said beyond its "visual splendor," the church must never forget the personal story behind it—the tragic death of Roger Stribling and the response of his family. They never gave up on life or gave way to bitterness. The organ was as much a "monument to courageous human coping as it was an instrument of great musical potential."[77]

The committee gave meticulous attention to detail in providing church worship with the best musical instrument possible. The Austin Organ, built by the Austin Organ Company of Hartford, Connecticut, was selected and touted for its skillful design. The committee thought that the organ's pipes would suggest the Trinity to the discerning observer, and the placement of a slender cross on the sanctuary's front wall would add to "the visible witness of the organ."[78] Installation of the organ was not without its problems. Heat from the sun, coming through the church's windows, changed the pitch of the pipes. Consequently, a small wall was built to block the sun from shining directly on the pipes—something the organ installers said they had never had to do before.[79] In subsequent years, according to organist Billy Trotter, tuning the organ continued to be a challenge because of the shining sun.[80]

The central role of the organ pointed to the serious liturgical nature of Northminster worship. Beginning in 1980, however, the church also took a Sunday break from the sanctuary to have outdoor worship at Rice Acres, the

---

[76] N Minutes 11 12 78; N News 3 28 79; N News 3 10 81.

[77] John Claypool, "God Has No Grandchildren," sermon, Northminster Baptist Church, March 29, 1981.

[78] N History 3 22 81.

[79] Sweat, interview, 6.

[80] Billy Trotter, interview by Aaron Weaver and Doug Weaver, May 7, 2017.

recreational facilities of the Hinds-Madison Baptist Association.[81] In summers, the church still had worship, but, as it did when Dudley Wilson was pastor, reduced the number of activities. According to Claypool, the reduction matched the "change of pace that summer is in the lives of church members."[82] Wednesday evenings throughout the year included choir but not worship.

Ministry of Education and Service: Small Groups

Soon after his arrival, Claypool urged the creation of small groups for personal and communal devotion, a ministry not unique to Claypool or Northminster but ahead of its time for many Baptist churches. In January 1977, he offered a personal growth group, which met during the day and was capped intentionally at ten participants. Two months later he added a group that met on Sunday nights.[83] The personal growth group often focused on a book study such as Harry Emerson Fosdick's classic book on prayer—led by the pastor. On another occasion, the group took the Minnesota Multiphasic Personality Inventory as a means of exploring spiritual growth.[84] Sunday evening church activities not only focused on personal growth groups; adult education discussion groups, which had been created before the Claypool years, were continued. These groups were not the traditional Southern Baptist "training union"; rather, they provided a variety of special topics, reflecting the congregation's desire for a theologically educated laity. For example, in fall 1977, the adult discussion group studied religious themes in popular movies.[85] On another occasion, a Hindu believer visited and discussed his religion.[86] As noted earlier, Hank Guest led academic studies of the Old Testament and New Testament. Claypool frequently praised this teaching side of Northminster's ministry and enthusiastically commented that the Sunday evening ministry opportunities reflected the church's openness to diversity.[87]

---

[81] N News 5 12 81.
[82] N News 6 21 78; N News 5 30 79.
[83] N News 1 5 77.
[84] N News 9 13 78; N News 9 5 79.
[85] N Deacons 7 10 77; N News 8 22 77.
[86] N Bulletin 4 8 79.
[87] N News 3 1 78; N News 12 6 78; N News 1 24 79.

Small groups have historically, at times, been tempted to be insular, but the adult discussion group demonstrated an interest in outward missions. They continued "the Christmas project" effort to provide 300 sacks of basic essentials to people who lived in boarding houses on the west side of Jackson (some of the residents had spent time in the state mental hospital). As part of Northminster's Advent observance, church families delivered these Christmas packages.[88] The ministry—ongoing in 2017—has made a significant impression on church members. Mike Peters commented, "I was out at a boarding home, and it's a moving target. You show up, and they had said there were thirty there but [there are] forty.... You have to remember it was right at dusk one day, and I was out of bags. These people were all standing there on the front porch; they didn't get their bag. I looked at them and I said, 'Look, we're coming back, we're coming back.' We ran to Walmart, put together some bags and brought them back, and I remember hearing them say as I walked away, 'They came back, they came back.'"[89]

Claypool did not continue the pastor's participation in the orientation program for new members that was initiated by Dudley Wilson. Orientation was incorporated into the Sunday school offerings. Kelley Williams Sr. and Lue Ann Claypool were active organizers, and Jan Purvis worked with the orientation program for several years.[90] Youth activities were bustling during this era of the church's life. With American culture moving away from the "church always comes first if there is a conflict with a club or sports activity" perspective, youth workers sometimes had difficulties finding space in busy family schedules. The later phrase "soccer mom" was not yet commonplace, but some church leaders confessed that they were "ready to pull out their hair," trying to get commitments for church events.[91] It was a sign of things to come for religion in America.

Crisis Ministry: The Flood of 1979

Crisis ministry was called for when much of northeast Jackson was flooded by the Pearl River on Easter, April 15, 1979. Church members were directly affected; about fifteen families had their homes flooded and nine-

[88] N News 11 29 78; N News 1 19 79.
[89] Peters, interview, 12–13.
[90] Jan Purvis, interview by David Stricklin, February 29, 1992, 14.
[91] Claypool, "God Has No Grandchildren."

teen businesses related to church families experienced flood damage.[92] Charlie Johnson, still serving as college intern, recalled that he and Claypool took a canoe "up to the eve of a roof" to help rescue one family trapped by the flooding.[93] The Jackson *Clarion-Ledger* reported on Claypool's message to the church that the Christian concept of grief must be expanded to include flood victims and their damaged possessions.[94] The message was consistent with Claypool's personal experience of grief in the tragic loss of his daughter to leukemia during his ministry in Louisville, Kentucky, and his subsequent well-known written account (*Tracks of a Fellow Struggler: Living and Growing Through Grief*), which the newspaper noted. Northminster received some financial assistance for the flood victims from the Home Mission Board of the Southern Baptist Convention, and Claypool encouraged church members to accept it as a "sacrament of compassion" from fellow Baptists. Church members helped their friends and neighbors—and the church held a family-night supper called "A Time of Gratitude." Hank Guest especially pointed out the "energy and quiet assertiveness" of Lue Ann Claypool as a source of strength and judgment during the crisis of the flood.[95]

Women in Leadership and Ministry

Leadership roles that had traditionally been filled by men at Northminster became more available to women in the mid-to-late 1970s. In August 1977, two of the eight nominees for deacon were women—Nancy McDaniel and Linda Shelton. However, the congregation elected neither. Three women—Jann James, Jan Purvis, and Dot Taylor—were elected to serve on the Committee on Committees, the group that recommended positions for the various committees in the organizational structure of the church.[96]

The following years, women were always on the deacon ballot and often elected to one or two spots. In August 1978, two of the four deacons elected were women—Suzanne Boone and Nancy McDaniel—and this was the first time two women were elected at the same time. In 1979, interest-

[92] N Deacons 4 22 79; N News 4 8 79.

[93] Johnson, telephone interview.

[94] "Claypool: Flood Victims Sensing 'Grieving Process,'" *The Clarion-Ledger Daily News*, June 1979.

[95] N News 4 25 79; N History 6 6 79; N Deacons 5 27 79.

[96] N News 8 22 77; N Minutes 8 28 77.

ingly, no women were elected though one was on the ballot. Women were again serving on the Committee on Committees (Judy Parker and Margaret Phillips). In August 1980, two women, Margaret Phillips and Jan Purvis, were again elected as deacons. This time, they were two of the five deacons elected.[97]

Church educational activities also began to provide space for discussion of the changing roles of women in the life of the (Baptist) church—a topic of increased attention in churches across the United States. In April 1978, the Sunday evening discussion group had a three-week study on the topic. One week featured Dr. Lee Reiff of Millsaps College, who presented on women and the Bible. In 1980, Mae Eleanor Mosley helped organize a conference held at Northminster on "Women in the Church."[98]

At the outset of 1980s, the journey to electing women to key positions of lay leadership had taken more forward steps. As mentioned above, Pat Travis was named minister of Christian education in March 1980. What was left was affirming women in the Northminster pulpit. A sign of things to come occurred in June 1981 when Sarah Frances Anders of Louisiana College, who would be known for her work on behalf of women in ministry in Southern Baptist circles, preached. In noting that Anders would fill the pulpit, the deacons' minutes listed her name and put "(female)" beside it.[99]

Social Ministry/Race Relations

Northminster focused attention on social missions and service during the Claypool years and supported a variety of ministries such as Bread for the World, and church members volunteered for Jackson Mobile Meals (the early version of Meals on Wheels).[100] The church also helped with the YWCA program at Camp Turnage for low-income children. Other social ministries for children included support for families from out of town whose children were cancer patients at University Medical Center. Church members, led by Linda McGehee, worked with the families and helped maintain the Candlelight House, the temporary housing for these out-of-town

[97] N Minutes 8 27 78; N Minutes 8 26 79; N Minutes 8 24 80.
[98] N News 3 30 78; N News 2 27 80; N Bulletin 4 16 78; N Bulletin 2 24 80.
[99] N Deacons 6 20 81.
[100] N News 8 31 77; N News 9 29 77; N News 10 5 78; N News 10 17 80.

guests.[101] The church also supported a prison ministry at the state penitentiary at Parchman called B.A.I.C.—Born Again in Christ.[102] However, not all types of "social" ministry were accepted. In the July 1981 deacons' meeting, the deacons rejected an offer from someone to give a house to the church—to be raffled off—in a plan where the person would take part of the sale proceeds and the church the rest. The deacons said no to raffling.[103]

In his previous ministry, John Claypool had been known for his progressive advocacy on behalf of racial equality. In his first ministerial position after completing his education, Claypool served at First Baptist Church, Decatur, in Atlanta, Georgia. In 1960, he participated in a monthly minister's luncheon, which also included Dr. Martin Luther King Jr., who had returned to the city to co-pastor Ebenezer Baptist Church alongside his father. In April 1961, King Jr. gave a lecture—which made many white Southern Baptists unhappy—at Southern Baptist Theological Seminary in Louisville, Kentucky. Claypool had moved to Louisville and assumed the pastorate of Crescent Hill Baptist Church. After the lecture, King Jr. and Claypool had coffee together, and a picture of the socializing made for controversial headlines in the *Louisville Courier*. Claypool and his family received hate mail and threats, and some church members left Crescent Hill, especially after Claypool led the congregation to integrate. Its first member of color was a seminary student from Nigeria. During his time in Louisville, Claypool also chaired the Louisville Baptist Interracial Ministers Conference from 1962 to 1968.[104]

Claypool maintained his investment in the arena of race relations and thus increased its presence in the visible life of Northminster. He preached about racial issues as a valued aspect of the church's commitment to diversity. In the early days of 1978, Claypool highlighted race in several church newsletter columns. He mentioned that he had great respect for John Perkins, the most prominent African-American social justice activist in Mississippi and his work with "Voice of Calvary." This ecumenical ministry fo-

[101] N News 6 21 78; N News 9 26 79; N News 1 30 80; N News 3 12 80; N Bulletin 9 23 79.

[102] N News 1 24 79; N Bulletin 3 4 79.

[103] N Deacons 7 5 81.

[104] "Door Interview: John Claypool," *The Wittenburg Door* 42 (April–May 1978): 10–11; Ratliff, *Life is Gift*, 27, 86.

cused on "human needfulness," which included Operation Vision, an effort to collect 50,000 pairs of old eyeglasses to distribute to the poor of Haiti. Northminster responded, and its missional identity incorporated this ministry into its giving.[105]

In February 1978, Northminster participated in the Southern Baptist-sponsored calendar emphasis, Race Relations Sunday. The African American West Jackson Community Choir was a guest in worship. Claypool commented, "It will be a very different cultural form than the one to which Northminster is accustomed…to enrich our awareness of such diversity."[106] Two weeks later, the Sunday evening adult discussion group heard Dr. S. L. Bowman, pastor of Greater Clark Street Baptist Church (and pastor of Calvary Baptist Church in Yazoo City when it was set on fire in 1965), speak on the topic, "Where We Are Today in Race Relations in Jackson." Claypool again noted, "I hope this will be a day of growth and expanded horizons for all of us here at Northminster. Come prepared to lengthen the cords of your understanding."[107] The topic of race also received attention from Northminster Women when Dr. Margaret Walker Alexander, of Jackson State University, spoke at their luncheon that October. In spring 1980, the church's Missions Committee invited two leaders of the Voice of Calvary, Dolphus Weary and H. Spree, to preach, and the African American Mendenhall Ministry Singers visited as well.[108] The question of language as part of race relations was still far away, however, seen clearly when the youth had a fundraiser with the slogan, "Slave for the Day."[109]

Ministry of Cooperation: Ecumenism

Northminster's commitment to an ecumenical identity was nurtured and enhanced during the Claypool years at practically every level of church life. Interactions started young. Children attended a children's choir camp at Fondren Presbyterian Church, and Fondren Presbyterian also invited the

---

[105] N News 1 25 78. On John Perkins, see Randy Sparks, *Religion in Mississippi* (Jackson: University Press of Mississippi for the Mississippi Historical Society, 2001) 267–68.

[106] N News 2 2 78; N Bulletin 2 12 78.

[107] N News 2 8 78; N News 2 15 78

[108] N News 9 13 78; N News 3 12 80; N News 6 10 80.

[109] N News 4 7 81; N Bulletin 10 8 78; N Bulletin 3 16 80; N Bulletin 6 8 80.

youth of Northminster to a "houseboat party."[110] Junior high youth of the church and Beth Israel had an interfaith weekend during which they worshiped at both places.[111] Activities of the Northminster singles group often crossed denominational lines with joint meetings with St. Andrew's Episcopal Church and Christ United Methodist Church among other churches. Baptists from Broadmoor Baptist Church also participated.[112]

Northminster worship featured ecumenical emphases. In 1978, Beth Israel invited the church and other congregations to a special Sabbath observance to remember victims of the Holocaust.[113] In 1979, Claypool announced Lenten Services to enrich the celebration of Easter that would be held on Wednesday evenings with Briarwood Presbyterian Church, Covenant Presbyterian Church, and Fondren Presbyterian Church.[114] Claypool announced that the services "represent the beginning of a kind of 'grassroots ecumenism' that could lead to other cooperative ventures" and could, in terms of worship, "do for Easter what the Advent season is doing for Christmas." In spring 1981, however, Claypool lamented to the deacons that there was little interest in Holy Week services in the immediate community.[115]

In October 1980, Northminster sponsored a joint preaching workshop with these same Presbyterian churches that featured well-known African-American minister Dr. James Forbes of Union Theological Seminary, New York. Forbes preached on the topic of "The Liberating Power of the Holy Spirit." The meeting doubled, in a sense, as a time to examine the role of the Holy Spirit in worship in a decade where many churches—though not Northminster—were grappling with the growth of the Pentecostal-charismatic traditions and their focus on the Holy Spirit, speaking in tongues, and spiritual gifts.[116]

The women's ministry of the church was certainly ecumenically focused in its participation in the ministry of Church Women United. This group was a national movement made up of women from Protestant, Catholic, and

---

[110] N News 1 12 77; N Bulletin 6 17 79.
[111] N News 9 20 78.
[112] N News 4 21 77; N News 4 16 80; N Bulletin 2 24 79.
[113] N News 1 19 78.
[114] N Deacons 1 28 79.
[115] N News 1 31 79; N News 3 19 80; N Deacons 4 18 81.
[116] N Deacons 9 21 80; N Bulletin 10 12 80; N Bulletin 10 19 80.

Orthodox Christian groups. Northminster women participated in their "Ecumenical World Community Day" and "World Day of Prayer." Church members, including Jan Purvis, were also program participants at local meetings of Church Women United.[117]

Southern Baptist Convention Conflict

From the outset, Northminster's clergy and laity expressed concern about the "Holy War" that erupted in the Southern Baptist Convention. In June 1978, Claypool praised Jimmy Allen, the president of the SBC, for helping to defeat the election of Anita Bryant—singer and television personality known for her conservative social activism on matters of sexuality and strident rhetoric against gays and lesbians—as vice-president of the convention.[118] That would essentially be the last time Northminster ministers could easily voice pleasure with Southern Baptist leadership. While conflict and skirmishes had previously occurred among Southern Baptists on a host of cultural and theological issues, unity amid diversity around a shared sense of missions and evangelism and a set of Baptist principles (e.g., soul freedom, authority of Scripture, local church autonomy, religious liberty) had existed.[119] The year 1979 is now regarded as the official start of the ten-year fundamentalist takeover plan of convention boards and agencies (later called the Conservative Resurgence by Southern Baptist leaders). Immediately after the SBC meeting in early June 1979 that launched the purge of "moderate" Baptists, Claypool told the deacons that the SBC annual meeting was a "very political meeting and a discouraging time."[120]

Given the keen interest in events at the convention meeting in Houston, moreover, Claypool then addressed the topic of the SBC in a sermon titled "Baptists in Crisis" on June 24, 1979. He lamented the intolerant attitude found in speakers such as Texas evangelist James Robison, who said anyone who did not affirm the inerrancy of the Bible was a "snake in the

---

[117] N News 4 21 77; N News 10 26 77; N News 1 31 79; N Bulletin 2 25 79; N Bulletin 10 28 79.

[118] N News 6 21 78.

[119] There is a host of books on the Southern Baptist conflict. A short overview can be found in chapter eight of C. Douglas Weaver, *In Search of the New Testament Church, The Baptist Story* (Macon, GA: Mercer University Press, 2008).

[120] N Deacons 6 17 79. A fuller description of the conflict in the Southern Baptist Convention will be offered in the next chapter.

household" and must be destroyed. Claypool bemoaned the rumor—which came true—that Adrian Rogers of Memphis, Tennessee (the newly elected SBC president), would select only leaders who affirmed the litmus test of biblical inerrancy (i.e., the belief that the Bible is without error in all matters, including science, history, and theology). Claypool said he never heard a convincing argument about inerrancy, just that it had to be accepted by "naked authority." He hoped that the future of the SBC could be preserved by the Baptist genius of walking alongside each other in conversation and persuasion rather than intolerance of differences.[121]

In a January 1980 sermon, which was not devoted to Baptist issues, Claypool decried religion that addressed the complexities of life by oversimplifying and then absolutizing the answers as litmus tests that must be obeyed for authentic faith. According to those Baptists attempting to take over the Southern Baptist Convention, Claypool said, "It makes no difference what else a person believes or does in his or her Christian commitment"; all they "want to know about is where you stand on the subject of plenary verbal inspiration of the Scripture." Claypool added, "This could be as destructive to our Baptist fellowship as single-issue pressure groups could be to our nation."[122]

Two church members, Clark and Margaret Hensley, attended the annual SBC meeting in St. Louis in 1980, but the fundamentalist victory led Claypool to tell the deacons in November that the church needed to have its full allotment of ten messengers to attend the 1981 gathering in Los Angeles, California.[123] Just before the meeting in June 1981, Claypool told the congregation that he was worried: "This could be the most fateful convention in many decades…with a well-organized attempt by one faction to take over the Convention." While Southern Baptists had always had differences, the "militant" group with the "inerrancy focus" was unwilling to cooperate. "Southern Baptists are not a radical people, and the inerrancy faction are radicals," Claypool warned. But then as most moderate leaders believed at that time, he suggested, "The great power of the moderating center will

[121] John Claypool, "Baptists in Crisis," sermon, Northminster Baptist Church, June 24, 1979.

[122] Claypool, "Simplicity, Complexity and Our Present Crisis."

[123] N News 6 10 80; N Deacons 11 2 80.

probably hold in the long run."[124] After the convention, despite the election of the takeover candidate, Bailey Smith, Claypool, in retrospect, was too optimistic when he thought that Smith was more conciliatory than his pre-convention rhetoric. Still, Claypool noted that for either side in the conflict "to try to purge the other completely would amount to destroying the whole structure." He again relied on the moderate refrain that Southern Baptists had unity in "shared tasks" rather than in theological agreement.[125] Northminster would grapple with the SBC conflict throughout the 1980s.

Ministry of Stewardship: Growth and Giving

Northminster experienced significant growth during the Claypool years. For example, in 1979, twenty-six families joined in a five-month period. The preschool aged group was bustling (seventy-two children one Sunday in April 1981), and worship services were often packed. By the end of Claypool's ministry, the church had 563 resident members and 668 total members.[126]

As the church's membership grew, so did its budget. In 1978, the budget was $204,831; by 1981, the budget increased dramatically to $303,340 (the first year the deacons were willing to approve a budget not fully pledged). Missions giving likewise increased. The $6,000 given to the Southern Baptist Cooperative Program at the outset of 1977 was raised to $7,200 in the next budget cycle. The church supported the traditional Baptist missionary offerings, but the goals were never nearly as high as many sister Southern Baptist churches who gave in the thousands of dollars (for example, 1977: Lottie Moon, $682; Annie Armstrong, $ 212.40). Missions giving was often diverse with restricted gifts to several charities. Social ministries like Good Samaritan, Operation Shoestring, and Beginning Again in Christ received consistent support. Regular gifts to Mississippi Baptist min-

[124] N News 6 2 81. See also John Claypool, "New Faces, Old Battles," sermon, Northminster Baptist Church, June 7, 1981. In the sermon Claypool elaborated on his conception of Scripture in terms of progressive revelation and how inerrantists attributed an absolutizing character to the Bible when that was reserved for God alone. He asked, "Which will it be, the gods that we have made out of our needs and desires or the God Who made us?" Claypool was quoting Paul Scherer.

[125] N News 6 16 81.

[126] N News 3 28 79; N Deacons 5 27 79; N Deacons 4 18 81; N Deacons 7 19 81.

istries (Gulf Shore Baptist Assembly) and the Hinds-Madison Baptist Association were also included.[127]

John Claypool's Resignation

In April 1978, the Christian satirical magazine, *The Wittenberg Door*, published an extensive interview with John Claypool. He had been pastor of Northminster Baptist Church for eighteen months. The interview—never mentioned in church records and published in a magazine most Southern Baptists had never heard of—was remarkably confessional and revealing regarding Claypool's view of his move to Jackson. Claypool said that while reasons were complex, the overriding factor was a battle with fatigue, expressed in an inability to pace himself and set limits in dealing with the excessive demands at the 5,000-member megachurch, Broadway Baptist Church in Fort Worth, Texas. Claypool had gone to Fort Worth to see if he could work with the powerful in the community, and the attempt had been taxing and tough. He was attracted to the slower pace promised in Jackson as well as the ability to study more. For the first six months at Northminster, however, Claypool confessed to his interviewer that he probably should have talked to the leaders in Fort Worth to see if adjustments to his ministry could be made. After accepting the call to Northminster—but even before he had begun ministry there—Claypool realized that he had acted impulsively and had not been perceptive enough in facing his utter fatigue. Friends complicated his thought processes as they reacted in disbelief that he would leave a church of 5,000 for a new church of 450 members. "My friends at Ft. Worth said I had an affair with this church, that I was seduced at the point of my fatigue," Claypool noted.[128] Claypool confessed that he was dealing with "a measure of self-reproach for having misread myself. And then when I realized I had even misread the situation, I just walked around holding my hands saying, 'What am I doing here?' I had gone out here and cut off an arm just to take care of a fingernail. It was a very, very humbling experience to see how deep my fatigue had pushed me out of touch with

---

[127] N News 3 3 77; N Minutes 11 13 77; N News 10 25 78; N Deacons 3 15 81; N Deacons 1 28 12.

[128] "Door Interview: John Claypool," 12–13.

reality."[129] When the interviewer asked Claypool if he had made a mistake in going to Jackson, Claypool responded vividly:

> I thought I had actually jumped out of an airplane with no parachute. I spent the first six months in dismal second guessing. I had no cultural reinforcement for what I did. I mean everybody else was so shocked when I said I was going to do it and then they began, you know, to concoct a lot of theories. "There was really something wrong and he had to do it." Which of course isn't the case, but you know you're vulnerable to all kinds of gossip. Even the people here in the Jackson church wondered why I came. The great host of folks here are just like anybody else and they think that the better you are the bigger a place you ought to try to go to. So I found a lot of consternation here—why would you do this?[130]

After revealing such a blunt assessment of the start of his ministry at Northminster, Claypool strongly affirmed that he was happy to be at the church. He noted that after six months he forgave himself for how he handled the move:

> Now I am delighted to be in Jackson, and to be frank, I would not want to be back where I was. There are many things that I see here that are possible that never would have been. Theologically I would say that it's incredible what God can do with our stuff and with our bumblings and our impulsive attempts. I have more sense that God is the God of fertilizer. That He can take dung and bring things of beauty out of it. It is incredible what He can still salvage out of what we do.[131]

When Claypool resigned from Northminster just over three years later, his reasons were much the same as those he had listed for leaving Fort Worth—fatigue and the inability to set limits on attempting to be successful.

In early 1981, the Northminster congregation made efforts to provide Claypool some financial security to be the church's pastor. They wanted to help him in the purchase of a home. The church received a gift of stock, and the proceeds ($17,980) were set aside as a Dr. John R. Claypool Special

---

[129] Ibid., 14.
[130] Ibid.
[131] Ibid., 18.

Fund.[132] However, Claypool resigned on May 17, 1981, to be effective at the end of August. He left to do a year-long residency in clinical pastoral education at the Southern Baptist Hospital in New Orleans. Claypool said he was at a "seam moment" in his ministry. "I have nothing but gratitude and good will for the Northminster reality," said Claypool in his letter of resignation. "There is no church in the world I have enjoyed serving more, and were it not for this 'invitation to grow,' no other church in which I would rather be."[133] Lue Ann Claypool added, "How very much I regret leaving Northminster."[134]

In his first sermon after the resignation, Claypool explained his decision. He said he was dealing with two major life issues—internally, emotional fatigue ("burnout"), and externally, relational inadequacies. He had followed the American white, middle-class path of prioritizing a successful career over developing relationships, which is what he said was part of his problem at Broadway Baptist Church in Fort Worth. Claypool was grateful for Northminster's compassionate perspective that characterized its total ministry. Northminster did not shoot her wounded but accepted "that in all the army of the Lord, all are wounded."[135] With John Claypool moving to New Orleans, Lue Ann Claypool returned to Fort Worth. According to Claypool, Lue Ann did not agree to the move to New Orleans, and divorce was the result.[136] The Claypools, according to their son Rowan's later reflections, had grieved in different ways over the tragic death from leukemia of their ten-year-old daughter, Laura Lue, in 1970, and the marriage ultimately did not survive.[137]

---

[132] N Deacons 1 18 81; N Minutes 2 15 81.

[133] N News 5 19 81; N Minutes 5 24 81

[134] N News 7 7 81.

[135] John Claypool, "Pressing Toward the Mark," sermon, Northminster Baptist Church, May 24, 1981.

[136] Art Toalston, "Former local pastor besieged by ultra-conservative Baptists," *Jackson Daily News*, June 17, 1982, 6.

[137] In his sermon reflection about his father's ministry, Rowan Claypool commented, "My parents had grieved in very different ways: my Dad taking his grief outward making it visible and Mom taking hers inward and private. Inevitably, this became one of the major fractures leading to their divorce ten years later. It was the dividing fork in their relationship that they never resolved. Each had sought to heal their wounds and those paths led them apart" (John Rowan Claypool V, "View from

In his last sermon to Northminster Baptist Church on July 19, 1981, Claypool reflected on the original vision he brought to the congregation more than four years earlier. He wanted to reflect on the "mysterious boundary where the Divine and human intersect." Put another way, the primary goal was "To stay close to God, to stay close to you, and to do what I could to bring the two of you closer together." Because of this goal, Claypool's typical closing benediction after a sermon ended with the words, "Depart now, in the fellowship of God the Father." Not surprisingly then, Claypool closed his final sermon at Northminster with similar words: "God is, you are, and the two of you are made for each other. It is enough that we should die alone. There is no need to live alone. The journey can be shared with Him. Therefore, go, go with God, be not afraid."[138]

After Claypool left Jackson, a group on the Pulpit Committee tasked with finding the next pastor discussed briefly bringing Claypool back. One committee member recalled that Claypool told the committee that he would never hurt the church and asked committee members to discuss with their spouses the ramifications of a return, given his family matters might be an issue for some. Discussions really never progressed inside the committee—nor did Claypool give an indication he would return—and the church soon looked for and found another highly educated pastor, but this time, much younger and at the start of a ministerial career.[139]

---

the Second Row," sermon, Crescent Hill Baptist Church, Louisville, Kentucky, January 17, 2011, http://chbcky.org/sermon-archive/2011/1/17/january-16–2011.html).

[138] John Claypool, "As You Go, Remember…" sermon, Northminster Baptist Church, July 19, 1981; N Bulletin 7 19 81.

[139] Peters, interview, 16.

Chapter 4

The 1980s and the Ministry of John Thomason: Developing "Caregiving" Lay Leadership and Confronting Baptist Identity

Finding a Pastor

Following John Claypool's departure in August 1981, a new Pulpit Committee was convened to seek his successor. Over the next eighteen months, the committee, led by Leland Speed, examined the resumes of more than 100 individuals, spoke with fifty applicants, and visited fifteen candidates. Three candidates visited Jackson. The committee thought it had found its next pastor in Dr. Walter Shurden, very popular professor, dean, and noted Baptist historian from Southern Baptist Theological Seminary in Louisville, Kentucky—until Speed received a call from Shurden, who told him, "Leland, I hate to call and tell you this, but my wife and I have prayed over this situation, and we have concluded that we should stay where we are." A long process had culminated in being "back to square one," as Speed explained.[1]

A couple of months later, Speed and his wife, Bessie, were in Chicago and decided they would rent a car and drive to Champaign, Illinois, to hear one of the applicants the committee had not interviewed. The informal service at Temple Baptist Church was nothing like that of Northminster, but the Speeds took notice of the young pastor, John Thomason. "The service was not at all like ours, but as soon as John started talking, we looked at each other and said, 'I think we've found our man,'" Speed said. Upon returning to Jackson, Speed shared his praise of Thomason, and on February 8, 1983, the pastor search concluded with the committee's unanimous nomination of Thomason to be Northminster's third pastor in its almost sixteen-year history.[2]

---

[1] Leland Speed, interview by Aaron Weaver, February 23, 2016.
[2] Ibid. See also N Deacons 2 8 83.

The thirty-four-year-old John Thomason had served as pastor of Temple Baptist Church since 1976 and received his master of divinity degree from Southern Baptist Theological Seminary. He also served as a pastoral assistant at Crescent Hill Baptist Church in Louisville, a church John Claypool pastored from 1960–1971. A Texan, Thomason was born and grew up in Corpus Christi and graduated from Baylor University in 1970 with a bachelor of arts in history and was minister to youth at Seventh and James Baptist Church on Baylor's campus in Waco. He also pursued additional study in theology and culture at Oxford University (1971–1972) and doctoral studies in theology at the University of Chicago Divinity School (1974–1976). Thomason married Polly Stokes of Waco in 1972 and came to Northminster with two young children: Kate (five years old) and Beth (one year old).[3] In the Chicago area, Thomason had been deeply involved in local denominational affairs, serving in a variety of leadership roles with the East Central Illinois Baptist Association.

The Board of Deacons and Finance Committee of Northminster approved the recommendation of the search committee, which included a $30,000 salary and a $15,000–$20,000 housing allowance as well as four weeks of vacation and an additional four weeks of leave for church-related conventions, continuing education, and other meetings. Thomason was also provided a twelve-week sabbatical every fourth year in lieu of the eight weeks of vacation or leave for purposes of "study, refreshment or replenishment" (Claypool, a more established pastor, had received nine weeks and a sabbatical every three years).[4]

Donning a robe and stole, Thomason preached his first sermon at Northminster on April 3, 1983. Later in May, a worship and installation service was held on Pentecost Sunday. Special guests who brought greetings included J. W. Brister, director of the Hinds-Madison Baptist Association; Dr. Earl Kelly, executive director of the Mississippi Baptist Convention; The Right Reverend Roderick L. Murray, dean of St. Andrew's Episcopal

---

[3] Ibid.

[4] Ibid. See Leland Speed to John Thomason, February 7, 1983. The family also purchased a home in Jackson, and the church loaned the Thomasons $25,000 toward that purchase for a period of ten years at 8 percent interest (see N Deacons 3 3 83).

Cathedral; and Rabbi Richard Birnholz of Beth Israel.[5] This ecumenical and interfaith gathering was the first of many during the church's history in the 1980s, which featured a heightened commitment to fellowship and cooperation with other Christians as well as Jews.

Ministry of Worship

The music ministry of Northminster Baptist Church became more vibrant and evolved throughout the 1980s as the church went through several periods of transition. In late 1985, Karen Gilfoy, who had directed the adult choir since the church's first service on May 7, 1967, resigned after a seven-month leave of absence. Gilfoy was credited in the church newsletter for having "challenged the adult choir and congregation by presenting many of the classic works of the Christian music tradition" during her eighteen years of service. She was lauded for devoting her time and energy to providing the church with special music events and recruiting and coordinating guest musicians.[6]

Following Easter in 1986, Dr. Richard Joiner began serving as minister of music. Joiner came to Northminster from Mississippi College, where he had been a music professor and conductor of the concert choir since 1980. At Northminster, he led the adult choir rehearsal on Wednesday nights and directed the choral anthem during Sunday morning worship.[7] After two years, Joiner stepped down. His last Sunday was August 7, 1988. Reflecting on the music ministry and worship traditions at Northminster on the occasion of his one-year anniversary, Joiner shared:

> After 12 months of service as music minister at Northminster, several worship traditions have become very obvious to me: Northminster seeks an organization in its worship which gives each worship moment its greatest impact; Northminster tenaciously protects and encourages lay leadership in worship, both in written liturgy and spoken direction; Northminster is proud of its musical standards; Northminster has become one of the citadels of fine organ music in the area. We have a unique combo in an outstanding Austin organ and Billy Trotter, who

[5] John Thomason, "An Ecumenical Service of Worship on Pentecost," sermon, Northminster Baptist Church, May 22, 1983; N News 5 17 83.

[6] N News 10 8 85.

[7] N News 8 2 88; N News 4 29 86.

> uses his magnificent artistry effectively because he is a believing worshipper himself.[8]

Joiner's commentary captured the ethos of Northminster's ministry of worship, with worship at the center of congregational life and lay leadership as the defining quality of congregational identity.

Other worship traditions evolved during the 1980s. Less than a year into Thomason's tenure, the Worship and Music Committee planned (and the Board of Deacons approved) more frequent communion services. As was typical with many Southern Baptist churches, Northminster observed communion on a quarterly basis. Under this new plan, Northminster would share communion eleven times during the year and at different services, including Sunday morning worship, Sunday evening worship, and on special observances such as Maundy Thursday and Christmas Eve.[9]

"How often should our church have the Lord's Supper?" Thomason asked during a sermon. "We might better ask: 'How often should we eat?' We usually eat three meals a day. Admittedly, not all of our daily meals are special or full of significance.... We might respond to the question: 'How often should our church have the Lord's Supper? By asking, how often should we commune with the risen Christ? Is once every three months enough? Hardly."[10]

Another change was the introduction of the lectionary to Sunday morning worship. In October 1987, Thomason announced his plans to preach from the lectionary beginning with the first Sunday in Advent. He assured the Board of Deacons that following the Common Lectionary would not inhibit the "freedom of the pulpit" because the lectionary allowed topical flexibility for local emphasis. Thomason explained in *Northminster News* that the lectionary was a scriptural guide for Christian preaching and worship, containing suggested lessons for each Sunday of the Christian year and for special occasions—with readings covering most of the New Testament and large portions of the Old Testament spread across a three-year cycle. He noted that the lectionary is the product of an ecumenical team of biblical scholars and used by most major Christian denominations for the

---

[8] N News 6 9 87.

[9] N News 5 22 84.

[10] John Thomason, "As Often as You Eat and Drink," sermon, Northminster Baptist Church, September 23, 1984.

purpose of ensuring that "the Body of Christ is united in its weekly proclamation." The lectionary was not designed to limit a preacher's message, but to assist ministers in stretching into areas of the Bible they might have avoided or neglected if left to personal preference, Thomason said.[11]

During fall 1985, Northminster Baptist Church adopted recommendations from the nine-member Long-Range Planning Committee with the goal of "reaching our potential" over the next five years. The plan aimed to better incorporate and appreciate the congregation's growing diversity with regard to age, faith tradition, and theological maturity as well as offer new growth strategies to effectively equip the church to respond to changes in its neighborhood and broader community. It also proposed cultivating responsible discipleship and a more active membership. The plan encouraged strategies to communicate Northminster's "unique" identity built around "grace, freedom, acceptance, relationships, and an honest struggle with the questions of our faith."[12]

Four "reasons for existence" were offered in the plan: creative worship characterized by reverence for God and liturgical expression; appreciation for the church's Baptist heritage, history of the Christian tradition and revitalization of the important symbols of the Christian faith; freedom of participation based upon accepting grace; and growth in Christian relationships within a family of believers. The committee noted that Northminster achieved growth in its early years through attracting a large number of non-Baptists, many of which were young families (Baby Boomers); individuals nominally connected to the church; and others looking for a more meaningful expression of their Christian faith. From this diversity of perspectives, Northminster developed a "specialized identity" with an "intentional set of congregational values." The church's "specialized-intentional" nature allowed Northminster to "draw its members from a broad set of neighborhoods and a diverse make-up of people," according to the committee. This assessment displayed the church's understanding of its "uniqueness" within an exclusively theological framework, rather than an understanding of "di-

[11] N Deacons 10 6 87.

[12] "Reaching Our Potential, 1986–1990 A Summary Report of the Long-Range Planning Committee," Northminster Baptist Church, Fall 1985, 2.

versity" that relied on popular measurements such as race, ethnicity, and socio-economic status.[13]

The Long-Range Planning Committee suggested strategies to communicate Northminster's identity in Jackson, ways to use media to increase community outreach, spur church growth, increase giving and ecumenical cooperation, strengthen education ministries, heighten hands-on missions involvement, promote Christian citizenship, focus on facilities and staffing needs, and nurture church-wide fellowship. The committee also offered the goal of continuing to develop the congregation as a worshiping community—a cornerstone characteristic of Northminster from its inception:

> Worship has been the center of church life from the beginning, and there is a consciousness among the members of the uniqueness of the worship experiences at Northminster. The worship experiences at the church are one of the ways in which the uniqueness of the church is communicated and cultivated among those members and to those who visit the church.

The committee recommended that Northminster continue to educate congregants in the observance of the Christian year and to continue scheduling worship and fellowship events with other churches—both of which continued to occur throughout the 1980s.[14]

Thomason's Ministry of Preaching

Through his sermons, Thomason often highlighted and celebrated Northminster's unique identity while also challenging and sometimes chiding the congregation to engage more deeply in its surrounding wealthy community, pushing members to chart a creative path toward greater community outreach. "We can live nostalgically in the past; we can calcify in our present routine; or we can re-group and plan creatively for our future,"

---

[13] Ibid., 1.

[14] Ibid. Less than a year later, the Publicity Committee designed a logo that combined the church's two most prominent features of its sanctuary: the cross in the chancel and the window in the transept. The logo was intended to reflect the nature and purpose of Northminster, with the cross serving as a reminder of the congregation's Christ-centered life and the window as a symbol of the congregation's openness (N News 6 17 86).

Thomason said in his "State of the Church" sermon at the outset of his tenure in 1984. He continued,

> Have we made all the inroads we can into the neighborhood around us? Have we begun to discover and treat the wounds that fester behind closed doors in hundreds of homes in northeast Jackson? Are we to presume that because our neighbors are well-housed and well-fed and well-heeled that all is well within their souls? Friends, if we were simply to ask, what are the five most pressing personal, relational and spiritual problems of affluent people in northeast Jackson, we could generate so many new ministries that our heads would spin.[15]

The following year, Thomason again challenged the congregation to place a greater emphasis on community ministry. "Is it possible, however, that we have been hiding our lamp under a bushel, that we have been too laid-back, too passive in relation to our community?" he asked. Thomason challenged members to spread the word about Northminster in northeast Jackson, noting that "outreach" must be a top priority in the coming years.[16]

Thomason would strike a similar chord two years later in a 1987 sermon where he gently scolded the church, rhetorically asking if Northminster was "too much the clubhouse and not enough the life-saving station." While pointing out that just a year prior the congregation had adopted a long-range plan focused on outreach and missions, Thomason suggested a loss of energy around these goals due to being "heavily invested in our own buildings and programs." "Sometimes I wonder whether our hearts are really in it," Thomason preached. "Have we forgotten how to reach the lost sheep of the house of Israel? Do we even try? ...This morning, I have a pretty good idea who the lost sheep are and how they got lost and where they might be found. But I'm wondering where the shepherds are, and if they're willing to seek and save that which is lost?"[17] No doubt, the young Thomason's preaching was at times boldly courageous.

---

[15] John Thomason, "The State of the Church," sermon, Northminster Baptist Church, January 15, 1984.

[16] John Thomason, "Reaching Our Potential...In Outreach," sermon, Northminster Baptist Church, October 6, 1985.

[17] John Thomason, "A Sense of Proportion, Please," sermon, Northminster Baptist Church, February 1, 1987.

Ministry of Stewardship and Missions

Appeals to tithing as a basic commitment to financially support local and direct missions work were a regular refrain from the pulpit throughout Thomason's tenure. "Friends, our church building is surrounded by a mission field we have hardly begun to explore or penetrate; if only we had eyes to see it," exclaimed Thomason in a March 1984 sermon.[18] He noted the following year that the Bible requires a "higher standard of giving than the simple ten per cent…we are not free to escape the tithe; we are only free to exceed it."[19]

Thomason frequently challenged the congregation to double-down on its commitment to missions through the adoption of a large budget. Indeed the budget grew greatly—growing 116 percent from 1978–1986. And in 1986, the church adopted a record budget of $442,000.[20] The Missions Committee aimed for Northminster to allocate 20 percent of its total budget to mission ministries by 1988—a lofty goal for any Baptist church. Northminster came close but fell slightly short in 1987 with 17.75 percent to missions and 18.5 percent in 1988. Reaching this goal was deferred due to financial obligations to expand church facilities.

Missions giving in this record 1988 budget was divvied up between the Southern Baptist Convention (50 percent), local and direct missions (35 percent); and the Hinds-Madison Association, Crestwood Mission Centers, ACTS—the television network of the SBC, and Baptist Children's Village (15 percent). Several other missions and ministries such as Mississippi Mission and the Southern Baptist Alliance received separate support.[21] Thomason said that the 1988 budget reflected the congregation's desire to "lengthen our building" and "strengthen what we offer inside this building." "It reflects a commitment to stretch ourselves in mission to the community and the world, and at the same time, to secure the ministry we provide to

[18] John Thomason, "New Visions, New Frontiers," sermon, Northminster Baptist Church, March 11, 1984.

[19] John Thomason, "The Truth about Tithing," sermon, Northminster Baptist Church, November 17, 1985.

[20] John Thomason, "Reaching Our Potential...In Giving," sermon, Northminster Baptist Church, November 10, 1985.

[21] "Proposed Northminster Budget—1988."

our own people," Thomason commented. "'Either/or' will not do. 'Both/and' is the only acceptable strategy."[22]

Hands-on involvement in and direct financial gifts to a variety of ministries remained a part of the day-to-day activities of many members of the congregation. One notable example included support for The Sims House, a temporary shelter for homeless women founded in early 1983. Northminster accepted an invitation to participate in the ministry alongside other area churches during summer 1984 and helped with efforts to paint and furnish the house in preparation for its December opening.[23] Other ministries included the Good Samaritan Center, a social service agency established in March 1974 to assist families and individuals in transitional crisis situations in Jackson. Northminster was one of more than eighteen area churches supporting the center.[24]

Northminster Women also became formally involved in Meals on Wheels alongside other Jackson churches. Church members had previously volunteered for Jackson Mobile Meals, Meals on Wheels' predecessor. In February 1982, Northminster Women named Meals on Wheels as one of its mission action projects. Led by Mission Action chairperson Suzanne Boone, women volunteers purchased groceries and cooked, packaged, and delivered meals to twenty-four elderly and homebound persons one day each month.[25] Later Meals on Wheels expanded to three days a month and included male volunteers.

The Christmas Boarding Homes Project, the church's most unique outreach ministry, continued to thrive throughout the 1980s alongside these other local mission efforts. "This annual ministry has become a personal favorite of mine because it helps me put the Christmas season in its proper perspective from the very start," wrote Northminster member Ruth May in November 1987. "You might say, it gets me in the right 'frame of heart,' when there are so many distractions that can blur the true meaning of the holiday."[26] Members would gather to assemble 400 care packages for needy

---

[22] John Thomason, "Maintenance and Mission," sermon, Northminster Baptist Church, November 1, 1983.

[23] N News 1 7 86, "Lengthen and Strengthen."

[24] Ibid.

[25] N Deacon 3 28 82; N Bulletin 2 16 82.

[26] N News 11 17 87.

boarding homes residents and then make the deliveries, a project spearheaded by Mike Peters and funded outside the missions budget via special offerings and private donations—direct local missions giving of Northminster members above and beyond that reflected in the 18.5 percent budget allocation.[27]

Missions: North Jackson Baptist Mission

In May 1984, the Missions Committee voted to sponsor North Jackson Baptist Church as a mission of Northminster Baptist Church in partnership with the Hinds-Madison Association. North Jackson was a predominantly African American congregation in a transitional neighborhood. The struggling church, which would decertify to become a mission, expressed the need for a partnership characterized by mutuality as it sought to become a self-sufficient church. The fledgling congregation requested primarily nonfinancial support, including teachers for Sunday school classes, volunteers for children and youth activities, a music director, and office assistance.[28] "The people of North Jackson do not need our money; they need us," Thomason told the Northminster congregation during a June 1984 sermon. He continued,

> We may have only five loaves and two fish—but in God's economy, that has been proven again and again to be more than enough. I am told that only one-fourth of our adults are presently enrolled in a Sunday school class. That would seem to indicate that we have some who could give of themselves at North Jackson without sacrificing a current place of study or fellowship. ...And as for our own church, we would lack nothing. The challenge from North Jackson would stretch us, but not break us. From what I know about you and what I know about God, the resources are there, and the power is there to see it through.[29]

At a church-wide business meeting later in the summer, the congregation voted to proceed with sponsoring the mission and approved a financial commitment of $3,000 for 1984.[30] Barry Barr was appointed interim chair of

[27] Ibid.
[28] N Deacons 5 20 84; N Deacons 6 17 84.
[29] John Thomason, sermon, Northminster Baptist Church, June 24, 1984.
[30] N Minutes 7 8 84; N Deacons 7 11 84.

the North Jackson Baptist Mission Committee.[31] Led by Barr, Northminster members worked to organize a staff of Sunday school teachers for the mission and helped to organize a Vacation Bible School held at North Jackson in August.[32] A "service of commitment" between the two congregations was held on August 12, 1984, with Thomason preaching on being "partners in the gospel." He compared the relationship of Northminster and North Jackson to that of the Apostle Paul and the church at Philippi:

> The epistle to the Philippians is a good case in point. The church at Philippi was the first congregation formed by the apostle on European soil. He was their initial "sponsor," if you will, and their ongoing mentor, advisor, and helper. He had seen their Sunday finery and smelled their dirty laundry. He had every right and every reason to come across to the Philippians as Big Brother. But the opening lines of his letter reveal a more human, vulnerable side of Paul: "I thank my God in all my remembrance of you, always in every prayer of mine for you all making my prayer with joy, thankful for your partnership in the gospel from the first day until now."
>
> Paul, you remember, was in prison when he wrote these words. His thoughts and prayers are filled with remembrance and thanksgiving. Even as he prays for the Philippians, he takes heart that they are praying for him. The giving and receiving are moving both ways. The help is mutual because the need is mutual. One word in verse 5 says it all. It is the word "partnership." He who holds the title to sponsorship affirms the role of partnership. As the discussions between North Jackson and Northminster have developed over the last several weeks, one word has been used more than any other to describe our working arrangement—the word "partnership." Early this summer, you sought a sponsor, and we accepted a mission, but we both got a partner. If we take Paul as our model, it could not be otherwise. In Christ's economy, adjectives like "large" and "small," "strong" and "struggling" all become relative. We are becoming your sponsors because you are worthy to be our partners, and only hope that we are worthy to be yours. We are offering our help

[31] N Deacons 7 15 84.
[32] N Deacons 8 19 84.

> not because we fear for your future, but because we believe in it, and believe in you.[33]

One year into the sponsorship, Thomason provided the church with an update on the partnership with North Jackson Baptist Mission. During a July 1985 sermon, he focused on how to assist the congregation in a non-paternalistic way:

> "Helping" another congregation is a delicate and difficult task. How does one help without "creating" dependence or triggering resistance? How does one help without hindering the growth of another's self-esteem and self-sufficiency? We have learned by trial and error, negotiation and re-negotiation. Through it all, the goal of our partnership with North Jackson has never been in doubt. We are working toward that day when North Jackson will again be a fully autonomous and vital congregation.

Thomason reported that a year into the partnership, North Jackson was better able to staff its programs and ministries, had added new members, and had called an interim pastor. He explained that North Jackson felt called to provide a Southern Baptist witness in a racially mixed neighborhood. "They are honestly striving to be a color-blind, open communion—and to make that model of ministry viable in a denomination that is nearly all white," Thomason said. "North Jackson has a worthy reason for being, and Northminster has a worthy reason for being their partner as long as we are needed."[34]

Two and a half years into the sponsorship, Northminster voted to discontinue a budget allocation for North Jackson. Barr said that the mission had not requested any funds, but were a need to arise, he would bring the matter to the attention of the deacons.[35] Ultimately, enthusiasm for the mission was limited to a small number of involved and committed members responsible for making the sponsorship a reality.[36]

---

[33] John Thomason, "Partners in the Gospel," sermon, Northminster Baptist Church, August 12, 1984.

[34] N News 7 30 85.

[35] N Minutes 11 2 86.

[36] "Memo from Kelley Williams Sr.," June 14, 2004.

Ministry of Cooperation: Ecumenism

Northminster Baptist Church continued to enjoy a special friendship with Beth Israel throughout the 1980s. In February 1984, a group of twenty-five members from the church and synagogue came together for an event Thomason humorously described as "historic" but "not without historic precedent" and detailed the shared history of the two congregations. He commented, "Before we had our own 'temple' on Ridgewood Road, we were tent-dwellers and nomads in the best Hebrew tradition; one of the stops on our itinerary was Beth Israel, which served as home for our congregation from 1967 to 1968. Last as a house-warming gift and gesture of goodwill, Beth Israel gave Northminster some of the paraments [altar-cloths] which help to highlight the seasons of the Christian year."[37]

Thomason noted that many Northminster members had formed relationships around shared civic issues with members of the Jewish community. He added that Rabbi Richard Birnholz of Beth Israel immediately offered his friendship upon accepting leadership of the synagogue in 1983. "When I moved to Jackson last spring, it was no accident that Rabbi Richard Birnholz immediately offered himself as a friend and colleague, and that I gladly reciprocated," Thomason wrote. In his sermon two days before the scheduled fellowship, Thomason proudly and, for a Southern Baptist pastor, provocatively proclaimed the shared theological identity and journey of Christians and Jews: "One cannot be a good Christian without being a good Jew," Thomason told the congregation. "For the very Lord who brought us out of death's domain into a new creation is the same Lord who brought us out of Egypt and led us into the promised land. To all who would make that common journey, I say *Shalom!*"[38]

Northminster rooted its close friendship with Beth Israel in its Baptist identity and commitment to Baptist principles, specifically a focus on freedom—freedom of the individual and freedom of the local church. At the shared fellowship with Beth Israel, Thomason explained that Northminster's efforts to "encourage freedom" had made possible its ecumenical and interfaith relationships. "Northminster has encouraged considerable free-

[37] N News 1 31 84.

[38] John Thomason, "Christians Are Good Jews," sermon, Northminster Baptist Church, February 26, 1984.

dom, the freedom to embrace Christians from other backgrounds and the freedom to break bread with Jews," he said.[39]

A second interfaith gathering was held with the Beth Israel congregation three months later on January 29, 1985. Thirty members of each congregation met at Northminster for a joint supper and a time of conversation.[40] The following January, Thomason and his wife, Polly, represented Northminster at the 125th anniversary banquet of Beth Israel, which was chartered in 1861 by the governor of Mississippi. Northminster and Beth Israel would hold a third interfaith gathering just one week after the celebratory banquet.[41]

Two additional events further solidified the special bond between the two congregations. During fall 1988, Rabbi Eric Gurvis led a three-week Sunday evening study at Northminster on the basic beliefs and practices of Judaism.[42] Then, the two congregations sponsored a shared dinner on November 9 to commemorate the fiftieth anniversary of Kristallnacht—the "Night of Broken Glass," one of the first acts of Nazi terrorism against the Jews prior to World War II. This special service included readings and responses and Rabbi Gurvis and Thomason offered a Jewish and Christian perspective respectively on Kristallnacht. In his opening introduction, Rabbi Gurvis shared why, fifty years later, Kristallnacht should be commemorated: "Americans should remember the tragedy of 'Kristallnacht' as an event which demonstrates the need for national resolve to respond to government-sponsored persecution anywhere in the world. Remembrance also calls for national rededication to the principles of tolerance and freedom of choice which form the very foundation of our democratic society."[43]

Northminster Baptist Church also remained a regular participant in ecumenical events. In 1983, Northminster women joined women from African-American denominations at Mt. Helm Baptist Church for a program and fellowship focused on healing and reconciliation between all people.[44]

---

[39] John Thomason, "The Christian Distinctive," sermon, Northminster Baptist Church, February 26, 1984.

[40] N Bulletin 1 6 85.

[41] N News 1 28 86; N Bulletin 1 19 86.

[42] N Bulletin 11 6 88.

[43] "Kristallnacht: Fiftieth Anniversary Observance," Beth Israel Congregation and Northminster Baptist Church, November 9, 1988.

[44] N News 5 3 83.

Northminster took part beginning in 1984 in rotating ecumenical advent services with Ascension Lutheran Church, St. James' Episcopal Church, and St. Richard Catholic Church, hosting a "Hanging of the Greens" service.[45] Other examples of a maturing ecumenism included a special celebration of Independence Day in 1987 with the previously mentioned churches as well as Northeast Jackson Christian Church, with St. Richard Catholic Church hosting the fellowship featuring prayer, food, games, and music.[46] Then, in 1989, Northminster held a dinner dialogue with Pearl Street African Methodist Episcopal Church to discuss race relations in Mississippi—past, present, and future. Church members gathered for conversations around topics such as housing, public schools, business, and the economy with the goal of building bridges within the community.[47] The plethora of contacts with African-American Baptists and churches from other Christian denominations—Protestant as well as Catholic—revealed a congregation making sincere efforts to avoid the tribalism and triumphalism that was present within Northminster's denominational home, the Southern Baptist Convention. Through these gatherings and events, the church was, without a doubt, striving to extend the right hand of fellowship to other Christians across the boundaries of race and theology.

Ministry of Caregiving

The Board of Deacons administered a survey in late 1983 to gauge the congregation's interest in a potential lay-led pastoral program. Northminster members, according to the survey, indicated via their responses that the church needed to be more intentional about involving new members in the life of the congregation and an effort was needed to reestablish contact with and engage inactive members.[48] From this survey, the Lay Pastoral Care Subcommittee of the Board of Deacons, comprising Barry Barr, Suzanne Boone, Alan Perry, and John Thomason, proposed a program for a lay ministry of caregiving. The plan called for laity to be trained as "caregivers" with the task of staying in touch with church members, paying attention to spe-

[45] N News 11 27 84; N News 1 20 87.

[46] N News 6 23 87.

[47] N News 4 4 89.

[48] Lay Caregiving: Report from the Lay Pastoral Care Subcommittee of Board of Deacons, Northminster Baptist Church, May 1, 1984.

cial needs and cultivating friendship and providing fellowship throughout the congregation.

Suzanne Boone remembered that the seeds of the caregiving ministry developed at a deacons' retreat attended by deacons and spouses. Group discussion centered on recapturing the early days of the church's history when the congregation was smaller and people knew each other better. According to Boone, Dick Barnes commented, "I believe that we need to look back towards some of those days and find a way for us to be involved in each other's lives again." Some of the deacons were not predisposed to participate and objected, "Well my family's all together. We're doing fine. We don't need this, and I don't want to do that and that's not my gift." Despite the initial hesitancy, the congregational survey was taken, and energy for a ministry of care and friendship had begun to form.[49]

As the caregiving plan unfolded, approximately twenty-five caregivers were selected, and the congregation was divided into geographical districts with at least two caregivers per district. Each caregiver was assigned between ten to twelve families with a term of service of one year. Caregivers were expected to keep records on those under their watch and be attentive to birthdays, anniversaries, and special circumstances. Caregivers were also asked to participate in a monthly meeting for other caregivers to offer mutual support, report needs of the congregation, update the ministry staff and receive continued training. Caregivers would make regular contacts with assigned members via cards, phone calls, and in-person visits as well as assist new members in becoming involved in all aspects of the congregation's life.[50] The deacons and congregation affirmed this innovative and inclusive lay-led ministry and included funding in the 1985 budget for the pastoral care program.[51]

The Caregiving Ministry was blessed and launched during a service of commissioning on January 13, 1985. Twenty-two persons were commissioned as part of this new ministry, which signaled a doubling down on Northminster's cornerstone commitment to be a lay-led congregation. "We are laying to rest one of the oldest, saddest heresies of Christendom; namely, that ministry belongs only to the hireling clergy," Thomason said in his

[49] Suzanne Boone, interview by David Stricklin, March 1, 1992, 10.
[50] N Minutes 10 21 84.
[51] N Minutes 11 4 84.

charge to the first class of caregivers. 'We have heard in the Christian church a lot of theological jargon about 'the priesthood of all believers' and 'equipping the saints for ministry.' What would it mean to take these terms out of the realm of cliché and actually build our church's ministry around them?"

Thomason explained the caregiving program had been the "brainchild of the laity." "You recognized the need; you resolved to do something about it. The caregiving program has been your ministry from conception to birth. It has not been foisted upon you by the professional staff. You have owned this ministry, and that will insure its success." Members of the Caregiver Steering Committee included Suzanne Boone (chairperson), Barbara Barnes, Gloria Martin, Guy Parker, and Jim Travis. The first twenty-two caregivers were a mix of women and men: Dick Barnes Sr., Judy Bigham, Hilda Calhoun, Marcia Carlson, Pauline Cochran, Maurice Gregory, Anne Guidry, Rosemary Hester, Budd Hughes, Linda McGehee, Judy Parker, Margaret Phillips, Helen Ridgway, Emily Smith, Mildred Smith, Bessie Speed, Elizabeth Taylor, Polly Thomason, Sandra Toler, Tom Turner, Jean Williams, and Jane Winston.[52] Within a year, the number of caregivers grew from twenty-two to twenty-eight with sixteen individuals signing up for a second one-year term and twelve new additions.[53] Each caretaker received a towel of service to remind them of Jesus' ministry of care to his disciples when he humbly washed their feet (John 13). About the only hiccup in the caretaking program was when Thomason included foot washing in a commissioning service, and he discontinued the practice after some church members objected.[54]

On the one-year anniversary of the Caregiving Ministry, Thomason wrote in his *Northminster News* column a letter of appreciation for the steering committee and caregivers, especially Suzanne Boone, who served as caregiving director: "Suzanne's attention to detail, her belief in lay ministry and her own loving spirit have provided a model for caregiving to all concerned."[55] Boone remembered being asked to speak to the congregation

[52] "A Service of Commissioning: Northminster Caregiving Ministry," January 13, 1985.

[53] N Deacons 2 16 86.

[54] S. Boone, interview (1992), 10.

[55] N News 1 7 86.

about the Caregiving Ministry after Thomason had left Northminster. She recalled the occasion as the first time a lay person preached at Northminster Baptist Church: "I wasn't sure that it was the thing to do, or that I could do it.... In making my decision and imagining where different people sat in the congregation, I realized there was not a person in that congregation who would want me to fail. That certainly everybody would be there for me just as I hoped to be there for them. It was a rich experience."

Appropriately, Boone spoke "about the priesthood of the believer and how we were all called to be caregivers. I mean everybody; on the back of our bulletin we're all commissioned to serve, and we just have to find our way of serving."[56]

Caregivers developed into a cornerstone ministry of the congregation to the congregation. The deacons also established a "Caregivers Fund" in 1986 for use to aid Northminster members in times of special need.[57] More than thirty years later, this lay-led effort continues to offer Northminster members an outlet to follow the model of Christ in their service to one another. Reflecting on the importance of this ministry, longtime member Jann Puckett said that it "was one of the things that touched me the most as a young adult in the church." She said that young adults were always encouraged by caregivers to attend church suppers. "There was always this encouragement from the people that were in more stable incomes and older in the church, trying to encourage us to be there, even if it meant just coming straight from work and not being able to go home and cook a casserole," Puckett said. "Just that kind of care and concern came across [from the Caregivers]." Puckett said that she will "never forget" that when her mother died, caregivers and other members came from ninety miles away to the funeral in Meridian, and when her father moved to Jackson to an assisted living home, caregivers would send him cards. "Caregivers were ready to do whatever was needed to show compassion and love for that person," Puckett said. "Care-

[56] S. Boone, interview (1992), 10. See also Bill Boone and Suzanne Boone, interview by Aaron Weaver, February 22, 2016, 14. Other church members commented on the importance of the caregiving ministry. For example, see Elizabeth Dean, interview by Aaron Weaver, February 22, 2016, 5.

[57] Ibid.

givers made a huge impact on everybody's lives for a long time…offering loving support."[58]

Celebration of Church Anniversaries

Two milestones were celebrated during the 1980s: the tenth anniversary of the dedication of the Northminster sanctuary and the twentieth anniversary of the church's founding in 1967. The former was celebrated on February 19, 1984, with a special service of worship titled "What Mean These Stones?" in which the congregation's uniqueness and heritage were honored. In his pastoral greeting, Thomason said the two primary purposes of a sanctuary should be to "glorify the God we worship and serve the needs of the worshiper." During the service, the congregation sang the same hymns sung at the sanctuary's dedication in 1974. The litany of dedication from 1974 was also repeated. Members Jack Sweat and Hilda Calhoun offered reflections on the meaning behind the architectural design, including the chancel (the area of the sanctuary beginning with the communion table), nave, and narthex. Theological explanations had been offered when the building was originally dedicated, but remembering and reiterating this architectural theology were surely acts of faith and joyful celebration. Sweat reminded the congregation that the Northminster sanctuary was designed so that worship leaders—choir, lay reader, and clergy—could enter from the rear and approach the chancel while singing the opening hymn of praise. This processional was intended to symbolize the congregation's entrance to worship, praise, and pray.[59]

The lectern was placed on the floor level where calls to serve are sounded and the lay reader leads the congregation in the call to worship. "The pulpit itself is raised to give symbolic priority to the significance of its function as the place where the Word of God and His message are proclaimed," Sweat explained. "Beyond the pulpit is the Baptistry backed by live greenery, which speaks of the life and vitality that come from being born into Christ." Sweat noted that since funds were not available for a pipe organ at the time the sanctuary was built, adequate space was left for the church's impressive organ. He added that the three pyramids of pipes are symbolic of the Holy

[58] Jann Puckett, interview by Aaron Weaver, February 4, 2016, 3.

[59] "What Mean These Stones," A Service of Worship Marking the Tenth Anniversary of the Dedication of the Northminster Sanctuary, February 19, 1984.

Trinity and of congregants' prayers reaching up to God. The cross behind the organ console, Sweat said, "provides not only a reminder to us of our hope in Christ Risen but also serves as a visual link between the various offices of the chancel." The choir stall area was placed on the same level as the church pews to symbolize the fact that all participants at Northminster are part of "one worshiping family," Sweat added.[60]

Calhoun offered reflections on the Building Committee's theological intentions in designing the nave and narthex:

> From the beginning, it was determined that we would want a building where God's people could truly worship Him in spirit and truth and be renewed to go out to serve as Christ commanded. It seemed that if our building were designed in the shape of a cross—or of the cruciform—that would be a good beginning. Our architect agreed, saying that such construction could be seen from the outside as well as the inside, so that when one entered the sanctuary, the long nave with its wide center aisle, flanked by colonnaded side aisles would lead to the crossing. Here would be the communion table, symbolizing the shared life of the church family. Tall, clear glass windows would be used—it would be a well-lighted place—the outside light pouring in—the light from the worshipers going out.[61]

Indigenous materials were used throughout the building, with the warm textures and colors of brick and wood predominating, Calhoun added. Low-backed pews of warm-toned wood were to be almost open-ended, signifying the openness of Northminster's fellowship. The vaulted ceiling was designed with small and great beams of the same wood to be a place of comfort to the physical body and a place of spiritual renewal for the soul, she said. Calhoun concluded her interpretive reflection with a captivating verbal walk through of the sanctuary, to visually depict the worship experience at Northminster:

> We enter through the wide double doors on the east into the narthex, the light shining in through the floor length windows of the south wall. Fresh growing plants are here. We notice the antique furnishing, the tapestry on the table, the pottery, the beautiful handmade wall hanging—the old signifying our faith in the Christian traditions of the

[60] Ibid.
[61] Ibid.

> past—the wood paneled wall on the north and the plants reminding us of the constant newness of life in Christ. We are met and welcomed by members of the Outreach Committee and quietly visit before being handed the Order of Service for the day by an attentive usher. There is a hush in the air as we enter the sanctuary for we are reminded that we have entered here for a time of true worship of God—not a time for visiting with friends until the service is over.
>
> Now we walk down the nave and take our seats in the open-ended pews with our fellow church members and welcome visitors. We do not kneel physically, but there is time for inward prayer and kneeling as we follow the Meditation offered in the order of service. We lift our inward prayer and kneeling as we follow the Meditation offered in the order of service. We lift our eyes to the clear windows and see the bright sky, or the clouds rushing by, or birds come in view and again we remember that not even a sparrow escaped His notice.... Now with the notes from the beautiful organ pealing out, we are ready to participate in the worship to rise and sing praise to God as the choir processes, to join the lay reader in the Call to Worship, to bow in prayer, to hear glorious music as we bring our offering, to listen attentively to the reading from the Bible, to have our hearts lifted by the message song from the choir, to hear and be challenged and encouraged as our pastor brings a thoughtful sermon, to be a part of the invitation to Christian discipleship, and to join in a closing hymn and prayer. We have entered to worship and now we leave inspired to serve.[62]

Calhoun's comments, consistent with earlier renditions of explaining the church's architectural design, added the depth of experience and perspective.

In his remarks, John Thomason lauded Northminster's embrace of a faith that defied popular stereotypes of Baptists, striving to be an ecumenical, innovative, intellectual, service-focused, and worship-centered church. Preaching from Joshua 4, he called the sanctuary a "kind of memorial [that] recalls an event in church history when thirty-four Jackson families crossed the Jordan on dry ground and felt as if they had inherited a Promised Land." They had spent a long time in the wilderness and had "begun to question whether it was possible to be both Baptist and ecumenical, to be committed to the faith and yet open to fresh ways to express that faith to members of a

[62] Ibid.

family instead of numbers in a bureaucracy, to be reverent in worship and adventuresome in study and generous in service," he said.[63]

Thomason challenged the congregation to never forget that Northminster Baptist Church was a fellowship of persons long before it came to be identified with a pile of stones. "When these stones were finally gathered, they were intended to be a memorial to God's creation and redemption of a particular people," Thomason said. "This is why we have the stones, and why we must interpret the stones in every generation, because they point unfailingly to the One with whom we have to do."[64]

Three years later, another celebratory worship service was held to commemorate the twentieth anniversary of the church's founding. At the "Service of Covenant Renewal" on May 3, 1987, congregants remembered the birthing of Northminster. Charter members were recognized, and the church covenant was read aloud. Dr. Roy Honeycutt, president of Southern Baptist Theological Seminary in Louisville, Kentucky, offered a sermon to help launch the church into its third decade of ministry and an anniversary party or "dinner on the grounds" was held following the service. The day of worshipful celebration concluded with a dialogue with Honeycutt on the future of the Southern Baptist Convention and the significant challenges it and the seminary faced.[65] One of Northminster's traditions has been to celebrate its anniversaries as expressions of remembrance and praise and hope for the future.

New Facilities as "Integrated Ministries"

When Northminster Baptist Church formed in 1967, it began with just thirty-four families. Nearly twenty years later, the church had grown to include more than 300 families with a total membership of more than 700. This sustained growth resulted in a need for the congregation to review its facilities, and the Board of Deacons appointed a Facilities Planning Committee in late 1983. Four months later, the committee released its final report to the church, which included numerous recommendations outlined in terms of priority, such as new education and youth facilities to address severe

---

[63] Ibid.

[64] Ibid.

[65] N News 4 6 87.

overcrowding, additional office space, expanded fellowship facilities, and an enlarged children's playground.[66]

Acting on these recommendations, the congregation approved a motion from the deacons to direct the Building Committee to take the next step of developing a plan for a building project.[67] Almost two years later, the Building Committee put forward a plan for the construction of new buildings to the east and south of the existing church buildings for a large fellowship area with kitchen facilities, twelve new education classrooms, a library and media center, new office space, an expanded music suite, enlarged preschool facilities, and additional parking with access to Eastover Drive. A courtyard with a bell tower was to be the centerpiece of the church complex, which would form a contiguous quadrangle.[68]

The entire plan came with a price tag of $1.6 million. A brochure describing and depicting the building project called for "a quality of commitment." "Such an undertaking requires a quality of commitment that goes beyond our ordinary giving," the brochure read, noting that the church's 1973 building was full of light, "with a distinct feeling of openness to the world." This quality of light would be extended to other church ministries. The purpose for the new building was "to receive the light, to proclaim the light, and in the process to become the light of the world."[69] A letter from Building Committee co-chairmen Dick Barnes Sr. and Leland Speed noted that the planning had "required many meetings and some hard decisions."[70]

After both the deacons and congregation adopted the plan from architect and Northminster member Jim Eley, a pledge drive began encouraging "sacrificial giving" to ensure that the fundraising effort did not have a negative impact on the church's annual budget.[71] Within three months, more than one million dollars had been pledged to the project—with a shortfall of fifty pledge cards and just over $450,000. Thomason encouraged sacrificial giving in a June 1986 sermon, asking congregants who had not pledged to do so and suggesting that others with conservative pledges to reconsider as

[66] N Minutes 4 29 84; N Deacons 4 15 84.
[67] N Minutes 4 29 84.
[68] N Minutes 3 16 86.
[69] N History 3 16 86.
[70] Dick Barnes Sr. and Leland Speed, March 4, 1986.
[71] N News 3 18 86; Northminster Baptist Church, "A Quality of Light," brochure, March 16, 1986.

he and his wife, Polly, had. He warned that if the entire amount was not pledged, the balance would have to be borrowed, resulting in a $60,000 increase to the regular annual budget to cover the interest.[72]

Despite the pledge shortfall, six months later, the church ratified a recommendation by the Board of Deacons to enter into a contract with Nickles and Wells Construction Company for $1,469,839 and to seek short-term financing for the remaining balance.[73] A groundbreaking ceremony was held December 21, 1986. At the ceremony, deacon chair Ed Wall recalled the Northminster's founding in his opening remarks:

> At the groundbreaking for our original building, young people from the church family were prominent in the photography in the *Northside Sun*. The inference was that Northminster was building for the future. Today, we continue that journey to fulfill God's purpose for our congregation. We will erect a building from steel, brick and mortar. However, in reality, we will add needed space for education of young people and adults in God's word, space for fellowship to share experiences and reinforce Christian relationships.

The new education and fellowship spaces were completed and dedicated during a special service on September 18, 1988. The four-year project concluded with an open house to showcase the new facilities, which included a Great Hall for fellowship activities, education space, rooms for music ministry, and an administration area for church staff—completing Northminster's "complex" and creating a courtyard tying together the old and new buildings, "an idea reminiscent of older European-style edifices that utilized the courtyard as a central gathering place within the church-house." The new facilities were described as symbolizing the "integrated ministries" of the church and serving as a positive witness to the larger community of Jackson of the importance of education and fellowship in the total life of the church.[74]

---

[72] John Thomason, "Making the Best of Babylon," sermon, Northminster Baptist Church, June 15, 1986.

[73] N Minutes 12 14 86; N News 12 16 86.

[74] "The Dedication of the Education and Fellowship Additions to Northminster Baptist Church," September 18, 1988.

Staff

After serving for five years as youth director, Bryan Rodgers left Northminster in October 1983 for a job in Nashville, Tennessee.[75] A few months later, Chuck Barlow, a twenty-one-year-old senior majoring in English and religion at Mississippi College in nearby Clinton, was hired to lead the Northminster youth group.[76] In 1985, Weaver McCracken began a three-year tenure as youth director, a position renamed as minister to youth. Associate Minister Robert Dibble credited McCracken with bringing "great strength and stability in the leadership and organization of the youth program."[77] Ricky Harvey succeeded McCracken as youth minister in February 1989. A Mississippi College alum and former pastor, Harvey had spent two years at Southern Baptist Theological Seminary before becoming a student at the University of Mississippi School of Medicine.[78]

For more than a year from 1986 to 1987, Northminster was without a second full-time staff minister. Then, during spring 1987, the church called Dr. Robert "Bob" Dibble to be associate minister of education and administration.[79] Dibble served as associate minister for just over two years before departing in August 1989 to take a similar position at River Road Baptist Church in Richmond, Virginia.[80] Dibble succeeded Pat Travis, who had served as minister of religious education, from May 1, 1980, until February 9, 1986. Travis's husband, Jim, had served the church in an interim pastor role prior to the pastorate of John Thomason.[81]

Other staff transitions, additions, and recognitions included the "retirement" in December 1987 of Barbara Webb as church clerk after twenty years of service in that position.[82] Maurice Gregory was elected and served three years. Webb was elected to serve as church clerk again in September 1990 and still served in that position in 2018. The church also recognized Northminster custodian James Jefferson, affectionately known as "Mr. J.," in

[75] N News 10 25 83.
[76] N News 2 14 84.
[77] N News 5 10 88.
[78] N News 2 14 89.
[79] N News 3 31 87; N Minutes 4 5 87.
[80] N News 8 1 89.
[81] N Bulletin 2 9 86; N Bulletin 5 1 80.
[82] N Deacons 4 26 87; N Minutes 9 14 86

February 1989 on his seventh anniversary.[83] In April 1984, Joann Blankenship began as the new church secretary, following Ann Martin who had resigned earlier in the year due to health reasons.[84] Earl Owen began his duties as minister of music on August 28, 1988, and served Northminster through 1996.[85]

Religion and Politics

Throughout the 1980s, Northminster Baptist Church did not shy away from the popular-but-difficult conversation about the proper role of religion in politics. In fact, John Thomason addressed the congregation's approach to this often divisive topic during a Wednesday night discussion during his first year as pastor, affirming the important role of faith in politics and its impact on how one votes. "If I know the people of this church at all, we tend to agree that there is an important relationship between religion and politics," Thomason preached. He continued,

> We affirm that Christ is the Lord of all life—public and private. We believe that we are called to serve Christ beyond the walls of the church, so that the world of our living becomes more like the kingdom of our Lord. We seek to bring our Christian conscience to bear on the realm of Caesar. And this requires direct and deliberate involvement in the arena of politics, at least at the level of the ballot box.[86]

This commitment to ethics and public morality—or what Thomason dubbed as the "necessary 'mixing' of religion and politics"—was reflected in Northminster's regular observance of worship services focused on special social concerns in the 1980s. From Race Relations Sunday to World Hunger Day to Christian Citizenship Day to Religious Liberty Sunday to the Day of Prayer for World Peace, Northminster joined with millions of other Southern Baptists in recognizing the biblical mandate to seek justice and reconciliation.[87] These services varied in style and approach. Congregants were encouraged to celebrate World Hunger Day through generous giving

---

[83] N News 2 28 89.

[84] N Deacons 4 15 84; N Deacons 3 18 84.

[85] N Bulletin 8 28 88; N Deacons 3 21 97.

[86] John Thomason, "First Wednesday Talk," sermon, Northminster Baptist Church, November 2, 1988.

[87] N News 11 16 87.

to a hunger offering.[88] In 1986, Northminster member and United States senator Thad Cochran delivered a talk titled "Christian Citizenship—A Washington Perspective" to commemorate Christian Citizenship Day.[89] In 1987, members heard a sermon from Rev. Nancy Sehested, leader of the Baptist Peace Fellowship of North America, to observe the Day of Prayer for World Peace and were encouraged by associate minister Bob Dibble to join the pacifist group.[90]

Northminster's Christian Citizenship Committee (renamed as Christian Life Committee in 1987) often sponsored events in conjunction with these special observances. Mississippi Supreme Court Justice Reuben Anderson, the first African American in that position, spoke to the congregation in 1987 about his journey and experiences with regard to race relations and steps still needed to secure racial justice and understanding in the state.[91] Other events included a series of Sunday evening programs to celebrate religious liberty and the Baptist heritage to commemorate the 200th anniversary of the United States Constitution in September 1987.[92] The Christian Life Committee also sponsored an adult retreat in 1988 at Lake Tiak O'Khata with Foy Valentine of the SBC Christian Life Commission and a dinner and dialogue later in the year with Oliver "Buzz" Thomas of the church-state watchdog, the Baptist Joint Committee on Public Affairs.[93]

Most notably, in 1989, Northminster observed Sanctity of Human Life Day, which was established on the Southern Baptist worship calendar in 1985 by the denomination's new fundamentalist leadership to focus on the single issue of abortion. However, the Christian Life Committee made a point of explaining to the congregation that this observance would not be limited to a singular focus on abortion. "It is right to observe Sanctity of Human Life Day, for Southern Baptists have historically held a biblical view of the sacredness of human life," wrote Bob Dibble. He continued,

> But it is the intention of our Christian Life Committee to observe this day not myopically but holistically; to promote a consistent pro-life

[88] N News 10 8 85.
[89] N News 6 24 86.
[90] N News 8 3 87.
[91] N News 2 17 89; N Deacons 10 6 87.
[92] N News 8 31 87.
[93] N News 11 22 88; N News 4 12 88.

> ethic that focuses not only on abortion, but also on world hunger, poverty, war and peace, and capital punishment.... I believe we can develop an ethic which works to promote both the right to life and the quality of life. But it can only be fashioned from a holistic vision of the interconnectedness of all human life. With God's help, we can offer the world a positive model of Christian love that is committed to the sanctity of human life.[94]

The Christian Citizenship Committee also became involved with service projects in the late 1980s. In 1987, the committee, chaired by Dot Taylor, submitted a proposal to the Board of Deacons that Northminster formally adopt Spann Elementary School, a predominantly African-American public school in Jackson located a short distance from the church. The committee requested that the church join the Adopt-A-School program of the Jackson Municipal Separate School District, a partnership between religious, business, and community organizations and the schools. Pointing out that numerous churches in Jackson had adopted public schools, the committee explained that the purpose of the program was to "serve children in need" and offer personal attention and much-needed tools and opportunities to improve their educational experience such as tutoring, library materials, incentive awards and enrichment activities (class parties, guest speakers, field trips, etc.). Adopting a school was a way to increase student motivation and to show appreciation for teachers, the committee said: "Through our participation we could demonstrate our desire to be good citizens by aiding all students to receive a quality education and to let the community know of our interest and concern in public education."[95]

Following a discussion about the Adopt-a-School program and the proposal, the Board of Deacons voted not to formally adopt the school, but said the committee "may participate with Spann School as they are willing to do so."[96] However, at the deacon's next monthly meeting, the board changed course and formally joined seven other Jackson churches and more than sixty local businesses as participants in the Adopt-A-School program.[97]

---

[94] N News 1 10 89.

[95] Letter from Christian Citizenship Committee to Northminster Board of Deacons, March 10, 1987; N Deacons 3 15 87.

[96] N Deacons 4 26 87.

[97] N News 5 26 87; N News 9 15 87.

Adopt-a-School would become an important and lasting ministry spearheaded by Dot Taylor and Elizabeth Dean. They started going to Spann Elementary to conduct eye tests, read books to the students, help with homework, make cakes for the school's annual cake walk, host an end-of-year luncheon for Spann staff and faculty, and volunteer in other ways. "We have the fifth graders come in each year and give them an illustration about the [Northminster] organ," Dean related in 2016. "Then, we take them to the Great Hall and feed them pizza and sing. We also have the kindergarten kids come once a year, and they come and sing Christmas carols to us. We have a very active program there with the children and the church."[98] Ten years after its inception, the Adopt-A-School program was hailed by then-pastor Roger Paynter as "one of the most quietly successful mission efforts" of Northminster.[99]

In the lead-up to the 1984 presidential election between incumbent President Ronald Reagan (Republican) and former vice president Walter Mondale (Democrat), John Thomason preached a series of sermons on Christian citizenship in which he decried partisan endorsements of candidates from the pulpit while emphasizing the pastor's role in speaking to a wide array of moral and ethical issues. Thomason, who recognized and understood the political diversity within the congregation, was careful in these sermons to note that the Bible could not be used as a public policy manual.[100] Speaking to Reagan's "peace through strength" foreign policy posture and Mondale's proposals for "peace through disarmament," Thomason said,

> As a Christian, I have always wished that the Bible could be used as a manual of public policy. If only we could sift through the Scriptures

---

[98] Dean, interview, 4.

[99] N News 9 85 96. In 1998, the deacons added a standing Adopt-a-School Committee. Previously, it had been a subcommittee of the Christian Life Committee (N Deacons 4 23 98). The following year, the deacons voted to remove the Christian Life Committee from its list of standing committees per a request of the Committee on Committees, which decided that the CLC's work was filled by other committees, primarily Adult Ministries and Adopt-a-School (N Deacons 11 21 99).

[100] John Thomason, "On Minding Your Own Business," sermon, Northminster Baptist Church, July 1, 1984. Northminster member and U.S. Senator Thad Cochran was on the ballot in November 1984 in his re-election bid to a second term in the Senate. Cochran handily defeated his Democratic opponent, William Winter.

> and find simple, clear answers to the dilemmas of war and peace. It is obvious that the biblical writers are longing for peace on earth and proclaim it as God's goal for creation; but, alas, they are fuzzy about details and silent about methods. The Bible cannot be read as a textbook on the conduct of foreign policy or military strategy. The material just isn't there.[101]

Thomason elaborated on this approach to mixing religion and politics ("without merging church and state") in an October 7 sermon just one month prior to the 1984 election. He argued that the notion that there is an obvious and unambiguous way in which Christians should vote is "dangerous in the extreme" because such a belief "misuses the Bible to which it appeals." "The Scriptures are not a Judeo-Christian counterpart of the Communist Manifesto," Thomason said. "The Bible does not endorse a political program or party or philosophy—either left or right or down the middle. The Bible gives us principles by which to make political decisions; but it does not give us specific prescriptions for defending human liberty and promoting the general welfare. The Scriptures are at best suggestive; they are not definitive."[102]

Baptist Battles

The 1980s was a decade rife with denominational controversy and Northminster Baptist Church was not immune from the "Baptist battles" that beset the Southern Baptist Convention. Baptist historian Walter Shurden has argued that the story of Southern Baptists is a story of almost perpetual controversy.[103] Indeed, the latter half of the twentieth century witnessed numerous theological conflicts in the nation's largest Protestant denomination. The first notable conflict was the "Genesis Controversy" of the 1960s that erupted when Broadman Press, the publishing agency of the SBC Sunday School Board, published a book by Baptist seminary professor Ralph Elliott asserting than an affirmation of the historicity of the first elev-

---

[101] John Thomason, "Can We Love Our Global Enemies," sermon, Northminster Baptist Church, August 5, 1984.

[102] John Thomason, "On Casting a Christian Vote," sermon, Northminster Baptist Church, October 7, 1984.

[103] Walter B. Shurden, *Not a Silent People: Controversies that Have Shaped Southern Baptists* (Macon, GA: Smyth & Helwys Publishing, 1995).

en chapters of Genesis was not necessary to express a strong affirmation of their theological truth.[104] Elliott's suggestion in *The Message of Genesis* (1961) that Adam and Eve were not historical figures led a number of outspoken Southern Baptist pastors to cry "liberal" and accuse Elliott of not believing the Bible. Ultimately, Elliott lost his position at Midwestern Baptist Theological Seminary.[105] A second controversy occurred over biblical interpretation in 1970 when Broadman Press published a commentary in which British author G. Henton Davies denied that God had literally told Abraham to practice child sacrifice (Genesis 22). These two controversies convinced many conservatives that the leadership of the Southern Baptist Convention was fostering or allowing a liberal drift in denominational agencies and seminaries.[106]

Throughout the 1970s, these conservative critics developed networks to oppose alleged liberalism in the convention.[107] As the convention was mobilizing for "Bold Mission Thrust" in the late 1970s, a missionary effort to share the gospel with the whole world by the year 2000, a group of fundamentalists was formulating a political strategy to gain complete control of the SBC. The main architects of this planned takeover, Paige Patterson of the Criswell Biblical Institute, and layman Paul Pressler, a Texas appeals court judge, sought to elect as SBC president men who were committed to biblical inerrancy. Patterson and Pressler recognized that the president, though historically considered a figurehead, had the power to appoint leaders to committees who would then select trustees to the various denominational agencies. With a series of presidential victories, trustee boards of SBC

[104] Ralph H. Elliott, *The Message of Genesis: A Theological Interpretation* (Nashville, TN: Broadman Press, 1961). For Elliott's memoir about the controversy surrounding his book, see *"The Genesis Controversy" and Continuity in Southern Baptist Chaos: A Eulogy for a Great Tradition* (Macon, GA: Mercer University Press, 1992).

[105] Elliott, *"The Genesis Controversy,"* 67–68.

[106] Jerry Faught, "Round Two, Volume One: The Broadman Bible Commentary," *Baptist History & Heritage* 38/1 (Winter 2003): 94–114.

[107] David Stricklin, *A Genealogy of Dissent: Southern Baptist Protest in the Twentieth Century* (Lexington: University Press of Kentucky, 1999) 145. One such group formed was the Baptist Faith and Message Fellowship.

institutions and thus the institutions themselves could be completely remolded.[108]

Despite the fundamentalist criticism, most Baptists across the SBC believed that historic love for cooperative missions would hold theological infighting in check. Baptist historian Bill Leonard has argued that for most of the twentieth century the diverse constituencies that existed throughout the SBC were held together by a "Grand Compromise." This "Grand Compromise" was an understood agreement not to let any ideological party, whether on the left or the right, take control of the denomination. Instead, the Southern Baptist Convention would be held together by a large group of centrists, who for the sake of missions and evangelism, found unity amidst diversity. According to Leonard, "There was less a synthesis than a Grand Compromise based in an unspoken agreement that the convention would resist all attempts to define basic doctrines in ways that excluded one tradition or another, thereby destroying unity and undermining the missionary imperative."[109]

The fundamentalists' first victory came in 1979 with the election of Memphis pastor Adrian Rogers as the president of the SBC. While several of the presidential elections in the 1980s were close, Patterson and Pressler's political strategy worked. Each year the candidate supported by the "conservative resurgence" won. By 1990, the Patterson-Pressler coalition had gained complete control of the Southern Baptist Convention. Leaders trumpeted a new Reformation in religious history. The SBC had turned the tide back on the evil of liberalism, and according to the victors, historic Baptist conservatism had been restored.[110]

The group of Baptists opposed to the so-called "conservative resurgence" came to be referred as "moderates" or "moderate Baptists"—who viewed the SBC controversy not as a conflict over conservative versus liberal theology or a "battle for the Bible," but as a political power struggle. The real issue at stake was Baptist freedom, with moderates rejecting the funda-

---

[108] Bill Leonard, *God's Last and Only Hope: The Fragmentation of the Southern Baptist Convention* (Grand Rapids, MI: W. B. Eerdmans Publishing Inc., 1990) 138–39.

[109] Leonard, *God's Last and Only Hope*, 29–38.

[110] Note the title of Jerry Sutton, *The Baptist Reformation: The Conservative Resurgence in the Southern Baptist Convention* (Nashville: Broadman and Holman, 2000).

mentalists' demand for doctrinal conformity, creedal litmus tests, and attempts to squelch dissent and stomp out theological diversity. Moderates argued that the charges of widespread theological liberalism in Southern Baptist seminaries and denominational agencies were false, repeatedly affirmed the centrality of biblical authority, but resisted inerrancy as dogmatism.[111]

A leading "moderate" congregation in Mississippi, Northminster Baptist Church became more deeply engaged in denominational affairs during the 1980s, sending messengers every summer to the SBC annual meeting. Denominational controversies were a frequent subject of sermons as John Thomason began to establish himself among his peers and within the congregation in the early 1980s as an outspoken critic of Southern Baptist fundamentalists. "We Baptists have taken to the battlefield. This time, we are not waging war against the powers and principalities, but against our own flesh and blood. The name of the game is denominational fratricide," Thomason said during his sermon following the 1983 SBC meeting in Pittsburgh, Pennsylvania.[112]

Thomason told his congregation that despite their diversity and progressive reputation in the state as a different kind of Baptist church, the Southern Baptist struggle was one of importance for the church:

> I realize that Northminster Baptist Church has always emphasized the word "church" over the word "Baptist"—I realize that we are something of a melting pot of many Christian traditions, that dozens of you are relatively new to Baptist life, that your ties to the Baptist family may be vague or half-hearted. I realize that, as a congregation, we have always marched to the beat of a different drummer among Mississippi Baptists. But any church that was born under the sponsorship of sister Baptist churches, any church that belongs to no fewer than three Baptist bodies, any church that gives a portion of its budget receipts to the wider Baptist cause, cannot be just incidentally or accidentally or nominally Baptist. We have a stake in the current Baptist dispute. It has eve-

[111] Shurden, *Not A Silent People*, 86–87 See also Leonard, *God's Last and Only Hope*, 149–51, 181.

[112] John Thomason, "Will the Real Baptists Please Stand Up," sermon, Northminster Baptist Church, June 19, 1983.

rything to do with us. We need to understand the issues and be actively involved in their resolution.[113]

In 1984, messengers to the SBC went on record as opposed to the ordination of women, adopting a resolution stating, "We encourage the service of women in all aspects of church life and work other than pastoral functions and leadership roles entailing ordination."[114] Thomason; Pat Travis, Northminster's minister of religious education; and member Suzanne Boone returned from the meeting in Kansas City and reported to the deacons about the "distressing" resolution and "other disturbing trends" within the SBC.[115]

Later in the summer, Thomason highlighted the distressing resolution in a sermon, describing his near twenty years of pastoral experience serving alongside ordained women and outlining his biblical rationale for championing women in ministry. "I hardly need to remind you that the Bible was written in a patriarchal culture," Thomason said. He went on,

> Men held the positions of authority in the home, the marketplace, the temple and the halls of government. In biblical times, women were regarded as the property of men. They stood on the fringes of every institution in Hebrew society. They were denied the right to teach in the Jewish synagogue because they were denied the opportunity for an education. Women were considered incapable of understanding religious truth, when in fact, they were rarely given the chance to understand.[116]

Unlike many on the "moderate" side of the Southern Baptist aisle, Thomason did not buy the simplistic depiction of SBC fundamentalists as merely opportunists in search of political power at any means necessary. Rather, Thomason understood fundamentalists to be motivated in large part due to sincere theological convictions about the truth and nature of the Bible. "A lot of moderates believe that biblical inerrancy is just a motto, that the real motivation of this campaign is political not theological. It is supposed that the fundamentalists are not on the defensive for the Bible; they

---

[113] Ibid.

[114] "Resolution on Ordination and the Role of Women in Ministry," Southern Baptist Convention, Kansas City, MO, 1984, http://www.sbc.net/resolutions/1088/resolution-on-ordination-and-the-role-of-women-in-ministry.

[115] N Deacons 6 17 84.

[116] John Thomason, "Learning to Let Go," sermon, Northminster Baptist Church, August 26, 1984.

are on the offensive for personal power," Thomason preached in a sermon during fall 1984.

> Friends, I believe that this is selling the ultraconservatives short. Whatever their real motivation, our fundamentalist colleagues have raised a critical issue.... A real question of truth is at stake here: what is the truth about the Bible? What is the healthiest way of viewing its authority? Does the unique place of the Bible depend on its being divinely written or does it suffice to say that the Bible was divinely inspired though written through human agency? We Baptists firmly believe in the authority of the Bible, but this is because the Bible has brought us face to face with Jesus Christ. God confronts us in a living person, not merely in information about that person.... [The Bible] was never meant to be an object of worship; it was meant to direct us toward the only true object, the living God.[117]

During fall 1986, a small group of moderates who had been fighting the fundamentalist movement convened on the campus of Meredith College in Raleigh, North Carolina, to explore the possibility of forming an organization that would work to preserve historic Baptist principles of freedom.[118] The formation of the "Southern Baptist Alliance" was announced on February 12, 1987, at press conferences in Charlotte, Raleigh, and Atlanta, where alliance founders offered the following statement of purpose: "The Southern Baptist Alliance is an alliance of individuals and churches dedicated to the preservation of historic Baptist principles, freedoms and traditions and the continuance of our ministry and mission within the SBC."[119] Northminster

---

[117] John Thomason, "The Medium and the Message," sermon, Northminster Baptist Church, September 9, 1984.

[118] Alliance of Baptists, "History," http://www.sitemason.com/files/cQ4qR2/Alliance%20of%20Baptists%20History.pdf.

[119] Bill J. Leonard, ed., *Dictionary of Baptists in America* (Downers Grove, IL: InterVarsity Christian Fellowship of the USA, 1994) 19. Oakhurst Baptist Church, a well-known Southern Baptist progressive congregation, became the first church to join the Southern Baptist Alliance. See also Oran P. Smith, *The Rise of Baptist Republicanism* (New York: New York University Press, 1997) 220–22. See also Stan Hastey, "Highlights of Alliance History," Alliance of Baptists (unpublished history, Baylor University, J. M. Dawson Institute of Church-State Studies). Two additional organizational meetings were held at Providence Baptist Church in Charlotte in January and February of 1986.

deacons adopted a motion one month later that the church join the newly-formed alliance, becoming just the third church to do so, and that Thomason attend the alliance's convocation in May.[120] Thomason stated in his *Northminster News* column that the alliance was not a political action group, but instead was formed to be a vehicle of communication between like-minded Baptists and the convention at large as well as "a means of advocacy for embattled ministries and institutions" such as the Baptist Joint Committee on Public Affairs, the SBC's religious liberty watchdog.[121] Later, during its November meeting, the church adopted a motion from John Clark to approve $3,000 to support the fledgling alliance.

The following year, John Thomason, who had become a recognized national leader among progressive pastors in the SBC, was selected as the president of the Southern Baptist Alliance.[122] Several months later, Northminster deacons formed a denominational study committee to examine the church's affiliation and financial support of the SBC as well as study denominational alternatives, such as financial support and dual alignment possibilities with the American Baptist Convention.[123] In September 1988, Northminster hosted a "Baptist Freedom Rally" of the alliance featuring Grady Cothen, the retired president of the SBC Sunday School Board, and Frank Stagg, professor emeritus of New Testament of Southern Baptist Theological Seminary, as guest speakers.[124]

Six months into his term, Thomason resigned from the alliance presidency, stating he needed to be more available to his family. "Over the past few months, I have given renewed attention to my private self—that is, my relationship to my own being, to God, and to my family," Thomason wrote.

> In the midst of these changes, something had to give. Simply stated, I took a long look at my outermost priority circle and decided to resign the presidency of the Southern Baptist Alliance. I have assured the SBA directors that my decision in no way signals a retreat from the

[120] N Deacons 3 15 87; John A. Bolt, "Alliance of Moderate Baptists Says Goals are Freedom, Unity," (IN) *Post-Tribune*, March 27, 1988, A4.
[121] N News 3 23 87.
[122] N Deacons 2 21 88.
[123] N Deacons 6 19 88.
[124] N Bulletin 9 18 88.

SBA's stated mission. I believe Northminster will be well-served to remain actively affiliated with the SBA.[125]

Northminster staff and lay leaders continued to participate in the alliance as Jan Purvis, Janey Stubbs, Bob Dibble, and Alan Perry attended the 1989 convocation in Greenville, South Carolina. Perry reported in *Northminster News* that he was encouraged at the convocation "by the realization that we at Northminster are not alone." "There are other Baptists who share our vision of what church can be," Perry wrote. "There are many articulate leaders—men and women—to speak for that vision. And I have more hope for the survival of an open, inclusive and intelligent Baptist witness than I have had for many years."

John Thomason's Resignation

Just two months after his resignation from the presidency of SBA, John Thomason submitted his letter of resignation to the church, announcing his intent to return to graduate school and pursue a doctorate at Southern Baptist Theological Seminary in Louisville, Kentucky. Thomason said that he grieved leaving the church after five years. "Our years together have been full of change for the church and full of grace and growth for me," he wrote. "You are a challenging congregation to serve, and as loving and encouraging as you are challenging. Thank you for the countless ways you have embraced me and my family in friendship."[126]

In his final sermon, Thomason expressed his gratitude for the church:

> On many occasions, I have said to prospective members that there are two Northminsters.... There is the one that meets the eye, that has all the spit and polish, success and affluence. Then there's the other Northminster, the one that is not so easily seen. It is composed of people who came here out of some experience of pain or failure and heard for the first time in their lives that "there is no condemnation to those who are in Christ Jesus" (Romans 8:1). As a pastor and as a fellow human being, I can tell you that those two Northminsters are one and the same! Behind many a high salary lies a low self-esteem. Behind many a smiling face lies a broken heart.

---

125 N News 9 27 88.

126 N News 11 14 88.

> But far from being a handicap, this is the secret of our energy and effectiveness as a church. There is surprisingly little pretense or one-upmanship in this congregation. For we are all partakers of grace, and thus we are better able to offer grace to others. Don't ever forget that the best healers are wounded healers. God's power is made perfect, not in wealth or strength, but in weakness (cf. II Cor. 12:9). When you try to comfort someone who has lost a loved one, or survived the nightmare of addiction, or filed for bankruptcy, they don't want to see your resumé, for God's sake; they want to see your heart; and if your heart is fully human, then you can comfort them with the comfort of God.
>
> Nearly six years ago, I became a partaker with you of grace. It was honor enough that you called me to be your pastor and preacher. But you gave me a much higher honor than that; you invited me to be a fellow church member. You told me that belonging to this church is more basic than leading it. Over the years, you have given me—a clergyperson on the payroll—the same grace and patience that you give to a lay volunteer. You have allowed me to grow into this job. You have motivated me more by encouragement than criticism. When I have struggled or hurt, you have not banished me to the land of fallen idols; you have invited me to join the human race. Somebody has said that the Christian church is the only army in the world that shoots its own wounded. That may be true of the Church at large, but it is not true of Northminster. For we are all partakers of grace.[127]

Thomason and his family were honored at the Thanksgiving Supper and received a love offering from the congregants. Earlier in the year, to celebrate Thomason's five-year anniversary, *Northminster News* featured laudatory reflections from church leaders. Jan Purvis, who served as chair of the Board of Deacons in 1984–1985 as well as on the committee that hired him in 1983, said that after experiencing five years of his leadership her enthusiasm had not waned. Purvis praised Thomason for his "recognition of the need for organization and lay leadership" as well as his contributions to the Sunday morning worship hour. "As a worship leader his reserve, poise, and speaking skill contribute to the creation of a worshipful atmosphere," Purvis said. "The service is kept vital and real and satisfying through his and the congregations' participation. John honors the gospel message and worshipers

[127] John Thomason, "In Remembrance of You," sermon, Northminster Baptist Church, November 20, 1988.

through careful sermon preparation. His messages are well balanced, bringing to us the grace, forgiveness, hope and challenge of the gospel."[128]

[128] N News 4 5 88.

Chapter 5

The Early 1990s: A Place of Healing and Hope and the Ministry of Roger Paynter

Calling a Pastor

The search for the next pastor of Northminster Baptist Church began in earnest two weeks after John Thomason's departure with a special called business meeting to appoint a Pulpit Committee. In accordance with the bylaws, the committee comprised the chairman of the Board of Deacons, Sunday school director, president of Northminster Women, two young adults (thirty or younger), and two members of the congregation at large. Unlike the previous search, which lasted eighteen months, this one was rapid. Just shy of seven months later, the Pulpit Committee, led by chairperson Alan Perry, recommended Roger Paynter to the Board of Deacons on June 25, 1989. Like Thomason, Paynter's compensation package included a twelve-week sabbatical every four years.[1]

Paynter came to Northminster from Lake Shore Baptist Church in Waco, Texas, where he had served as pastor since 1982. Prior to his tenure at Lake Shore, Paynter was pastor of Austin Heights Baptist Church in Nacogdoches, Texas (1978–1982), and associate pastor of Highland Park Baptist Church in Austin, Texas (1975–1978). Like his predecessor, John Thomason, Paynter was a graduate of Baylor University (BA, 1972) and Southern Baptist Theological Seminary (MDiv, 1975). He also completed a doctor of ministry degree at Texas Christian University's Brite Divinity School in 1982 and, again like Thomason, had studied at Oxford University. At the age of thirty-nine, the same age as Thomason upon his departure, Paynter also brought with him a young family: wife, Susan Youngblood; Grayson (age six); and Mary Kathryn (age four).[2]

---

[1] N Deacons 6 25 89. The twelve-week sabbatical, to begin in 1992, was in lieu of vacation and other leave and to be used for "study, refreshment, replenishment, or such activity as deemed appropriate."

[2] "Resumé of Roger Paynter," Pulpit Committee Minutes, June 9, 1989.

Similar to Thomason, Paynter was deeply engaged in denominational affairs, serving on the board of directors of the newly formed Southern Baptist Alliance as well as the board of trustees of the Texas Baptist Christian Life Commission. His wife, Susan ("Suzii"), was also active in denominational life and just over fifteen years later would emerge as a national leader on the Baptist stage as director of the Texas Baptist Christian Life Commission and later as the executive coordinator of the Cooperative Baptist Fellowship. She was the first woman to hold these positions.

Paynter preached his first sermon on August 20, 1989, and expressed his excitement and nervousness as he began his tenure as pastor of Northminster Baptist Church: "So, here I am and there you are. And I'd like to think that the Wind of God's Spirit has blown us across each other's pathways, and that we will sow some good seed together. I'm more than a little overwhelmed at the excitement and expectations that have preceded me. I mean, I know me, and I don't get that excited."[3] Two months later, Paynter was formally installed as pastor and introduced to the Jackson community. Baptist pastors and other leaders as well as clergy from Jackson's ecumenical community participated in the installation service, featuring Dr. Hardy Clemons, senior pastor of First Baptist Church in Greenville, South Carolina. This installation service exemplified Northminster's commitment to ecumenism and being a mediating Baptist voice or "a different kind of Baptist" church in the Jackson community where Southern Baptist conservatism and fundamentalism still reigned supreme.

Celebrating Twenty-five Years of Northminster

Just shy of Paynter's three-year anniversary, Northminster Baptist Church celebrated its own silver anniversary marking twenty-five years since the founding of the Northeast Jackson Baptist Mission in May 1967. A Saturday evening banquet dinner at River Hills Club was held May 16, 1992, and featured the church's first full-time pastor, Dudley Wilson, and church co-founder, Bob Guyton, as guest speakers. Guyton, who served as chairman of the Mission's Steering Committee in 1967, described the founding

[3] Roger Paynter, "Of Thieves, Hirelings, and Shepherds," sermon, Northminster Baptist Church, August 20, 1989.

of the church as the "most meaningful experience of my life."[4] "The task undertaken by the Steering Committee and Northminster's founding families in the late 1960s was impossible, but it was done and today, we have a strong, vibrant and meaningful church," Guyton said. "But it was done because it was God's will and we were carrying out His will. Certainly, we could not have done it alone and I am convinced He was carrying us every step of the way."[5]

In addition to emphasizing God's hand in the birthing of Northminster, Guyton noted that the founding came during a time of incredible change both within society and the larger church—pointing to struggles for equality on behalf of both African Americans and women. Guyton attributed these cultural challenges and changes as reasons for Northminster's success. "I believe this change, the need for equality, and the need of God for an effective change agent, and the desire of God for a young, dynamic institution that would not be afraid to try new approaches to worship, was paramount in our commitment and our success."[6]

Worship was primary. It was the central concern of Northminster's founding in Guyton's retelling—the *raison d'être*. He emphasized that the main motivating factor of the founding group was "the desire and need to worship reverently with anyone wishing to do the same, to study and learn and grow in the knowledge and love of God, and to involve ourselves and our whole family in building God's kingdom on earth as Jesus had commanded."[7] "We never considered being anything but a Baptist church," Guyton said. He continued,

> We wanted to belong and yet we wanted to provide new ways to worship in our urban society, and we wanted to provide opportunities of involvement for everyone. We worked long and hard. We covered all the bases, we got support from the right people and the energy flowed. This energy fed on itself, and the excitement was fueled by the commitment of so many people to being involved in doing God's work.

---

[4] Bob Guyton, "Northminster Celebration" (Northminster Baptist Church 25th celebration, May 16, 1992).

[5] Ibid.

[6] Ibid.

[7] Ibid.

> While it was hard work, it was also fun. We had a sense of community, of togetherness, of love for each other and of God.[8]

Guyton added that Northminster Baptist Church had experienced many changes in its first twenty-five years, and church members had provided leadership in the Jackson community and beyond through participation in denominational and ecumenical activities. Laity had been the backbone of the congregation. "Families have drawn closer, and children have grown up in places where God was important," Guyton said.

> And the community of Jackson and the state of Mississippi have benefited by this beacon of light. What we have today is an active, vibrant, committed community of faith—striving to live as Christ in the world. We've changed, we've all gotten so much more out of this than we've given. Commitment has been the hallmark of this church and it will remain the nucleus of the future of this church.... We were called, we responded, and today God is celebrating with us.[9]

The following morning, Northminster devoted its Sunday worship service to commemorating the twenty-fifth anniversary. Jan Purvis led the congregation in a responsive reading of the church covenant, and former pastor Dudley Wilson offered the Lord's Prayer. Members of the Mississippi Symphony performed John Rutter's *Te Deum* and the congregation sang a celebratory hymn penned by fourteen-year member Randy Weeks and harmonized by organist Billy Trotter titled "Now Is the Time of Celebration."[10]

Paynter read the Scripture—verses from Numbers 13 and 14 on the journey of the Israelites exploring Canaan. Ken Chafin, a well-known Southern Baptist leader and retired pastor of Walnut Street Baptist Church in Louisville, Kentucky, preached from this text with a sermon titled "Standing on the Banks of Tomorrow." Additionally, the worship bulletin listed the church's historic milestones and charter members. The Flower Committee was responsible for a special array of flowers throughout the sanctuary, Great Hall, and at the covered-dish luncheon in the courtyard held following the anniversary service. Northminster children designed banners in their Sunday school classes, which were hung in the church to com-

---

[8] Ibid.

[9] Ibid.

[10] N Bulletin 5 16 1992; N News 5 19 92.

memorate the anniversary, and Tom Cochran gave the church a watercolor of Northminster.[11] Once again, Northminster anniversary celebrations were detailed rituals of memory and inspiration.

Crisis and Community: Barbara Oliver

In 1994, the Northminster family began a journey together that would end in the tragic loss of the congregation's beloved associate pastor, Barbara Oliver. Three years earlier, in April 1991, Oliver had been hired as Northminster's associate pastor for childhood and adult education. She was diagnosed in 1994 with chronic myelocytic leukemia. The announcement of Oliver's illness, which shook the congregation to its core, prompted invitations to pray in the sanctuary and write her notes full of love and encouragement. "The Chinese character for crisis is the same character for opportunity," Paynter wrote in *Northminster News* at the time of the announcement. "This crisis presents us an opportunity to grow as a community of prayer, a community open to God's surprises, a community of 'love-in-action,' and a community of deep faith, on Barbara's behalf, but also on behalf of all those we touch who need our care. Let us become a church of deeper love and prayer."[12]

The church helped launch a bone marrow drive the following month, in late June 1994, which was publicized in Jackson's newspaper, the *Clarion-Ledger*. Several months later, an eligible donor was identified, and the church established a medical mission fund and held a rummage sale to raise funds to help with the exorbitant costs of Oliver's treatments. More than 110 families from Northminster participated in the sale and raised $11,200 for the fund.[13] A "sending service" was held on March 12 for Oliver at her request as she relocated to Atlanta for treatment and a bone marrow transplant at Emory Hospital. The Personnel Committee, led by Bill Lee, recommended and received the Board of Deacons approval to keep Oliver on full salary for six months after her departure until her disability insurance took effect.[14]

---

[11] Ibid.

[12] N News 6 15 94.

[13] N Deacons 10 16 94; N News 6 22 94; N Deacons 11 20 94.

[14] N Deacons 2 22 95.

This period of fear and pain in the life of the congregation could be felt in sermons Paynter preached in May 1995, which revealed the shared anxieties of the congregation as they watched their beloved friend's struggle:

> This past year, Barbara's body was invaded by chronic myelocytic leukemia. At the same time, in a way that we surely did not fully realize, this Body, the Body of Christ as Northminster was also invaded by this illness. Her illness became our illness, her anxieties have become our anxieties, her fear has become our fear. And now, the reality is that no matter how much we extend our love and our prayers it is ultimately Barbara who must face this. But I hope you know, that I think we know, on the other hand, that we all face this Jerusalem together. It is frightening to go to Jerusalem. It is painful to go to Jerusalem. But it is only by going through Jerusalem that life is to be found. There is no easier way unfortunately. What awaits is hard and scary, but who awaits is already here, the Spirit of the Living God who shall be with you, Barbara, and who shall be with us.[15]

Just one year after receiving her diagnosis, Oliver received a transplant from a donor in France. Paynter called on the congregation to pray for Oliver's healing during the 100 days of critical recovery. "My fondest hope is that a year from now [the donor] would be able to come to Jackson and be introduced to us by Barbara—what a joyful moment that would be," Paynter exclaimed to the congregation.[16] Sadly, two months later, Northminster would hold Oliver's funeral following her death on August 3, 1995, at the age of thirty-eight.

Two days later, on August 5, Northminster Baptist Church hosted a service remembering their beloved friend—"A Witness to the Resurrection and Celebration of the life of Rev. Barbara Ann Oliver," which included the participation of Paynter as well as Oliver's friends: Dr. Steve Pressley, associate pastor of First Baptist Church, Greensboro, North Carolina; Rev. Sarah Shelton, associate pastor of Riverchase Baptist Church, Birmingham, Alabama; and Rev. Stan Wilson, associate pastor of Northminster Baptist Church. "We gather also, in great gratitude, for the rich and generous life of

---

[15] Roger Paynter, "Encountering Jerusalem," sermon, Northminster Baptist Church, May 21, 1995.

[16] N News 6 7 1995.

the Rev. Barbara Ann Oliver, Barbara or "Barb" to so many of us here," Paynter said. He said in his meditation,

> We gather to drink deeply of happy and touching memories that encase our hearts and minds this morning. She lived life to the fullest in our midst and to the end. She ministered to us in word and deed, heart and spirit, and we shall always be grateful. Most of all, we gather as Barbara would truly want us to do, not just to pay homage to her, but to worship the Living God, the One who is Lord over life and death and life beyond death, the One seen most clearly and understood most profoundly in the face of Jesus, Savior of us all. He is the One who is the Living Word and thus is the last word over death. For it is in the power of his Resurrection that we gather in hope.
>
> How we deeply wish this day had not come. How we thought it would not. How we feared it might. How we abhor that it has. And yet, it cannot steal from us our profound gratitude. Gratitude for the great and glad gift that Barbara has been to us. Each of us is deeply blessed with some sustaining memory of how she impacted our living and the life of our church and the life of our faith. We have gratitude for her remarkable family that demonstrated what the agape love of Christ is all about in their steadfast and tender care of her. Gratitude for the way she allowed her illness and suffering to be used by the Spirit to secure us to one another. Gratitude, in the end, for coming home and allowing us to stand on sacred ground as one we love passed from this journey to the next. Gratitude above all, for as the Great Hope that is ours in the sure knowledge that Jesus the Christ has defeated death's ultimate power. That Barbara is well, even now, and in the Presence of the Living God, and that the deep longing that we feel is God's sign that someday that longing shall be made complete in a Great and Glad reunion.[17]

Missions and Ministries

Missions remained a central focus of Northminster Baptist Church during Roger Paynter's tenure as the congregation continued its involvement with numerous ministries such as Stewpot (a soup kitchen run by local churches), Meals on Wheels, Baptist Children's Village, and Habitat for Humanity. From 1990–1994, church volunteers, including the Northmin-

[17] Ibid.

ster youth group, helped to construct four Habitat homes for low-income families in Jackson.[18] A dedication service was held April 29, 1990, for the church's first Habitat building project.[19]

In 1992, Northminster became one of the sponsoring churches of Mission Mississippi—a three-day event to bring together black and white citizens for purposes of friendship, prayer and worship and to promote racial reconciliation. Northminster member Victor Smith served on the Executive Committee of Mission Mississippi, and Paynter in his *Northminster News* columns encouraged church members to "be a part of pursuing this calling of reconciliation."[20] Through sermons and columns, Paynter reminded the congregation of the importance of missions in their own local community, referring to Northminster as a "mission outpost on Ridgewood Road." "We have before us an enormous mission task of proclaiming good news to people right here," Paynter said. "We are not a religion club for people with discretionary income. We are either the church of Jesus Christ, a mission outpost in a growingly secular world, a place of healing and hope and inclusion and grace, or we are wandering 'off-center.'"[21]

Starting under the leadership of Barbara Oliver, mission trips for Northminster adults became a staple activity of the congregation during the summers. A group of Northminster adults spent a week in June 1993 at Richboro Baptist Church in Staten Island, New York, where they completed popular mission trip tasks such as providing community meals for indigent persons, operating a clothes closet, restoring church facilities, painting, and leading Bible studies combined with arts and crafts projects.[22] The week in Staten Island followed a 1992 trip to inner-city Chicago, where participants set up a Bible school, served meals to the homeless, and led wellness, nutrition, and parenting classes for women. In 1994, the group traveled to Berea, Kentucky, for hands-on ministry projects in partnership with the Appalachian Ministries Education Resource Center (AMERC)—the largest consortium of theological schools in the United States, which aimed to ad-

[18] N News 10 20 93; N Bulletin 2 6 94.

[19] N Bulletin 4 29 90.

[20] Ibid.

[21] Roger Paynter, "What Is the Mission of the Church," sermon, Northminster Baptist Church, November 19, 1995.

[22] N News 3 23 93; N News 6 23 93.

dress the spiritual, economic, education, and social concerns of the impoverished communities of Appalachia.[23]

The following year, twenty-five Northminster adults went on a mission trip to Honduras to help build houses with Habitat for Humanity.[24] Northminster members would engage in future years in a variety of ministries during their visits to Honduras, including providing medical and dental care clinics, hosting Vacation Bible School, distributing food, and supporting Honduran ministers and worship. This trip to Honduras would become an annual summer mission experience for the church into the second decade of the twentieth-first century.[25]

Throughout the 1990s, Northminster continued to develop and expand its various community ministries, providing members with a plethora of opportunities for service. Some of these ministries would last for just a few short years while others continued at least into 2018. Examples included a mentoring program launched in 1994 for sixth graders. This unique discipleship training program intended to foster relationships between adults and sixth graders through a structured, experientially-based learning program.[26] Northminster youth minister Gene Corbin also organized an "Adopt a College Student" initiative in 1990 for members to provide a monthly meal and foster relationships with college students attending Northminster.[27]

Northminster Baptist Church had long been a supporter of the Boy Scouts of America and began sponsoring its first troop in February 1984.[28] Six years later, the church celebrated National Scout Sunday on February 4, 1990, to commemorate the eightieth anniversary of the Boy Scouts. Cub Pack 5 and its fifty members were guests during the worship service.[29] "Scouting has long been viewed as one of the most wholesome activities in which boys could participate outside the realm of their church activities for building character and an appreciation for the devotion to our country and to other human beings," wrote Pat Travis, Northminster's minister of education, announcing the church's first celebration of National Scout Sunday

[23] N News 2 23 94.
[24] N News 8 10 95.
[25] N News 3 20 96; N News 7 15 08; N News 3 04 09.
[26] N News 10 11 95.
[27] N News 9 18 90.
[28] N Bulletin 2 5 84.
[29] N Bulletin 2 4 90.

on February 2, 1985.[30] Ministries such as the sixth-grade mentoring program, "Adopt a College Student" initiative, and sponsorship of a Boy Scouts troop were just a few examples of Northminster's desire to mold and better the lives of the next generation.

Ministry of Stewardship

From 1984 to 1992, Northminster saw a steady increase in the size of its annual budget. Each year, the budget growth ranged from 7 percent (1989 and 1992) to 16 percent (1987 and 1990), with an average annual increase slightly over 12 percent. The annual budget grew from $360,000 in 1984 to just shy of $850,000 by 1992—a $581,860 increase over the eight-year period.[31] Between 1988 and 1993, the church significantly expanded its facilities and added full-time staff. Barbara Oliver (associate pastor for children and adult education) and Gene Corbin (associate pastor for students and community ministries). Northminster's missions budget also increased 67 percent between 1988–1993.[32]

Despite increases in average pledges and annual budget, revenues struggled to keep up with the costs of Northminster's expanding ministries and operating expenses. From 1988–1991, Northminster experienced excess expenditures over revenue, forcing the deacons and Finance Committee to emphasize fiscal restraint. In 1992, this trend reversed as revenues began to steadily surpass expenditures: $8,387 (1992), $51,145 (1993) and $38,126 (1994). The fiscal health of the church continued to improve throughout the mid-1990s as the following percentages of its annual budget were collected: 93.5 (1993), 99.2 (1994), 95.7 (1995).[33] The adopted annual budget in 1993 slightly surpassed $850,000 but was decreased to $803,225 in 1994 and $843,813 in 1995.[34]

Roger Paynter frequently preached sermons on tithing. In 1989, Paynter commended tithing as a "disciplined means of supporting [the] church," while speculating that very few members gave 10 percent. He said,

---

[30] N News 1 28 85.

[31] N Deacons 9 18 91.

[32] N Deacons 1993; N Deacons 9 22 91.

[33] N Deacons 2 18 96.

[34] Ibid.

> I look at the symbols of affluence in this congregation, and I have a hunch that if we gave 10 percent of what those symbols cost we would far exceed our budget. So I suspect we have very few tithers and that makes me sad for us. I believe in it. Although, I'll have to admit that tithing isn't a New Testament teaching. The New Testament calls for sacrificial giving, which for many of us may be a good bit more than ten percent or a good bit less.

Paynter urged congregants to consider a 5 percent gift and increase it 1 percent each year until the 10 percent tithe threshold was met.[35]

Ministry to Children

Northminster Baptist Church experienced rapid growth six months into Paynter's pastorate with the addition of ninety-five people in 1990–1991—sixty-five new members and thirty children. Although no formal attendance statistics were taken, church leaders estimated a Sunday school weekly average of 300–350 people and 400 in worship. The children's ministry flourished during these years. Weekly children's ministry activities included Sunday early evening Mission Friends for preschoolers, graded missions classes for elementary school students, followed by choir practice for the different age groups such as Music Makers for first and second graders. Older elementary-aged students took part in Bible drill competitions. In 1993, Barbara Oliver began a Bible drill program featuring twelve weekly sessions to prepare the children for associational and statewide competitions.[36] Each summer, Vacation Bible School boasted more than 100 children.[37] The 1996 VBS included nearly 140 children and more than two dozen volunteers and was described as the "best ever" at the time.[38]

This new growth created "good problems" as Paynter explained in a May 1991 newsletter column. "Our facilities are beginning to be put to the test as extra space becomes an increasingly precious commodity," Paynter said. "The fifth grade meets in a converted storage area, the Youth House is filled, and there seems to be no place to add any additional classes. In addi-

---

[35] Roger Paynter, "The Sermon on the Amant," sermon, Northminster Baptist Church, November 12, 1989.

[36] N Deacons 1 17 93.

[37] N News 4 20 94; N Deacons 6 20 93.

[38] N News 6 18 96.

tion, there is very little storage space for children's and custodial supplies." These "good problems" led to extended conversations about and plans for additional facilities in the coming years. The lack of extra space also pointed to the increasing health of the congregation. While many other churches were facing stagnant growth in the early 1990s, Northminster Baptist Church was experiencing the opposite with a growing number of families with young children, perhaps the ultimate visible sign of a healthy congregation.

Staff

During fall 1989, the Long-Range Planning Committee, Personnel Committee, and the Board of Deacons sponsored a series of fourteen "home meetings," where members were invited to share their thoughts on several subjects such as the nature of the church staff. Out of those meetings, the committees recommended the creation of two new ministry positions: minister of family education (later renamed associate pastor for childhood and adult education) and minister to youth/pastoral intern. The minister of family education would oversee preschool and elementary ministries as well as adult education programs. The second position would focus on youth ministry while also assisting the pastor in pastoral care and helping guide the church in the area of local and global missions. The minister to youth/pastoral intern position was part of a ministry residency program of Southern Baptist Theological Seminary in Louisville, Kentucky. Through this two-year program serving at a "partner church," the pastoral intern would receive twenty-five hours toward a doctor of ministry degree.[39] The program was a further expression of doing creative, onsite theological training started during John Claypool's ministry.

Gene Corbin, a twenty-seven-year-old student at Southern Seminary, was soon hired to fill the newly created youth minister/pastoral intern position.[40] In 1992, at the conclusion of his two-year term, Corbin was promoted to a full-time position with the new title of associate pastor for students and community ministry, which encompassed a wider range of duties and responsibilities.[41] Just a year into this new position, in August 1993, Corbin

---

[39] N Minutes 2 4 90; N News 1 30 90.
[40] N Deacons 5 22 90.
[41] N Deacons 9 18 92; N Minutes 11 1 92.

resigned to become executive director of Stewpot, a community ministry partner of Northminster.[42] He continued, however, as interim youth director until April 1994.

In May 1994, the congregation voted to call Stan Wilson, a newly minted graduate of Duke University Divinity School, to succeed Corbin in the position of associate pastor for students and community ministry. While in seminary, Wilson had served as a youth minister at Watts Street Baptist Church in Durham, North Carolina, as well as on the staff of First Baptist Church in Greenville, South Carolina, as an undergraduate student at Furman University. Prior to attending Furman, Wilson was a student at Mississippi College for a year. Paynter outlined the role he envisioned for Wilson in his *Northminster News* column:

> I envision Stan joining Barbara and me in a full partnership of ministry, sharing in worship leadership, pastoral care, teaching and missions. In addition, I see Stan as someone who can do a lot of work towards deepening our sense of community at Northminster through the creation and nurture of a stronger small-group ministry in our church as well as guiding toward greater hands-on involvement in ministry in our community.[43]

Following the death of Barbara Oliver in August 1995, who had served as associate pastor from April 1991 until her "sending service" in March 1995, Northminster called Rev. Nancy Hollomon Peede in May 1996 to serve as associate pastor. A native of Warner Robins, Georgia, Peede graduated from Southern Seminary in 1984 and was ordained in 1990 while serving as the Baptist chaplain to Harvard University. She came to Northminster having completed her coursework for a masters of theology in spiritual formation at the Weston School of Theology, a Jesuit seminary related to Harvard.[44] With the hiring of Peede and return of Paynter from a sabbatical during summer 1996, Northminster was "comforted as a church family to now have all of our ministers in place," according to a note in *Northminster News* titled "New Beginnings."[45] The creation of these new staff positions allowed for a more robust teaching ministry as additional clergy allowed for

[42] N Deacons 8 15 93.
[43] N News 5 18 94.
[44] N Minutes 5 26 96.
[45] N News 8 14 96.

a more professional and informed approach to Northminster's ministry to youth and families.

Long-Range Planning: Community and Congregational Perspectives

A 1995 survey commissioned by the Long-Range Planning Committee offered a glimpse to the perspectives of both the community and congregation regarding the identity, strengths, and weaknesses of Northminster Baptist Church. The survey, conducted by a marketing research firm, found that 57 percent of respondents from the surrounding community were not familiar with Northminster. A significant majority of those who were familiar with Northminster to some extent (43 percent) described the church as being liberal (63 percent), open (73 percent), warm (73 percent), intellectual (70 percent), spiritual (78 percent). Fifty-four percent described Northminster as being "community oriented." However, only 13 percent of those surveyed were familiar with Northminster's ministries and partnerships in Jackson.[46]

An in-depth survey completed by church members revealed that the congregation was largely in agreement that more needed to be done to connect with the surrounding community, specifically with other churches in Jackson. Sixty-one percent stated that Northminster needed to strengthen relationships with churches in other denominations as well as the Cooperative Baptist Fellowship (62 percent) and Alliance of Baptists (52 percent). Notably, 35 percent—a number unchanged from the 1990 survey of the Long-Range Planning Committee—indicated a need to strengthen relationships with Southern Baptist Convention churches. Meanwhile, 34 percent strongly disagreed that those relationships needed to be strengthened—an increase from 26 percent five years prior. These findings pointed to the continued denominational identity crisis that congregations on the "moderate" side of the SBC controversy faced into the 1990s as many members desired to stay connected to some degree with their Southern Baptist identity while other members were ready to cut ties and move on from any connection to the denomination of their upbringing—74 percent of Northminster members surveyed grew up as Baptists.[47]

---

[46] Northminster Baptist Church, 1995 Community Survey Executive Summary.

[47] Ibid.

Nearly two-thirds of the respondents stated that Northminster needed to have more contact as a church with individuals from different social, economic, and racial backgrounds. The survey also pointed to the affluence of the congregation with 38 percent of those surveyed having a household income of more than $100,000 and 17 percent with an annual income surpassing $200,000. Only 3 percent had an income of less than $20,000, below the median household income of $26,538 of Mississippi residents in 1995.

While acknowledging the need for diverse outreach and greater connection with its community, church members signaled strong satisfaction with the internal aspects of Northminster, from worship to preaching to opportunities for ministry service. Ninety-one percent said that the worship service broadened their understanding and deepened their commitment to God, the message of the Bible, and the work of the church, and 94 percent expressed strong satisfaction with the "thought-provoking" content of the worship service, including the liturgy and sermon. Members praised Roger Paynter for his preaching and teaching (91 percent), church leadership (86 percent) community involvement (83 percent).[48] Nine out of ten surveyed said the Sunday services met their worship needs and stated they were satisfied overall with Northminster. Members said that they were provided with adequate opportunities for involvement and leadership in the life of the church (90 percent) and sufficient information about financial needs for ministry and missions (84 percent). However, members noted several ministry areas in need of improvement, including more effective ministries for single adults, senior citizens, and shut-ins.[49] Overall, the survey revealed an incredibly strong support from its members for the ministries, preaching, worship and other aspects of church life.

---

[48] Ibid.

[49] Ibid. Following the 1995 report, a thirty-four-member Long-Range Planning Task Force was created to draft a vision and mission statements for the church as well as action plans to achieve the objectives of those statements. The committee comprised a diverse array of Northminster members including four individuals from the existing committee alongside a representative of each adult Sunday school class, a member of the youth group, a deacon representative, and a representative of each of the other standing committees of Northminster (N Deacons 12 95; N Deacons 1 21 96).

Ministry of [Racial] Reconciliation

Racial reconciliation received some attention during Roger Paynter's tenure with the formation in 1990 of the North Jackson Clergy Network, the first ministerial alliance between white and black clergy in North Jackson since the 1960s. Led by Rabbi Eric Gurvis of Beth Israel, the ecumenical and interfaith network existed for "mutual support" and "creative action," hosting a prayer service for peace in September 1990 following the deployment of American troops to Saudi Arabia in preparation for the Gulf War. In 1991, the group held a worship service on January 20 in celebration of Dr. Martin Luther King Jr. and focused on how to "be more constructive disciples for efforts toward peace."[50] Northminster participated the following year in the second Martin Luther King Jr. worship service. The service was held at Anderson United Methodist Church, and the Northminster youth group gathered for pizza and small group discussion prior to the service with youth from Anderson United, St. Andrew's Episcopal Cathedral, and Beth Israel.[51]

In 1994, Paynter organized the well-attended annual MLK worship service and invited Rev. Sharon Austin, co-pastor of Ebenezer Baptist Church in Atlanta, the congregation once led by Dr. King and his father, Martin Luther King Sr.[52] The 1994 service was held at St. Richard Catholic Church. Paynter also participated in the Jackson Reconciliation Project, a primarily clergy-led civic group that included the mayor and aimed to foster better race relations. Paynter was selected as chairman of the project in 1992.[53] Although the impetus of this emphasis on racial reconciliation was clergy-initiated and clergy-led—a product of Paynter's desire to see divisions healed and relationships formed between African American and white people of faith in the Jackson community—these special worship services and periodic fellowships set the stage for more meaningful relationships between Northminster and African Americans through the church's Wider Net initiative in the Mid-City/Georgetown community less than a decade later.

[50] N News 1 18 91.
[51] N News 1 15 92.
[52] N News 1 12 94.
[53] N Deacons 1 19 92.

Ministry of [Interfaith] Friendship: Temple Beth Israel

Northminster Baptist Church remained in relationship with Beth Israel throughout the 1990s, living into its special friendship forged during its formative years. In addition to participating alongside Beth Israel in the annual Martin Luther King Jr. worship service sponsored by the Jackson Clergy Network, the two congregations announced plans in 1993 for a joint interfaith study tour of Israel scheduled for 1995 alongside members of St. Andrew's Episcopal Cathedral.[54] The following year Northminster hosted an eight-week interfaith study of the Jewish and Christian traditions. The study included members of Beth Israel, St. Andrew's Cathedral, as well as members from other Jackson congregations.[55] Other examples of joint fellowship included an April 1993 service at Beth Israel commemorating the Holocaust and attended by Barbara Oliver and Northminster Women members and a memorial service at Beth Israel in November 1995.[56]

Roger Paynter wrote a column in *Northminster News* in 1992 expressing his gratitude to Rabbi Eric Gurvis of Beth Israel and reflecting on the importance of the Jackson Clergy Network following news of Gurvis' departure to serve as rabbi in Teaneck, New Jersey:

> I have known [Rabbi Gurvis] best through the Jackson Clergy Network. This organization, which began with a group of Northeast Jackson Clergy being invited to lunch at the Temple's annual Bazaar, now stretches in membership from Canton to Clinton, is thoroughly interracial and has over fifty active members. In a very brief time, this organization has actively sought to be a voice of compassion and healing in our community. Eric Gurvis has been the primary force behind the birth and solidification of this enterprise.... I've known several rabbis, but I've never had a rabbi for a friend before. His leaving is a personal loss.[57]

The Northminster youth also held several joint gatherings with the youth of Beth Israel during the early 1990s. In late October 1991, the two youth groups attended the Stewpot Celebration, and three years later the

[54] N Deacons 3 28 93.
[55] N News 8 24 94
[56] N Deacons 4 18 93; N News 4 6 93; N Deacons 11 19 95.
[57] N News 3 27 92.

youth visited Beth Israel to learn from Rabbi Engel about Judaism.[58] These times of fellowship were just a few examples of the clearly special and unique relationship between these Baptist and Jewish congregations.

Baptist Battles, Continued

Conflict in the Southern Baptist Convention remained a regular topic in the church newsletter and pulpit into the early 1990s. Like his predecessor John Thomason, Roger Paynter was extremely active in Baptist life, involved in both the Southern Baptist Alliance (later renamed as Alliance of Baptists) as well as the Cooperative Baptist Fellowship, which was formed in 1991. At the 1990 annual meeting of the SBC, fundamentalists had secured complete control of the nation's largest Protestant denomination with the election as president of fundamentalist pastor and Mississippian Morris Chapman. A delegation of ten Northminster members, including Paynter, attended the 1990 SBC meeting as messengers. Paynter returned fired up and preached a sermon provocatively titled "Baptists and the AntiChrist Spirit." In the sermon, he urged Northminster to "begin the search for authentic freedom," asserting, "We can no longer be part of the Southern Baptist 'Flat Earth Society' and maintain any self-respect.... This is a 'Kairos' moment if there ever was one and we need to act. This will surely mean a new direction for the money left over after we make our 66 percent Cooperative Program contribution to Mississippi Baptist causes."[59]

Paynter said that he was unsure of what the future might hold, suggesting the possibility of alignment with the American Baptist Convention or the evolution of the Southern Baptist Alliance into a full-fledged denomination. "Others across the SBC are going to be looking to Northminster to take the lead because we have taken the lead in many areas in our brief history," Paynter said.[60] Indeed, Northminster had emerged as a respected congregation able to position itself within the mainstream of both the liberal Alliance of Baptists and much more moderate or centrist Cooperative Baptist Fellowship.

---

[58] N Bulletin 10 27 91; N Bulletin 2 27 94.

[59] Roger Paynter, "Baptists and the AntiChrist Spirit," sermon, Northminster Baptist Church, June 17, 1990.

[60] Ibid.

With the formation of CBF in 1991, Northminster quickly devoted much of its denominational energy and resources into the new fellowship, while also continuing to support the SBA. Paynter frequently used his column in *Northminster News* to highlight major denominational events and encourage support for and participation in CBF. He lauded "heroic" efforts by soon-to-be founding CBF executive coordinator, Cecil Sherman, and CBF moderator, John Hewett, to support missionaries in Europe who wished to leave the SBC. "Is [CBF] the beginning of a new denomination?" Paynter asked. "That is still to be determined. One thing is for sure. This is the end of the old denomination as we have known it.... We need to stay involved at the state level to see that this never happens to Mississippi Baptists and their institutions. And, for my money, we need to be very visible in the Cooperative Baptist Fellowship."[61]

Paynter noted that Northminster had "excellent representation" at the 1991 Convocation in Atlanta where CBF was birthed, and he encouraged an even larger showing at the 1992 General Assembly in Fort Worth, Texas.[62] His wife, Suzii, served on the first CBF Coordinating Council from 1991–1993.[63] Over the next two years, Paynter continued to champion the fledging fellowship to his congregation, reminding of the importance of supporting theological education and emphasizing the CBF's efforts to embrace diversity—with African-American and Asian-American speakers, women in leadership roles, and platforms for laity and young people. "None of this ever happened in the old SBC or the new SBC," Paynter said.[64]

Paynter did not paint an entirely rosy picture of CBF to his congregation, acknowledging its growing pains. "There will always be one step forward, steps backward, then two steps forward and one step backward," he wrote. He worried aloud that the young fellowship would lose its openness, creativity, and energy as it went through a process of institutionalization in the mid-1990s—all challenges that longtime Northminster members faced as they formed something new on Ridgewood Road two decades earlier.

---

[61] N News 1 21 92.

[62] Ibid.; N Deacons 4 19 92. Eleven members would attend the 1992 General Assembly in Fort Worth.

[63] N Deacons 1 19 92.

[64] N News 5 11 94.

Paynter succinctly captured the issues the new fellowship faced in a May 1994 column:

> One of the not-so-good points is fairly inevitable. Born out of a crisis, the CBF no longer has the 'feel of urgency' that it did four years ago. Now the task is to take that initial life force and turn it into a building process while maintaining the early energy.
>
> Institutionalization works against this and it will take enormous effort for the CBF to maintain its original openness and creativity. The growth among the CBF is now coming from churches and individuals who have been very cautious about doing anything other than traditional SBC and the spirit they bring to the CBF is one that is quite hesitant. They need the CBF and find it to be a place of both security and freedom. But they also will need to be continually challenged to face into the future rather than always longing to "return to Egypt."[65]

In 1995, on the recommendation of the Denominational Relations Committee, Northminster Baptist Church proposed an amendment to the church's bylaws and covenant to denote its affiliation with CBF. However, this request was referred to the Bylaws Committee. The bylaws would later be updated, but that revision was not made to the church covenant.[66] Five years prior, the church had voted to add the Southern Baptist Alliance to the bylaws and church covenant.[67]

The fundamentalist takeover of the SBC inspired similar conservative uprisings in Baptist state conventions and local associations across the country. While Northminster had long been regarded as "a different kind of Baptist church" locally in Jackson as well as across the state, the congregation faced greater attention and consequently increased scrutiny due to its role in Baptist life as the leading "moderate" congregation in Mississippi. Although Northminster was the eighth-largest contributor (third-largest per capita) to its local association (Hinds-Madison Baptist Association) and had several members who had served as trustees at Mississippi College, the executive board of the association took aim at the church in 1991 over its baptism practices. The association's moderator, Gowan Ellis, sent Paynter a letter dated January 16, 1991, on behalf of the association, admonishing the

[65] Ibid.

[66] N Deacons 8 27 95.

[67] N Minutes 8 19 90.

church to discontinue its long-held policy of granting membership to individuals from other Christian denominations who had not received "baptism by immersion." The letter cited the 1963 version of the *Baptist Faith & Message*, the confessional statement of the Southern Baptist Convention, which stated, "Christian baptism is the immersion of a believer in water in the Name of the Father, the Son, and the Holy Spirit.... Being a church ordinance, it is prerequisite to the privilege of church membership and the Lord's Supper." While the letter stated that there was "no malice in the intent of this letter," it declared that "people who are unwilling to be immersed are really not Baptist and do not need to be members of a Baptist church." The letter concluded with a subtle threat and not-so-subtle theological judgment:

> This letter is simply a reminder to you as leaders of the churches of this Association that we have agreed to the requirements of the Constitution of this organization. We believe these requirements to be in keeping with the command of Christ. Therefore, we admonish all member churches to seek, as soon as possible, to discontinue this practice and give our Lord the obedience which He deserves.[68]

Throughout the SBC Controversy of the 1980s, the *Baptist Faith & Message* was used as a coercive creed, rather than as a confession, to ensure doctrinal conformity across the convention. This associational letter, which also took aim at Northside Baptist in Clinton—a sister congregation with similar baptismal practices—raised serious concerns that the association was beginning to embrace the tactics of national fundamentalist leaders. In his newsletter column to the congregation describing the association's letter, Paynter said Northminster needed to respond to the letter but not do so hastily. He offered words of respect with non-Baptist baptismal experiences:

> Furthermore, we have said that regardless of the mode, we respect your baptismal experience as meaningful to you, that God's grace was present in your baptismal experience as meaningful and that "re-baptism" is an affront to both the notion of salvation and baptism. In effect, we

[68] Gowan Ellis and Hinds-Madison Baptist Association to Roger Paynter, January 16, 1991.

have said that while it is important to be Baptist, it is more important to be Christian. That, in point of fact, is good Baptist doctrine![69]

The letter from the Hinds-Madison Association was sent to every member of Northminster and several Sunday school classes used it as a basis for discussions on baptism and church membership. Several members also wrote their own individual responses to the association. The Denominational Relations Committee and the Board of Deacons worked over the next three months to formulate a reply from the church. In a letter dated April 23, 1991, and signed by Roger Paynter, Bill Boone (Denominational Relations Committee chair), and Ken Toler (Board of Deacons chair), Northminster expressed its disagreement to the association: "With all due respect for our common bond in Christ, we must disagree with you, for we believe that our policies do demonstrate respect and obedience to the Lord." The letter continued:

> As you state in your letter, you are well aware of our baptismal practices which have been in effect since 1968. Quite honestly we are confused as to why this request to change these policies has come now, twenty-three years after we began admitting Christians who have not been immersed into membership. Northminster practices believers baptism by immersion for all who come to faith in Jesus Christ under the ministry of this church. However, for those Christians who come to us with different baptismal experiences, our test of faith is not, "Were you immersed?" but rather, "Is Jesus Christ the Lord of your life?" If the answer is yes, we welcome them into the fellowship of our church. To ask anything more of them is to exceed the requirement of the New Testament....
>
> We have done extensive research of the biblical witness regarding baptism including examination of every Scripture listed in the *Baptist Faith and Message*. We cannot find any Scriptural evidence requiring baptism for church membership. Baptism is an important symbol of Christian commitment, but it is secondary to the primary commitment of embracing Jesus Christ as the Lord and Savior of one's life. We recognize that our policy is not in the mainstream of recent Baptist tradition, but we believe that it faithfully serves the New Testament, the Lordship of

[69] N News 1 29 91.

> Christ, and gives glory to God. We believe those to be the only crucial criteria.[70]

While this letter certainly did not resolve the issue in the minds of concerned associational leaders, they refrained from further associational action regarding the matter. This incident revealed the challenges of theological diversity within the context of a local or state Baptist organization comprising Southern Baptist churches as well as "former" Southern Baptist churches like Northminster Baptist Church. Freedom and fundamentalism inevitably collide—a truth that Northminster would experience again, most notably with the Mississippi Baptist Convention as the congregation approached its fiftieth anniversary.

Revisioning Stewardship: The Northminster Plan

Prior to the fundamentalist takeover of the Southern Baptist Convention, Northminster Baptist Church contributed all of its financial support for denominational missions and ministries through the Cooperative Program (SBC), the stewardship mechanism many Southern Baptists considered almost sacred. These funds were sent directly to the Mississippi Baptist Convention, where they were distributed to state and national entities according to a formula set by the state convention. In 1989, 63 percent of Cooperative Program dollars were kept by the state convention, and 37 percent were sent to the SBC Executive Committee in Nashville, Tennessee, where those gifts were distributed to the six SBC seminaries, Foreign Mission Board, Home Mission Board, Christian Life Commission, and other denominational entities.

Due to the new fundamentalist direction of the SBC, the Board of Deacons voted in June 1990 to freeze its contributions to the Cooperative Program until further decisions could be made following the outcome of the summer meeting of the SBC in New Orleans. At that meeting not many days later, the fundamentalists secured their final contested presidential election, defeating moderate leader Daniel Vestal, and the national takeover was completed.[71] Two months later, a group of moderate Baptists, including Northminster members, gathered in Atlanta for a convocation to discuss the

[70] Northminster Baptist Church to Hinds-Madison Baptist Association, April 23, 1991.

[71] N Minutes 6 3 90.

future (sponsored by the organization Baptists Committed). Out of that meeting, an alternative funding mechanism was created for moderates to support select missions and ministries, including some SBC efforts, without contributing gifts through the traditional Cooperative Program, now controlled by the fundamentalist leadership. In the aftermath of that meeting, Northminster's Denominational Relations Committee hosted congregational conversations following Wednesday night suppers to discuss the church's future financial support of Southern Baptist causes.[72] The Denominational Relations Committee had been formed in July 1988 to examine the church's affiliation and support of the SBC and to explore alternatives for denominational affiliation and monetary support.[73]

Soon after these conversations, the congregation voted to divvy up its denominational contributions through a new methodology that sidestepped the traditional Cooperative Program model. The congregation decided that designated portions of its funding would be sent directly to the Mississippi Baptist Convention and the Metro Baptist Association (formerly Hinds-Madison Baptist Association, renamed in 1996) with instructions that those funds be used by those organizations and not routed through the Cooperative Program formula that sent 37 percent to the SBC in Nashville. Instead, this 37 percent portion of Northminster's gifts that was typically sent to the SBC would be allocated to various ministries based on the direction of church members. Each year, Northminster would hold an annual pledge card drive allowing each pledging family or individual the freedom to designate their giving to either the "Northminster Plan" or the Cooperative Program of the SBC. The Northminster Plan allocated its funding to different Baptist organizations on the recommendations of the Denominational Relations Committee—recommendations first approved by both the Board of Deacons and the entire congregation. This process ensured that the committee would stay informed regarding developments and trends in denominational life.[74]

---

[72] N News 8 28 90.

[73] N Minutes 7 17 88.

[74] "A Brief History of Northminster Financial Support of Baptist Denominational and Cooperating Bodies and Other National and World Baptist Missions," Northminster Baptist Church, September 2007.

In proposing the creation of the Northminster Plan, the Denominational Relations Committee offered an interpretive statement:

> For over a decade, a group within the Southern Baptist Convention has systematically moved away from the historically held Baptist positions of the right of the individual to interpret Scripture for themselves, the freedom of the local church to shape its own life and mission, the necessity of a free church in a free state, and the servant role of pastoral leadership. Those of us who differ from their agenda of control of all SBC boards, agencies and foundations find ourselves without an official voice. We, as a body of Baptist believers, desire to voice our opposition to the direction the SBC has been taking. At the same time, we want to voice our strong hope for the new directions in which we think God's Spirit is leading.
>
> The action of this congregation should be viewed in two ways. First, it is an action of protest. We do not accept many of the changes taking place, and we can no longer support the directions that have been set. Second, it is an action of support for new ministries and institutions which will allow our strong position of religious freedom to continue. The money we direct to these new ministries will give us a recognized voice, as well as providing a challenging vision for our future.
>
> We would be guilty of the same control that we are rejecting if we did not give each member of Northminster Baptist Church a choice as to what his/her gifts are to support. Therefore, each member will have a choice in the 1991 budget year between supporting a Northminster Missions Plan, or the traditional Cooperative Program of the Southern Baptist Convention. Our prayer is that we will be faithful in seeking God's direction for our church, consistent with the life and teachings of our Lord Jesus Christ.[75]

From the first year of the Northminster Plan in 1991 through 1996, the plan supported a wide variety of emerging moderate Baptist organizations, including the newly-formed Baptist Theological Seminary at Richmond, Associated Baptist Press, Baptist Center for Ethics, as well as Baptist Women in Ministry. The plan also supported the Baptist Joint Committee

---

[75] "Proposed Recommendation: Action of the Congregation of Northminster Baptist Church at a Business Meeting Held November 4, 1990," Northminster Baptist Church, November 1990.

on Public Affairs and Ruschlikon Seminary in Switzerland, both which had been defunded by the SBC in 1990. Allocations for these entities ranged from 5–10 percent of the plan.[76]

The Northminster Plan also supported two national Baptist denomination-like organizations: the Alliance of Baptists and the Cooperative Baptist Fellowship. Northminster leaders, including both John Thomason and Roger Paynter, had provided leadership to the alliance and the church had hosted the alliance's annual convocation in 1990. However, Paynter and other Northminster members were also deeply invested in CBF, which was formed in 1991—the same year the Northminster Plan took effect. In its first two years, CBF existed primarily as an alternative missions funding mechanism to the SBC. When CBF established itself as a missionary-sending organization in 1993, the Northminster Plan began to devote a significant percentage to CBF. In 1993, 20 percent was allocated to CBF Global Missions and Operations. Northminster increased its allocation to 35 percent in 1994 and gave 30 percent in both 1995 and 1996. Contributions to the Alliance of Baptists (which, unlike CBF, did not support missionaries) remained constant from 1992–1996 at 10 percent.[77]

After the 1993 budget year, the Northminster Plan ceased supporting the Lottie Moon Christmas Offering of the SBC Foreign Mission Board, which funded SBC missionaries. This change came as CBF began to commission and send missionaries to locations around the world, specifically focusing on placing missionaries (called "field personnel") in countries located in the "10/40 Window" encompassing the Middle East, Saharan and Northern Africa, and much of Asia where Christianity was the least prevalent. During fall 1993, Keith Parks, then the new coordinator of CBF Global Missions and former president of the SBC Foreign Mission Board, visited Northminster and challenged the congregation to increase its support for CBF.[78] David Jones, chair of the Denominational Relations Committee, described Parks's presentation and the rationale for upping support for CBF in the Northminster Plan for the 1994 budget year:

> [Keith Parks] challenged us at Northminster this September with compelling evidence that the vision of CBF Global Missions is something

[76] N Minutes 10 22 95.
[77] N Minutes 10 24 93.
[78] N News 9 15 93.

that we can enthusiastically support. He also informed us that many SBC foreign missionaries no longer feel that they can work with the Foreign Mission Board with a clear conscience and the freedom to minister as they feel directed by God. The CBF has become the place of service for many missionaries of conscience, like Dr. Parks himself, unable to sign doctrinal statements or serve under the recent fundamentalist direction of the Foreign Mission Board. The Cooperative Baptist Fellowship has already appointed 26 missionaries. Twenty of these formerly served with the SBC Foreign Mission Board. Three were new young appointees that would at one time have applied through the Foreign Mission Board, but no longer felt that they could have been accepted through that path. Another 20 missionaries are expected to be appointed through the CBF by May 1994.[79]

Contributions to CBF in the 1994 budget would increase from 10 percent to 35 percent. Since CBF's inception in 1991, approximately 95 percent or more of pledging families and pledging individuals have chosen to designate their gifts through the Northminster Plan, and Northminster continues to offer members the freedom and opportunity to support missions through the Cooperative Program of the SBC.[80]

The Ministry of Worship

Advent and Holy Week. The Christian calendar continued to guide Northminster's liturgical practices during Roger Paynter's pastorate. Members were encouraged to attend all four of the Advent worship services featuring hymns, prayers, readings, anthems, and sermons to "create a space in your soul in which the Spirit can lodge." The congregation sought creative ways to center themselves on the season of Advent, creating wreaths for daily or weekly use, lighting candles, using a book of Advent meditations prepared by members, as well as stopping by the sanctuary to discover "quiet and stillness" in the midst of much noise and busyness.[81]

"Open your eyes to the Holy in your midst be it in the office or crowded mall, living in anticipation of the truth that especially in the chaos is God

---

[79] N Minutes 11 9 93.

[80] "A Brief History of Northminster Financial Support of Baptist Denominational and Cooperating Bodies and other National and World Baptist Missions," September 2007.

[81] N News 11 22 94.

with Us to be found," Paynter wrote to the congregation. "And may this be a most blessed Advent for each of us and for all."[82]

During Holy Week, Northminster opened its sanctuary each day for a time of individual reflection and communion. Members were encouraged to visit the sanctuary on the way to work, during lunch, or anytime in between to "receive the nourishment and restoration of our most merciful and loving Holy Spirit." On Maundy Thursday, the church celebrated the Passover supper with a Seder meal in the Great Hall. Children were encouraged to be at the tables because Jewish tradition requires the youngest person to ask the questions that signal the start of the special meal. Following the Seder meal, the church observed communion at the tables "just as Jesus gave new meaning to the Seder symbols on the night before his death."[83]

In 1990, Northminster started a new tradition during Holy Week, the "flowering of the cross." A wired cross was placed ("the Rugged Cross") in front of the church on Maundy Thursday, where it remained bare and desolate as a reminder of Christ's suffering. On Easter morning members transformed it into a symbol of new life and beauty with flowers. Paynter noted that "Dark" Friday would then become "Good" Friday and that the "life-taking" cross would become the "life-giving" cross.[84]

Northminster had in years past held an Easter vigil on Saturday evening. However, the church decided in 1991 to, for the first time in several years, worship on the evening of Good Friday to reflect on a central event of the Christian life, the death of Christ. This service included a sermon, choral music, readings, and a service of Tenebrae.[85]

For the first time, in 1994, Northminster Baptist Church held two worship services on Sunday morning. These Easter Sunday services attracted 200 people at 8:00 and an additional 450 during the 10:30 service. "Numbers have never been the issue here, but they do give us one yardstick by which to measure our effectiveness," Paynter wrote to the congregation. "These numbers tell us that if we had not conducted the early service, we would have been forced to seat people in the hallways or turn them away—

[82] Ibid.
[83] N News 3 12 91.
[84] N News 3 12 91; N News 4 12 17.
[85] Ibid.

neither is an acceptable alternative."[86] The popularity of Northminster's expansive Easter service offerings was clear.

Communion to the Homebound. In 1994, Northminster deacons began serving communion to the homebound and hospitalized each Communion Sunday. During fall 1993, the deacons did a successful trial run of home communion.[87] David Jones, vice chair of the deacons, said that the practice of serving the homebound had an impact on him personally. "I believe it may have been as helpful to me as it was to those served," Jones said. "There is something unexplainable that happens in the intimate spiritual contact between Christians serving and receiving this gift."[88] This ministry to the homebound and hospitalized—members who are often neglected in many churches—demonstrated one aspect of Northminster's commitment to being inclusive and holistic in its approach to caregiving.

Past Pastors. John Thomason, Northminster's third pastor, returned to the church's pulpit on April 30, 1995, for the first time since his departure in late 1988. Thomason, who was then pastor of the Eustace United Methodist Church, a small town of fewer than 800 people in East Texas, preached a sermon titled "The Lord Is Your Keeper" based on the lectionary Scripture of Psalm 121. A reception following the morning service was held to welcome Thomason. While all past pastors had been invited to attend the twenty-fifth anniversary celebration in 1992, Dudley Wilson was the only one to attend.[89] In July 1993, Wilson returned to the Northminster pulpit and preached a sermon titled "Lost and Found" from the lectionary text of Luke 15:1-10. He returned once more three summers later on July 28, 1996.[90] Other public mentions of past pastors included a remembrance of Harvey Whaley upon his death in 1991. Wilson officiated the memorial service at Calder Baptist Church in Beaumont, Texas.[91] John Claypool returned to the Northminster pulpit on October 17, 2004, while serving as

[86] N News 4 6 94.
[87] N News 6 1 94.
[88] N News 4 13 94.
[89] N News 4 26 95; N Bulletin 4 30 95; N Deacons 6 7 93.
[90] N Bulletin 7 25 93; N Bulletin 7 28 96.
[91] N Bulletin 5 16 91.

visiting professor of preaching at Mercer University's McAfee School of Theology.[92]

Ordinations. Northminster Baptist Church hosted two clergy ordination services during Roger Paynter's tenure. On October 14, 1990, Gene Corbin, minister to youth and pastoral intern, was ordained. Glenn Hinson, mentor and widely respected Baptist leader as well as Corbin's Southern Seminary professor, preached the ordination sermon. Prior to Corbin, Northminster had not held a clergy ordination service since 1981 when the church ordained Morris Thompson, a Southern Seminary graduate and church member.[93] Just six years after ordaining Corbin, Northminster ordained Jo Smith Hollman on the second Sunday of Christmastide on January 5, 1997. Paynter, who had departed three months earlier to become the pastor of First Baptist Church in Austin, Texas, returned to give the ordination meditation titled "On Being One of God's Amateurs."[94] The newly ordained Reverend Hollman would step into the Northminster pulpit as the guest preacher six months later on July 6, 1997.[95]

Deacon ordination services were an annual occurrence at Northminster. Each year during the pastorates of Thomason and Paynter, the church ordained at least one new deacon and as many as five new deacons. During this thirteen-year period, at least one woman was ordained each year with one exception as well as two years when no man was ordained. Overall, women made up roughly 40 percent of all deacon ordinations.[96]

Church Bells. In 1990, Northminster received a donation from the Lucian Harvey family for the purpose of purchasing and installing three cast bells for the church's bell tower. John Clark, chair of the Board of Deacons, appointed a committee (Dr. Richard Joiner, Dr. Earl Owen, Billy Trotter, and

---

[92] N Bulletin 10 17 04.

[93] N Bulletin 5 3 87.

[94] "The Ordination Service of Jo Smith Hollman," Northminster Baptist Church, January 5, 1997.

[95] N Bulletin 7 6 97.

[96] N Bulletin 9 18 83; N Bulletin 9 16 84; N Bulletin 9 15 85; N Bulletin 1 11 87; N Bulletin 1 17 88; N Bulletin 1 29 89; N Bulletin 1 21 90; N Bulletin 1 13 91; N Bulletin 1 12 92; N Bulletin 1 17 93; N Bulletin 1 16 94; N Bulletin 1 22 95; N Bulletin 1 28 96.

Dave Peterson) to make recommendations regarding the bells. The group recommended bells C4, E4, and G4 appropriate for ringing as a call to worship, marriages, funerals, times of celebration and chimes. The bells, made by Peccord in France, were capable of operating automatically as well as manually via controls installed near the organ console. The deacons voted to accept the gift and the group's recommendation. The congregation also unanimously affirmed accepting the gift.[97] Three years later, the deacons accepted a second gift from the Lucian Harvey family to commission and install two more bells for the church's carillon, completing the ensemble.[98]

Rice Acres Sunday. Northminster continued to hold its annual Rice Acres Sunday, first begun in 1980, an outdoor service, each April/May. The special Sunday event (held at a lodge located adjacent to a lake) included outdoor worship followed by "dinner on the grounds" and an afternoon of recreation for all ages. In 1990, Rice Acres Sunday fell on Earth Day (April 22), and the congregation celebrated God's creation during worship. Linda McGehee, Jim Sones, and Roger Paynter spoke in worship on the role of the environment in their personal lives as well as in their understanding of God.[99]

Roger Paynter's Resignation

Roger Paynter announced to the deacons at their September 1996 meeting that he would be preaching in view of a call at First Baptist Church in Austin, Texas, and would soon be resigning as senior pastor. Board chair Bill Lee expressed the deacons' appreciation of Paynter. In his final two sermons as senior pastor (October 6 and October 13, 1996), Paynter preached on the benediction, which he described as "one of the most important parts of worship." "One of the wonderful traditions of this church is that each minister who has served here, including Jim Travis as an interim, has had a benediction with which they have been identified," Paynter noted in his October 6 sermon. "I've enjoyed going into your homes and finding framed copies of benedictions of my predecessors. And you have been so generous in your response to the benediction that I have used these seven

[97] N Minutes 12 23 90.
[98] N Deacons 2 21 93.
[99] N News 4 17 90.

years."[100] He added in his October 13 sermon titled "A Final Blessing": "When we rise and when we go to bed and when we leave our worship, we need the sound of benediction in our ears. Your God will bless you and keep you. Your God will bless and keep you."

Paynter concluded his seven-year tenure as Northminster's fourth pastor with his benediction, adapted from the ancient benediction in the book of Numbers, a sermon from William Sloane Coffin of New York's famed Riverside Church, and the Scottish Book of Prayer: "The Lord will bless you and keep you and shine upon you. And remember, to risk yourself for Christ's sake and live by the harmony of truth and love. And never forget to let God take your minds, lips and hands and put them to his use. And live always: with your hearts set on fire! Amen."[101]

During the Paynter years, the congregation saw the need of being blessed and being kept. Coping with personal tragedy (the death of Barbara Oliver) and the persistent challenges of Baptist denominational conflict, Northminster Baptist Church, in turn, sought to be a place of healing and hope.

[100] Roger Paynter, "The Power of Holy Memories," sermon, Northminster Baptist Church, October 6, 1996.

[101] Roger Paynter, "A Final Blessing," Northminster Baptist Church, October 13, 1996.

Chapter 6

Missions on Our Mind: Ministry during the Tenure of Chuck Poole

Calling a Pastor

After a seven-month search process, Charles E. Poole was called as the fifth pastor of Northminster Baptist Church. During the Sunday morning church business meeting on May 18, 1997, the Pastor Search Committee (David Jones, chair; Jean Williams, vice chair; Mary Foose; Cliff Johnson; Bill Lee; George Purvis; Donna Sones; and Dudley Wooley) stood before the congregation and testified to the qualifications of "Chuck" Poole, describing the native Georgian as a great preacher with a passion for pastoral care.[1]

"It is our honor to present for your consideration Charles E. Poole as the next pastor of Northminster Baptist Church," wrote Jones in a letter to the congregation on behalf of the committee. "Your charge to the Pastor Search Committee was to find someone who was a truly gifted preacher, someone who would provide pastoral care to our varied needs, and someone who was committed to the Baptist heritage. As we sought advice from friends of Northminster across the nation, asking who would fit these qualifications, the name of Chuck Poole, without fail, was the first recommendation. Over and over again we were urged to consider him."[2] Jones continued,

> As the committee began to know Chuck, our sense of God's leadership grew. We listened to Chuck's life story, to his complete commitment to Christ, and to his vision of what it means to be the church. We found our own lives growing in a spiritual commitment as our discussions with Chuck developed. Chuck tested the rightness of his fit to Northminster by challenging our understanding of what this church needed as we move into the next phase of our development. As we struggled to

---

[1] N Minutes 5 18 97.

[2] N Minutes 5 18 97 (Exhibit 1).

answer as honestly as possible, Chuck's sense of God's call evolved as well.[3]

Poole; his wife, Marcia; and their children, Joshua (sixteen) and Maria (twelve), came to Northminster from the First Baptist Church of the City of Washington, DC, the historic church in the nation's capital where Poole had served as senior pastor for the two years prior (1995–1997). A native of Macon, Georgia, and a graduate of Mercer University, Poole was called at the age of thirty to serve as pastor of First Baptist Church of Christ in his hometown—a congregation he served from 1986 to 1995. Unlike all four of his predecessors at Northminster, Poole was not a graduate of Southern Baptist Theological Seminary. Instead, after graduating from Mercer University, Poole moved to Wake Forest, North Carolina, to complete his master of divinity degree at another Southern Baptist institution—Southeastern Baptist Theological Seminary. After graduation, Poole returned to Macon to be associate pastor of Highland Hills Baptist Church. A prolific writer, Poole was Northminster's most published pastor since John Claypool; he had written three books, contributed to preaching commentaries, and was the author of numerous Bible studies featured in Smyth & Helwys's popular *Formations* curriculum used by hundreds of churches across the southeastern United States affiliated with the Cooperative Baptist Fellowship.[4]

Ministry of Youth: On a Pilgrimage

Two months into Poole's tenure, the Northminster youth led a special evening worship service, which concluded with a dedication of the newly completed recreation and fellowship areas and a cookout.[5] An annual youth-led service had become a regular staple of the Northminster worship calendar—reflecting the growing vibrancy of a very "hands-on" youth ministry. Northminster youth continued to take part in mission trips and community missions as well as participate in community-wide events such as the Martin Luther King Jr. Day Project, where more than fifty youth joined with other youth groups across Jackson to work on service projects. To honor MLK Day in 1999, for example, sixty Northminster youth spent the day working with the Olin Park Neighborhood Association, painting front porches of

[3] Ibid.

[4] N Minutes 5 18 97.

[5] N News 9 24 97.

homes in the area.[6] The next year, the youth gathered at Galloway United Methodist Church to take part in a variety of service projects. Northminster's junior high and senior high youth groups often took MLK Day as an opportunity to remember and reflect on the civil rights movement, focusing specifically on the involvement of students in the struggle for equality.[7]

Associate pastor Stan Wilson emphasized the centrality of Northminster "youth"—a term he had come to reject in favor of the descriptor "young people"—in a column preceding a 1998 youth-led worship service:

> I roll my eyes whenever I read that someone's new Bible Study curriculum is based on the needs of "today's teenager." Oh, please. If there were such a monolithic entity as "today's teenager," I can assure you that students of the Bible, myself included, would be the last to discover it. Before young people need any special developmental expertise, they need honesty and love, challenge and acceptance—just like you and I do. As the Youth Committee has joined the long-range planning process, there has been a lot of talk of "welcoming our young people into the church." The young people in our "youth" house are not the church of tomorrow; they are, with you and me, the church of today. We do not await the day when they will emerge from the stage of adolescence and join us in adult faith, we hope for and expect maturity in all of us. We are together on a pilgrimage.[8]

In October 1997, Wilson recommended Malcolm McLaurin, a local student at Hinds Community College, to serve as youth intern. Like previous youth interns, McLaurin assisted with activities during the week and helped coordinate and lead summer mission trips as well as camps. Despite the congregation's desire and inclusive perspective, the integration of the church's membership had been a challenge. When McLaurin joined the church in January 1998, he became the first African-American member of Northminster in its near thirty-one-year history.[9] When McLaurin left Northminster in May 1999, Wilson recognized and thanked him for "two years of dedicated and consistent ministry with our youth and their families." "Thank you, Malcolm, for being a friend to so many, an excellent

---

[6] N Deacons 1 23 99.

[7] N News 1 5 00.

[8] N News 8 12 98.

[9] N Deacons 4 18 99; N Deacons 10 18 97; N News 1 28 98.

Christian example for all of us, and for providing a spark for our entire youth ministry. We will miss you," Wilson wrote.[10]

Ministry of Worship: Baptism and Communion

Communion was shared with increasing frequency during mid-to-late 1990s at Northminster. The church's practice of sharing communion on the first Sunday of each month was firmly established. The Lord's Supper was also offered Monday through Friday during Holy Week. Not surprisingly given its theological diversity, no uniform understanding of communion and all its specifics (sacrament vs. symbol, eligibility, etc.) existed among Northminster members. Yet, the congregation did agree that communion was about "remembering," according to Poole.[11]

"Communion is such a complex issue that one could write a doctoral dissertation about it and still not know everything there is to know," Poole told the church in his weekly *Northminster News* column. He continued,

> And yet communion is also deceptively simple. We as Christian believers participate in communion because long ago Jesus said to his disciples, "Do this in remembrance of me." At its core, communion is about remembering. Here at Northminster we participate in the Lord's Supper as a congregation on the first Sunday of each month. However, we also offer communion at other times because, let's face it, most of us need to remember what Christ has done for us more than once a month, and although we may not need the ritual of communion in order to remember, sometimes it really does help.[12]

In August 2003, Amy Joyner, who had joined the staff as associate pastor the previous summer and was ordained by the church in January 2003, asked the deacons to affirm a new option for children whose parents wished for them to wait until after their baptism to take communion. Joyner proposed that children be invited to come forward during communion and receive a blessing from the servers. Children would come forward and cross their arms over their chest, and the communion servers would, instead of offering bread, give the child a blessing.[13]

---

[10] N News 5 26 99.
[11] N News n.d.
[12] Ibid.
[13] N Deacons 8 17 03.

The deacons unanimously backed this proposal. Previously, children had two options: stay seated while their parents went forward to receive communion or take communion with their parents at the front of the church. The addition of this third way offered an inclusive option for children whose parents affirmed the historic Baptist belief and practice that communion was reserved for professing believers.[14]

Less than six months later, Joyner offered a proposal for the church's practice of its other ordinance—baptism. She proposed, and the deacons affirmed, to offer a baptismal service on the evening of Palm Sunday 2004.[15] As a letter to the congregation explained, "Northminster Baptist Church is a community of people from many different backgrounds and faith traditions. This diversity offers many rich blessings for our community as we learn, grow, and work together as a church. One of the meaningful experiences in the life of a person and a church is the celebration of baptism."[16]

"For example," the letter continued, "an individual might wish to be baptized at Northminster but be apprehensive about doing so during a regular Sunday morning worship service. Perhaps this individual is an adult who would feel awkward being baptized alongside the young people of our church. Or perhaps this individual was baptized in another faith tradition and wants to experience baptism by immersion without being disrespectful of his or her religious heritage. Having a special baptismal service would offer individuals such as these the opportunity to be baptized amidst the community of Northminster, but in an atmosphere that is more intimate and comfortable."[17]

The letter carefully concluded with an ecumenical disclaimer that the pastoral staff, deacons and music and worship committees "are in no way seeking to discount or repudiate the baptisms of other faith traditions":

> All forms of baptism are respected and celebrated at Northminster. Individuals who desire to be baptized by immersion and who have already been baptized in another faith tradition can rest assured that the spirit of the Palm Sunday baptismal service will demonstrate respect for their

---

[14] Ibid.

[15] N Deacons 1 18 04. See Amy Joyner and Tripp Martin to Northminster Baptist Church, March 1, 2004.

[16] Ibid.

[17] Ibid.

> previous baptism. The Palm Sunday baptismal service is meant simply to offer a sensitive and respectful opportunity for anyone who believes Christ is leading him or her to seek baptism by immersion.[18]

This Palm Sunday baptismal service became an annual tradition. Northminster members hoped that the baptismal service further served to model to other Baptist churches how to live into a rich ecumenical identity while remaining rooted in the Baptist tradition and respectful of historic Baptist beliefs and practices.

Facilities: Chapel Dedication

The new Northminster chapel was dedicated during a special litany and prayer of consecration on June 21, 1998. Funding for the chapel was made possible via a gift from the Lucian Harvey family in March 1996. The chapel was first opened (and used) March 31, 1997, and completed and fully furnished in 1998. The new chapel was designed as a place of prayer, worship, reflection, and devotion.[19]

"We dedicate today this special place, the Northminster Chapel, a place where people can come to sit in silence and kneel in prayer, to be still before God and to listen for God in a space created for that holy purpose," the chapel's devotional guide read.[20] Church members were invited to visit the chapel to spend time in reflection and prayer and receive the Lord's Supper. Prior to the dedication, the chapel had been used during Holy Week and as a place of worship for preschoolers, who used the chapel as a way of learning what to expect when they began attending regular worship services with their parents.[21] A special Sunday afternoon service was held on June 21 to dedicate and consecrate the Northminster chapel. This service followed a litany of dedication and prayer of consecration during the morning worship service.

Ministry of Creation: Blessing of the Animals

In 1998, Northminster held its first-ever Blessing of the Animals service—a liturgical experiment that would take place for a handful of years.

---

[18] Ibid.

[19] N Bulletin 6 21 98.

[20] Ibid.

[21] N News 6 10 98.

Members were asked to bring their furry friends along with a monetary donation to support an animal welfare organization. This tradition would support organizations such as Jackson Friends (a shelter for homeless pets) and the Mississippi Animal Rescue League. Donations of dog and cat food, cleaning supplies, and pet toys and treats were also collected.[22] The animal blessing service reflected Northminster's efforts to embrace various liturgical practices of the larger church as such blessings had been a long-established tradition in the Catholic Church, Episcopal Church, as well as other mainline Protestant denominations. The service also sought to remember the witness of St. Francis of Assisi, the twelfth-century patron saint of animals who continues to be celebrated for his love of the natural world as expressed in his *Canticle of Creatures* (known as "All Creatures of our God and King" in older Baptist hymnals). Numerous other Baptist churches have embraced this increasingly popular practice of blessing animals during the Feast of St. Francis (first Sunday in October).

Ministry of Missions and Stewardship

As Northminster aged, it displayed a strengthened passion for global mission work and community ministry. In his weekly column in July 2003, Chuck Poole described the church's concerted commitments and the church's vibrant portfolio of missions and ministries:

> If someone were to ask you where they might find Northminster Baptist Church, the simple answer, obviously, would be "3955 Ridgewood Road in Jackson, Mississippi." That is always an accurate answer, but it is rarely the only answer. For example, this week, you could find part of Northminster at the Youth Mission Trip in Smyrna, Tennessee. Next week, another part of Northminster will be serving in Honduras with Salt and Light Ministries, while a larger part of our congregation will be engaged in the wonderful work of Vacation Bible School back here on Ridgewood Road.
>
> Where might one find Northminster? Well, depending upon the day, various parts of Northminster might be at Grace House, Billy Brumfield House, Operation Shoestring, Stewpot, Mid-City or Spann School to mention a few places where our church can be found from

[22] N Bulletin 4 19 98; N Bulletin 2 3 99; N Bulletin 6 4 00; N News 7 14 99; N News 10 5 04; N News 6 3 03.

> time to time. This week and next, we can also be found up in Tennessee and down in Honduras. You can always find Northminster on Ridgewood Road. And sometimes you can find Northminster here and there, near and far, far and wide; bearing quiet, steady witness to the love of God, as the wind of the Spirit scatters the seed of the gospel to more places than we can name or count or know.[23]

In addition to its plethora of hands-on mission endeavors, Northminster's growing commitment was also evident through increased budget allocations to missions. From 1968 through 1979, Northminster designated a paltry 6 percent of its budget to missions in only four years. Although its total missions giving increased during this period, it never surpassed 6.4 percent of budget (1973)—vastly less than the typical missions giving standard of Southern Baptist churches of at least 10 percent of budget just to the SBC Cooperative Program.[24]

Throughout the 1980s, Northminster Baptist Church designated an average of nearly 13 percent of its budget to missions causes. This reflected a steady increase from 5.13 percent in 1980 to an impressive 20 percent in 1989. In fact, from 1968 through 2001, the church's total missions giving only decreased in four years—extremely marginal decreases of merely $250 or less in three of those years (1970, 1972, and 1977). In 1981, the church experienced a near $7,000 decrease in missions contributions from $31,139 to $24,131.[25]

Although any observer would be impressed by such steady growth in terms of both total budget and total giving, Northminster's missions contributions did plateau from 1992 through 1996 with only a modest increase in 1997 of less than $2,000.[26] During this period of plateau, the church's total budget dramatically decreased from 1993 ($850,284) to 1994 ($803,225) but by 1996 had rebounded and surpassed 1993 levels at $855,851. Yet, in each of those years of plateau, the church devoted 20 to 21 percent of its annual budget to missions causes—a statistic that most churches would surely en-

[23] N News 7 8 03.

[24] "NBC Missions Contributions: 1968 to 2001," Northminster Wider Net Archive.

[25] Ibid

[26] Ibid.

vy.[27] In addition, while both the missions contributions experienced a steady increase for years, the church collected less than 100 percent of its budget from 1990 to 1995, averaging 93.46 percent of budget collected in those years. Beginning in 1996, Northminster experienced a surplus that would continue for five consecutive years, from 1996 to 2000. In 1996 and 1997, the surpluses were modest at $10,000 and $11,000 respectively. However, the 1998 surplus was more than $80,000, which prompted serious conversations among deacons and other members about how to allocate these gifts.[28]

In a letter to Charles Parrott, chair of the Finance Committee, Chuck Poole requested that the board spend the entire surplus in support of missions. "I know that we have some institutional needs to which we could direct portions of the money," Poole wrote. "In this case, however, it seems to me that we find ourselves as the recipients of an extraordinary gift of grace and, thus, in a unique position to make extraordinary gifts to undergird gospel missions and ministries in our city. Theologically and biblically, it seems to me that this is the right thing to do."[29]

Consequently, the Finance Committee recommended and the deacons approved that $70,000 be designated to local direct mission efforts, with the remaining $10,000 allocated for church office needs such as new computers, a website, telephone, and other related expenses.[30] With this surplus, the deacons further strengthened its support of Stewpot Community Services with a gift of $15,000 for its community center and another $15,000 for Stewpot's personal care home ministry—an extension of Northminster's Christmas Boarding Homes Project, which enabled Stewpot to hire Rev. Jo Hollman as a chaplain to the personal care homes. Northminster had ordained Hollman in 1997. A nonprofit community organization, Stewpot formed in 1981 when seven congregations, including Northminster Baptist Church, provided volunteers and funds to start a soup kitchen. Over the years, the scope and services of Stewpot grew drastically, and by 2000 Stewpot Community Services featured the involvement of more than seventy

---

[27] Ibid.

[28] "Historical Comparison of Pledges, Budget and Collection," 2003.

[29] Charles E. Poole to Charles Parrott, January 28, 1999.

[30] N Deacons 2 21 99.

Jackson-area congregations as well as hundreds of businesses, clubs, and individuals.[31]

The church also designated $20,000 to Calvary Baptist Church Community Ministries, an area ministry focusing on relational work in the West Park neighborhood of Jackson, which included weekly Bible clubs for more than 200 children. New Horizon Ministries also received $15,000 to help with its purchase and renovation of Olin Park Place, a ten-unit apartment complex in West Jackson, which was planned as a home for individuals in a rehabilitation program, struggling families, as well as women recently released from prison and experiencing addiction. A final $5,000 was given to the Olin Park Neighborhood Association to help build a playground for the children of this low-income neighborhood.[32] Future surpluses were spent on a wide array of missions, ministries, and other initiatives: funding for job training via Christian Women's Job Corp; scholarships to send Stewpot children to Camp Kanuga; improvements to the Northminster Youth House; the Kauma Orphan Support Initiative to assist with the building of a group orphanage in Malawi; a mission trip to Tchula, Mississippi; and funding for the Rauschenbusch Metro Ministry (a partnership of the Cooperative Baptist Fellowship), which served the homeless in the Hell's Kitchen neighborhood of New York City.[33]

In 2000, Northminster Baptist Church enjoyed an historic budget surplus of approximately $218,000, collecting 116.5 percent of its annual budget. With the gift of continued surpluses came the difficulty of democratically deciding how to allocate the excess funds. The deacons had recommended to the church that the $218,000 be divided equally between the Missions Committee and the Denominational Relations Committee for distribution. However, when this recommendation was presented to the congregation, a substitute motion was made by Kane Ditto to amend the deacons' recommendation and allocate only half of the budget surplus between the two committees. This motion proposed to reduce the surplus amount designated to missions and ministries from approximately $110,000 to only $55,000.

[31] Cindy Griffin, "Reports from recipients of special gifts from 1999 Northminster Budget Surplus," N News (Spring 2000): 2–3.

[32] Ibid.

[33] Cindy Griffin to Gloria Martin," October 4, 2000; Charles E. Poole to Gloria Martin, March 22, 2000; Mark Wiggs to Gloria Martin, April 3, 2000.

After discussion for and against the motion by numerous members, the congregation voted 55–49 to adopt the substitute motion and decrease the surplus allocation.[34]

Debate over the proposed equal allocation of the historic surplus between the two committees had bubbled up at the previous meeting of the deacons. Ditto had noted his belief that Northminster's missions priorities should be local whereas the missions and ministry priorities of the Denominational Relations Committee were more national and global in scope. Both Ditto and Kelley Williams Jr. expressed their desire to set aside at least $50,000 in case the church decided to pursue a special missions or building project. The deacons voted 8–5 to recommend the equal split between the two committees, but Ditto and Williams Jr.'s comments reflected a desire to see the congregation weigh both options.[35]

Following the vote of the congregation, Chuck Poole offered pastoral words to affirm the process, despite the stated disagreements among the members, and to temper the potential for division. "We do lots of talking at Northminster, as well we should, about Baptist distinctives and congregational church polity," Poole said. He continued,

> Today is a wonderful example of how that looks when it really happens. We, as a congregation of people of good faith, goodwill, and good vision, bring ideas; and the congregation has the opportunity to speak to those ideas and embrace them according to the will of the congregation. Sometimes we think that everything is cut and dried in church life, but Baptist polity at its best has congregational demonstrations, so I just wanted to say thanks to all for your participation. It's important and it's a good example of congregations as families of faith having real conversations and making real decisions.[36]

The two committees used the $55,000 to support denominational ministries and missions as well as numerous local and state ministries. The Denominational Relations Committee split its allocation between scholarships for students of Mississippi Baptist Convention colleges (Blue Mountain College, William Carey College, and Mississippi College), scholarships for students at Cooperative Baptist Fellowship-partner theological schools

[34] N Minutes 5 20 01.
[35] N Deacons 4 29 01
[36] Ibid.

(Wake Forest University Divinity School, Baptist House Studies program at Duke University Divinity School, Baptist House Studies program at Emory University's Candler School of Theology, and the Baptist House Studies program at Texas Christian University). Funding was also provided to CBF of Mississippi and its Mississippi Delta Poverty Project, to a volunteer mission fund in China, and to CBF missionaries in Albania. The committee also allocated funds to Associated Baptist Press, the independent Baptist news organization where church member Christopher Hedglin was completing a summer internship. Local missions and ministries receiving financial gifts included the Baptist Children's Village, a shelter for battered women (project of Catholic Charities), Operation Shoestring (a community service organization in Jackson designed to help people overcome the problems of poverty and racism to become self-sufficient), and Stewpot Community Services, among others.[37]

During this period of budget surpluses, Northminster Baptist Church placed a heightened focus on local and direct ministries and missions. The congregation participated in dozens of hands-on ministries, using funding from the annual budget as well as, in many instances, private financial support. The 20-plus percent devoted to missions did not adequately capture the extent of Northminster's financial commitment and personal involvement. Examples included a week-long blitz construction of a house for a low-income family with Briarwood Presbyterian Church in August 2000; construction of a house in partnership with Habitat for Humanity in 2001 (continuing a partnership birthed in 1989 between Habitat and Northminster); participating with other CBF-affiliated churches in a mentoring program for school-aged children in the Mississippi Delta town of Tchula (long dubbed one of the poorest communities in the United States); tutoring at Barr Elementary, a program coordinated by church member Mary Hendrick; reading to elementary-aged children at New Horizon Academy; mentoring families at Olin Park Apartment Project; volunteering at nearby Spann School; and providing hundreds of care packages during the first weekend of Christmas (a beloved Advent tradition started November 21,

[37] N Minutes 5 20 01; "Northminster Baptist Church Denominational Relations Committee Special Funding Recommendations for 2000 Budget Surplus," May 5, 2001.

1978, called the Christmas Boarding Homes Project).[38] Northminster supported many other ministries including Hospice of Central Mississippi, Magnolia Speech School, Mendenhall Ministries, and Mississippi Food Network to name just a few.[39]

During fall 2002, the church's Adopt-A-School Committee was honored with the Golden Achievement Award by the Jackson Public Schools' Partners in Education program for its volunteer work at Spann Elementary School. In 1987, Northminster joined the Adopt-A-School program, and for fifteen years members had volunteered there in a variety of ways, from providing vision screenings to hosting Christmas parties for students and luncheons for teachers to tutoring and reading books with the students.[40] Northminster was again recognized in 2003 when member Mary Levereault was recognized at the Adopt-A-School program's twenty-fifth anniversary celebration for serving as the church's community coordinator from 1998 to 2003.[41]

The late 1990s saw a sustained focus on ministry to those living with HIV/AIDS. In May 1997, the deacons approved a recommendation of the Missions Committee to pay for the unfunded drug care of one HIV/AIDS patient for the remainder of the year.[42] "The foundation of our faith is to love one another with the grace and compassion demonstrated to us by Jesus Christ," the deacon board wrote. "Without their life sustaining and enhancing drugs, most of these cut from funding face certain illness and death."[43] The drug-providing program harkened back to some of the earliest social ministries the congregation engaged in under the leadership of Dr. Jim Hendrick in the early 1970s.

Northminster's focus on the HIV/AIDS epidemic came as the state of Mississippi struggled to slow the crisis, reporting an increase in the effects of the disease in 1997 especially in the African-American community, which along with females, accounted for the majority of new HIV infections and

---

[38] N Deacons 1 18 01; N Deacons 9 30 96; N News 9 6 00; N News 8 23 00.

[39] "Questionnaire about Missions: Evaluating our Current Mission," 1999.

[40] N News 10 16 02.

[41] N News 4 15 03

[42] N Bulletin 6 1 97.

[43] Ibid.; N Deacons 3 19 95. Northminster had previously supported care for AIDS patients with a $500 contribution to the Episcopal Aids Committee in 1995.

AIDS cases.[44] The church hosted several informational meetings for members and the community who were interested in learning more about ministry to those with HIV/AIDS and how to advocate on behalf of those with HIV/AIDS.[45]

In 1999, Northminster Baptist Church made a weekly commitment to provide support to the thirty residents of Grace House, a home in Jackson for people living with HIV.[46] Under the leadership of Anne Guidry, church members signed up and delivered dinner for the residents. Volunteers were invited to either drop off the food at the two-story house on Millsaps Avenue or stay and share the meal with the residents.[47] Nearly twenty years later, this ministry of compassion and friendship continues.

Baptist Denominational Affairs

In 2000, the Southern Baptist Convention significantly revised its confessional statement, the *Baptist Faith & Message*. While the updated confession did not use the controversial language of "inerrancy," it was panned by non-fundamentalists for its deletion of the Christocentric criterion for interpretation of Scripture; the diminishment of the doctrines of soul competency, priesthood of the believer, and local church autonomy; as well as for its extremely narrow interpretation of the role of women in marriage and the church—prohibiting women from serving as pastor. The revisions sparked outcry from Baptists and non-Baptists alike. Chuck Poole used his weekly column in *Northminster News* to address the new developments in the SBC just days after the adoption of the updated confession in June 2000. Poole wrote,

> This kind of public spot-light on the Southern Baptists has left me feeling a rather strong sense of internal dilemma. On the one hand, it would suit me just fine to never offer another word of commentary on the pronouncements of Southern Baptists. For one thing, I haven't attended a Southern Baptist gathering in nearly a decade. As a matter of personal conscience and theological conviction, my denominational en-

---

[44] Mississippi State Department of Health Annual Report: 1997, p.16–17, http://msdh.ms.gov/msdhsite/_static/resources/47.pdf.

[45] N Bulletin 10 12 97; N Bulletin 6 15 97.

[46] N News 11 1 00.

[47] N News 9 22 99.

> ergies flow through other Baptist channels.... It seems to me that one simply has to be silent when one can be silent with integrity, and then one must "speak truth in love." To that end though I know that the convention's decisions are none of my business and that their pronouncements do not in any way affect Northminster's day-to-day life, let me say here, as I have in the last two weeks in more public forums, that the proposed revisions to the SBC's *Baptist Faith and Message* do not, in my judgment, reflect the spirit of Christ, who is the ultimate measure by which all Scripture is to be interpreted. To not say that would be, for me, a failure of integrity.[48]

As the SBC continued to follow its fundamentalist impulse, Northminster Baptist Church strengthened its ties to the Cooperative Baptist Fellowship and its network of like-minded partners. In fall 1999, Northminster hosted a gathering for Baptists in Mississippi to honor CBF global missions coordinator Keith Parks upon his retirement. Five years later, Northminster was honored with the Associated Baptist Press Founders Award. ABP was founded in 1991 as the nation's first and only independent Baptist news service—a reaction to the fundamentalist-controlled news agency, Baptist Press. Northminster had been a longtime financial supporter, providing the independent news entity with $46,000 from 1991 to 2004, and church member Rebecca Wiggs had previously served a term as chair of the ABP Board of Directors.[49]

Ministry of Interfaith Ecumenism

Northminster continued to hold annual opportunities to gather with its friends at Beth Israel and learn about the Jewish faith. Interfaith cooperation remained an important distinctive of the congregation. During summer 1999, church members were encouraged to visit and volunteer to guide tours of an exhibit of Jewish history and heritage.[50] Two years later, Rabbi Egolf, who had served the Beth Israel Congregation since 1997, led an interfaith study on Judaism as part of Northminster's Adult Studies program on Sunday evenings.[51] Additional Adult Studies interfaith programs were held in

[48] N News 6 14 00.
[49] N News 3 23 04.
[50] N Bulletin 4 26 98.
[51] N Bulletin 11 11 01.

future years.[52] In 2004, Northminster members attended the Interfaith Holocaust Memorial Program led by Rabbi Valerie Cohen at Beth Israel, and two years prior Northminster joined the Jewish Congregation for Friday evening services in the synagogue to hear from the Shirim Choir, a widely recognized volunteer choir at Beth Israel.[53] The Northminster youth shared in fellowship with Beth Israel youth, with its high school basketball team playing against the Beth Israel team. The youth also took part in conversations with the Beth Israel rabbi over supper to learn more about the Jewish faith, and a "Jam with the Jews" event featuring a Havdalah service was followed by a joint party between the two youth groups.[54]

Staff

In April 2002, nearly eight years after joining the Northminster staff as associate pastor for students and community ministry (later renamed associate pastor for youth and community ministry), Stan Wilson announced his resignation to accept the pastorate at fellow progressive Baptist church, Northside Baptist Church in Clinton—just eleven miles away. A cookout was held to honor Wilson, his wife, Jennifer, and young daughter, Jane.[55] In a letter to the Northminster deacons upon the church's purchase of a barrister bookcase for their new home in Clinton, Wilson wrote, "Northside is a good church, and I am very grateful to be here. I am eager for our two congregations to work together, and I am sure there will be many opportunities in the future. Thank you for your generous gift."[56]

"God has clearly called Northminster to its own distinctive ways of worship and witness and will give you what you need to fulfill those callings," Wilson wrote. Reflecting on his eight-year tenure, he continued,

> Your mission is vital. Because you follow Christ the way you do, you offer true light and new life in a way no other church could do, and you offer living bread and living water to people all around Jackson. I will always pray for you in hope and thanksgiving. I am particularly thankful and hopeful for *our* youth. Thank you for your friendships. I feel

[52] N Bulletin 4 25 04.
[53] N Bulletin 4 18 04; N Bulletin 10 6 02.
[54] N Bulletin 3 2 03; N News 11 20 00.
[55] N Deacons 4 21 02.
[56] Stan Wilson to Deacons of Northminster Baptist Church, October 8, 2002.

> like most of our time has been spent on a bus or in vans, and the journey itself has been a taste of our final destination in the joyful kingdom of God.[57]

After announcing his departure, Wilson wrote a letter to the Personnel Committee recommending the employment of Jill Barnes, a second-year seminarian at Boston University, as a pastoral intern for summer 2002. Wilson also asked the committee to approve the request of the Youth Committee to hire church member Courtney Allen as the church's summer youth intern to be supervised by Barnes. Both of Wilson's recommendations were approved.[58]

Wilson would enjoy a friendly relationship with Northminster over the next fourteen years, throughout his tenure as senior pastor of Northside Baptist Church in Clinton. He returned to the Northminster pulpit in May 2004, as did former pastor, Roger Paynter, following the departure of Chuck Poole.[59] In 2003, Wilson also organized a joint pizza supper for Northside and Northminster youth in Clinton.[60] Wilson participated in the ordinations of Amy Joyner (2003), Jill Barnes Buckley (2007), and Courtney Allen (2011); he even chaired Joyner's ordination council.[61]

Following Wilson's exit to Northside, Northminster called Joseph M. Martin III (known as Tripp) in May 2003 to the position of associate pastor for students and community ministries, and tasked him with leading the church's youth program and local missions outreach. Martin came to Jackson from Winston-Salem, North Carolina, where he had recently graduated from Wake Forest University School of Divinity.[62]

Three years earlier, the church had experienced another staff transition. In 2000, Associate pastor Nancy Hollomon Peede resigned to pursue her passion for spiritual direction and retreat leadership. Chuck Poole said that Hollomon Peede had called the congregation to a "deeper walk with our Lord." "She has shown us the way to a more God-centered life," Poole

---

[57] Stan Wilson to Congregation of Northminster Baptist Church, March 22, 2002.

[58] N Deacons 4 21 04.

[59] N Bulletin 5 16 04

[60] N Bulletin 3 23 03.

[61] N Deacons 10 20 02; N Bulletin 10 14 07; N Bulletin 7 31 2011.

[62] N Deacons 5 18 03.

wrote at the time of Hollomon Peede's departure. "She has loved all our children, and guided our spiritual formation and Christian education, while also giving administrative leadership to several areas of the life of the church."[63]

Northminster called Amy Joyner to succeed Hollomon Peede in the role of associate pastor in June 2002. A graduate of Wake Forest University School of Divinity, Joyner had served as interim youth minister at Myers Park Baptist Church in Charlotte, North Carolina, and came with the strong recommendations of moderate Baptist leaders and Wake Forest Divinity's dean, Bill Leonard, and Wake Forest professor Frank Tupper.[64]

In 2004, the congregation voted to call Jill Barnes as its associate pastor for community ministry, a new position created with the adoption of the church's Wider Net missions initiative (see chapter 8). Barnes, who had served as a pastoral intern during summer 2002, completed her master of divinity degree at Boston University School of Theology with a concentration in urban ministry and had returned to Jackson to work again for Stewpot.[65] In this new associate pastor role, Barnes was responsible for coordinating and facilitating the church's efforts to support and carry out its Wider Net ministry in the Mid-City/Georgetown neighborhood, working closely with area churches including Wells United Methodist Church, New Mount Zion Missionary Baptist Church and agencies such as Operation Shoestring, Habitat for Humanity, and the LifeShare foundation.[66]

Other staff hires included the calling of Tim Coker as minister of music in spring 2004. With the departure of Earl Owen in 1997, who had served as minister of music since 1988, the church called Bill Pharr to this part-time role in April 1998 to direct the adult choir.[67] At the time of his hiring, Pharr had been a member of Northminster for twenty-three years. He served until his death in February 2004, at which point Coker was asked to join the staff. An experienced musician, Coker was chair of Performing Arts and professor of music at Millsaps College. He had served as the inter-

[63] N News 10 11 00.

[64] N Deacons 6 26 02.

[65] N Deacons 8 15 04.

[66] Charles Parrott, chair of Board of Deacons, to Northminster Baptist Church, September 3, 2004.

[67] N Deacons 4 19 98.

im music minister since September 2003 while Pharr battled illness.[68] Coker had previously led the choir at Jackson's Covenant Presbyterian Church.[69]

Deacons

When Northminster Baptist Church was founded in 1967, it began with just nine deacons. The size of the Board of Deacons increased to twelve in 1975 and to fifteen in 1981, in accordance with the church's bylaws requiring the board to increase by three each time resident membership grew by 100 persons. In 1998, the board grew again from fifteen to eighteen as Northminster surpassed the 600-resident member mark.[70] Eight years prior, in 1990, the Board of Deacons had recommended several changes to Northminster's bylaws, most notably a provision to allow for absentee voting in deacon elections by members unable to attend the congregation's annual business meeting. The deacons' proposal would have allowed members to visit the church office and vote at any time during the ten-day period prior to the annual meeting. However, the congregation voted down the proposal.[71]

Another proposal for absentee voting in deacon elections was made fifteen years later in 2005. The deacons proposed that any church member be allowed to cast an absentee ballot for the election of deacons during church office hours the five weekdays preceding the election. They also proposed a new requirement that the names and photos of the deacon nominees be circulated to church members in advance of the election.[72] This proposal was hotly debated and generated much discussion from members at the business meeting. A motion to table the proposed changes until additional conversations could take place was defeated. Another motion to limit absentee voting to only individuals who would be out of town on the day of the annual meeting also failed to pass. The changes to the bylaws were eventually approved on a final vote.[73]

---

[68] N Deacons 3 21 04.
[69] N Deacons 9 21 03.
[70] N Minutes 9 13 98.
[71] N Minutes 9 9 90.
[72] N Minutes 5 22 05.
[73] Ibid.

State of the Church

Reflections from deacons' retreats in 1997 and 2003 shed insight into Northminster's perceived strengths and weaknesses. Bill Boone, who was beginning his fourth term on the board, emphasized that the congregation had not experienced significant change in its thirty-year history, noting that he could not think of another institution with the same level of stability. Others shared how Northminster had excelled at nurturing and mentoring its children as well as fostering the formation of deep relationships across the congregation. The deacons discussed the need to welcome diverse views and embrace change, while stressing the importance of remembering the church's history and "what birthed us."[74]

At the 2003 retreat, deacons were asked to offer a word or phrase to describe what attracted them to Northminster. They cited the church's theological diversity, an emphasis on lay leadership, tolerance, gender inclusiveness, missions philosophy, and the "safe place" that it provided.[75] Kelley Williams Sr. echoed many of these descriptors' comments at the retreat later titled "A Keeper of the Cairn." In his remarks, Williams Sr. described himself as the "keeper of the Northminster Cairn," noting that on the tenth anniversary of the dedication of the church's sanctuary, pastor John Thomason preached a sermon titled "What Mean These Stones?" in which he described Northminster's distinctive features.

"The keeper of the cairn is typically the role of an elder in primitive societies and is appropriate for me.... I think of the stones in the Northminster Cairn as the values or norms we share. They are what we stand for. They bind us together," Williams Sr. said. He continued,

> We are the church. The church is not the sanctuary. It is not the pastor or the staff. It is not the convention or association. It is the congregation. We are the body of Christ and the hands and feet. Northminster began life without a church building or a pastor. We have survived interims without a pastor. These have challenged us, united us and brought out the best in us. We are a laity led church. We do the work of the church with help and guidance from the pastor and staff. But we don't hire them to do church for us. It is important for us, for us to do

[74] N Deacons 10 18 97.

[75] N Deacons 3 22 03.

church. It is important for our children to see us doing church and see that it is meaningful to us.

We are family. We care for and about one another as members of our church family. We care especially for our children. We minister to each other. We are our brother and sister's keeper. We may not like what some of our biological family members do or say. In fact, we may not even like some of them. But we love them because they are family. It is the same with us as members of the Northminster family.

We are tolerant. We began life as a diverse group. Many of us were malcontents or rebels with causes—but different causes. We challenged each other. We were forced to examine what we believe and what we did or didn't do. Some of us changed—some. But we were and are still different. This is one of our strengths. It keeps us vibrant.

Worship is serious and meaningful. We value Scripture-based excellence in the pulpit. We expect to be challenged, taught, inspired and comforted. We are reverent in the sanctuary and respect the history and tradition of the paraments. We value the formality of the liturgy and the fine music.

All are called. We are all called from time to time to be servant leaders and followers according to the church's needs and our talents and gifts. There is no hierarchy of status or vested positions for servant leaders or qualifications as to age or gender. We are expected to listen for and be responsive to God's call. The pastor is our spiritual leader and teacher as we seek to grow in wisdom and understanding of God's way and will for us.

Our cairn is not finished. These stones mark our heritage and speak our values. This is our Northminster identity. Our children and those who join Northminster should know it and value it. Yet more stones will be added. We are not finished growing as persons, for we are still being redeemed. We are not finished growing as church either, and Northminster will change. But let us add stones carefully and wisely and in accordance with God's will.[76]

---

[76] J. Kelley Williams Sr., "A Keeper of the Cairn," Deacons Retreat, March 21, 2003.

No doubt, Williams Sr. had captured the self-perception and the perceived tradition of the fundamental identity of Northminster Baptist Church.

Poole's Departure and Interim Period

In June 2003, six years into his tenure as Northminster's fifth senior pastor, Chuck Poole announced his resignation to take a position with the LifeShare Foundation to serve underprivileged children in Mississippi. Poole would serve as the LifeShare community minister, working in Jackson's inner-city neighborhoods and other areas with great need throughout the state. Poole told the congregation that his family planned to stay in Jackson and be active members of Northminster Baptist Church.

"During these years in Jackson, I have experienced an ever-deepening sense of call to serve alongside Mississippi's most disadvantaged families," Poole wrote to Northminster members.

> This gravity toward those who are in poverty has grown out of long study of the Gospels and many visits to Jackson's neighborhoods where need is great and hope is small. That growing gravity and deepening call have now converged with an opportunity for ministry. That convergence of call and opportunity brings me to write this letter of resignation as Pastor of Northminster Baptist Church so that I can begin full-time ministry among some of Mississippi's most disadvantaged families.[77]

Northminster would hold a blessing service for Poole on his last day in the Northminster pulpit on September 13, 2003.[78] Following Poole's departure, a Pulpit Committee was assembled, comprising Dudley Wooley, chair of the Board of Deacons; staff ministers Amy Joyner and Tripp Martin; and eight lay members. The committee sought to fill three Sundays a month. The first Sunday of each month was reserved for communion and a staff minister filled the pulpit.[79] Supply preachers were used over the course of twenty months before the church's next senior minister was called. Guest preachers included numerous notable Baptist pastors and leaders including

[77] Chuck Poole to Northminster Baptist Church, June 23, 2003.

[78] N Bulletin 9 14 03.

[79] Report of the Pulpit Supply Committee to Deacons of Northminster Baptist Church, September 21, 2003.

Walter Shurden of Mercer University, whom the church had unsuccessfully attempted to call decades earlier following the resignation of John Claypool; Frank Tupper of Wake Forest University School of Divinity, who preached at least ten times; Charles Bugg of the Baptist Theological Seminary of Richmond; noted Bible scholar Phyllis Trible; Loyd Allen of Mercer University, whose wife Libby directed the church's children's center years earlier when Allen was a professor at Mississippi College; Brent Walker of the Baptist Joint Committee on Public Affairs; contemporary Christian musician Kyle Matthews; and Brad Braxton and Bill Leonard of Wake Forest University School of Divinity. Former staff ministers and pastors also preached, including Dudley Wilson, Stan Wilson, Chuck Poole, Roger Paynter, Gene Corbin, and John Claypool.[80]

[80] Supply calendar, May 2005.

Chapter 7

Every Member a Minister: The Ministry of Brian Brewer

New Pastor

After a twenty-month interim, Brian C. Brewer was called on July 31, 2005, to serve as senior pastor—the sixth senior pastor of Northminster Baptist Church. Brewer came to Jackson from Oklahoma City, where he had been senior pastor of Spring Creek Baptist Church since 2001. At thirty-four, Brewer was the youngest pastor, alongside Thomason (also age thirty-four), in the church's nearly forty-year history. A graduate of Drew University and Princeton Theological Seminary in New Jersey, Brewer was the first pastor since John Claypool to hold a PhD, which he received in 2003 from Drew with a dissertation on the sacramental theology of sixteenth-century Anabaptist and radical Reformation leader Balthasar Hubmaier. Like John Claypool, John Thomason, and Roger Paynter before him, Brewer was a graduate of Baylor University, where he received his undergraduate degree in religion in 1993 before attending Baylor's then-new seminary, George W. Truett Theological Seminary, to earn his master of divinity degree.[1]

Brewer and his wife, Amy, a pediatrician, had two young daughters: Brittany (six) and Ashley (four). He preached his first sermon on September 18, 2005, paying homage to his predecessors:

> I do not stand in this pulpit believing that I somehow "deserve" to be here. Many of those who have gone before me in this place are now regarded as legends and senior statesmen in our Baptist and greater Christian world. And it seems particularly astounding to be standing here in this place just two weeks after the passing of one of your and our greatest preachers. I will make no plans and I cannot attempt to fill anyone's shoes in this place. But I must stand on their shoulders through your loving support and witness.[2]

---

[1] N Deacons 7 26 05; N News 8 16 05; N Minutes 7 31 05.

[2] Brian Brewer, "On Seeing Jesus," sermon, Northminster Baptist Church, September 18, 2005.

Brewer was referring to John Claypool, Northminster's high-profile and much-beloved second senior pastor (1976–1981), who died on September 3, 2005, from complications related to treatment for multiple myeloma. Claypool was seventy-four years old and had been serving as professor of preaching at Mercer University's McAfee School of Theology and as an associate priest at All Saints Episcopal Church in Atlanta. His memorial service was held at Crescent Hill Baptist Church in Louisville, Kentucky, where he was pastor from 1960 to 1971. At the service, a tree was planted to honor his life with soil from Claypool's previous churches, which included Northminster.[3]

Hurricane Katrina

Brian Brewer began as pastor just a few days after Hurricane Katrina struck the Gulf Coast, making landfall first in southeast Louisiana, causing severe destruction for 400 miles from central Florida all the way to Texas. The death toll surpassed 1,800; nearly 1,600 people had died in Louisiana, largely because of the systematic failure of New Orleans' levees during the storm's surge. The hurricane also devastated parts of Mississippi—causing more than $150 billion in damage and the deaths of nearly 250 people—and left thousands of Mississippians homeless and in a state of disarray. Northminster leaped to action and established a "Katrina Fund" to collect money for the relief efforts, and the church pledged to support ten displaced families who had no nearby relatives or any means to securing housing. They also supported the Cooperative Baptist Fellowship's disaster response efforts.[4] Just a week after Hurricane Katrina hit land, the deacons voted to send $9,000 to CBF of Mississippi to hire someone to direct relief efforts in the state.[5]

Three weeks into the efforts, the church had helped five displaced families from New Orleans get settled in Jackson; in the first month, the church had given more than $40,000 to the Katrina Fund.[6] Associate pastor Jill Barnes Buckley organized the hands-on volunteer efforts in Jackson, providing the congregation with lists of items needed for displaced families

---

[3] N News 9 7 05.
[4] N News 9 7 05.
[5] N Deacons 9 05.
[6] N Bulletin 9 25 05.

relocated to the area. Members donated clothing, household items, furniture, and their time—assisting displaced families in moving from shelters to residences and providing transportation to the families in and around town. Barnes Buckley also published bios and stories about the families aided in the weekly church newsletter.[7]

By the end of the year, the church had raised more than $50,000 and helped fifteen displaced families relocate to Jackson from Gulfport, Mississippi; New Orleans and Slidell, Louisiana; and Houston, Texas. The church also assisted ten more people with emergency needs such as food, gas, clothing, and living expenses. Many of the evacuees receiving aid continued to face personal struggles, such as difficulties finding work as well as deaths in their immediate families, not to mention grief, anxiety, and depression.[8]

Through its support of the Cooperative Baptist Fellowship's disaster response efforts, Northminster aided the long-term rebuilding efforts in Pearlington, Mississippi, a small unincorporated community of 1,500 people ninety miles southwest of Hattiesburg. In the eighteen months following Hurricane Katrina, Northminster members would join more than 1,300 CBF volunteers who traveled to this almost-forgotten town to help rebuild. CBF of Mississippi hosted more than 110 groups.[9] In the order of worship for Easter 2006, the liturgist, Gray Jackson III, recalled the Great Easter Flood of 1979, which left much of Northeast Jackson under water:

> This congregation has yet once again traversed the quiet darkness and deep introspection of Holy Week to arrive once more at the joyful gates of Easter. In a year marked by the tragedy of Katrina, I can think of no greater time to welcome that news as a reminder that God is always with us no matter what.
>
> Thinking on the challenges of Katrina during Holy Week, I was transported back to Holy Week of 1979 when I was just a nine-year-old boy. It was Friday, April 13, 1979, and the Pearl River was beginning a fast rise and flooding was predicted. By Easter morning on Sunday, April 15, 1979, thousands of Jacksonians were flooded out of their

[7] N Bulletin 10 16 05; N Minutes 9 11 05.

[8] N Bulletin 1 22 06.

[9] N Bulletin 4 22 07. Northminster members joined St. Luke's United Methodist Church and Wells United Methodist Church on a rebuilding trip in Pearlington, Mississippi, on May 4–6, 2007.

> homes, businesses were under water, and schools were an island. I can still remember heading down to the bottom of the hill with my friends to see our own neighbors paddling in and out of their homes in boats with whatever belongings they could collect together. The "Great Easter Flood," as it came to be known left an indelible mark on the city of Jackson as well as many members of this congregation.
>
> As I began to research the "Great Easter Flood of 1979," I asked Barbara Webb if there was a tape available from that Easter Sunday in 1979 when much of Northeast Jackson was under water. I thought it might prove interesting to hear what sermon topic John Claypool chose for that Easter Sunday. Her reply was that Claypool stepped up in the pulpit that Easter Sunday on April 15, 1979, and told those who were there to go home, put on their work clothes, and do what they could to help their brothers and sisters in need. In the year of Katrina, we have seen this sense of servitude at its finest. While floods and hurricanes may come and go, the spirit of the resurrected Christ lives on in each and every one of us.[10]

Jackson challenged members to embrace Claypool's words from twenty-five years prior and "move forward with a sense of discipleship and servitude as we aid our fellow brothers and sisters in a world rebuilding after the storm."[11]

One year after Hurricane Katrina struck the Gulf Coast, Northminster's Katrina Fund had provided assistance to more than thirty-five families with a wide variety of needs, from providing a tank of gas to a night's stay in a hotel to money for rent and household items. Fifteen families had received assistance resettling in Jackson, and eight of those families had returned to New Orleans for a fresh start. Several families were not able to recover, however. "At least two of 'our' families have not been able to recover at all really," Barnes Buckley wrote in her update to the congregation. "Their lives are a continuing chaos of addiction relapses, abuse, money mismanagement, or indecision. For those who were already vulnerable in some way, the force of the hurricane was not only in the wind and water."[12]

---

[10] N Bulletin 4 16 06.

[11] Ibid.

[12] N News 8 29 06.

Barnes Buckley called the families "some of the strongest, most courageous people I know." She recalled the story of Edward, who, after losing everything he owned in the flood, lost his son to gun violence in New Orleans in early 2006. Yet, he remained committed in his faith. "The Lord gives and the Lord takes away. Blessed be the name of the Lord," Edward told her. "For my part, the strength of these families has helped me to get to the other side of my own pain and grief; sharing their recovery has been a blessing beyond the telling," Barnes Buckley shared with the congregation. "But this story is not complete without a deep and sustained 'thank you' to everyone who contributed to the Katrina Fund. Without you, this work truly would not have been possible. Not once did I forget that any help that I could offer on behalf of Northminster was due to your generosity. God bless all of you."[13]

Denominational Identity

Cooperative Baptist Fellowship leaders remained frequent guests in the Northminster pulpit during the 2000s. In 2006, CBF missionary Ben Newell spoke on the fellowship's rural poverty initiative called Together for Hope in the twenty poorest counties in the United States. For some years, Northminster Baptist Church had been a consistent supporter of this initiative in the Delta region of Mississippi.[14] The church also heard from former member Holly Hollman, who served as general counsel to the Washington, DC-based Baptist Joint Committee for Religious Liberty, a moderate Baptist organization committed to defending church-state separation and extending religious freedom for all. Hollman, whose mother, Jo, had been ordained by Northminster, joined the church while a student in Mississippi College in 1986.[15] Twenty years later, she returned as one of the nation's foremost experts on the First Amendment's religion clauses to share with the congregation about current events and trends in church-state relations. Over the years, Northminster had been a faithful backer of the Baptist Joint Committee, especially during the tumultuous 1980s when Southern Baptist fundamentalists (eventually) successfully defunded the religious liberty watchdog, which had for more than fifty years brought together Baptist

[13] Ibid.
[14] N News 1 21 06.
[15] N Bulletin 2 2 86.

groups in the United States from across the theological spectrum. Several Baptist Joint Committee staff members, including former executive director and noted firebrand James Dunn, had been guests in Northminster's pulpit and Sunday school classrooms.[16]

Ministry of Ecumenism, Interfaith Witness

Since its founding in 1967, Northminster Baptist Church had displayed a commitment to forming ecumenical friendships with Presbyterians, Episcopalians, Methodists, and Catholics, as well as nurturing an important interfaith relationship with the Beth Israel Congregation. In 2005, the congregation on Ridgewood Road expanded its interfaith witness to include Muslims, hosting the church's first "Ramadan Feast" in partnership with the Institute for Interfaith Dialog. Northminster joined local Muslims in celebrating Eid ul-Fitr, the three-day period marking the end of their holy month of Ramadan—the ninth month of the Islamic calendar commemorating the first revelation of the Quran to Muhammad.[17]

Not surprisingly, Northminster had long demonstrated an openness to Muslims that was uncharacteristic of the average Baptist church. In the immediate aftermath of the 9/11 terrorist attacks, the Adult Studies Committee hosted a study of Islam led by William Waheed, former Imam of Masjid Muhammed and curator of the International Museum of Muslim Cultures in Jackson.[18] At a time when society at large viewed Muslims with increased suspicion and as the FBI reported a spike in hate crimes against Muslims, Northminster welcomed an imam to share with the congregation about the history and beliefs of the Islamic faith.[19] This time of study exemplified the church's open posture and desire to be an inclusive and positive witness in the Jackson community.

Opportunities for mutual learning continued the next year as Northminster hosted Charles Kimball, a Baptist minister and professor of comparative religion at Wake Forest University, to speak about the wide theo-

---

[16] N Bulletin 1 9 06.

[17] N News 10 6 05.

[18] N News 10 24 01.

[19] "Data: Hate crimes against Muslims increased after 9/11," Public Radio International, September 12, 2016, https://www.pri.org/stories/2016–09–12/data-hate-crimes-against-muslims-increased-after-911.

logical diversity that exists within the Muslim world and to encourage greater understanding between Muslims and Christians.[20] In 2006, Northminster hosted a special gathering of faith groups called the Festival of Faiths—an effort to educate, promote understanding, and celebrate the various faith traditions of Jackson, including Muslims. The festival served as a kick-off for Jackson's first "Peace House"—a joint Habit for Humanity build project that featured volunteers from Jackson's various faith communities, including Northminster members.[21] The church also participated in the construction of the second Peace House in 2007 alongside worshipers from other Christian churches as well as Temple Beth Israel, a Unitarian Universalist congregation, and two Jackson mosques.[22]

Ministries to Children and Youth

The children's ministry continued to thrive in the mid-2000s with a diverse offering of opportunities for preschool and elementary-aged children of Northminster such as the annual Easter Egg Hunt, PASSPORT*kids!* summer camp, chapel on Sunday mornings, and Children's Atrium on Wednesday evenings (later changed to Sunday evenings). Children's Atrium was designed as an hour-long program based on the Montessori method of education with a contemplative approach to spiritual formation, including choir and missions study.[23]

An important development was the adoption in June 2006 of a set of policies and procedures for the protection of minors as well as vulnerable adults. Associate pastor Amy Joyner worked with the deacons in this effort to formalize policies to protect children, youth, and vulnerable adults who were part of any of Northminster's programs. The new policies and procedures established in writing long-standing practices of the church, Joyner said, such as requiring written permission from a parent or guardian before any minor could participate in any overnight activities. The policies were modeled after policies in place at First Baptist Church in Jackson, the Catholic diocese in Jackson, and Myers Park Baptist Church in North Caroli-

[20] Sophia Halkias, interview with Dr. Charles Kimball, *Jackson Free Press*, February 1, 2006, http://t.jacksonfreepress.com/news/2006/feb/01/dr-charles-kimball/.

[21] N News 5 6 06.

[22] N Bulletin 5 13 07.

[23] N Deacons 08 06; N News 7 17 07.

na—one of the first Baptist churches to formalize a comprehensive policy of its kind in response to the sex abuse scandals affecting faith communities across the nation, most notably the Catholic Church. "It is sad to think that the times in which we live warrant our church developing 'Policies and Procedures for the Protection of Minors and Vulnerable Adults,' but hopefully our church's efforts to be proactive rather than reactive will help to ensure the safety of our children, youth, and vulnerable adults," Joyner wrote to the congregation.[24]

The youth ministry continued to strengthen into the 2000s with heightened participation in hands-on service projects. Northminster youth displayed their commitment to the Jackson community through Habitat for Humanity builds, annual MLK service projects, as well as joining in disaster relief efforts in the aftermath of Hurricane Katrina. During spring 2006, the youth took part in a trip to Bayou La Batre, Alabama, to assist with the disaster relief work, bringing with them donated tools to leave behind for Volunteers of America. The previous year a youth fundraiser raised money to benefit those affected by the December 2004 tsunami in Southeast Asia, which killed more than 200,000 in Sri Lanka and Indonesia and devastated hundreds of thousands of families in the region.[25]

Ministries of Missions and Stewardship

Financial support of missions continued its uptick throughout the mid-2000s. An impressive 21 percent of the annual budget in 2006 and 2007 was designated directly to missions. Local and direct missions support through the Missions Committee featured a diverse array of ministries such as Baptist Children's Village; Beginning Again in Christ, a nonprofit preparing those in correctional institutions for re-entry into society; Catholic Charities; Exchange Club Parent Child Center, an organization working to prevent child abuse and improve quality of life for families at-risk of abuse; Habitat for Humanity; Hospice of Central Mississippi; Mustard Seed, a ministry serving adults with special needs; Salt and Light, a local ministry seeking to holistically serve the poor in Honduras (born from a Honduras ministry of Northminster and other Mississippi churches); Magnolia Speech School; Mission Mississippi; Mississippi Food Network; New Life for

[24] N Deacons 06.
[25] N News 1 18 05; N News 5 1 07; N News 3 29 06.

Women, a residential treatment program for women battling addiction; Operation Shoestring; Stewpot Community Services; Young Life, a mission focused on reaching adolescent youth; and Grace House, a Jackson ministry supporting people living with HIV/AIDS.[26]

Northminster also continued to support a significant number of local, national and global Baptist organizations and initiatives through its Denominational Relations Committee such as the Metro Baptist Association, Mississippi Baptist Convention, Baptist World Alliance, Alliance of Baptists, Cooperative Baptist Fellowship, CBF of Mississippi, Associated Baptist Press, Baptist Joint Committee for Religious Liberty, Baptist Women in Ministry, Wake Forest University School of Divinity, McAfee School of Theology at Mercer University, Central Baptist Theological Seminary, George W. Truett Theological Seminary at Baylor University, Baptist House of Studies at Duke University, Baptist Theological Seminary at Richmond, Advent Spirituality Center and Christian Ethics Today. The church's longtime support for many of these organizations revealed a focus on and faithfulness to supporting missions and ministries in the state of Mississippi as well as most of the major organizations within Cooperative Baptist Fellowship life devoted to global missions, theological education, religious freedom, and an independent Baptist press. With support for six different seminaries, Northminster demonstrated a strong desire for diverse theological education options in Baptist life.

Despite several consecutive years of budget surpluses, Northminster's collections fell slightly short of its annual budget in 2001. From 2001 through 2005, the church collected more than 99 percent of its budget in three years with slight dips in 2003 (92.9 percent) and 2004 (97.5 percent). In 2006, collections totaled 109.1 percent of annual budget. In late 2006, just prior to annual budget pledge cards being sent out to members, Brian Brewer preached a sermon encouraging increased financial support. Like his predecessors, Brewer made the oft-heard plea for members to tithe, noting that the church's budget could easily be doubled to more than $2.5 million if the 450 active families of the church "tithed the minimum 10 percent." He pointed out that only 261 of the church's 450-plus families gave financially in the previous year. "For the last several years here at Northminster we have crossed our fingers and hoped not that we met the budget but that we met at

[26] N Minutes 10 18 05; N Minutes 10 17 06; N Minutes 11 11 07.

least our expenses at year's end," Brewer said. "Isn't that a shame? Think of the incredible ministry we could have for Christ if we just all of us tithed."[27]

Ministry of Worship

In 2007, Northminster Baptist Church celebrated the completion of its magnificent pipe organ to its original design. When the church's sanctuary was built in 1973, funds were not left for the purchase of a pipe organ, so an organ fund was started. Donations trickled in and accumulated over time. Meanwhile, an electric organ accompanied the choir and congregation. Five years later, in 1978, the Austin Organ Company began designing a pipe organ for the sanctuary, thanks to the fund and major gifts from Roger Stribling Sr. and Ben Puckett in memory of beloved member Roger Wilson Stribling Jr., who had died in a plane crash in 1975. The organ builders, Bernard Higgins and Zoltan Zsitvay, designed and constructed what has been hailed as "one of the finest organs in the world" and a "work of art in and of itself."[28]

The original design of the pipe organ included pipes, which the church was not able to afford in 1978 but which were installed in 1981. In 2006, the Stribling family made a gift in memory of Mattie Lou Stribling, mother of Roger Stribling Jr. and a patron of the arts, to complete construction of the organ—a longtime dream of hers. The new pipes, installed by organ builder David Finch, were said to give the organ more "versatility, breadth, and depth." A special service was held on August 26, 2007, to dedicate and bless the completed organ. Northminster organist Billy Trotter and the church choir and music minister Tim Coker led the celebratory late afternoon service. In an invitation to the event, the worship-centered identity of Northminster was highlighted:

> Since its beginning in 1967, Northminster has been a worship-centered church. The Charter Members of Northminster blended the best elements of the early Christian church, our Baptist heritage and the rituals of "high church" to establish Northminster's God focused worship tradition.... Worship at Northminster has always been about God and God's interaction with us. Scripture readings, thoughtful selection of written meditations, meaningful prayers and music all lead us to be

[27] Brian Brewer, "The Sermon on the Amount," sermon, November 12, 2006.
[28] N News 8 15 07.

> spiritually and mentally sensitive to God's presence. Music is a fundamental element of worship. Sacred music transcends the mental and communicates directly with the heart, directly with the spiritual and emotional part of our being. Music at Northminster is selected to reflect the same timeless and permanent quality that characterizes the other elements of the worship service. The choir and organ together lead and encourage the congregation to participate in the act of worship. God call us to make a joyful noise.[29]

The church hosted a celebratory concert on September 12, 2008, featuring world renowned organist Todd Wilson, who served as professor of organ at Indiana University's Jacobs School of Music. In the concert program, Trotter shared more about Northminster's Austin organ and its role in the context of the church's worship-centered identity:

> An organ by nature is a unique instrument that combines multiple sound characters that can be used individually or in a myriad of combinations. The room in which the organ is played also greatly influences the character of its sound. The most skillfully built organ will never sound entirely pleasing in a room without natural resonance. Likewise, an organ with deficiencies may sound very good in a room that is very resonant. The uniqueness of the Northminster organ is partially due to the fact that all pipe organs are designed and built for a particular location and no two will sound exactly the same. The Northminster organ is also unusual in that there exists a fortunate unity between the way the organ was designed and built and the acoustical character of the sanctuary. Those responsible for designing and building the pipes seemed to have been inspired to make them suited to the room. Sounds from the softest to the loudest combine in a manner similar to multiple instruments played individually. This is one factor that contributes to its crispness and clarity.
>
> This organ was designed specifically for the worship of God as practiced at Northminster. Its primary function is to lead and support the congregation's participation in the singing of hymns. This requires a quantity of sound as well as a sound that clearly delineates the hymn tune and articulates the rhythm and beat of the music. These goals are completely achieved, and this contributes to its uniqueness. Another purpose of the organ is to accompany choir and soloists as well as play

[29] Ibid.

organ music for various parts of the worship service. The organ is also available to play music for weddings and funerals. All of these goals are superbly achieved.[30]

Brian Brewer elaborated on the centrality of worship and music to Northminster's identity in a May 2007 sermon celebrating the church's fortieth anniversary. "Our music and worship here, they have that power," Brewer said. "It is power from no human, but a power from above. The words we sang as children are those that sustain us or rebuild us as adults." Brewer noted that when the congregation heard the ancient words of Scripture and sang hymns from generations ago, they "join in with our parents before us, our children behind us and know in God's house we are home." "'Lord, you have been our dwelling place in all generations,' says the psalmist. That, I think in part," Brewer continued, "is what this congregation decided would be important, that God would be central. 'Distinctive but orthodox, different but nevertheless Baptist.' That describes Northminster, doesn't it?"[31]

Church Covenant

During spring 2006, Neva Eklund, chair of the Denominational Relations Committee, recommended that the Northminster Baptist Church covenant be amended to reflect the congregation's fifteen-year association with the Cooperative Baptist Fellowship. The proposal requested to amend the sixth paragraph of the covenant, which stated: "Committed to serving, we gladly enter the larger fellowship of the Christian community, especially into the Metro Baptist Association, the Mississippi Baptist Convention, the Southern Baptist Convention, the Baptist World Alliance and the Alliance of Baptists as we seek cooperatively to serve Christ in our world."[32] Since its adoption in 1967, the covenant had rarely been revised. In 1990, the church voted to add the Southern Baptist Alliance to both the bylaws and church covenant, and, at some point, the covenant was updated to include the new names of the church's affiliations: Metro Baptist Association and the Alliance of Baptists (formerly Southern Baptist Alliance). The Denominational

---

[30] N Bulletin 8 26 07.

[31] Brian Brewer, "In All Generations," sermon, Northminster Baptist Church, May 20, 2007.

[32] N Deacons 4 23 06.

Relations Committee had previously proposed amending the bylaws and covenant to denote Northminster's affiliation with CBF, but this proposal was referred to the Bylaws Committee, and no further action was ever taken.[33]

The deacons discussed the committee's recommendation, and some questioned whether it was necessary to list all of the church's Baptist partners in its covenant. Brewer told the deacons that most church covenants list beliefs and principles rather than specific affiliations. After much discussion, the motion to adopt the recommendation was tabled, and the committee was asked to reconvene and consider including beliefs and principles rather than listing affiliations.[34]

A month later, the Long-Range Planning Committee proposed revising the church covenant to list core Baptist beliefs such as priesthood of the believer, autonomy of the local church, authority of Scripture, separation of church and state, and believer's baptism. The committee also proposed removing references to specific Baptist groups.[35] "Our mission is what our members determine," they wrote. "First who, then what. This is how Northminster began. The first members vigorously debated what Northminster would be and do. The Covenant was the result. It is our mission statement. It is also the definitive statement of who we are and what we believe. It is our bedrock statement."[36]

The report of the Long-Range Planning Committee said that while the covenant had only one minor revision in forty years, it should be reviewed and changed "as times and members change." The covenant "still appears current and appropriate with one exception," the report read. This "one exception" was the listing of specific Baptist affiliations. The committee contended that "a more lasting and universal way to express our relationship with the Christian community is to state our fundamental Baptist beliefs and connections with churches that also embrace these principles."[37]

---

[33] Ibid.

[34] Ibid.

[35] Northminster Baptist Church Long-Range Planning Committee, Summary of Phase 2 Report, May 23, 2006.

[36] Ibid.

[37] Ibid.

To support its proposal, the committee solicited the perspective of the church's founding pastor, Dudley Wilson. In a letter, Wilson observed that the covenant had listed its Baptist affiliations in 1967 as a means to demonstrate its place within the mainstream of Baptist life and boost its credibility among other Baptists and prospective church members.[38] "It is my opinion that the statement was not intended to be irrevocable but would be subject to review and/or amendment at any point on the journey," he wrote. "It was a beginning point for the infant church, a church which would grow in many directions, changing as it progressed and matured."[39] Wilson suggested that a revision should "express appreciation for the vital principles that have historically characterized Baptists." The covenant, he related, "should be viewed as dynamic, not stagnant; subject to periodic review, and, where necessary, change that reflects the life of the congregation."[40]

At its March 2007 meeting, the Denominational Relations Committee received a formal recommendation from the Long-Range Planning Committee to revise the covenant's sixth paragraph to add the following statement of core Baptist beliefs and remove references to affiliations. The proposed paragraph read (new language in italics):

> Aware that as bearers of His name we personally embrace His Lordship, we shall strive in all of our ways and relationships, in our families, the church and the wider community, to honor and serve Him. *We hold these core beliefs: the autonomy of the local church, the soul competency of the individual, the priesthood of the believer, the authority of the scriptures, religious freedom, and believer's baptism.* Committed to serving, we gladly enter into the larger fellowship of the Christian community *with other churches that hold these beliefs* as we seek cooperatively to serve Christ in our world.[41]

In proposing this recommendation, Kelley Williams Sr., chair of the Long-Range Planning Committee, explained that the references to other Baptist groups needed to be removed for a variety of reasons. "Over time

---

[38] Dudley Wilson to Northminster Baptist Church, April 19, 2006.

[39] Ibid.

[40] Ibid.

[41] "Recommended Changes to and Restatement of Northminster Baptist Church Covenant," Denominational Relations Committee, March 2007.

these organizations changed, and our membership changed," Williams Sr. wrote.

> Some members now support some of the organizations and oppose others. Some members don't know what the organizations stand for and have little interest in what they see as denominational politics. The inclusion of these relationships in the Covenant is divisive for some members and irrelevant or meaningless for others. As a result, the Covenant is not being used in worship and embodied in our church life as it once was.[42]

Williams Sr. noted that the proposed Baptist beliefs were "the foundation on which our Northminster values and distinctives rest." "They are not subject to changing organizations or denominational politics. They are also clearer and more meaningful than the existing statement of organization affiliations and are more likely to be understood and accepted by our members," Williams Sr. wrote. He added that Brian Brewer, as well as past pastors Dudley Wilson and Chuck Poole, had expressed support for the proposed changes.[43]

The Denominational Relations Committee made several tweaks to the Long-Range Planning Committee's recommendation, changing "the priesthood of the believer" to "the priesthood of all believers"—the latter phrasing commonly viewed as offering a greater balance between the biblical emphases on the individual and community.[44] The original recommendation stated, "Committed to serving, we gladly enter into the larger fellowship of the Christian community with other churches that hold these beliefs." The committee revised this to read, "Committed to serving, we gladly enter into relationships for mission and ministry with other Baptist churches that share these beliefs and into the larger fellowship of the Christian community." This revision gave the covenant a more intentional ecumenical emphasis. The committee also tweaked the proposal to affirm a belief in "the practice of believer's baptism," rather than simply "believer's baptism"—language that fit better with the church's open and ecumenical approach toward baptism.[45] The deacons adopted the Denominational Relations Committee's

---

[42] Ibid.
[43] Ibid.
[44] Ibid.
[45] Ibid.

proposal and the church then approved the changes.[46] At the end of the evaluation and planning process, church members affirmed a general Baptist identity of historic principles, but in a way that most any Baptist in almost any Baptist group could affirm. Not identifying specific affiliations in the church covenant was seen to be helpful to those who really did not care about Baptist identity. They could accept the principles as compatible with their larger Christian identity or simply as part of the faith community called Northminster. The lack of specific affiliations in the church covenant, given that the document previously had them, appeared as a way to approach the diversity of opinion in the congregation about denominational affiliation. Left unsaid, in 2006, was that in hiring, in worship, in the approach to interfaith witness and ecumenism—in other words, in the practice of faith at the church, the congregation's identity was a moderate Baptist one, a progressive Baptist community. At the same time, they were, as they always had been, strong supporters of the Mississippi Baptist Convention. In 2006, the majority of ministry monies were allotted to the Cooperative Baptist Fellowship and to the Mississippi Baptist Convention—the leadership of the latter increasingly not in tune with the CBF. A decade later, having a covenant of basic Baptist principles would not be enough to avoid the tensions of what being Baptist meant as the Mississippi Baptist Convention became increasingly uncooperative with Northminster Baptist Church.

Ministry of the Laity: Every Member a Minister

During John Thomason's pastorate in the late 1980s, the phrase "Every Member a Minister" began to take shape as an unofficial motto of Northminster. Proudly a lay-led church, "Every Member a Minister" was first included in the Sunday worship bulletin on July 19, 1987.[47] The phrase began to appear under the heading "The Ministry of the Church" on the bulletin's back cover with paid personnel listed beneath the motto. For years prior, the subheading had read simply "Church Staff," but beginning in 1987 the bulletin featured this motto and ministry-focused subheading. The weekly *Northminster News* began to include the motto as well with the August 11, 1987, issue.[48] In 1991, Roger Paynter mentioned the motto and offered his

[46] N Deacons 7 8 07.
[47] N Bulletin 7 19 87.
[48] N News 8 11 87.

understanding of its meaning, which is instructive for interpreting the church's purpose and understanding for what would later become a very popular and arguably overused slogan in moderate and progressive Baptist life:

> And every week, we print these words in the bulletin: "Every member a minister." Which simply stated means, "Every member a representative of Jesus Christ." "Every member an ambassador for Christ." Wherever you are, whatever you do. You see, any task we take on must grow out of that foundation. We perpetuate the ministry of Jesus Christ because it is the shared life in Christ that is our reason for being. We have not been called into being by a common task. We are not here to be a different kind of church. Rather, we are here because Christ called us together, and if we share that calling with one another in honest commitment, we will be a different kind of church. Because, precisely because, most churches are formed around the task.[49]

The 1998 report of the Long-Range Planning Committee noted the centrality of the motto to Northminster's identity as a lay-led church. "There remains an unswerving commitment to the Northminster philosophy of 'Every Member a Minister,' making as much effort as possible to 'do church ourselves,' keeping professional staff to a minimum."[50]

Brian Brewer referenced the popular motto several times in sermons during his brief tenure. Describing "Every Member a Minister" as the church's "hedgehog concept," he emphasized that living out this motto made the church "both biblical and unique":

> Though Northminster shares in similar ministries to other churches and does many of our ministries well, what makes Northminster distinctive is our conviction and practice of "Every Member a Minister." This is our hedgehog concept. Northminster values the input of laity and places the responsibility of ministering not just in the hands of a few, but each one to all the others. "Every Member a Minister," from Luther's concept of the "Priesthood of All Believers," comes as both a liberating privilege and a burdensome responsibility. What must continue to be Northminster's single focus is not any program or mission,

[49] Roger Paynter, "The Task of the Church," sermon, Northminster Baptist Church, October 10, 1991.

[50] 1998 Long-Range Planning Committee Report.

> but that all our missions and ministries appropriate this conviction, with clergy and laity partnering together. This makes our churches both biblical and unique.[51]

Brewer again referenced the motto in his Reformation Sunday sermon later in the year on October 29, 2006:

> Now we are obliged to one another, to be priests to one another, to pray for one another. Because Christ is our eternal and perfect High Priest, we are freed to be priests and to minister to each other. This is why Northminster, through its forty years of existence, has kept the motto: "Every Member a Minister." It is because we bear a responsibility to one another—"the priesthood of all believers."[52]

And in his next-to-last sermon at Northminster, Brewer again brought up this "hedgehog concept," suggesting, notably that perhaps the church had overreached in its application of "Every Member a Minister" and caused confusion with regard to the role of the pastor: "Now, to be honest, there are times I think we at Northminster have understood this principle so well of 'Every Member a Minister' that it makes the role of pastor uncertain. And I hope in the coming years this church will have a more balanced approach to lay and pastoral leadership. But the basic Protestant principle must remain: we must minister to each other, all of us."[53]

Despite this suggested uncertainty at times in the leadership relations between pastor and laity, Northminster Baptist Church without a doubt had publicly reclaimed the priesthood of all believers through the adoption of this motto, perhaps to such an extent to cause frustration, at times, to staff ministers. In addition, the timing of the embrace of this restated Christian principle of the Reformation was no coincidence. The "priesthood of all believers" or soul freedom/soul competency had been under assault by fundamentalists in the Southern Baptist Convention throughout the 1980s. In 1988, the year following the church's first use of the motto in Sunday worship, this cornerstone theological concept would come under attack. A reso-

---

[51] Brian Brewer, "What Wondrous Love," sermon, Northminster Baptist Church, May 15, 2006.

[52] Brian Brewer, "Our High Priest," sermon, Northminster Baptist Church, October 29, 2006.

[53] Brian Brewer, "A Royal Priesthood," sermon, Northminster Baptist Church, April 29, 2007.

lution, which was narrowly adopted by SBC messengers at the denomination's annual meeting, declared the Baptist distinctive as a "recent historical development" that had "been used to justify wrongly the attitude that a Christian may believe whatever he so chooses and still be considered a loyal Southern Baptist."[54]

That the church would make this their "hedgehog concept" in 1987 demonstrated its commitment to a Baptist identity rooted in an uncoerced faith—a faith which valued and recognized the necessity of an active laity. Since its founding in 1967, Northminster had attempted to live more fully into what it understood to be a biblical expectation to be involved in ministry through service to the church and the world.

Staff

During spring 2006, Northminster Baptist Church celebrated two retiring staff members: Shirley Foster and Betty Beasley. Beasley, the financial secretary since August 1993, and Foster, the office manager, had served the church staff for a combined twenty-five years. Brewer honored the women in his weekly *Northminster News* column, praising their quiet service. "So as they leave, they leave a gap here," Brewer wrote.

> But this gap is not one simply filled by hiring other employees. For Betty and Shirley were far more than "employees." Their love for this church and their gifts of working with its details were ministries to us all. So the vacancies will be found less behind their desks and more in our own hearts. Countless times they were interrupted when checks suddenly had to be cut, reminder cards suddenly sent, or special services suddenly rendered. Betty and Shirley quietly helped staff, committee chairs, deacons and other members whenever the need arose. And so, their rest from their labors comes well deserved.[55]

Northminster also celebrated organist Billy Trotter and community minister Jill Barnes Buckley in 2007. Trotter was recognized on January 21, 2007, for thirty years as the church's organist. To celebrate the occasion, Northminster hosted an afternoon anniversary recital by one of Trotter's

[54] "Resolution on the Priesthood of the Believer," Southern Baptist Convention, June 1988, http://www.sbc.net/resolutions/872/resolution-on-the-priesthood-of-the-believer.

[55] N News 4 25 06.

former students, Len Bobo.[56] Later in the year, Northminster ordained Barnes Buckley. Guest worship leaders at the October 14 service included Jo Hollman; former Northminster associate pastor Stan Wilson; Chuck Poole; and Buckley's brother, Terry Barnes, a minister at Parkview Baptist Church in Monroe, Louisiana.[57]

Brewer's Departure

Nineteen months into his tenure at Northminster, Brian Brewer informed the congregation of his plans to join the faculty of Baylor University's George W. Truett Theological Seminary as an assistant professor of Christian theology. Brewer said that he had been struggling with his "ultimate calling as a Christian minister and how best to use my gifts to further God's Church and Kingdom." He explained to the congregation that the invitation to return to Baylor's Truett Seminary, his alma mater, was a "dream come true."[58] Brewer added that he had been drawn to academia since his days as a freshman at Baylor University in the late 1980s. He shared that an opportunity to teach simply had never presented itself and so he was "called in to the traditional church pastorate." "While being a pastor has been enjoyable and rewarding beyond what I could imagine, the ministry of teaching continued to tug at my heart, though I made my best attempts to suppress it," Brewer wrote to the congregation. "And so it is through many prayers and tears that I feel led to inform you all of the status of my spiritual pilgrimage. I hope you will understand that in many ways this [2007] Lenten season has been a desert experience for me like none other I have experienced." He emphasized that he had questioned his own motives, God's timing, and God's will for Northminster as well as the seminary, and, yet, believed he was "following God's leadership" in the decision to depart.[59]

In his column in *Northminster News* at the end of May 2007, Brewer offered a few additional parting words, emphasizing that Northminster had been a home to him like no other previous church: "I thank you for that," he said. "I thank you for teaching me how to become a better pastor, preacher,

---

[56] N News 1 10 07.
[57] N Bulletin 10 14 07.
[58] Brian Brewer to Northminster Congregation, March 20, 2007.
[59] Ibid.

counselor, friend. Thank you for being patient with my foibles, open to my ideas, and forgiving of my missteps. I thank you for the gifts of your time, your listening, your gifts, your presence. I thank you for loving me as I tried to work to minister to you."[60]

Interim Period

A search committee was formed six weeks before Brewer's final sermon, and in July the deacons voted to affirm the recommendation of the Pulpit Supply Committee to call Bill Hill as interim pastor. Hill was an Old Testament scholar who had served as a dean at Central Baptist Theological Seminary in Kansas City, Kansas.[61] After these events, associate pastor Amy Joyner encouraged the congregation to use this interim period to reflect on Northminster's purpose and seek to discern what is "essential":

> As a community of faith, we find ourselves once again in an interim period. This is the perfect opportunity for us as a congregation to ask the question of ourselves, "What is essential?" The answer to this question will tell us much about who we are and who we want to call as our next senior pastor. What is essential to our communal life as a family of faith and to our individual lives as followers of Jesus? What is the "one needful thing" that God wants to shape our lives? What is Northminster's purpose here on the corner of Ridgewood and Eastover? Many things can be helpful and even good, but not everything can be essential. May we all have the discernment to seek what is essential and the courage to hold lightly that which is not.[62]

Just six months into its work, the search committee, chaired by Kelley Williams Sr., had found its candidate to present to the church. With a unanimous recommendation, the committee selected Brian Brewer's predecessor and Northminster's fifth senior pastor, Chuck Poole, to return to his previous position.[63]

Undoubtedly, this was a very unusual move for a search committee to make. However, it was not without precedent in the community. Frank Pollard, the renowned preacher and much-beloved senior pastor of First Baptist

---

[60] N News 5 30 07.

[61] N Deacons 7 2 07; N Minutes 4 15 07

[62] N News 7 31 07.

[63] N Minutes 11 4 07.

Church in Jackson, had served the historic congregation from 1976 until 1983 when he was named president of Golden Gate Baptist Theological Seminary in San Francisco, California. Three years later, Pollard would return to the FBC Jackson pulpit as pastor and stay put until his retirement in 2002.[64] Northminster members hoped Poole would follow the same path as Pollard.

Since his departure in 2003, Poole had served as community minister of the LifeShare Foundation, a Jackson-based nonprofit foundation striving to meet unmet needs in the lives of at-risk and underprivileged children in Mississippi. Poole had also served as an interim at nearby Madison Baptist Fellowship during this time. "Our committee knows [Poole] to be an authentic man of God, who is blessed with tremendous gifts as a preacher, teacher and pastoral care-giver," the search committee wrote to the congregation. "We believe that he meets each of the criteria set forth at the beginning of our search, and we believe that both our committee and Chuck have been led by God to this decision."[65]

After the church voted to call Poole, he wrote a note of reflection on the unlikely direction of his ministry journey:

> Seven or eight years ago I was in the pastor's study at Northminster, reading from Wendell Berry's beautiful book, *A Timbered Choir*, when I stumbled across his marvelous sentence, "We live the given life, not the planned." So struck was I by the truth of those words that I stopped reading, borrowed some scissors from Barbara Webb, cut the sentence from the page and taped it to the top ledge of the middle drawer of the big desk. Last week, I stopped by the church, went into the study and opened the drawer, just to see. Sure enough, there it was; a bit yellowed by the years but staring back at me nonetheless: "We live the given life, not the planned."
>
> Indeed we do. Ten years ago when Marcia and I moved to Jackson with sixteen-year-old Josh and twelve-year-old Maria, if someone had told us we would serve Northminster for six years, leave to serve the community for four years, then return to serve a second time at Northmin-

---

[64] "Dr. Frank Pollard," obituary, *The Clarion-Ledger*, http://www.legacy.com/obituaries/clarionledger/obituary.aspx?pid=121039207.

[65] Northminster Pastor Search Committee to Northminster Baptist Church, October 22, 2007.

> ster, we would have dismissed that as the most unlikely of travel plans. And yet, here we are, living "the given life, not the planned." When we came to worship, learn and serve with you ten years ago it was, for us, a gift from God. Our lives were formed, shaped, challenged and stretched by our years among you. When I left your pulpit four years ago to serve as the LifeShare Foundation's community minister, that too was a great gift. Never has a minister had more freedom to do more good in more places than I have had for these four years of ministry in Jackson's inner-city, as well as in areas of need from Canton to Tchula to Eupora. And now, to return to worship, learn and serve with you again is a gift of grace revisited. About all of the above, I can only say, "We live the given life, not the planned." For all of the above, I can only say "Thanks be to God."[66]

In 2001, Northminster began its Wider Net initiative during the first tenure of Chuck Poole and sustained it during the ministry of Brian Brewer. As Wider Net increasingly became central to the ministry of the church, there was no one more equipped—head and heart—to work with staff like Jill Barnes Buckley and the larger congregation than Poole, long known for his deep and abiding commitments to ministry to the oppressed and disadvantaged.

[66] N News 11 14 07.

Chapter 8

A Wider Net: Community Missions in a New Century

Beginnings

Just as the tenure of Chuck Poole was beginning in early 1997, a Long-Range Planning Committee was beginning its work to study every aspect of the church, including staffing, membership, finances, programs, and especially its facilities. Such committees were nothing new—committees for Long-Range Planning had been used at intervals, often every five years, to assess Northminster's present situation and focus on the future. After a nine-month process, the Long-Range Planning Committee, chaired by Mary Foose, brought forward numerous recommendations for the congregation's consideration. Most notably, the committee recommended constructing additional education space and a columbarium. The committee also urged the completion of the sanctuary balcony—a long expressed desire of many members, who took note that worshipers were often forced to sit in the narthex on Sunday morning due to overcrowding.[1] Foose embodied the lay led leadership present in the congregation and her support for the balcony project was pivotal. A member of Broadway Baptist Church, Fort Worth, Texas, when John Claypool was the pastor there, Foose had moved to Jackson and earned the respect of fellow church members at Northminster Baptist Church.

The committee also suggested that another committee focused on a special missions project be formed to identify an opportunity for "deep and broad involvement in a particular neighborhood that could provide permanent programs in which church members would be active over a sustained period of time." "Work could be achieved in partnership with institutions (religious or otherwise) currently involved in the area," the recommendation said. "A goal of the project would be to identify a specific area of need that is not being addressed and establish plans to provide necessary support."[2]

---

[1] 1998 Long-Range Planning Committee Report.

[2] Ibid.

From this report, an ad hoc Building Study Committee was created, chaired by John Clark. This committee recommended to the deacons on October 16, 1999, that Northminster proceed with construction of the sanctuary balcony and additional educational space. Two months later, the congregation voted to appoint a Building Committee to develop specific plans for these facility additions and improvements as well as appoint a Special Missions Project Committee to work in tandem with the Building Committee and develop plans to fulfill the Long-Range Planning Committee's recommendation for a concentrated and sustained long-term missions effort in Jackson. Cheryl Allen and Jim Warren were named to chair the Special Missions Project Committee and Building Committee respectively.[3]

Chuck Poole preferred that the church not invest in the construction of a balcony. As the congregation continued its planning, he expressed his desire to see, in light of a building project, a dollar-for-dollar commitment to missions. Consequently, as the church adopted plans to move forward with a building project, it did so with a commitment to making a comparable investment "outside the walls" of Northminster. In his report to the congregation on behalf of the ad hoc Building Study Committee, John Clark said that the group was aware that many members shared the aphorism of its pastor that the church should "Do the minimum where we are, and the maximum where we aren't."[4] "Theoretically, the committee agrees with this aphorism," Clark wrote. "However, on balance, the committee feels that adding to the capacity and comfort of our physical facilities in modest ways such as those proposed is likely to attract more worshipers-donors and increase our financial ability to expand our missions effort—not detract from it." Clark contended that the building recommendations would not result in "taking water from the missions bucket" but, through attracting more members, would "attract more water to that bucket."[5] Practically speaking, it was effective long-range planning to do something inside the church's walls to encourage new innovation outside the church's walls.

The new Building Committee hired Jim Eley of Eley & Associates to begin its work. Nine months later, the deacons received reports from both

---

[3] "The Timeline for 'A Wider Net.'" Documents related to Wider Net can be accessed via the church's Wider Net Dropbox archives.

[4] John Clark to Northminster Congregation, November 22, 1999.

[5] Ibid.

committees with proposals for construction of a balcony, columbarium, and educational space as well as a new neighborhood ministry focusing on the Mid-City/Georgetown community of Jackson.[6] According to the United States Census of 2000, the Mid-City/Georgetown community was just over 97 percent African-American with a household median income of $18,000 for Georgetown and $13,000 for Mid-City, below the national poverty line and significantly lower than the nearly $34,000 median income for Hinds County (Jackson).[7]

The Special Missions Project Committee proposal, titled "A Wider Net," aimed to "begin and nurture a community ministry that would bring hope and opportunity to the people in the Mid-City/Georgetown area of Jackson, Mississippi, by touching their lives spiritually, physically and socially and by leading them to resources and cooperative activities that will empower them in the name of Christ." The committee was tasked to formulate a strategy to devote "a significant amount of money in places other than Northminster's own facilities."[8] The initiative suggested an asset-based and cooperative approach—a commitment to hear and incorporate the needs and desires of the community when planning activities through ongoing communication with neighborhood residents, associations, businesses, and partnerships and coordination with churches and agencies with ministries in the neighborhood.[9] Suggested ministries included home building in conjunction with Habitat for Humanity; adult literacy classes; after-school program for children and youth in cooperation with Operation Shoestring, a ministry partner of the church; home repair, especially for elderly homeowners; upgrading of community spaces such as parks and playgrounds; food pantry; drug and alcohol rehabilitation; job training and computer classes; and other activities based on community needs.[10]

According to member Courtney Allen, who wrote her seminary thesis on the Wider Net initiative and whose mother chaired the Special Missions Project Committee, the committee "understood their work as beyond the

---

[6] "The Timeline for 'A Wider Net.'"

[7] United States Census, 2000.

[8] Courtney Allen, "A Wider Net: Beyond the Walls and the Possibilities Which Lie Before Us" (master's thesis, Wake Forest University School of Divinity, 2010) 3.

[9] "A Wider Net Proposal."

[10] Ibid.

walls of the church and beyond the congregation's current realm of presence." During their many meetings, committee members shared personal experiences involving missions and covenanted to pray as individuals and pray as a committee for the congregation and the Wider Net initiative. The committee hoped to offer Northminster Baptist Church "a specific gospel deed (or deeds) that would embody the spirit of Christ, reflect the spirit of Northminster, and make a real difference in Jesus' name"—and desiring that its deed would be "something that might not occur if it were not for our efforts."[11]

During its discernment process, the committee spoke with Jackson community leaders and sought to ascertain the most important unmet need in Jackson while learning from local nonprofit leaders about inner-city ministry—hearing their experiences, both successes and failures. Over the course of eleven months, the committee held more than twenty-five meetings, not including many separate small gatherings with individuals and community leaders.[12] The committee, according to Allen, understood its efforts to be consistent with Northminster's covenant, which concludes, "Sharing a personal commitment to Jesus Christ and a deep concern for the world, and bound by the bonds of love and understanding, we seek to allow the church to be instrumental in accomplishing God's purpose in the world."[13]

After a lengthy study, countless hours of discussions, and tours of various local urban areas, the committee settled on (or "felt drawn to") the Mid-City/Georgetown neighborhood of Jackson—an area with significant needs that had been overlooked by other local faith-based organizations and nonprofits. Through conversations with residents, the committee learned that the neighborhood felt "left out" in the community. Additionally, the committee had connected and consulted with prospective partners Operation Shoestring, a neighborhood nonprofit serving children and families, and Wells United Methodist Church, a congregation in the neighborhood.[14] From this process of discernment, the committee articulated a vision based on three components: a person, a place, and a ministry. It proposed hiring a community minister "who would be a conduit between the needs of people

[11] Ibid.
[12] Ibid., 5.
[13] "A Wider Net," 2.
[14] Ibid., 5–6.

and families [in the neighborhood] and our congregation." It was also determined that a physical presence in the neighborhood—"a place"—was needed, whether that involved sharing space with a partner organization or purchasing a building. Finally, "a ministry" would be necessary to give church members opportunities to put their faith to action through hands-on missions, e.g., supporting Habitat for Humanity projects and volunteering with other already-established neighborhood programs.[15]

A church-wide meeting in March 2001 updated members on the work of the Special Missions Project Committee and Building Committee and offered a forum for conversation and feedback. An additional congregational "town meeting" was held on April 22, 2001 for purposes of education, information, feedback, and input. Members of the two committees also visited youth and adult Sunday school classes to answer questions regarding the building and missions proposals.[16]

The Board of Deacons approved the recommendations of the two committees on June 3, 2001. The building and missions projects of the committees—described as "one effort with two dimensions"—was named "A Wider Net." The name "A Wider Net" was chosen because the special missions committee felt Jesus' image of the Kingdom of God as a net far flung and filled full was a powerful metaphor for the mission of the church. Citing Matthew 13:47 ("The Kingdom of heaven is like a net that was thrown into the sea and caught fish of every kind"), Allen explained that the imagery of a "wide net" invited the congregation to embrace those beyond its walls. "It was in this spirit that *A Wider Net* was chosen as the moniker for Northminster's efforts to create new and lasting structures that would result in 'a wider place to gather within our walls as well as a wider embrace of others beyond our walls,'" she wrote.[17]

Prior to the introduction of Wider Net, Chuck Poole had preached numerous sermons challenging the congregation to leave its comfort zone in service of others, emphasizing the themes of "embrace" and "boundaries." "Jesus had long arms that reached over walls across hard lines and around weary souls," Poole preached. "Aren't you glad? I know I am because if the long arms of God's love did not have room to embrace everybody, I would

[15] Ibid., 6–10.
[16] "The Timeline for 'A Wider Net.'"
[17] Ibid., 13.

be as likely to be left out as anyone. And so would you…everyone is embraced, welcomed, and received by the long-armed love of God."[18] Poole's sermons "shaped and molded the membership at Northminster," according to Allen, preparing the congregation for this next stage in their journey together.[19]

In adopting the Wider Net proposals, the deacons recommended that Northminster Baptist Church immediately begin constructing the balcony and making other improvements to the existing building as well as begin the missions initiative in the Mid-City/Georgetown neighborhood. The deacons voted to use the remaining $109,000 of the budget surplus from 2000 along with short-term financing to subsidize the balcony construction. The remaining construction of the 5,500 square feet of educational space would not begin until $2 million in pledges had been received. The congregation voted the following week to move forward with A Wider Net.[20]

The total cost for the Wider Net initiative was nearly $3.3 million, with 31 percent ($1,048,960) devoted to the long-term missions commitment in the Mid-City/Georgetown neighborhood. This made Wider Net the most expensive project Northminster had ever undertaken and significantly increased the church's financial commitment to missions. When Northminster contracted to build its Ridgewood Road sanctuary in September 1971, it did so at a cost of $480,000, and its construction of the Great Hall, bell tower, additional educational space and expanded parking in 1986 was $1.5 million.[21]

To offer support for this project, a "frequently asked questions" document was produced outlining the significant member growth that Northminster had experienced since its 1971 building project. The church's facilities had become a hub throughout the week for numerous community activities. Northminster had grown from a church of 56 families and 133 members at the time of its founding in 1967 to a congregation of 360 families totaling 650 persons. Throughout the week, outside organizations used the church's facilities, serving as the meeting place for two troops of Girl Scouts, two Brownie troops, four packs of Cub Scouts, five women CoDA

[18] Allen, "A Wider Net," 31.
[19] Ibid.
[20] Ibid.
[21] "Frequently Asked Questions: Wider Net," handout.

members (Co-Dependents Anonymous), twenty book club participants, the Mississippi Children's Choir, and seventy children in the Northminster Children's Center. Church groups that met weekly included a Christian businessmen's prayer group, women's Bible study, men's prayer group, caregivers' meeting, and Meals on Wheels, to name a few.[22]

Wider Net: Continued Planning, Financing and Construction

The missions dimension in Mid-City/Georgetown kicked off during summer 2001 with a Northminster-sponsored picnic in Jaycee Park, regarded as the geographical center of the neighborhood. Even though the park was known in and outside the community as "dangerous" and under the control of the Wood Street Gang, nearly 100 people showed up for the event, and twice-a-week breakfasts and devotionals at Operation Shoestring also spurred the project along.[23]

As construction of the balcony at the church in north Jackson began during fall 2001, Northminster members built their first Habitat for Humanity home in the Mid-City neighborhood—the first of twenty new homes the congregation had committed to support over a five-year period (at a financial commitment of $570,000).

The fundraising campaign for A Wider Net officially began in May 2002 with a church-wide mailing of a brochure and pledge cards.[24] In March, the congregation had elected members to serve on the Pastor Search Committee to name an associate pastor for community ministry as part of the Wider Net initiative. The search committee sought a person who fell somewhere between being a sort of "village priest" with theological training and a traditional community organizer with a social-work background. Just over two years later, the committee called Jill Barnes to this role.[25]

The fundraising campaign was not an immediate success. Contributions stalled several months into the effort, and by fall 2002, only $1.3 million had been pledged.[26] At the one-year mark, the campaign was $200,000 short of the $2,000,000 pledges and payments needed to begin the second

---

[22] Ibid.
[23] Allen, "A Wider Net," 14.
[24] "The Timeline for 'A Wider Net.'"
[25] Allen, "A Wider Net," 16–18.
[26] N Deacons 8 18 02; N Deacons 10 20 02.

phase of construction. It took another full year for the campaign to reach the $2 million mark.[27]

In 2004, the Building Committee recommended that a columbarium be constructed alongside the education building. A columbarium subcommittee had been appointed in 2001 to determine the policies and regulations for the future home of members' urns, which would be situated in a garden between the sanctuary and the planned education building. The columbarium would have space for up to 600 urns, and the intention was that revenues from the niches in the columbarium—$1,500 for a single niche and $3,000 for a double niche—would help to pay for its construction and ongoing costs.[28] Those eligible to purchase a niche included Northminster members and clergy as well as former clergy or their surviving spouses. Several years later, in 2005, the terms of eligibility were broadened to include "friends of Northminster"—non-members who had a "substantial, long-term association and friendship with Northminster" as determined by the Columbarium Committee.[29]

A new estimate from Harvey Construction in 2005 put the cost of the next phase of construction at the church at $2.8 million—$800,000 more than the earlier estimate. The increase resulted, in part, from added scope to the parking lot and the columbarium. As the Building Committee finalized its plans and entered into a construction contract, the committee discovered that there had been an unprecedented increase in building costs due primarily to Hurricane Katrina and a worldwide rise in commodity prices. The estimate soared to $3.8 million, which included $400,000 for the columbarium and garden, which was regarded as self-funding—to be paid for with proceeds of niche sales.[30]

The congregation approved the new estimate and financial plan to fund the education building, columbarium/garden, and expanded parking lot during a special business meeting on February 12, 2006. During the groundbreaking service on April 23, 2006, members of the Building Committee led the congregation in a litany of dedication (Jean Williams), prayer of invoca-

[27] N Deacons 4 17 04.

[28] "Report to Deacons from Building Committee," November 29, 2004; N Deacons 10 13 99.

[29] N Deacons 10 15 06; N Deacons 5 20 07—"Columbarium Time Line."

[30] Kane Ditto, "Talk to Congregational Meeting," June 1, 2008.

tion (Susan Pratt), dedicatory remarks (Stewart Boone), and Scripture reading (Dana Kelly). The service concluded with the committee and architect, Jim Eley, and builder, Lucian Harvey, breaking ground.[31] Two years later, in March 2008, the project was completed. The total cost for the building dimension of A Wider Net was $4 million with $1.6 covered by pledges and contributions and $2.4 converted to long-term debt—resulting in a near $200,000 general budget line item for debt service.[32]

Forming Partnerships

With construction underway, Wider Net's missions initiative continued its commitment to build houses in the Mid-City/Georgetown area in partnership with Habitat for Humanity. As the initial act of ministry, Northminster members helped to build six Habitat houses and to purchase fourteen additional lots as future sites for Habitat homes. In March 2006, Northminster Baptist Church took part in Habitat's New Neighbor program to build ten houses for families displaced by Hurricane Katrina and Hurricane Rita.[33] Other early efforts included home repair projects, sponsorship of a youth internship at Operation Shoestring, art classes at Mid-City Community Center, and the hiring of Jill Barnes as associate pastor for community ministry in 2004. Also in 2006, for the sixth year in a row, Northminster members provided volunteers to the Project KIDS summer program of Operation Shoestring, leading short devotionals and serving breakfast each Tuesday and Thursday during the summer camp of seventy-five children ages five to twelve.[34] As many as fifty Northminster members usually assisted with the camp.[35] Barnes Buckley later reflected on this particular aspect of Wider Net:

> Lately, I've been looking through old photos from Summer Kids Clubs past. There are so many good memories. Many children from that first summer have moved away, but for those still in the neighborhood, our friendships are still going strong. In 2005, when we began this summertime ministry, our plan was simple. We showed up at the Commu-

---

[31] N Bulletin 4 23 06.
[32] Ibid. See also "A Brief History of Wider Net Funding."
[33] N News 3 1 06.
[34] N News 5 23 06. See also N News 6 10 09.
[35] N News 5 7 08.

> nity Center on Wood Street with games, food, and crafts and waited to see how many kids would come. We hired teens from the community as summer interns so that they could gain some work experience. By the end of the summer, we had amassed a core group of about 15 kids. Summer Kids Club 2009 will be the best summer yet. I admit: it's ambitious. Our plans include practicing reading, performing a play, taking swimming lessons, attending Upward Basketball camp at Mission First, painting and decorating children's bookcases with the youth, learning Bible lessons, doing crafts, cooking, eating lunch AND hanging out. I am both energized and exhausted just thinking about it![36]

In 2012, the goals of the summer camp had again evolved. Barnes Buckley told the congregation that summer camp had begun to focus "mainly on combating summer learning loss." There would be fun activities, but also math work and reading and language skills exercises. Barnes Buckley had facilitated several "dreaming" sessions with members of the ad hoc Wider Net Vision Committee with parents of children from the Mid-City. Her commentary summed up the worth and goals of the summer camp: "At those meetings, I was reminded that the hopes parents have for their children are the same almost everywhere: safety, good friends, good opportunities, and good mentors."[37]

Forming partnerships with community organizations and authentic relationships with community residents were two priorities of Wider Net in its first half-dozen years. During a presentation to the congregation in June 2001, Cheryl Allen, chairperson of the Special Missions Project Committee, emphasized the absolute importance of building relationships with the community. "That means listening to the people who live there and finding out what their concerns are," Allen said. "Not things that we think might be important or programs that we think might be a good idea. Building relationships within the community and partnering are two of the most important things that must be done."[38]

In 2002, a weekly Bible study was started in Mid-City. Chuck Poole led this Thursday morning class made up of ten residents and held at the Mid-City Community Center on Wood Street—or the "Yellow Church" as

[36] N News 5 3 09.
[37] N News 5 13 15.
[38] Allen, 38.

the neighborhood children began to refer to it several years later.[39] Poole recalls a "sacramental moment" that occurred at the Bible study. An offering was taken up by the small group of Mid-City residents to help pay for the medical bills of a Northminster member, whom they did not know. The group had been praying for the health and healing of the member for weeks, and on that Thursday morning collected $24, mostly wrinkled one-dollar bills, and presented it to Poole. "We went to Mid-City with our love, compassion and money, and eight years later it came to us...and those 24 dollars probably represented more sacrifice than our one million," Poole said. "This powerful gesture by the Wood Street Bible Study group illustrates the two-way street of need in this transformative relationship."[40]

Mutuality in Ministry

Five years into the initiative, Jill Barnes Buckley offered her reflections on the successes and challenges of Wider Net. She noted that partnerships with established organizations in the community such as Operation Shoestring and Habitat for Humanity had given the church "ready, concrete, tried opportunities for service." By using space already available rather than purchasing or constructing a building, Wider Net had been able to more effectively maximize community resources and build partnerships, she explained. She did note, however, that the lack of a building presented challenges that affected the availability or accessibility of services. She stressed that the need in the neighborhood was "overwhelming" and beyond the capacity of Northminster Baptist Church alone. "There is an overwhelming cry for activities for kids and teens," Barnes Buckley wrote. "We do not alone have the capacity of responding."[41]

Barnes Buckley emphasized that the church faced the challenge of the tension that existed between doing *for* and doing *with*—providing a program *for* versus working *with* the community as it charted its own course for confronting an issue. This *doing for* versus *doing with* extended to North-

[39] N News 5 1 07; "Wider Net Ministry: Report to the Long-Range Planning Committee," November 18, 2012.

[40] Allen, "A Wider Net," 40–41. For another brief reflection, calling the class a "a sign of God's love and care, embodied in Christian friendship," see N News 5 2 12.

[41] Jill Barnes Buckley, "Wider Net Reflections," N News, December 12, 2006.

minster's ministry of sharing the gospel of grace and love of Christ. "We use every opportunity [at the community center] to teach the children about God," she added. "Hopefully, we are giving them a good experience of 'church' but more importantly, living examples of God's grace and love."[42]

Yet, in their ministry *to* the children, Barnes Buckley noted that Northminster members were also recipients. Their ministry in Mid-City was often a mutual ministry, a ministry *with* the families of the neighborhood. "In a reversal characteristic of gospel tenor, we are the ones hearing the Good News anew! Particularly those of us who have the opportunity to connect with the older residents of the neighborhood, many of whom are people of deep and abiding faith," Barnes Buckley reflected.[43]

This acknowledgment of the tension between "doing for" versus "doing with" pointed to the intentional effort of Northminster, a congregation with a "tremendous amount of intellectual and financial capital," to be mindful of its own paternalistic tendencies and work to avoid approaches that too frequently have characterized the missions efforts of wealthy, predominantly white churches and Christian groups in lower-income neighborhoods and among people of color. Barnes Buckley noted that, for the most part, Northminster members in these early years rightly understood that the residents of Mid-City were "people not projects." Wider Net's commitment to the Mid-City neighborhood was rooted in "respect for the history, lives, families and institutions there," according to Courtney Allen.[44]

In sermons and communications, Chuck Poole and Jill Barnes Buckley often referred to the "two-way street" of need between Mid-City and Northminster Baptist Church. The congregation and the neighborhood were recipients of each other's gifts. A 2001 sermon titled "Deep and Wide (But Not Always in that Order)" offered insight into this "two-way street" of need. Poole reflected on the church's introduction to the area at the picnic in Jaycee Park during the summer that year. He said he left the fun-filled event featuring food and games with a "wider net of acquaintance, a wider circle of friendship and a wider table of fellowship." This statement from Poole was the "clearest and earliest statement specifically describing Northminster's 'need' for relationship with Mid-City," Allen wrote. "From the

[42] Ibid.
[43] Ibid.
[44] Allen, "A Wider Net," 40–41.

early stages of relationship between Northminster and the Mid-City/Georgetown neighborhood, Northminster understood the relationship in terms of widening the circle of friends and as a wider embrace of those beyond the walls."[45]

Other developments in Wider Net's formative years included the launching of a summer youth club in 2006. During Christmas of the same year, Northminster's thirty-year tradition of delivering personal care bags to area boarding homes intersected with Wider Net as the Boarding Homes Project was expanded to include delivery to elderly residents in Mid-City. A community Christmas dinner was also held at the Mid-City Community Center in 2006 as Northminster members and Mid-City residents gathered for a time of fellowship and to discuss community goals. In 2007, an after-school program was started at the community center, and the first community cleanup was held with neighborhood residents. Northminster youth continued to participate in Mid-City events and efforts, such as painting projects and Habitat builds.[46]

Bustling with Activity

In April 2008, a month after the $4 million building dimension of Wider Net was completed, Northminster dedicated the new education facility and columbarium with a special service. During the service, the congregation remembered its founding as it looked to the future. "For those who birthed our church with faith and hope, we say 'Thanks be to God,'" the litany of dedication read. The litany continued,

> We dedicate this new space to the sacred work of teaching God's truth and learning God's ways. Within these walls may we, and those who come after us, find strength for the journey and light for the way. In these rooms, may our lives be formed for God and shaped by the gospel. From these rooms, may we be sent forth in the fullness of the Spirit to serve the world in the name of Christ.... We dedicate today our columbarium, and the fountain and the garden which surround it. We set apart this sacred space and consecrate it as our church's burial ground. May it be a refuge of peace, solace and rest for the people of God from generation to generation. May all the rooms and spaces we

[45] Ibid., 44.

[46] "The Timeline for 'A Wider Net.'"

dedicate today be used to honor God and lift the lives of those to whom we minister.[47]

While the building dimension was complete, the missions side of Wider Net continued to develop and expand. In June 2008, Northminster joined Habitat's venture called Park View Place to build eighteen homes on the backside of Jaycee Park. When Wider Net launched in 2001, the Special Missions Project Committee (later renamed as the Wider Net Missions Committee) had envisioned the park lined with homes and filled with families. One of the first steps toward fulfilling that vision occurred in 2006 when an interfaith coalition (including Northminster Baptist Church) formed to build the first "Peace House." This same coalition agreed in 2008 to partner with Habitat to fund and provide labor to landscape all of the houses in Park View Place with Jill Barnes Buckley as the coordinator of the effort—called Planting Peace.[48]

The Northminster youth joined Stewpot youth on Martin Luther King Jr. Day in January 2008 to clear the land behind Jaycee Park to make way for the eighteen-house Park View Place development. The work continued, and one year later, Northminster youth returned to the same site alongside 200 additional volunteers to plant shrubs and trees, put down sod, and spread pine straw for five new homeowners—marking the midway point for the Planting Peace project. Northminster youth and other volunteers gathered September 12 to celebrate the end of the interfaith effort, joining volunteers from Beth Israel, Galloway United Methodist Church, Fondren Presbyterian Church, St. Andrew's Episcopal Church, Unitarian Universalist Congregation of Jackson, and the Muslim community.[49]

New programs and other opportunities continued to be offered to Mid-City children in both the life of the church as well as the community. In 2009, children from the summer and after-school programs began to participate in Upward Sports at Mission First of First Baptist Church in Jackson. Additionally, some children from the after-school program began to attend Wednesday night supper and activities at Northminster. Northminster youth also continued their involvement in Mid-City, painting and performing clean-up of the Mid-City Community Center as part of its 2010 in-

[47] N Bulletin 4 20 08.
[48] N News 6 4 08.
[49] N News 9 2 09.

town mission project and completing painting projects on Erie Street in 2011. That same year, Knollwood Baptist Church of Winston-Salem, North Carolina, a Cooperative Baptist Fellowship-affiliated church in the backyard of Wake Forest University School of Divinity, hosted a weeklong children's camp at the Mid-City Community Center. Northminster Baptist Church also began sponsoring Mid-City children and youth to attend Passport summer camps with Northminster's children and youth.[50]

Chuck Poole reflected on the involvement of Northminster youth in Mid-City in a 2010 column in the *Northminster News*, stressing the importance of friendship within the context of this so-called "mission project":

> When I reflect on those outstanding days of service, punctuated by times of prayer and play, the word which looms largest in my mind is the beautiful, powerful, deep, strong word *friendship*. Watching all those Northminster youth and adults working on and around Wood Street alongside residents of the neighborhood, it was obvious that the Wider Net, nine years after its creation, is no longer a 'mission project' but is, instead, a deep, loving, respectful friendship. On those hot, hard June days of good labor, shared meals and much laughter, there were no givers and receivers, just friends. That sort of thing doesn't happen overnight. Rather, it happens over years. Thanks be to God, and to all of you, we are actually getting to see it happen. And when we see it, what we are watching is the kingdom come. Friendship by friendship, moment by moment, the kingdom we pray to come every Sunday is coming, little by little, year upon year.[51]

Poole had offered a more extended reflection on the Wider Net initiative during the previous summer, remembering the call of the Northminster covenant to "be Christ's servants" and "dedicate our lives to ministering in the world, ever alert to the voice of human need":

> When our church adopted those commitments in the winter of 1967, who could have imagined the shape they might take by summer 2009? Who would have predicted that, forty-two summers after our church adopted that world-embracing covenant, Northminster would travel to Hungary one month and Honduras the next? Who would have dreamed that living up to our covenant would one day include our

[50] "The Timeline for 'A Wider Net.'"
[51] N News 6 23 10.

> church's life-lifting, life-changing friendship with Mid-City and Georgetown, a friendship we all now know by the familiar name, "A Wider Net"? Who would have imagined that a small band of believers forming a new congregation in 1967 would quickly become so invested in mission and ministry within and beyond their church's walls?
>
> Northminster is a far from perfect church. We have our share of flaws and limits. But we also have much for which to give thanks. Among our blessings is a covenant to live up to. Those of us who were not here the day you adopted it owe a deep debt to those of you who were here on that December day in 1967. You made a vow then which forms our lives now. You adopted a big-souled, world-embracing covenant, and you did not let it sit, die, atrophy, or fail. You went to work immediately, keeping the covenant to which you promised yourselves. Thanks be to God for those who made the covenant four decades ago, and thanks be to God for those who have kept the covenant forty years of "ministry in the world, ever alert to the voice of human need."[52]

Ten-Year Assessment

In 2009, eight years into Wider Net, an ad hoc committee was appointed to review the initiative and offer recommendations for its future. From this review process, two recommendations were put forward: extend the contract of Jill Barnes Buckley as associate pastor for community ministry and continue the Wider Net missions dimension under the umbrella of Northminster's Missions Committee. When the congregation approved Wider Net in 2001, it approved five years of salary for the new community minister position. This budgeted salary was set to expire during fall 2009.[53] "Wider Net is largely about building relationships between Northminster Baptist Church and Mid-City/Georgetown, and Jill has the relationships," the review committee reported to the deacons. "In fact, our committee couldn't even conceive of continuing Wider Net without Jill. While many Northminster members have spent many hours in Mid-City/Georgetown, Jill is the face of Northminster there."[54]

The second recommendation was an answer to a persisting question of where to place Wider Net on a permanent basis within Northminster's gov-

[52] N News 6 24 09.
[53] N Deacons 08 16 09.
[54] Ibid.

ernance structure. Since its adoption in 2001, Wider Net had existed as an ad hoc committee, which, as the review committee pointed out, meant there was no clear venue for broader participation in Wider Net's governance. Many of the original committee members continued to serve eight years later, and "committee fatigue" had set in. The ad hoc group noted that this move would not impact the Missions Committee's budget for at least two years because the designated fund for Wider Net missions still had a balance of slightly more than $210,000.[55]

In 2011, the Missions Committee created a six-member Wider Net subcommittee to oversee the growing activities in the Mid-City/Georgetown area. The same year, the subcommittee recommended to the deacons that a standing committee devoted exclusively to Wider Net missions be formed. In response, the deacons appointed a Wider Net Transitions Committee to consider the subcommittee's requests. Together, the subcommittee and the Transitions Committee put forward several joint recommendations: 1) beginning in 2012, Wider Net expenses be folded into Northminster's general budget; 2) form an ad hoc Vision Committee responsible for long-range planning for Wider Net; 3) make Wider Net a standing committee. In addition, they recommended that the name "Wider Net" be kept.[56] The deacons approved these recommendations, and $50,000 was allocated to Wider Net missions in the 2012 budget.

Second Decade of Wider Net

To celebrate the tenth anniversary of Wider Net, the congregation reflected on the impact of the special missions initiative during worship on June 12, 2011. Following worship, a special luncheon in the Great Hall gave congregants an opportunity to share about the impact of this decade-long effort through pictures, reports, and personal testimonies. Barnes Buckley pointed out in her invitation that June 12 also marked another important day in the Christian calendar: the day of Pentecost. "At Pentecost, the Spirit empowered those gathered to continue the teaching, healing, proclaiming, reconciling work of Jesus," Barnes Buckley wrote. She continued,

[55] Ibid.
[56] Wider Net Vision Committee Report (2015), 6; N News 9 14 11.

> How fitting, then, that we celebrate the work of the Holy Spirit in our congregation on that day, the Spirit that has given us also the vision and guidance and strength to do the work of the kingdom in our own place and time. Who knows how we might be empowered for the next phase of our journey of friendship with Mid-City/Georgetown, as "we are all gathered in one place" (Acts 1:1) on this coming Pentecost Sunday?[57]

From 2012–2015, Wider Net continued its staple programming and activities, such as providing breakfasts and devotionals at Operation Shoestring, a Thursday Bible study led by Chuck Poole, a tutoring program, home repairs with Habitat for Humanity, Circle of Friends, an after-school program, funding of utilities and maintenance costs at Mid-City Community Center, and a summer camp with a heavy academic focus run by Northminster college students, among others. New events and activities included a Back-to-School bash at Jaycee Park led by Northminster youth (2012), hiring of an administrator (2012) and retired teacher (2013) to assist with the after-school program, and the addition of a summer intern from Wake Forest University School of Divinity (2013 and 2014). In 2012, Barnes Buckley organized Northminster volunteers to provide Mid-City children with Christmas presents—an effort which later expanded.[58]

Wider Net also took on the community's challenge of confronting blight due to foreclosures and abandoned lots. Numerous church members were active in the work, with Jim Johnston especially being cited for his commitment.[59] In 2013, the church joined the community in clearing twenty-seven lots. Church members helped clear sixty additional lots over the next two years. In addition to maintaining a dozen lots, members also assisted with removing trees, cultivating a community garden, and adding speed bumps in the neighborhood. The neighborhood experienced, according to a Habitat for Humanity report, a reduction in crime, an increased sense of safety, and improved appearance from 2008–2014.[60] Gang activity along the once-dangerous Wood Street had been eliminated, the report noted. With an increased positive police presence and swifter responses in the neighbor-

[57] N News 5 10 11.

[58] "The Timeline for 'A Wider Net.'"

[59] N Deacons 2 21 16; see also N Deacons 2 16 14.

[60] Wider Net Vision Committee Report (2015), 48–49.

hood, trust had grown between residents and Jackson police officers. Habitat also reported an increased pride among residents, better upkeep of properties, greater participation in the neighborhood association, an uptick in home values, and the emergence of a more cohesive community. "Residents look out for each other, and the older and younger generations communicate more," the Habitat report concluded.[61] Habitat emphasized the continued need for community partners to address ongoing challenges such as lack of economic development and jobs as well as the need to leverage the successes in Mid-City with local officials to attract market-rate housing and business investments.

Similarly, in 2015 Northminster's Wider Net Vision Committee received similar suggestions from church members as future areas of focus, including creating a job training program and career/skill development and resource center as well as advocacy engagement with the local government on behalf of the community.[62] While several Wider Net ministries and programs had come and gone from 2001 to 2016—"abandoned due to lack of participation or lack of energy and sometimes lack of success," according to the Vision Committee—a set of programs flourished and remained healthy endeavors, foundational to Wider Net. These included Poole's Thursday morning Bible class, after-school programming, summer youth and children's ministries, neighborhood lot maintenance, and a house repair program. To move forward into the next fifteen years of Wider Net, Northminster's relationship with Mid-City/Georgetown needed to be one characterized by "faithful presence" and a "continued commitment to listening and learning before speaking and acting," according to the Vision Committee, which again stressed the importance of reciprocal relationships:

> Our presence in the neighborhood and the presence of the neighborhood residents in our church force us to acknowledge the power and opportunities that we have and to consider ways to share. That presence forces us to see our own need for reconciliation and redemption. That presence forces us to seek the image of God in all of humanity. Our involvement should be a two-way sharing of skills. We should encourage empowerment of neighborhood people to lead the projects,

---

[61] Ibid., 29.

[62] Ibid., 28–29, 54.

> and the people in the neighborhood should be encouraged to share their gifts with us.[63]

The Vision Committee emphasized that the focus of Northminster's relationships should not be limited to church-led programs and events, but instead must center on the "creation of community"—"being on the receiving end of situations which spiritually, physically and socially empower all of us to be one community." Opportunities involving both giving and receiving were encouraged. "Not only should we give of our gifts and resources, we should also learn to recognize the gifts and resources of the community of which we want to be a part," the committee said. "In receiving, we recognize that a person has something to offer, something we need. We should provide opportunities that require us to practice receiving."[64]

When Wider Net was launched in 2001, the original proposal called for a "physical presence in the neighborhood," and $70,000 was put toward this objective. After using office space for a short period at the site of Operation Shoestring, Barnes Buckley relocated her office to the Northminster campus on Ridgewood Road. However, she quickly set up an unofficial office at the Mid-City Community Center—known as the "Yellow Church." The Yellow Church was owned by the Mid-City Community Association, a defunct nonprofit organization, with Mid-City resident, Horace Kelly, as the acting owner. For many years, Northminster Baptist Church contributed regularly to the cost of repairs and maintenance at the Yellow Church. In return, Northminster was allowed to use the center rent-free, and Barnes Buckley was responsible for opening and closing the facility.[65]

Horace Kelly offered the Yellow Church to True Vine Missionary Baptist Church, so it was unclear if the building would remain available to Northminster once it changed ownership. Additionally in 2014, Northminster received a $100,000 gift from an anonymous donor to be used to purchase a physical presence in Mid-City.[66] The next year, in response, the Vision Committee recommended that an ad hoc committee be appointed to assess Wider Net's property needs and identify property to purchase and renovate. The Vision Committee emphasized in its report that a temporary

---

[63] Ibid., 12–13.
[64] Ibid., 50.
[65] Wider Net Vision Committee Report, 42–43.
[66] N Deacons 11 17 13.

presence no longer satisfied Wider Net's long-term commitment to establish a "sense of place" in the Mid-City community. "Because of this expanded relationship, a 'sense of place' is no longer satisfied with a temporary presence," the report stated. "Our faithful presence in the neighborhood calls for a 'sense of place' that is permanent."[67] The Vision Committee based its recommendation for a permanent presence on the theological foundation that had long undergirded the work of Wider Net:

> Theologically, the church should listen to the community, work with the community, and be with the community as the community strives to attain their hopes and dreams.... By listening to the community through Mid-City socials held in the Yellow Church and organized through the Mid-City Neighborhood Association, we know that the residents of the neighborhood have hopes and dreams for their community. We, as a church, should not impose our own hopes and dreams on a community of which we are not a part.[68]

The Vision Committee also emphasized that ownership of property within Mid-City would give Northminster an "equal voice" with residents and organizations in the neighborhood. "Ownership would indicate a sense of faithfulness to our relationship and an indication that Northminster wants to be a permanent part of the community," the committee said. "Theologically, ownership creates an incarnational response."[69] The committee also recommended that Northminster continue to have a presence in the Yellow Church for the sake of its healthy relationship with the neighborhood. "The intent to own property in the neighborhood is the intent to increase our commitment and expand our relationship, not alter the current relationships," the report said.[70]

Numerous other important affirmations and recommendations were made by the Wider Net Vision Committee in its 2015 report. The committee reaffirmed its support for Jill Barnes Buckley's community minister position, described as a necessary catalyst for the relationship between Northminster Baptist Church and Mid-City/Georgetown. Since 2004, Barnes Buckley had become a "village priest" in these communities, according to

---

[67] Ibid.

[68] Ibid.

[69] Wider Net Vision Committee Report, 44.

[70] Ibid.

Poole, "filling a wide range of pastoral roles in the lives of residents in the Wider Net neighborhood." While credibility between the church and the community was first gained via partnerships with Habitat for Humanity and Operation Shoestring, Barnes Buckley was responsible for bringing a new level of respect and trustworthiness through her daily long-term presence in the neighborhood.[71] During the fifteen-year history of Wider Net, Northminster's relationship had evolved from providing "a person" to the neighborhood to being "a people" with the communities of Mid-City/Georgetown, according to the committee. More than 400 Northminster members had been involved in Wider Net in some capacity over the course of this period. Eight people from Mid-City had joined Northminster Baptist Church, and three were baptized at the church.

Faithful presence in the community required faithful listening, the committee reiterated. "Opportunities to dream together, to plan together, to work together should begin with our efforts to listen," the committee stressed. "Only when we have been accepted as a permanent part of the community will the community be willing and able to faithfully listen to us. Only then will we have the right to hope and dream for the community because only then will there be no 'us' or 'them.' There will only be 'a people' hoping and dreaming for 'our community.'" Regular conversations with residents and community partners were a vital ingredient of faithful listening, they said.[72]

Challenges

Resource-abundant church ministries serving in underprivileged communities must necessarily navigate socio-economic and cultural differences. This was true for the congregation at Northminster as members interacted and formed authentic and deep relationships with residents of the Mid-City/Georgetown community. Wider Net leaders strove to carefully negotiate perceived cultural boundaries and the challenges of inequality. These challenges required a thoughtful and well-considered approach to urban missions.

The Wider Net initiative was a laboratory of successes, albeit with some expected challenges, as church members and Mid-City/Georgetown

[71] Ibid., 35–37.
[72] Ibid., 50–51.

residents learned to relate to each other in more meaningful ways. Wider Net was not an isolated initiative, where missions work was confined to one aspect of the church's life. Rather, over time the initiative was integrated into virtually all aspects of the life of the congregation, including youth and children's ministries. Northminster youth were vital participants in Wider Net, taking part in countless clean-up projects and Habitat builds. In 2013, for example, Northminster youth led Mid-City children in various day-long activities—dubbed Wonderful Wednesdays—including a trip to the Mississippi Children's Museum and a tour of the Mississippi State Capitol. Meanwhile, several youth from the Mid-City/Georgetown community were active in the Northminster youth group, joining in Sunday and Wednesday evening activities, Sunday school and worship, youth service projects, weekend retreats, Passport summer camp, and a ski trip to Colorado. These Mid-City youth often arranged their own transportation and volunteered on weekends to raise funds for more expensive trips. Northminster members also provided transportation and covered the majority of costs to ensure that the experiences of the Mid-City/Georgetown youth were equal to those of the Northminster youth. These youth—with radically different life experiences and cultural backgrounds—would worship together, learn together, pray and read the Bible together, serve together, and travel and room together.[73]

The Northminster Youth Committee sought to enhance the quality of interaction between church youth and youth from Mid-City/Georgetown and work on cultural differences by building personal relationships with Northminster members—often referred to as "Godparents." From their perspective, the committee thought the best way to sustain interaction between diverse young people was through concentrated involvement in the Mid-City/Georgetown community via participation in Wonderful Wednesdays, cleanup days and other service projects. Joint activities were sought where the youth could "maintain a more symmetrical relationship at a neutral site around an activity that required teamwork and was a common interest among many of the youth."[74]

Negotiating the when and how of youth interaction made realizing the "wide net" that is the kingdom of heaven in the Gospel of Matthew a chal-

[73] Allen, 16–17.
[74] Ibid., 19.

lenge on occasion. Intent and reality do not always coincide. Several youth from Mid-City/Georgetown, however, remained involved in other activities at Northminster. These youth participated in weekly youth activities, Sunday school, worship, camps, service projects, and a mission trip to New York City. Three youth were baptized into the church, becoming members of Northminster.[75]

The children's ministry at Northminster also grappled with some challenges. In fall 2009, several children from the Wider Net after-school program asked to attend the church on Wednesday nights. These children had participated at Northminster in its Children's Bible Camp several months earlier. Chuck Poole hoped that Northminster children might find these as opportunities to minister to their friends made through Wider Net.[76] In his report to the deacons in November 2012, Poole acknowledged challenges regarding how to minister in church settings where children came from diverse social and cultural backgrounds. Volunteers were recruited and trained to assist with addressing behavioral needs and the programming was adapted to be more accessible to all of the children, who had varying degrees of familiarity with the Bible. Wednesday night "godparents" sat with the Mid-City children at supper and were responsible for discipline and providing transportation.[77]

Challenges continued and in fall 2012, church leaders decided to re-envision Wednesday evening children's programming. Rather than leave after supper for separate activities, the children remained with the adults for Wednesday night worship, and Poole adopted a "discussion-style meditation" geared to all ages. The godparent program ceased. With the changes, attendance patterns shifted as well. At the same time, Northminster children's ministry continued to be extensively involved in Wider Net activities.[78]

Legacy of Wider Net

In her 2010 graduate thesis, Courtney Allen explored at length how Wider Net had positively affected and challenged her congregation. One

---

[75] Ibid.

[76] N Deacons 5 15 11. See also N Deacons 10 17 10.

[77] Chuck Poole, Report to Northminster Deacons, November 11, 2012.

[78] N Deacons 11 11 12.

church member said that she had long feared crossing the Fortification Street Bridge leading into the Mid-City/Georgetown neighborhood. Because of tutoring in the Wider Net program, that fear dissipated, and Mid-City/Georgetown had become part of her community. "My community is bigger now," she told Allen.[79] This is just one of many similar examples shared regarding the positive impact of the initiative on church members themselves.

Allen, herself a "child of the church," wrote that Northminster Baptist Church "looks and feels different" from before the launch of Wider Net:

> The physical plant of Northminster is aesthetically different due to the completion of the balcony and the completion of the educational building and columbarium. But Northminster thinks, acts, and speaks differently than it did ten years ago because of the relationship with friends in Mid-City. The wider circle of embrace requires Northminster, a place rich with resources, to employ careful speech[80] about new friendships and those who were previously considered other. As one interviewee noted, "A Wider Net is at the heart of what we do [at Northminster]...it is not just going *down there to help poor people.*"[81]

She noted that the intentionality behind the Wider Net initiative and sensitivity to cultural boundaries and socioeconomic differences had a lasting impact on church members. "Language and understanding of community has shifted to include a broader swatch of the world, beyond previously understood boundaries and institutions," Allen wrote.[82]

Tenth Anniversary of Wider Net

That Wider Net was forming and transforming Northminster Baptist Church was evident during the tenth anniversary celebration of the special missions initiative in 2011. "It's important to understand exactly what we are celebrating," Barnes Buckley told the congregation.

> We do not celebrate that we've served hundreds of breakfasts at Operation Shoestring or that we've had nearly 175 children and teenagers come through our programs at the Yellow Church, though these things

[79] Allen, "A Wider Net," 58.

[80] A favorite term of Chuck Poole.

[81] Ibid., 72.

[82] Ibid.

> are worthy of note. We do not celebrate that nearly 350 Northminster members, both past and present, have physically gone to Mid-City/Georgetown, though that too is worthy of note.... We do, however, celebrate that our community is becoming more whole, that we are becoming more whole, that people in Mid-City (we pray to God) are becoming more whole, because we, as Chuck would say, "got in on what God was up to" in Mid-City/Georgetown. The Spirit was already moving. We had just jumped on board. And our lives have been blessed, have they not, because we opened ourselves to the wild and wonderful wind of the Spirit, letting it blow through our life together and send us out on a mission of healing, friendship and reconciliation.[83]

Also at the tenth anniversary celebration, Chuck Poole articulated a theological framework of A Wider Net for the congregation. He told the congregation that if he had to reduce this framework to a single sentence, it would read, "The gospel to which we have given our lives calls us beyond our own comfort to embrace, and be embraced by, the wider world around us." The theological foundations of Wider Net, Poole added, could be found in the "deep passion and wide compassion" of Jesus found in the Gospels of Matthew and Luke.

For Poole, the rationale or the "why" of Wider Net was merely a matter of answering Charles Sheldon's century-old question "What Would Jesus Do?"[84] "Reduced to its most rudimentary and elementary core, we did what we did because we thought it was what Jesus would want us to do, because the Jesus of the Gospels lived a life of walls down, arms out compassion," Poole said. "And, since Jesus is the Lord of the church, we thought we should do our best to do the same."[85] The words of Scripture to "be quick to listen and slow to speak," helped to explain the theological basis for the "how" of Wider Net. "For a congregation comprised of doers and fixers, that was a spiritual exercise which required the intentional spiritual disciplines of restraint, patience, meekness and humility," Poole said. "That is a simple example of how theology not only tells us why we do what we do, it also tells us how we do what we do: We listen and learn before we speak and

[83] Jill Barnes Buckley, remarks on the tenth anniversary of Wider Net.

[84] Chuck Poole, "The Theological Framework of Wider Net"; Charles Sheldon, *In His Steps* (1896).

[85] Poole, "The Theological Framework of Wider Net."

act."[86] He elaborated on the theological underpinnings for the "how" of Wider Net and revealed his ongoing goals and dreams:

> Our job is not to import our ideas about "what is good for them," but to join them in identifying community needs and community strengths (asset mapping) so that we work together to lift a community in need of help and hope. Closely tied to patient listening, this is a spiritual matter of genuine respect.... One of the ways thoughtful, prayerful, gospel theology shapes how we go about our work is by slowly, eventually, transforming mission to friendship.... Mission is a wonderful place to begin; that's what gets us "out there." But once we get out there, once we actually meet people and learn their names and faces, they cease to be the objects of our compassion and become instead, our friends. Friends learn from one another. Friends have their minds changed by one another. Friends need one another. Friendship is deeper, and more complicated, than mission. Friendship blurs the lines between in here and out there. As a church, we can make a congregational decision to adopt a mission program or project, but reconciling and redeeming friendship is the work of the Holy Spirit.[87]

Poole concluded his theological reflections and exhortations with an assessment of how the "success" of Wider Net should be measured, pointing out that "success" could be measured via a tally of Habitat houses built, homes repaired, abandoned lots cleared, classes led, and hours given by volunteers. However, there was a higher, more valuable form of measurement. "Thinking theologically, I would say that we measure the worth of our work in lives changed, friends found, hope given, and love embodied," Poole said. "Theologically speaking, our goal is to live the gospel in ways which match up with the spirit of Jesus. If that is our goal, then that means that the worth of our work is measured by the spiritual metrics of reconciliation, friendship, hope and joy."[88] Poole distinguished Northminster's mission with that of a nonprofit:

> We have to remind ourselves, from time to time, that we are doing this work, not as a nonprofit helping agency but as a church. Helping agencies are wonderful, vital, dynamic channels of God's work in the world,

---

[86] Ibid.
[87] Ibid.
[88] Ibid.

> but, as a church, our reasons, goals, and measures are guided and governed by a very peculiar set of theological, biblical, and spiritual commitments. So we pray, think, listen, serve, and measure our work in ways as odd, peculiar, particular and Christian as the Gospel itself.[89]

In May 2016, Chuck Poole reflected on the ministry of Wider Net as the deacons were beginning full-scale planning for the church's fiftieth anniversary in 2017. He remembered that in summer 2001, immediately after the adoption of the Wider Net vision, founding member Rubel Phillips called him and said he and fellow founding member John Palmer planned to visit the Mid-City area. When they arrived at Jaycee Park, the two founding visionaries pondered what could be done in the area. Poole commented,

> There was extreme blight and overgrown areas. Today, there are beautiful Habitat homes. Fifteen years later, a member of our congregation, who was baptized in this church, lives in one of those Habitat homes. Those two people who had a conversation about Mid-City had an earlier conversation on a street corner downtown about starting a new church. It is a lot to think about and ponder. It is the hard work of the Holy Spirit. There is much for which to give thanks.[90]

As of 2018, the Wider Net ministry was ongoing. Questions, no doubt, would arise. The question of a permanent "incarnational" place or facility in the Mid-City area was still an issue. In 2015, the Vision Committee had decided a permanent place in the Mid-City area was needed, but as of early 2018, no permanent facility had been established. The congregation was still using the "Yellow Church" as their base, but hoped to purchase property one day.

Jill Barnes Buckley's resignation from the church's ministerial staff in January 2017 to become executive director of Stewpot was essentially a part of the Wider Net story. According to Chuck Poole, the laity of the church "stepped up" to maintain the ministry. Chuck Poole had become the "face" or the "village priest" of Wider Net since Buckley's departure.[91] What shape the ministry would take permanently after Buckley's leadership was a question to be answered. Commitment to Wider Net remained strong.

---

[89] Ibid.

[90] N Deacons 5 15 16.

[91] Chuck Poole, phone interview by Doug Weaver, July 31, 2017.

Chapter 9

Chuck Poole Redivivus: His Second Tenure as Pastor

The calling of a pastor to a church a second time is rare in Christian ministry. It has happened, of course, but a "rebirth" of a ministry takes special gifts on behalf of the pastor and the congregation. Those gifts include the ability to see that the first pastorate was a good and blessed time, and that the departure of the minister was viewed, appropriately so, as an authentic call, not away from a bad situation, but to a new ministry that the minister and congregation concurred was a move of faithfulness in response to the Holy Spirit. When Chuck Poole returned to Northminster Baptist Church as pastor for a second time in November 2007, all of these gifts were evident. Poole's ministry with LifeShare Foundation had been fulfilling, but his ministerial heart was again called to a place he considered special. The Northminster congregation had not planned on a "Poole Two," but when the opportunity presented itself, the answer was clear. There was no better minister than Chuck Poole to help them be the church they believed they were called to be, a congregation that loved its heritage but was willing to forge forward in new ways of ministry in the twenty-first century.

Staff

In September 2009, the recently married Amy Joyner Finkelberg initiated conversations about shifting from full-time associate pastor for children and adults to a part-time role. She was looking for a simpler lifestyle, one where she slowed down, listened more, and sought "divine spaciousness."[1] After eight months of discussion, led by an ad hoc Staffing Committee, the congregation supported her move to the role of part-time associate pastor for adults. She began her new position on May 17, 2010.[2] After twelve years

---

[1] N Deacons 9 20 09. Finkelberg cited author Barbara Brown Taylor for the phrase "divine spaciousness."

[2] N Deacons 2 21 10; N Deacons 5 16 10; N News 5 26 10. Finkelberg had supervised Northminster's Children's Center.

of service, Finkelberg completed her ministry at Northminster on March 15, 2015, but remained actively involved as a church member.[3] At the reception honoring her service, Finkelberg commented after receiving a gift, "Whenever I wear my necklace, I will remember what the Northminster emblem represents to me: soulfulness, spaciousness, and graciousness—qualities to which every Christian should aspire, qualities that our congregation embodies so well."[4]

Alongside this staff transition, the congregation decided to create a new position, associate pastor for children. Holly Wiggs, chair of the Children's Committee, and other committee members provided leadership during an interim year. Lesley Ratcliff, a graduate of Mississippi College and Baylor University's Truett Theological Seminary, was called to the new position and began work on June 1, 2011. Beyond her responsibilities in children's ministries, Ratcliff was active on the board of the ecumenical Conference of Young Clergy Women.[5]

Jill Barnes Buckley had been hired as associate pastor for community ministry in fall 2004. Northminster ordained her on October 14, 2007.[6] She was active in Baptist life and became the moderator of the Cooperative Baptist Fellowship of Mississippi in 2010.[7] Her work with Wider Net ministry efforts was considered stellar. For example, in a May 2010 reflection, Chuck Poole commented that more than 300 church members had participated in the Mid-City/Georgetown neighborhood ministries to date, and that Barnes Buckley had been key to building the bridge from Ridgewood Road to Wood Street.[8] Buckley's twelve-year ministry at Northminster concluded on January 2, 2017, though her family continued as active church members. She assumed the position of executive director of Stewpot, an inner-city ministry the church had long supported. Despite the loss of a well-regarded staff member, Poole declared to the deacons that in his thirty years of minis-

[3] N Deacons 9 21 14; N News 10 1 14.

[4] N News 3 4 15.

[5] N Deacons 2 21 10; N Deacons 5 16 10; N Deacons 4 17 11; N News 5 25 11; N Deacons 8 18 13.

[6] N News 10 3 07; N News 10 16 17.

[7] N Deacons 10 17 10.

[8] N Deacons 5 16 10.

try he did not know "of another minister going to something that seemed more right than Jill Buckley going to lead Stewpot…a gift to our city."[9]

In the area of youth ministry, Tripp Martin concluded his service on November 6, 2009, in order to accept the call as pastor of Vineville Baptist Church in Macon, Georgia. He had worked at Northminster since summer 2003.[10] After Megan Kash served as interim youth director, Steven Fuller assumed his duties as associate pastor for students in February 2010, and he stayed six years. He left on December 11, 2016, to become pastor of First Baptist Church in Gastonia, North Carolina.[11]

As Northminster entered its fifty-first year, ministerial vacancies existed. Searches for two full-time positions, associate pastor for community ministry and associate pastor for students, were underway. With some concern about budget restrictions, the search for a part-time associate pastor for adults would come later. At the age of eighty-three, long time organist Billy Trotter retired on June 30, 2017. Barbara Webb and George Smith, church clerk and church treasurer respectively, continued in the positions they had held for decades.[12] In the last decade, office staff have provided stable, highly regarded work. Two long-tenured contributors were Donna Lewis (2009–), pastors' secretary/administrative assistant, and Sandra "Sam" South (2006–), financial secretary. A few retirements of note were highlighted in recent years. In November 2007, Von Watts was celebrated for twenty years of faithful work in the nursery and the Northminster Children's Center. In 2013, Doll Ree Boone was praised for working with children for twenty-seven years.[13] That same year, Barbara Stanton died. The *Northminster News* related that she had worked with the congregation's children for thirty years. "Since beginning her work here, at age eighteen, Barbara has nurtured our church's little ones with such constant and beautiful care that two generations of children have known Northminster as 'Miss Barbara's Church' long before they have known the name 'Northminster,'" the newsletter eulogized.[14]

---

[9] N Deacons 11 13 16; N News 11 30 16.

[10] N Deacons 9 20 09; N News 10 1 09.

[11] N Deacons 11 8 09; N Deacons 11 21 10; N News 2 16 11; N Deacons 10 16 16.

[12] N News 10 26 16; N Deacons 2 19 17. Smith had been treasurer since 1981.

[13] N News 11 28 07; N News 6 12 13.

[14] N News 10 2 13.

Two other members of the church staff lauded for their years of service to Northminster Baptist Church were James (affectionately known as "Mr. J") and Rosie Jefferson. Their custodial work at the church began March 1, 1982 (when Mr. J still had another full-time job). In 2005, the Jeffersons retired from full-time custodial work at the church but continued doing a variety of tasks, including "special hospitality" (wedding and funeral sextons) and cooking sausage biscuits for two men's groups and for the Billy Brumfield House ministry. In 2010, they decided they could no longer be responsible for Wednesday night suppers, but in reality, retirement did not retire much of their tireless work. Throughout their ministry at the church, they had served the congregation additional ways, from helping with Vacation Bible School during Mr. J's week of vacation to his being a member of the ordination council of Amy Joyner in 2003.[15]

Despite Mr. J's advancing age (79), the Jeffersons continued to work at the church in 2017.[16] Probably no story captured the warmth that the Jeffersons brought to Northminster than the story of little Megan. Annette Hitt recalled the story from early in the Jeffersons' time at the church:

> Thirty-three years ago four-year-old Megan and I were walking down the hall at Northminster when we met Mr. Jefferson. As was his custom with children, the Giant-of-a-Man-in-Everyway knelt to speak to Megan. Even kneeling he towered over her as he said, "Well, hello Little Lady," and as he patted her back, I noticed his large hand completely spanned her back. He and Megan engaged in a conversation for a few minutes while she told him some story about her dog and he listened intently. Then he bid her good day, patted her back and went on his way. As he walked away Megan looked from him to me and asked in a whispered voice, "Mama, was that God?" I smiled and thought and replied, "Very close, Darling. Very close!"[17]

Hitt's concluding reflection summed up the view that Mr. Jefferson revealed the heart of Northminster: "Mr. Jefferson still walks our halls and remains to this day a part of our lives, and still represents for me a very close look of how I think God must be."[18]

---

[15] N Deacons 7 1 84; N News 2 26 97.

[16] N Deacons 9 19 10.

[17] Annette Hitt, email to Doug Weaver, June 19, 2017.

[18] Ibid.

Since the days of Dudley Wilson, Northminster's first pastor, the congregation had offered occasional summer sabbaticals for its ministers. Wilson's was every third summer; perhaps more realistically, the church had moved to a sabbatical after five years of ministry. Both Amy Joyner and Chuck Poole took sabbaticals (2008 and 2013, respectively). Poole acknowledged the staff's appreciation to the church's lay leadership, noting that Sabbath seasons were times to step back, be still, come up for air, read, write, ponder, reflect and return.[19]

Northminster Baptist Church ordained several ministers during this era. By 2017, the congregation had ordained eight ministers in its history, six of whom were women. On July 31, 2010, Courtney Allen, who had grown up in the church, was ordained as she assumed the position of associate pastor for community ministry at the First Baptist Church of Dalton, Georgia. In 2015, when Allen was installed as pastor of Grace Baptist Church in Richmond, Virginia, several Northminster members attended the service.[20]

On May 31, 2009, the congregation ordained Holly Benzenhafer Redford (now, Holly Benzenhafer). She joined Northminster in 1993 and attended until 2003, when she moved with her family (husband, Ken, and daughter, Kristen Redford) to Massachusetts. Her parents, David and Emily Benzenhafer, remain long time church members. While at Northminster, Benzenhafer served two terms as moderator of the Cooperative Baptist Fellowship of Mississippi, chaired the congregation's Adult Ministries Committee, and sang in the sanctuary choir. She had graduated from Mississippi College before completing a Master of Divinity (2009) and entering the Ph.D. program at Boston University School of Theology in practical theology and spirituality. Benzenhafer "requested ordination from Northminster Baptist Church because the congregation remains her heart's home and spiritually formative talisman of being the church."[21]

---

[19] N News 6 17 08; N Deacons 3 7 13; N News 5 30 13.

[20] N Deacons 7 17 11; N Deacons 9 20 15.

[21] Holly Benzenhafer, email to Doug Weaver, June 20, 2017; N News 5 13 09; N News 2 19 14. In Massachusetts, Benzenhafer worked as a spiritual director with students and interim spiritual life coordinator before becoming associate pastor at First Baptist Church in Needham, Massachusetts.

On October 30, 2016, the congregation ordained Kristen Redford Hydinger, the daughter of Ken and Holly Benzenhafer Redford. Kristen was fifteen when her family moved to Massachusetts. In 2008, Kristen returned to Northminster as a summer intern in children's ministries. She graduated with a Master of Divinity from Boston University School of Theology and was working in Newton, Massachusetts, at the YMCA at the time of her ordination. According to Redford Hydinger, she desired ordination from Northminster because the congregation was "the family of faith that formed her."[22] No doubt it is rare that a parent and child are ordained at the same church, and the ordination of two women in the same family at the same church is rarer still; these ordinations symbolize Northminster's affirmation of equality in ministry.

Deacons and a Lay-led Church

Northminster Baptist Church had identified itself from its beginnings as a congregation with both a strong pastoral presence and a strong lay leadership. While the church frequently re-affirmed the conviction of lay leadership, circumstances also challenged the congregation to define what "lay leadership" meant practically. It is clear that being lay-led has always been anchored in a strong Board of Deacons and an extensive number of committees. In a 2012 historical reflection on the Board of Deacons, John Purvis noted that the spirit of being lay-led was seen in the fact that twenty-seven committees were active and working by 1976 when the church still was not a decade old.[23] By 2017, the church depended on thirty-four committees, members and chairs who were selected by an important Committee on Committees. The work of the church was a fine-tuned, businesslike process—a meticulous planning and decision-making process vetted through the committee structure and then the Board of Deacons.[24]

Northminster had always (rightly) acknowledged that the congregation was the final voice in all matters of the church—such was 400-year-old Baptist polity. But how the Board of Deacons and the pastor related was a natural question in a lay-led church. What responsibilities were solely the pastor's? What were the functions of the deacons? The long-range plan of 2006

[22] N News 5 21 08; N Deacons 4 27 14; N Deacons 6 26 16.
[23] N Deacons 1 28 12.
[24] N News 10 2 13.

had raised these issues after committee members read about the nature of leadership. In the report, the spiritual responsibilities of the pastor were affirmed:

> Leadership responsibilities are different from leadership style. All of our leaders should be servant leaders. But not all have the same responsibilities. The pastor is the spiritual and theological leader of the church. He proclaims the Word and challenges and leads us to follow Christ. He is also the church visionary and shepherd. He leads the professional staff and vets educational programs and materials theologically. He does not share leadership with the laity in the discharge of these responsibilities.[25]

The laity, Board of Deacons, and the church's committees were responsible for non-spiritual matters. Ministerial staff participated, but the laity led:

> According to the bylaws the deacon chair "...shall be the principal executive officer...and in general shall perform all duties customarily incident to the office of President and Chief Executive Officer of a corporation." The deacons are analogous to a board of directors and the members of the congregation, to shareholders. Members through the deacons and different committees hire and fire the pastor, make committee assignments, prepare the budget, and administer the church's financial affairs. The pastor and staff participate in committee assignments, budget, and financial affairs. But the laity leads. In other areas leadership responsibility is shared, and the pastor and the staff and the members working together perform the mission of the church. We are all our brother's keeper and we all are members of the priesthood of believers.[26]

In May 2008, Wilson Stribling, representing an ad hoc committee on deacon selection and by-laws, told the deacons that the church's bylaws described the role of the Board of Deacons, in particular, the chair of deacons, in excessively explicit business terms. Such was not surprising, given the long history of active, successful, business professionals in the congregation. Stribling's report, however, acknowledged that the use of a business model for understanding church polity needed revision:

---

[25] N Deacons 5 18 08.
[26] Ibid.

> Our bylaw description of the deacon chair as CEO is probably inappropriate because it is based on a business model with a power structure and executive authority that does [*sic*] not exist in a church. The deacon chair leads by example, persuasion, and consensus—not by executive authority or fiat. So do deacons and committee chairs.... There is another problem with thinking about the deacon chair as CEO, and that is that this title suggests authority over the pastor in his responsibilities as chief theologian and spiritual leader also described above which are solely his.[27]

In April 2009, the Board of Deacons was receptive to the revision of the picture of the deacon chair as a corporate CEO. They approved deleting from the bylaws the phrases "shall be the principal executive officer of the church" and "and in general shall perform all duties customarily incident to the office of President and CEO of a corporation." Deacons hoped this intentional effort would add to the focus on servant leadership alongside the ministerial staff.[28]

In 2010, an intentional effort was made to broaden committee leadership and committee participation. A study of the make-up of standing committees from 2000 to 2010 revealed that many chairpersons had served ten years in a row. Consequently, the chairs were shuffled, literally, and in 2011 new chairs or co-chairs totaled twenty-one with sixty-nine new committee members—either first-time appointees or people serving on different committees.[29]

The composition of the Board of Deacons also underwent revision as a result of the long-range plan of 2006. In 2008, Mary Foose chaired and led the ad hoc committee to recommend a change in the deacon nomination

---

[27] Ibid.

[28] N Deacons 4 19 09. The deacons recognized the challenges and importance of the ongoing process of defining what it meant to be a lay-led church. Again in 2010, the deacons, upon the suggestion of Paul Smith, had a discussion of the topic and affirmed that "laity take seriously the responsibility of 'doing church' so that we are strong during times when we have been without a pastor, and we don't step back when pastors are hired. We discussed the idea that being lay-led becomes more difficult as we get bigger and that there are no set rules for a lay-led church; hence, more grace, more careful speech, more institutional courtesy is required" (N Deacons 10 17 10).

[29] N Deacons 11 21 10. There were 398 members, chairs, or co-chairs on the thirty-two standing committees in 2011.

process to cease the practice of electing six of twelve nominees. The ad hoc committee suggested that persons selected in deacon elections were often the more visible contributors of the congregation, which proved disadvantageous to quieter servant leaders. Foose and the committee also voiced concern that people who "lost" elections might decline to be nominated again or might even leave the church. In 2009, the recommendation was approved that the number of deacons be capped at eighteen (originally nine in 1967), and that a slate of six candidates (who submitted to a selection-committee review process and had been active members of the church at least two years) be presented for each subsequent annual election of deacons. Not all deacons, including the pastor Chuck Poole, were in favor of the switch to a single slate of nominees. Dissenters noted the new approach was not very Baptist or democratic. The bylaw revision moved forward, however, and on November 15, 2009, received the approval of the congregation.[30] Observers credited the high regard church members had for Mary Foose and her influential lay leadership. In September 2010, at its annual business meeting, the congregation elected its first single slate of deacons—no one lost an election.[31] While the new process allowed for deacon nominations from the floor that might challenge the single slate, no names had been presented as of 2017.

By 2012, according to John Purvis, 137 different people had served as deacons at Northminster Baptist Church. Many had served multiple times, including Leland Speed a remarkable seven times. Bill Boone and Lucian Harvey had each served as chair three times. Since Jan Purvis's election in 1975, forty additional women had served, or about 30 percent of the total number of deacons. In subsequent deacon elections from 2012 to 2016, sixteen first-time deacons were elected, nine of whom were women.[32]

Chuck Poole, as pastor of the congregation, certainly affirmed the lay-led nature of the congregation and how it incarnated the concept of the priesthood of believers. He complimented the laity for participating and

---

[30] N Deacons 5 18 08; N Deacons 6 21 09; N Deacons 9 20 09; N Deacons 10 11 09; N Minutes 10 12 10.

[31] N Deacons 8 15 10; N Deacons 1 28 12; Kelley Williams Sr., email to Aaron Weaver, October 8, 2017.

[32] N Deacons 1 28 12. Barbara Webb tabulated the deacon numbers from 2012 to 2017 (Barbara Webb, email to Doug Weaver, June 19, 2017).

leading in ministries like Children's Bible Camp or the varied ministries of Wider Net. During the crisis with the Mississippi Baptist Convention about church contributions (explained below), he carefully worked with the deacons and the Denominational Relations Committee. At the same time, the pastor, like the congregation, had to ask how specific situations in the church's life were best modeled in the balance between minister and laity. In 2009, when Amy Joyner raised the issue of moving from a full-time to part-time ministerial position, Poole expressed concern to the deacons about his role in the process; how did a pastor appropriate his voice in a strongly lay-led church that "would not seem political or intended to influence the vote"? In 2011, he also suggested that the deacons reflect on the question, "What is my role as spiritual leader of the church?" during the context of dealing with some issues and problems that arose from Wider Net ministries at the church.[33] In such cases, Poole sought to be mindful of the thoughts of people in the congregation and at the same time, "embody the embrace of Christ."[34]

In a 2017 reflection, Chuck Poole without hesitation could say, "Northminster is probably the least pastor-centered church anywhere. It was designed to be a lay-led church, it is a lay-led church."[35] He elaborated that the DNA of Northminster was such that the laity were willing and able to do things without the pastor's blessing, a characteristic rare even in congregationally governed churches. On occasions, Poole opposed specific congregational actions out of his own ministerial conscience, but the minister-laity relationship remained intact. Poole never insisted that the church follow his preferences (and they sometimes did not), yet they maintained their love and respect for the pastor as their minister. For example, when the church voted to expand its facilities and build a balcony (2008), Poole thought the construction was unnecessary. He also spoke against revising the deacon selection process (2006) to eliminate the election of six of twelve nominees and move to an up or down vote on a slate of deacons.[36]

[33] N Deacons 10 11 09; N Deacons 6 13 10; N Deacons 5 5 11.

[34] Chuck Poole, phone interview by Doug Weaver, July 21, 2017.

[35] "Northminster Baptist Church," *The Northside Sun Magazine* 12/4 (June 2017): 24.

[36] Chuck Poole, phone interview.

Poole was undoubtedly a seasoned, experienced pastor highly respected for his untiring care and service for others. He possessed a quiet but strong calming demeanor and did not need to be authoritative. His spiritual leadership and his ability as a caregiver, a peacemaker, and a keen expositor of Scripture were never in dispute. He could speak on conflicted issues, but his goal was to speak with grace and careful speech. Observers watched Poole model leadership by example, but also demonstrate the humility of a co-sharer in ministry. Most Baptists talked lay-led ministry, but the Northminster paradigm, an extensive lay-led committee and deacon structure that worked alongside the ministerial staff, was rare—especially in settings where the preaching ministry was strong and provided leadership through proclamation. Poole was content and affirmed Northminster's uniqueness; not an ounce of stress over leadership dynamics was present.[37] After fifty years, it seems best to conclude that the importance of the pastor and staff and the importance of the laity in a church self-identified as a lay-led church were important dual emphases that were regularly affirmed and negotiated.

The Church's Architecture: Facilities

On April 20, 2008, Northminster Baptist Church dedicated new facilities, the balcony in the sanctuary as well as a new education building and columbarium. The new structures were part of the Wider Net vision formed in 2001—the enlargement of the literal walls of the church plant alongside the enlargement of the commitment to ministry in the Mid-City/Georgetown neighborhood. The dedication ceremony referred to the sacred garden with fountain in memory of Tommy Ramey. In 2001, the cost of the building phase of Wider Net was $2.3 million. By 2008, the cost had risen to $4 million (adding the columbarium to the original components), with 1.6 million received in pledges and contributions and 2.4 million converted to long-term debt service.[38]

In 2009, as part of the congregation's observance of All Saints' Day, a memorial dogwood was planted on the church's grounds in remembrance of each person interred in the new columbarium. The planting of memorial

[37] Ibid.

[38] N News 3 26 08; N News 4 23 08; N Minutes 11 13 11. A $192,000 line item was added to the annual budget for debt service.

dogwoods became a tradition each All Saints' Day. The first two internments in the columbarium had been for Sam Cox and Jim Hendrick.

Also in 2009, the deacons discussed the possibility of adding property to the church campus. An opportunity arose to purchase a home that faced Eastover Drive as a way to confront persistent parking issues. Given the economic depressed climate of 2009 in the region, however, the deacons declined to take on new debt. Chuck Poole thought that restraint was wise, noting that the congregation would do well to "be content with our possessions."[39]

In 2013, the congregation was forced to confront the safety of their facilities. A robbery and vehicle break-ins resulted in the increase of security guards at the church.[40] The church always was attuned to campus maintenance. In increasing technological times, Northminster did the obvious and made its facilities equipped with wireless internet.[41]

Additions also enhanced the music ministry at the church. Improvements that completed the original design of the Austin organ were completed in 2007—in memory of Mattie Lou Stribling, the mother of Roger Stribling Jr., for whom the organ had been dedicated in 1981. On September 12, 2008, a celebration of the new organ featured an organ concert by Todd Wilson, a world-renowned concert organist. In 2013, the church added a $375,000 choir suite renovation to its musical space.[42]

In 2012, the church began digitizing its significant historical archives. As Kelley Williams Sr. said, "Barbara Webb is a living, breathing storehouse of knowledge with a memory that's an awesome searchable data base. She has a lifetime warranty. But what then?"[43] Collecting and preserving the materials were part of the church's close attention to honoring the memory of its fifty-year heritage.

---

[39] N Deacons 9 21 08; N Deacons 1 18 09.

[40] N Deacons 3 30 08; N Deacons 4 20 08; N News 10 28 09; N Deacons 1 5 13; N Deacons 7 17 13; N News 8 21 13.

[41] N Deacons 6 14 15.

[42] N Deacons 3 17 13.

[43] Kelley Williams Sr. memo to Jason Greener, January 4, 2017; N Deacons 2 19 17.

Ministry of Worship

The serious observance of the cycles of the Christian calendar at Northminster continued unabated in the Poole years. Poole's love of worship was obvious to all and without question during Holy Week and the season of Lent. He invested significant energy to convey to church members the importance of the preparation for Easter for the congregation's communal identity and for personal journeys of faith. Poole pastorally and graciously reminded congregants that the observance was not "indispensable" for the Christian pilgrimage, yet he encouraged them to consider the "deep meaning" the observance brought to those that practiced the spiritual discipline.[44] In a *Northminster News* column, Poole vividly took his readers into the depths of Ash Wednesday at the beginning of the Lenten season:

> As I write these words the sun is rising on another Ash Wednesday, which means that, by the time these words are read, the church will be purple; dressed in her annual Lenten solemnity, feet to the path of another long Lenten journey which will lead us, at last, to the cross of our Lord, where death will have the next-to-last word. The last word will come later. Death will have the next-to-last word on the last Friday of the last week in Lent, and then, two days later, Someone Else will have the last word. But not yet. First, there is a purple road to walk, a steep path to climb, and a fierce cross to face. Easter is coming, but Lent is here.[45]

On another occasion, he focused on the significance of Holy Week for worship:

> Our church seeks to create moments and spaces that can help us keep faith with the deep rhythms of *"The Great Week."* Northminster's Holy Week schedule is printed below. The spaces it creates in the week are intended to help us ponder the suffering of our Lord as we prepare to embrace the joy of Easter. The hope and joy of the resurrection may be right around the corner, but you can't get there from here. There is uneven ground first to cross. There's a steep hill to climb and thick darkness to travel before the glad day dawns. We have an annual appoint-

[44] N News 2 18 09.
[45] N News 3 5 14.

> ment to keep with the great week before we can celebrate the great day.[46]

The church offered a full plate of Holy Week services: Palm Sunday vespers, Maundy Thursday, Good Friday Tenebrae, and daily Holy Week meditations and communion in the chapel before Easter Sunday worship. From 2004 to 2010, during Holy Week the Palm Sunday vesper service included the ordinance of baptism.[47] During the Lenten season, the church visually prepared as well. Purple paraments adorned the lectern, pulpit, and table, with a purple drape on the sanctuary cross. A church member carried a Lenten banner to lead the procession at the beginning of each Sunday worship service. At times, other special worship elements—sacred musical performances—were included under the leadership of Worship and Music Committee chair, Dr. Richard Joiner, and minister of music, Dr. Tim Coker. For example, in 2010 the singing of each Sunday's designated lectionary psalm was the call to worship. For Palm Sundays, the Northminster Choir performed Gabriel Faure's *Requiem* and Dan Forrester's "Requiem for the Living."[48]

Other key events of the Christian calendar were highlighted annually. Each fall (November) All Saints' Day was observed, appropriately, as a time to remember loved ones who had died the previous year and "preceded us into God's nearer presence." A dogwood tree was planted in the Stribling Garden in their honor and the names of the deceased were read aloud in a vesper service. In 2008 and other times, the church choir sang (John) Rutter's *Requiem* (an adaptation of a Latin Mass for the dead) as part of the service.[49]

The celebration of Advent was, of course, special. Poole admitted that the first week of Advent was his personal favorite:

> It's the one week of Advent which is just the right distance from Christmas; close enough to be close, but distant enough that we might actually have a chance to get it right this year; a chance to travel the church's purple road in the mindful, gentle, prayerful, thoughtful way we always mean to but rarely get to. This early in Advent, there is still

[46] N News 2 13 08. See also N News 3 12 08.

[47] N News 2 13 08; N News 3 4 09.

[48] N News 2 17 10; N News 3 31 10; N News 3 21 12; N News 3 18 15.

[49] N News 9 17 08; N News 3 19 13; N News 10 14 15.

> time for us to move through new December days with the deep repentance, constant prayer and quiet kindness which will bring us to Bethlehem centered, not fragmented. Who knows? By the time Advent's circle of light is full and finished, we could, ourselves, be all aflame with the coming of Christ. We could, ourselves, be lit up and luminous with holiness, kindness and love. After all, this is week one, so there's still time! It's not too late to walk the purple road again and get it right, for once.[50]

The Advent season had a candlelight Christmas Eve communion service, and sometimes a living nativity featuring elementary-aged children as part of the pre-service music for the evening. In the afterglow of Advent and Christmas, a church member might attend a communion service on New Year's Eve.[51] The New Year was brought in, since 2010, with an annual Baptism of the Lord vesper service—on Baptism of the Lord Sunday on the liturgical calendar—that complemented other baptismal services throughout the year. This evening service supplanted the Palm Sunday vesper baptismal service, but it maintained the opportunity for baptism in a smaller setting than the Sunday morning worship hour.[52]

The deacons often discussed worship and their participation. In 2010, such discussion led them to respond to a call to be more focused servant leaders. Gayla Purvis reported that various homebound church members had inquired about receiving communion at home. Purvis agreed to coordinate the lay ministry.[53]

One element often seen in more formal, liturgically oriented churches—compensating singers to enhance the musical quality of worship—was discussed in 2010 among the deacons. A request from the Worship Committee was submitted, but later withdrawn, to establish a designated fund to pay selected singers (non-church members; college students) for their choir participation.[54] Another worship element that became increasingly popular in the twenty-first century among congregations that emphasized spiritual formation and sharing ecumenical ideas was the labyrinth walk, a meditative

---

[50] N News 11 30 11.
[51] N News 12 17 08; N News 12 16 09.
[52] N News 12 16 09; N News 1 8 14; N News 12 3 14.
[53] N Deacons 4 11 10.
[54] N Deacons 1 17 10; N Deacons 2 21 10; N Deacons 3 21 10.

walk on a circuitous path from its outer edge to center. In 2009, the *Northminster News* began promoting the labyrinth experience for the spiritual growth of church members. The church never set up its own labyrinth on the church grounds but for several years borrowed a "portable labyrinth" that covered almost the whole floor of the Great Hall. The labyrinth was in place for a weekend or a week. David and Emily Benzenhafer were inspired to establish a labyrinth walk at their home in Prentiss, Mississippi. Numerous church members, including the children's ministry, visited and enjoyed it.[55]

Given the long tradition of liturgical worship rooted in the Christian calendar and lectionary readings and preaching, some new members from non-liturgical backgrounds had a steep learning curve regarding worship practices. Consequently, in 2010 and 2011, the Worship Committee (Richard Joiner, chair) sponsored a liturgy workshop. The workshop was also intended to help shepherd new members to participate as lay readers or liturgy writers, two important parts of the lay-focused element in Northminster worship.[56] Since Northminster was a progressive Baptist congregation, the use of inclusive language by the ministers leading worship was to be expected. For example, the term "Godself" was used rather than a masculine pronoun for God, and congregants were referred to in worship as "brothers and sisters."[57]

Experimentation in worship practices in strongly liturgical settings was much rarer than in more "low church" environments. The ancient practice of foot washing was a new ritual for most contemporary churchgoers. Historically, foot washing had been practiced in more rural, mountain, conservative (Free Will Baptist) churches but was becoming increasingly prevalent. In some congregations where Holy Week services were being offered, the ritual was a humble imitation of Jesus' act of foot washing with his disciples in the week before his death. After having a foot washing in a Maundy Thursday service in 2009, the church waited before doing it again. In 2017, the Wor-

[55] N News 3 31 09; N News 3 31 10; Barbara Webb, email to Doug Weaver, June 16, 2017.

[56] N News 3 3 10; N News 12 15 10.

[57] Doug Weaver, attendance at worship, Northminster Baptist Church, October 16, 2016.

ship Committee re-introduced foot washing to the observance of Maundy Thursday.[58]

Mixing worship and fellowship, the congregation—despite its preference for more serious liturgical worship—had an annual old-fashioned hymn sing, ice cream social, and "backpack blessing" (for students returning to school) at the end of the summer. While not worship, the worshiping community was encouraged to participate in fellowship like the annual church-wide Labor Day picnic.[59]

For fifty years, Northminster Baptist Church was known for its distinctive worship: a focus on reverence, a long-standing basic order of worship, reliance on the wondrous, booming sound of its organ, following the liturgical calendar, and the like. At the same time, the congregation desired strong preaching, with a focus on substance and homiletic brevity (in contrast to traditional Southern Baptist preaching), and was proud of its heritage of pulpit excellence. Chuck Poole's preaching undoubtedly fit the bill of excellence, and he contributed his own unique style of brevity. Poole's preaching was characterized by a poetic cadence, with intentional repetition of important words and phrases that stuck with the listener. He spoke with deliberate speed, and with slow, intentional pauses. He normally drove home one clear point from the lectionary text(s)—not the old-fashioned three-point sermon—and emphasized the need for careful speech (a major theme), non-judgmental discernment, and trusting faith. "When it comes to the great mysteries of suffering and loss, pain and prayer, disappointment and hope, I invite you to a life of careful speech," Poole suggested, instead of spouting the "slogans and certitudes of popular Christianity" in the Bible Belt.[60]

Poole made no secret that he was a person of constant prayer. This was reflected in his preaching when he emphasized that God is mystery, life can be hard, but God is good and loving. Poole could and would occasionally use a dry humorous wit (referring to the lectionary as the person Lex Shunnairy), but his preaching style highlighted the seriousness of the gospel mes-

---

[58] N Deacons 6 10 09; N Deacons 3 19 17.

[59] N News 8 21 13; N News 8 5 15.

[60] Charles E. Poole, *A Church for Rachel: Sermons for Those Who Mourn* (Macon: Mercer University Press, 2012) 4. The analysis of Chuck Poole's preaching is based on reading several of Poole's books of sermons, most recently *A Church for Rachel* as well as sermons on the church's website.

sage. He drew the listener into a deep sense of empathy and grace for those on the margins, those hurting, or simply all persons in need of an affirming word from Scripture.[61] Poole focused on the mercy of a gracious God for all people. He was inclusive and offered words that listeners often considered prophetic. For example, his sermon at the 2014 CBF General Assembly reflected these traits. He preached about a "gospel embrace" of diversity of all peoples.

> Maybe that's one reason why Jesus said, "when you give a dinner, don't invite those who are most like you. Rather, invite those who are least like you." I sometimes wonder if Jesus instructed us to set ourselves such a long table, and draw ourselves such a wide circle, in this life, so it won't take us so long to adjust in the next life; where, not only will the circle be unbroken, but the circle will be wider than anything any of us have ever imagined. Maybe Jesus wanted us to go ahead and live a big table, wide circle life now, so we won't be so surprised when we learn, over on the other side, that *we* is more than *us*. Maybe he was trying to get us ready for that far off someday when every creature in heaven and on earth and under the earth and in the sea will sing to God around the throne; every tongue, tribe, people and nation, every soul God ever loved, reconciled to God through the cross, just as God always wanted, hoped, willed and planned.[62]

Poole preached the universality of the gospel. Passages such as John 3:16 and John 14:6, long used by Christians to highlight an exclusive message, needed to be interpreted with reliance upon the Holy Spirit and experience so "what we believe is what rings most true in the depth of our soul." "Jews, Muslims, Hindus; people whose lives so fully embodied the Spirit of God that to believe they were going to eternal torment when they died, for no other reason than believing what their parents and grandparents believe,

[61] On careful speech, see Poole, *A Church for Rachel*, 1–4, 36, 40. See also at the church's website, Poole, "Careful Speech concerning John 3:16," (http://www.northminsterbaptist.org/sermon/careful-speech-concerning-john-316/) and "Careful Speech Concerning John 14:6." http://www.northminsterbaptist.org/sermon/careful-speech-concerning-john-316/.

[62] Charles E. Poole, "One Small Taste," sermon, CBF annual meeting, June 2014 (unpublished sermon manuscript); Poole, *A Church for Rachel*, 22.

the same way I believe what my parents and grandparents believe, eventually became something I could no longer pretend to believe," Poole preached.[63]

Weekly Northminster heard Poole preach a message in which every word counted. He delivered sermons with pathos and substance; instead of offering easy answers with certainty, he offered messages full of "incurable hope." As he told the congregation, "Personally, I have never had as much faith as I would like to have, but I do have a pretty good case of incurable hope.... There's nothing like living a life of faith. It limbers up your soul and gives you so much more to think about than just the facts on the ground. Faith makes room in the room for God."[64] Incurable hope did not mean all things turned out rosy or as people prayed, Poole agreed, but hope was unfailing: "it's awful what we have to go through in this life, and it's wonderful the way God, and God's people, go through it with us."[65]

Ministry of Education

Ever since the church's founding, church members sought a variety of educational avenues instead of simply relying on basic Sunday school literature. Academic studies were made available quickly, and the phrase, "teaching church" dated back to the ministry of John Claypool. Adult studies continued the tradition during the Poole years, including looking beyond the Baptist tradition for resources. For example, church members were encouraged to visit St. Peter's Cathedral and engage in a guided tour of the Stations of the Cross. In 2015–2016, the Adult Ministries Committee, co-chaired by Jo Ann Ratliff and Max Arinder, coordinated a two-year study on "Word and Spirit," building on a comment from the early church father Irenaeus: "God has two hands, Word and Spirit." The study included three elements: Bible study, church history, and stories about the Holy Spirit.[66] A focus on studying personality traits as a tool for spiritual growth—via the personality typing approach called the Enneagram—became popular in recent years across denominational lines. Northminster participated in these ecumenical workshops co-sponsored by several other churches, including St. Andrew's Episcopal Cathedral, Galloway United Methodist Church, St.

[63] Poole, "Careful Speech concerning John 3:16."
[64] Poole, *A Church for Rachel*, 8.
[65] Ibid., 46.
[66] N News 3 6 13; N News 9 2 15; N Deacons 1 16 16; N News 4 27 16.

James' Episcopal Church, as well as the Shepherd's Staff and the Center for Ministry at Millsaps College.[67] Poole also offered a brief times of study after Wednesday evening suppers. Topics close to Northminster's identity as Baptists were not missing among the studies. For example, what it meant to be a lay-led church was one topic for study, and Poole visited Baptist historic distinctives with the creative title, "Thinking Baptistly, Ten Minutes at a Time."[68]

Baptists had long had an annual winter Bible study. Northminster continued the tradition by scheduling winter lectures with trained specialists, male and female scholars, well-known Baptists (Fisher Humphreys, 2008; Bill Leonard, 2012) and non-Baptists (Steven Haynes, 2007; James Efird, 2010). Speakers often had prior connections to the church: former youth minister, Stan Wilson (at Northside Baptist Church, Clinton, in 2009); former pastor, Roger Paynter (at First Baptist Church, Austin, Texas, in 2013); former church member Holly Benzenhafer Redford (living in Boston in 2014); and former church member Holly Hollman (a member of Northminster from 1986 to 2003; daughter of Harold and Jo Hollman; general counsel of the Baptist Joint Committee for Religious Liberty, Washington, DC, in 2016).[69]

The annual women's retreat offered opportunities for study and spiritual formation. Guest speakers also included women with special connections to the congregation. For example, in 2011, Holly Benzenhafer Redford, who had been ordained by the church in 2009, led the retreat, and in 2014, Katherine Martin was the leader. Martin was married to Brent Martin, whose home church was Northminster. She was an ordained minister in the United Church of Christ who had graduated from Wake Forest University School of Divinity.[70] Ellen Gabardi was a frequent speaker for women's ministries' "Lenten Half-Day Retreat." Like Martin, Gabardi was trained in contemplative spiritual formation, a theme that Amy Joyner Finkelberg en-

---

[67] N News 1 13 13; N News 9 17 14; N News 1 6 16.

[68] N News 1 7 09; N News 9 15 10.

[69] Jo Hollman was ordained in 1998. Fisher Humphreys was a Baptist theologian at Samford University's Beeson Divinity School (Birmingham, Alabama). Bill Leonard was a historian of Christianity, especially Baptist studies, at Wake Forest Divinity School. James Efird taught New Testament at Duke Divinity School.

[70] N News 12 17 14.

couraged during her ministry.[71] The interest in spirituality and devotional life was also seen in the larger congregation with the special publication of a book of devotional reflections, *Echoes of Grace* (2015) by the senior citizens fellowship called PrimeTimers. Anne Guidry, Amy Williams, and Amy Finkelberg co-edited the volume.[72]

During the Poole years, other "teaching church" activities included participation in a Moravian love feast to celebrate the birth of Christ and to commemorate the early Christian practice of an "agape/love feast," a Jesus and contemporary film series, and a summer book study on former Mississippian's Charles Marsh's influential academic exploration of religion and the civil rights movement: *God's Long Summer: Stories of Faith and Civil Rights*. In 2014, Rebecca Wiggs and Jill Barnes Buckley led the study to remember and observe the fiftieth anniversary of the contentious "Freedom Summer" in Mississippi.[73] Chuck Poole reflected on the importance of remembering summer 1964, a time when he was an eight-year-old in Macon, Georgia. "Fifty years later, I can also say, 'I'm sorry' for the indignities and injustices that so many people have suffered," Poole wrote, "for no reason other than the color of their skin; indignities and injustices which came with being born on the other side of those 'White' and 'Colored' signs I can barely remember, but will never forget."[74]

Amid all the serious study events on the church calendar, the congregation also experimented with "foyer groups," groups of eight church members randomly put together to share a meal and fellowship. The congregation was encouraged to get to know more people than those in their usual circle.[75] Adult educational opportunities at Northminster simply spelled variety and were never in short supply.

---

[71] N News 3 2 11; N News 1 11 12; N News 10 31 12. Garbadi received training from Shalem, a contemplative spiritual formation institute in Washington D.C. and at the Center for Ministry at Millsaps College, Jackson, MS.

[72] N News 8 5 15; N Deacons 8 16 15.

[73] N News 10 10 08; N News 10 14 12; N News 5 14 14.

[74] N News 5 28 14.

[75] N News 8 22 12; N News 8 21 13; N News 1 22 14.

Ministry of Education: Wake Forest University School of Divinity

Northminster's important relationship with Wake Forest University School of Divinity continued during the second stint of Poole's ministry and revealed the congregation's interest in the relationship between theological education and ministry. Courtney Allen, a member of Northminster for fifteen years (daughter of David and Cheryl Allen and the sister of Camille Allen Snyder), received a time of blessing and affirmation from the congregation when she entered divinity school in 2007. She returned to preach in summer 2008 when she worked with the Cooperative Baptist Fellowship of Mississippi.[76] In 2011, Jill Buckley and Amy Finkelberg traveled to Winston-Salem, North Carolina, to represent Northminster and give the church's gift of a liturgical stole to Katherine Martin upon her ordination to the ministry in the United Church of Christ.[77] When Steven Fuller joined the church staff in 2010, he became the third associate pastor (Tripp Martin and Amy Joyner Finkelberg) who had graduated from Wake Forest Divinity School.

In 2013, divinity school student Rebecca Wright served eight weeks as a community ministry summer intern as part of the partnership the church and the divinity school developed. Jill Buckley noted that the genesis of the partnership was Courtney Allen's research project on the Wider Net ministry written at the divinity school. Divinity students worked with the Wider Net ministries in the Mid-City/Georgetown neighborhood (for example, assisting with devotionals, the Operation Shoestring summer breakfast program, and the summer camp for middle school students at Greater New Zion Baptist Church). In summer 2014, Christopher Coates was the second divinity school student to serve as a community ministry intern under the supervision of Jill Buckley. The partnership continued with intern Christopher Harris in 2016.[78]

Northminster also had connections to the leadership of Wake Forest University School of Divinity. In 2012, Bill Leonard, founding dean and popular professor of church history and interpreter of Baptist identity, and in 2015, Gail O'Day, current dean of the school, were the featured guest speakers for the church's annual Winter Lecture Series. During O'Day's vis-

---

[76] N News 12 19 07; N News 7 15 08.

[77] N News 2 20 11.

[78] N News 5 30 13; N News 5 28 14; N Deacons 6 2 13; N News 6 8 16.

it, members of Shady Grove Baptist Church (Ridgeway Street) attended because one of their members was also a student at the school.[79] The *Northminster News* also highlighted a gift the church received from Frank Tupper, a theologian at Wake Forest. Tupper sent a copy of the second edition of his book, *A Scandalous Providence*, to the congregation and dedicated it to "John R. Claypool and the congregation of Northminster Baptist Church of Jackson, Mississippi." In a letter to the church, Tupper called Northminster his "Mississippi church home" and thanked the congregation for the opportunity to preach at the church on numerous occasions, writing, "The opportunity to speak with openness and freedom proved uniquely significant for me, one of the most meaningful experiences in my entire life." Diann Arinder commented that such a "heartfelt expression" honored the "spirit of Northminster."[80]

The Wake Forest-Northminster connection is supported in other ways, in particular, through the alumni efforts of church member Rebecca Wiggs. Rebecca and Mark Wiggs have been longtime friends of the divinity school; Rebecca received her undergraduate degree at Wake Forest University, was on the divinity school's first Board of Visitors, and became the second chair of that board (then serving multiple terms). As Bill Leonard commented, "We owe Mark and Rebecca a lot."[81]

Ministry to Youth

The ministry of youth in Baptist settings is usually a mixture of Bible study, mission projects, and fellowship. Northminster had its share of all these activities throughout its fifty-year history. Ever since the congregation's development of its Wider Net ministries, youth were actively involved. On Martin Luther King Jr. national holidays, Northminster youth worked with neighborhood youth at Stewpot for a "mid-city work day." On other occasions, they helped clear lots in preparation of the construction of Habitat for Humanity houses. Northminster also sponsored summer internships at Operation Shoestring for members of the youth group. One youth to participate was Callie Daniels, a high school junior, who worked with a kids'

[79] N News 11 30 11; N News 1 7 15; N Deacons 3 15 15.
[80] N News 9 3 14.
[81] Bill Leonard, email to Doug Weaver, July 14, 2017.

camp.[82] In 2016, for the Martin Luther King Jr. holiday the youth traveled to Shaw, Mississippi, to work in a CBF-sponsored ministry, Delta Hands for Hope, with youth from University Baptist Church of Hattiesburg in what was described as "continuing a growing relationship."[83] All of these Wider Net related activities afforded church youth a race-relations laboratory for their Christian pilgrimage. While working with people from different walks of life, intentional dialogue was important. In 2014 the youth from Northminster and from Stewpot's after-school program had small group discussions to face "the challenges and hopes of race and diversity as people of faith, and then just hang out and play together."[84]

In July 2013, youth minister Steven Fuller led the youth on a mission trip to New York City. They ministered to ninety children during the week, with the work divided between two locations, Metro Baptist Church in Hell's Kitchen and Greater Restoration Baptist Church in Crown Heights, Brooklyn. Fuller noted,

> The youth seemed a bit surprised when we showed up at Metro Baptist Church.... After traveling from Jackson that morning, we had to carry our fifty-pound bags up 68 stairs to our dorm rooms. But they pulled and tugged, stepped and stuttered their way up there. To be honest, after getting my bag up there, I began to question our endurance.... They had a week of teaching, chasing, leading, and loving 90 children.[85]

Typical youth ministry featured some type of "youth week." In 2004, Northminster initiated an annual youth focus week. Noted Baptists Kay Shurden (2007) of Mercer University and Kyle Matthews (2009), contemporary Christian musician and minister of worship at First Baptist Church of Greenville, South Carolina, were guests.[86] Northminster youth also participated annually in summer Passport camps, the ecumenical organization that was the camp experience of choice for Cooperative Baptists. Every spring, the congregation attended a luncheon-auction where youth auctioned off donated desserts to raise funds for youth retreats and activities.[87]

---

[82] N News 12 12 07; N News 7 30 08; N News 1 7 09; N News 5 6 09.
[83] N News 1 6 16.
[84] N News 5 28 14.
[85] N News 8 7 13.
[86] N News 10 3 07; N News 11 4 09.
[87] N News 2 5 14; N News 4 30 14.

Youth ministry, of course, included a range of fellowship activities. Perennial favorites were the Colorado ski trips and the annual lake party to close out the summer. Ecumenical sports included paintball with the Episcopalians from St. James' Episcopal Church. The connection to mid-city ministry included sports. Northminster and youth from the after-school program at Stewpot played on "Stewminster" basketball teams, even winning a league championship in 2013.[88] Steven Fuller advertised "mystery trips" to attract youth. He also offered a combination of fellowship and Bible study with the uniquely titled breakfast devotional activity "God and Grits." He visited different locales and had breakfast with youth before their school day started. "God and Grits! Bible and Biscuits! Pancakes with the Paraclete! Do you wake up eager to eat of breakfast foods and the word of God?" Fuller wrote as he invited youth to participate. Spirit-led pancakes were no doubt a draw.[89]

Northminster Baptist Church, since its inception, did not follow strict age-based Sunday school classes, especially among the adults. Nevertheless, children and youth had their age groups. In typical Baptist chronology, each fall there was "promotion" from one aged class to another. At Northminster, a special event was the gift of giving Bibles for rising seventh-graders. As high school seniors left the youth group, children joining the group were given a Bible to begin the next phase of their life journey.[90]

One mentoring relationship with the youth of the Georgetown area and an outgrowth of the Wider Net initiative was featured not only on the front sports page of the *Clarion-Ledger* newspaper in Jackson but also on the front page of the online high school sports section of *USA Today*. The occasion was a football rivalry game between Jackson Prep and Jackson Academy on October 5, 2012. The featured player was Jamaal Clayborn, a 6'4", 320-pound senior offensive lineman from Jackson Academy, whose team was ranked number one in their classification (AAA). Two rival players from Jackson Prep were Zach and Jake Williams, sons of Kelley and

---

[88] N News 6 22 11; N News 10 26 11; N News 3 19 13; N News 6 11 14.

[89] N News 11 10 15.

[90] N News 2 21 16.

M'lee Williams. At the time of the game, Clayborn had lived at the Williamses' house the past three years.[91]

The story began when Kelley Williams Jr., as part of his volunteer work in the Mid-City area, was coaching the Georgetown Colts in a youth football league in 2006. He befriended Clayborn and developed a mentoring relationship. When Clayborn's mother had concerns about her son's grades as a freshman in a public high school, Williams arranged for Jamaal to be homeschooled in north Jackson. Because of the distance between his home and school, Jamaal lived with the Williams during the week and returned home for weekends, until he eventually moved in full time with the Williams family when he enrolled at Jackson Academy.

The relationship was reminiscent of *The Blind Side*, the 2009 Hollywood movie (starring Quinton Aaron and Sandra Bullock) that depicted the story of University of Mississippi football player Michael Oher. The Williams family understood the reference to *The Blind Side*, and Zach, Jake, and their sister, Anna Kate, worried about the comparisons. M'lee related, "We knew Jamaal way before *The Blind Side* came out. Kelley takes his mentoring seriously, so I always kinda thought someone would come live with us one day. I just kinda felt it was God's plan." Clayborn also rejected comparisons to *The Blind Side*, pointing out, "I didn't want people to think my mom wasn't there for me and all of that. My mom did her job but just saw this as a good opportunity for me." He added that *The Blind Side* was one reason that he did not want to go to Ole Miss as Oher had.[92] The Clayborn-Williams story demonstrated the Williamses' personal and family commitment and the church's role in youth-Wider Net ministries, and Clayborn embodied the dignity revealed in genuine cross-cultural relationships.[93]

Legacy of Youth Ministries: "Child of the Church"

At Northminster, the phrase "child of the church" refers to the numerous adults in the congregation who grew up in the church and either never

---

[91] Rod Walker, "A House Divided," *Clarion-Ledger*, October 5, 2012, C-1, http://usatodayhss.com/2012/ja-vs-prep-a-house-divided.

[92] Ibid. Clayborn was a starting center for two years on the football team at Mississippi State University, finishing his college eligibility in 2016.

[93] N Deacons 11 16 14.

left or returned to Jackson (perhaps after receiving their education) to worship at the church of their upbringing. These adults were influenced significantly by their experience in the Northminster youth group.

On April 2, 2017, the congregation had a special session on what it meant to grow up at Northminster as a "child of the church." Max Arinder, co-chair of the Adult Studies Committee, moderated the evening; panelists included Kelley Williams Jr., (parents, Jean and Kelley Williams Sr.), Dudley Wooley (parents, Easie and O. B. Wooley), and Gray Jackson III (parents, Eda and Gray Jackson Jr.). Arinder noted that the phrase "child of the church," coined by Chuck Poole, had deep meaning for the congregation and asked the panelists about their experience growing up there. Dudley Wooley commented that youth felt valued in the church and were expected to contribute as a "vibrant part of the community." When asked what core values their church experience as youth had given them, Kelley Williams Jr. said, "we are very loved and valued" and "are all special creatures of God." He added that the church communicated that a spirit of service was integral to life, even if it was not convenient. Wooley recalled the foundational phrase of the church's origins; people could agree to differ and still love each other and respect one another. "Unbelievable mentors" such as Mike Peters and Bryan Rodgers had influenced his life. Gray Jackson recalled the importance of his baptism as a teenager and applied a phrase from Poole to express it: "The water never dries off." He also mentioned the affirmation that at Northminster "every member is a minister." All the panelists agreed the church youth were almost like siblings because they spent so much time together, and the panelists explained that as they made decisions to stay at the church as adults, one motivator was that they "owed something back to this church" and wanted to pass the grace and distinctive heritage they had received on to their children. No doubt, being a "child of the church" at Northminster had left a significant impression on the congregation's first fifty years.[94]

In separate reflections, Kelley Williams Jr. recalled his experience and the effects on his future:

---

[94] Kelley Williams Jr., Dudley Wooley, and Gray Jackson III, cited in "Growing Up at Northminster," audio recording, Adult Ministries Evening Service, April 2, 2017.

> It is not an exaggeration to say that we might not be a family at all were it not for the youth group at Northminster. My wife M'lee and I got to be friends through the youth group. We sat through countless Sunday nights at the youth house together and went on numerous retreats with the youth. We never once dated in junior high or high school, but it was those formative years in the youth house that nurtured our friendship. Because we grew up following the same leaders, hearing the same lessons, and sharing the same experiences, we formed the same core values, which ultimately brought us together.[95]

Williams related that the youth workers (the same ones that Wooley praised during the panel discussion)—Mike Peters and Bryan Rodgers—were friends and mentors. Enduring friendships developed; Peters and Rodgers served as groomsmen for Kelley and M'lee's wedding seven years after they were in the youth group. Northminster's pastors have also been heavily involved in the ministry to youth. Both John Claypool and John Thomason accompanied the youth on some of their youth trips and retreats. Williams Jr. reflected, "I think Northminster viewed the youth program as the garden where the next crop of church members—be that at Northminster or elsewhere—were grown."[96]

On January 22, 2017, Northminster had its most recent Youth Sunday. The Sunday reflected some typical emphases for a youth Sunday in a Baptist church. The youth led in worship and there were multiple preachers. Along with Rose Daniels and Will Hicks, Anna Kate Williams, daughter of Kelley and M'lee, was one of the three preachers for the worship service. "So the influence of the youth group on us back in the late 1970s and early 1980s," Williams Jr. gratefully reminisced, "endures and has now been passed on to the next generation."[97]

Ministry to Children

Significant changes to Northminster's ministry to the children of Jackson occurred in 2009–2010. Over the previous twenty-seven years, a mother's morning out program had developed into the Northminster Childcare

---

[95] Kelley Williams Jr., "What the Northminster Youth Group Means to Our Family," email to Doug Weaver, January 22, 2017.

[96] Ibid.

[97] Ibid.

Center, which served children outside the church's membership. Sustainability of the center was a major challenge. In February 2009, the deacons discussed perpetual budgeting deficits—an annual deficit of $6,135.00 for the last ten years—from running the center. Hope remained that the center's ministry, which included employment for eighteen women, many of whom "represented a distressed part of our community and have few other options for work," would continue.[98] An advisory committee asked the deacons to consider making the center's work an element of the church's budget rather than a separate entity.

Challenges continued. In September 2009, deacons heard of continued enrollment issues and learned about the persistent loss of three-year-olds to developing elementary programs, particularly the one at Jackson Academy. An ad hoc advisory committee, chaired by Jeff Wilson, recommended a 20 percent hike in tuition fees, a cutback to limit the staff to the legal limit for student-teacher ratios, and a marketing strategy to allow for drop-ins in order to obtain an 80 percent capacity. If these recommendations were successful, the committee thought, the childcare center could be sustainable.[99]

By spring 2010, the Board of Deacons accepted a recommendation from the ad hoc committee to close the Northminster Children's Center in May after the spring session. According to the *Northminster News*, despite the good work of the center and those involved in its ministry, decreasing revenues and enrollment problems had become too significant to continue.[100]

Northminster as a "teaching church" certainly applied to its children's ministries. One unique program—at least for Baptists—was Children's Atrium. According to Amy Joyner, Holly Wiggs was most responsible for the enthusiasm, energy, and organization of the program's start and success. The Atrium was an approach to spiritual formation based on the Montessori teaching method, which was used primarily in Catholic, Episcopal, and some Methodist churches. The Atrium method paralleled the adult education focus at Northminster on contemplative spirituality and was "meditative, not didactic," with the goal that children would develop a relationship of love with Jesus, the Good Shepherd. Praying, learning Bible stories, and

[98] N Deacons 2 5 09. See also N Deacons 1 18 09.
[99] N Deacons 9 20 09.
[100] N Deacons 2 21 10; N Deacons 3 21 10; N News 4 14 10.

worshiping were key elements of the experience. Joyner's summer sabbatical of 2008, she noted, was tied to this innovative experience. She wrote, "It is primarily through my work in the Children's Atrium that a deep longing for silence and prayerful listening has been called forth in my soul."[101]

The congregation found special times and ways to honor children as they grew. At the time of a baby dedication, the infant received a silver dove on a chain to symbolize the presence of the Holy Spirit in the growing, developing life. White Bibles were also provided for the infants. A pewter fish was presented in the water of baptism to each newly baptized person (not necessarily a child) as a sign of the family of faith, and each child received a pottery cup upon his or her first communion. When children entered the first grade, they received a Bible inscribed with their name. While not using the language of sacrament, Chuck Poole's vision of the rich symbolism of the church's rituals offered believers a sacramental presence: "small signs of big moments; sacred turnings marked by the keepsakes of the church." Poole continued,

> One imagines that some lifelong Northminsterites have received all those tokens of grace; stored away, perhaps, in a box at home; dove and fish, Bibles and cup, all marking sacred moments and passing time as we "Grow in grace and in the knowledge of our Lord and Savior Jesus Christ," a lifelong journey we do not make all by ourselves, but surrounded and supported by the family of faith.[102]

Several additional educational moments were provided rising first-graders as they transitioned into a new phase of participation at church. They participated in worship classes in which they took a tour of the sanctuary, were taught how to use a worship bulletin and a hymnal, and learned about the purpose of worship. They attended their final children's chapel (which occurred twice a month and followed the same lectionary worship pattern as the larger congregation's service, except with kid-friendly, three-minute sermons) and made an "official" entrance into worship in the sanctuary where they received their new Bible.[103]

---

[101] N News 5 21 08; N News 9 2 09. The *Northminster News* added that the Atrium's method was adapted from "The Catechesis of the Good Shepherd."

[102] N News 8 19 09. See also N News 2 13 08.

[103] N News 9 17 08; N News 9 24 08; N News 8 19 09; N News 6 25 14.

Children were also given an opportunity to do service projects outside the church. In 2016, for example, the children of Northminster Baptist Church and Galloway United Methodist Church joined together to make welcome bags for the Methodist Children's Home. Similar to ministry efforts of the youth, the children of Northminster and the Yellow Church joined together in a service project to assist Syrian refugees on the Martin Luther King Jr. national holiday.[104] Lesley Ratcliff, associate pastor for children, said that "worship and friendship kind of guide everything that we do."[105]

Like the youth, children participated in PASSPORT*kids!*, the ecumenical summer camp from Passport. They traveled to various out-of-state locations. Vacation Bible School, a staple of summer children's ministry, still needed creativity and new energy to be sustained. In 2008, the Vacation Bible School Committee considered taking a sabbatical from the summer program but decided instead to reformat the ministry with more focus on learning Bible stories (with less entertainment) and rename it Children's Bible Camp. Seventy-five volunteers anchored the week's work. The theme was "Beach Party—Surfin' through the Scriptures" and children from the Mid-City Summer Kids Club, sponsored by the Wider Net ministries, also attended and were invited to Sunday worship.[106] After the worship experience in which all the children placed gifts on the altar, Chuck Poole commented, "All in all, it was Northminster at its best; Northminster looking and sounding like the kingdom of God." Children's Bible Camp, Poole believed, was an excellent illustration of a lay-led church.[107]

A recent Children's Bible Camp revealed the energy and joy still invested in children's ministry. The 2017 camp theme was super heroes. Lesley Ratcliff, Carolyn Browning (Lesley's mother), and Cathy Davis sewed eighty capes with the Northminster logo affixed for the children who attended the camp. Chuck Poole told the legendary story of Martin Tours, the fifth-century church leader who ripped his cape in half to give to a person in need. Poole wanted to dramatize the story for the children, so Ratcliff

[104] N Deacons 1 16 16; N News 7 6 16; N Deacons 8 21 16.

[105] "Northminster Baptist Church," 25.

[106] N News 2 27 08.

[107] N News 7 1 08; N News 6 10 09; N News 6 23 10; N News 5 10 11; N Deacons 10 17 10.

cut a slit in his cape in order for it to tear easily. "Chuck wore the cape into the sanctuary during the assembly and told Martin's story, but when he got to the moment where he needed to tear the cape, he couldn't get it to rip," Ratcliff recalled. "I was standing right there so I jumped in to help and we ripped the cape apart. I told him afterwards that it was the quality of the sewing, not his strength, that stopped him."[108]

Ministry of Missions

Northminster's identity continued to have an anchor in missions as it entered its second half-century. In May 2009, twelve youth and four chaperones traveled to Pécs, Hungary, for a week of mission work. The group, working with Glen and Clista Adkins, former missionaries of the Cooperative Baptist Fellowship, hosted an English camp for Roma students who faced prejudice because of their ethnicity and poverty.[109] The primary focus of international missions continued to be the work in Honduras. In 2008, for example, the church's newsletter reminded church members that they had done mission work in Honduras for almost fifteen years. Reservations were set aside for up to forty-five participants from Northminster. The one-week summer (July) trip was a combined ecumenical effort with other churches (Galloway United Methodist Church, Christ United Methodist Church and Bellwether Church), and seventy people made the journey. Typical mission activities in Honduras included building homes, offering medical and dental services, distributing food, training local pastors, and conducting a Vacation Bible School for hundreds of children. The mission work was itself strongly ecumenical as the Mississippians served alongside Mennonite, Pentecostal, and Catholic Honduran friends.[110] Chuck Poole theologized that the trips were "a convergence of Matthew 25:31-46 ("I was hungry and you fed me, sick and you visited me") and Matthew 28: 16-20 ("Go therefore and teach all nations").[111] In 2009, the church was unable to go to Honduras because of political unrest there, but mission trips continued

[108] Lesley Ratcliff, email to Doug Weaver, June 12, 2017.
[109] N Deacons 4 9 09; N News 5 3 09.
[110] N News 2 27 08; N News 7 1 08; N News 3 4 09.
[111] N News 7 15 08.

in subsequent years.[112] The *Northminster News* did not advertise a trip in 2016 (church-led trips to Honduras had ceased), but in 2017, Covenant Presbyterian Church invited Northminster to join them on a trip to Honduras.[113]

Though Northminster continued its support for international missions by contributing to Cooperative Baptist Fellowship's general fund, Northminster missions energy focused primarily on Mississippi, with a focus on Jackson via Wider Net. The local focus was seen in Poole's emphasis, not on the word "missions," but on ministry to those in need as friendship and relationship. In other words, mission was re-conceptualized as friendship servanthood. With such a perspective, an international consciousness was present, though not as embodied or expressed as regularly.[114] Of course, as many observers of Mississippi could point out, a half a tank of gas could take someone to the Delta region of the state and find "any need imaginable."[115]

As the church entered its second fifty years, mission support was 25 percent of the total church budget. Mission efforts were divided into three broad areas, local and direct missions, denominational relations, and Wider Net ministries. Committees for each area of missions made recommendations regarding which ministries the congregation engaged in and provided close oversight of mission allocations (the Wider Net subcommittee of the Missions Committee became a free-standing committee of the church in 2012).[116]

In Northminster's fifth decade, local mission efforts continued to be extremely diverse and more plentiful than ever. Commitment to Wider Net ministries was stronger than ever. Local mission efforts tied to Wider Net continued to include Habitat for Humanity, Stewpot Ministries, Operation Shoestring, and the Yellow Church (Mid-City Community Center). A November 2015 report noted that since 2001, more than 350 Northminster

---

[112] N News 7 8 09; N News 4 14 10; N News 6 22 11; N News 2 6 13; N News 12 17 14.

[113] N News 3 29 17.

[114] This language of this section, particularly missions as friendship and the material regarding international consciousness is derived from an interview (Chuck Poole, phone interview).

[115] This comment about missions is based on several conversations.

[116] N Deacons 10 19 14.

church members had participated in ministries in the Mid-City/ Georgetown neighborhood.[117]

Other local mission efforts included Meals on Wheels, Catholic Charities, Magnolia Speech School, and Voice of Calvary Ministries. Two ministries that regularly caught the eye in the *Northminster News* were the Grace House (a home for people who were HIV-positive) and the Billy Brumfield House. Northminster Baptist Church had been involved with the Grace House since 1999, with volunteers providing meals for residents every Thursday evening. Deacons' minutes provided directions for deacons to participate in the ministry to Brumfield: the volunteer was to buy forty-eight eggs and one or two gallons of orange juice! Members, including deacons, delivered the food; Chuck Poole at times stayed to help prepare it.[118] Focus on alleviating hunger was expressed in other ways as well. In 2013, for example, the Adult Ministries and Denominational Relations committees set aside $2,500 to "Stop Hunger Now," an action, about which the *Northminster News* exclaimed, "That means that our congregation can package 10,000 meals!"[119] In 2017, the congregation remained strongly committed to its four-decade-old Advent tradition they called the "Boarding Homes Project." Church members provided and delivered food, clothes, and toiletries for people with mental health issues who lived in the personal care homes in Jackson. Like many churches, Northminster had an "angel tree" during Advent so that church members could pick a name of a child in need (often one connected to the Wider Net Ministries) to provide gifts for Christmas.[120]

Mission money also was directed toward Baptist entities. In 2017, support for denominational relations often focused on the work of the Metro Baptist Association, the Mississippi Baptist Convention (see separate story below regarding the future of these contributions), and the ministries affiliated with the Cooperative Baptist Fellowship (state and national level) though individual contributions might go to other Baptist groups (even on a rare occasion, the Southern Baptist Convention). When annual contributions to the church budget ended a year with a surplus, the Denominational Relations Committee divided its allotment in a variety of ways. In 2011, for

[117] N Deacons 11 8 15.

[118] N News 7 30 08; N Deacons 11 13 11; N Deacons 1 5 13; N News 8 5 15.

[119] N News 9 18 13.

[120] N News 12 3 08; N News 10 26 16.

example, the committee recommended $4,000 to place roofs on two new churches in Malawi; $5,000 to the local Metro Baptist Association, and $4,000 to the Madison Baptist Fellowship.[121]

Ministry of Stewardship: Budgets and Long-range Planning

In its fifth decade, Northminster Baptist Church accomplished financial goals most churches might only dream about—budget surpluses. In 2008, a surplus of $113,081 was reported on the 2007 budget. Surplus funds were used to pay for construction costs on the new education building ($88,656) with the remainder given to the Missions and Denominational Relations committees to disburse (60 percent and 40 percent, respectively). The amount committees were authorized to spend without deacon approval was raised when Bill Thompson recommended to fellow deacons that the Missions Committee be allowed to spend up to $5,000 on a particular cause without deacon approval. After deacon discussion, Holly Wiggs offered an amendment to authorize $2,500 spending authority. With the approved amendment, any allocation exceeding $2,500 to a new entity would need deacon approval. The interaction of committees and the deacons was evidence of the ongoing identity of a lay-led church being worked out.[122]

Budget amounts climbed annually. In 2009, the budget was $1,489,076, a 5.6 percent increase over the 2008 budget. Of particular note was the increase of $16,881 to the missions component in order for the total budget to have a minimum of 20 percent allocated to missions. The church bylaws were revised to guarantee that any surplus funds when allocated would include the same percentage for missions that was in the annual budget. The 2012 budget climbed to $1,723,067, a 9.2 percent increase over the 2011 budget; in 2015, the budget was $1,865,751, a 3.7 percent increase over the 2014 total of $1,799,656.[123] Budget surpluses continued to grace the ministry of stewardship ($89,361 in 2008; $121,772 in 2009; $91,066 in 2010). When a much smaller surplus was reported in 2012 from the 2011 budget ($21,665), still, the financial message was "the Church remains in an

[121] N Deacons 6 17 12.

[122] N Deacons 2 17 08; N Deacons 3 30 08; N Deacons 9 21 08.

[123] N Deacons 10 19 08; N Deacons 4 9 09; N Deacons 10 16 11; N Deacons 10 19 14.

enviable financial position." A high surplus returned in 2013: $143,865.62.[124]

Deacons and finance leaders began to express some concern about giving in 2014. The number of church members who were pledging was decreasing annually (and it was acknowledged that older members were more prone to pledge, which was an older standard stewardship method in Baptist churches). In 2010, 74.1 percent of the budget had been pledged; in 2015, the figure was 65.8 percent. In October 2014, deacons learned that the congregation was $109,288.83 behind budget. In December, David Allen, chair of the Finance Committee, wrote to the congregation in the *Northminster News* that an end-of-the-year budget deficit "seemed imminent." This was not a message the church normally heard. The deficit of $7,763 stood in sharp contrast to the surplus of almost $144,000 the previous year.[125]

Budget concerns continued in 2015. While receipts were actually up $35,000 over 2014 at the same time, the deficit was $59,000 higher ($178,000 to $129,000). Consequently, Mike Peters made a motion that the deacons ask committees to cease nonessential expenditures the rest of the year.[126] Fears were allayed, however, when 2016 rolled around and year-end giving—typically the strongest giving period at any church, including Northminster—resulted in a surplus of $97,000. Deacons were pleased to see that expenditures had been carefully managed ($63,701 underspent), coupled with receipts in December that totaled $431,704 ($397,000 was needed to meet the year-end budget), a Northminster record. The congregation had come through—and the deficit in 2014 had probably been a blessing in disguise of sorts—making urgent appeals in light of the historically high deficit in fall 2015 seem necessary and real.[127] In March 2016, the congregation's financial health was reported: $10,156,744 total assets, with unrestricted cash of $499,591 and restricted cash in designated funds of $589,827. The total debt was $1,511,080. Budget planning was based on 430 families/giving units.[128]

---

[124] N Deacons 3 18 12; N Deacons 3 17 13.

[125] N Deacons 10 19 14; N Deacons 11 16 14; N Deacons 12 17 14; N Deacons 2 15 15.

[126] N Deacons 9 20 15.

[127] N Deacons 1 16 16.

[128] N Deacons 3 20 16. The actual figure of 429 families comes from the 2015 Long-Range Planning Report.

The budget for Northminster's fiftieth year was $1,926,807, a 2.4 percent increase over the 2016 budget of $1,880,910. Broad categories included: $341,690 for pastoral ministries, $113,341 for education ministries, $113,070 for music ministries, $444,138 for supportive ministries, $453,842 for building and grounds ministries and $45,000 for contingency. Twenty-five percent—a standard amount in recent years—was set aside for missions: $415,726 (divided among local and direct missions, denominational relations and Wider Net ministries). Church leaders still expressed caution in light of financial scares the previous two years. The number of members pledging continued to decrease, John Purvis, Finance Committee chair, wrote the congregation. He told the deacons that new members, especially the young, needed focused education about the vital importance of stewardship, both pledging and giving, for the financial health of the church and its ministries.[129]

The ministry of stewardship at Northminster was approached with the care expected of a church keen on being faithful stewards of its significant resources. Reminiscent of its earliest history, the church applied seasoned business acumen to managing its financial health. Detailed historical comparisons of pledges, budgets, and collections were a regular feature of planning. Challenges, even for a congregation with more wealth than other congregations its size, were still real when ministry efforts were so extensive. Meticulous business analysis did not stop innovation either. In spring 2017, online giving was planned—a sign of the times and likely a new technological aid to maintain the viability of the pledge card-contribution process in an age of online banking.[130]

Long-range planning was another sign of the efficiency of the business-professional giftedness and orientation at Northminster. It was considered an important part of the church's ongoing visioning process in order to remain a healthy and vibrant congregation. In the past, both the Wider Net Ministries and the Caregivers had developed out of long-range plans. Every five years or so the Committee on Committees appointed a new Long-range Planning Committee to "prayerfully ponder the 'big picture' of the congre-

[129] N Minutes 11 13 16; N News 11 30 16; N Deacons 1 14 17. The Finance Committee planned to have prepared an updated Reserve Study (the first since 2011) to analyze expected future expenditures (N Deacons 6 26 16).

[130] N Deacons 2 19 17.

gation's life together."[131] In 2012, the planning process began that produced the long-range report of 2015. Cheryl Allen was chair of the committee, and Kelley Williams Jr. wrote the report. Baptist leader Bill Wilson of the Center for Congregational Health in Winston-Salem, North Carolina, met with the committee. The Long-range Planning Committee met with the ministerial staff, and in 2014, held three lunches for the congregation to discuss long-range hopes and dreams. The report focused on four themes: worship, fellowship and community, teaching church, missions and outreach.[132]

The study of worship—noted as a distinguishing feature of Northminster—unsurprisingly said "if it ain't broke, don't fix it." The committee wanted people to be greeted for worship but insisted that worship remain reverent and God-centered per the Northminster tradition. To remain a teaching church, another long-standing theme of the congregation's identity, the committee asked, "How can the church's past with its emphasis on theological literacy, be passed on to spiritual heirs?" One recommendation was to consider implementing a pastoral residency program (a two-year program for a recent seminary graduate). The plan sounded reminiscent of the program used during the ministry of John Claypool. The continuing education of church members was also a significant theme, with ideas ranging from designing a "Pre-K to 12" curriculum (what should youth know by the time they graduate from high school) to more in-depth understanding of a theology of missions to support Wider Net and other ministries. Special attention was given to using technology to further ministry goals (e.g., upload sermons online, livestream worship services, email the church newsletter, facilitate online giving, and use the church website to educate and offer members opportunities to be involved in Wider Net ministries).[133]

The report recognized the importance of planning for fellowship and community in light of the changing demographics surrounding the church plant. In 1976, only 7 percent of the congregation's members lived in Madison, Ridgeland, Brandon, Clinton, or beyond. By 1987, the figure had doubled to 14 percent, and by 2012, the increase had reached 37 percent. Northminster's reach had expanded significantly, but community was also

---

[131] N Deacons 2 19 14.
[132] N Deacons 11 17 13; N Deacons 1 10 15.
[133] Long-Range Planning Committee Report, 2015; N Deacons 5 17 15.

being redefined. No doubt, long-range planning was going to continue as a regular practice for the congregation.[134]

Ministry of Ecumenism

In the summer 2008, Amy Joyner and Arthur (Arty) Finkelberg became engaged to be married. That October, Chuck Poole wrote a letter to the deacons because several members of the church had asked for theological assistance to affirm the marriage of a Baptist minister on the church's staff to a member of the Jewish faith. Amy was a beloved staff member, but the situation was admittedly unique, Poole noted. His response built on the church's unique heritage and friendship with Beth Israel:

> Northminster, from its birth forty-one years ago, has been a church where rare and special things could happen. Indeed, while Amy and Arty's marriage is about two people, not two congregations, I would say that it has been a part of Northminster's "DNA" from the beginning that a love like theirs might someday be seen and celebrated. Beth Israel gave us shelter when we were first being born back in the sixties. (I recently heard one of our long-time members proudly say, "We joined the church at Beth Israel.")[135]

Poole affirmed that the congregational friendship between Northminster Baptist Church and Beth Israel could exist because it was built on a theological foundation,

> which recognizes that our Jewish friends are our fellow children of God. As Paul said in Romans 4:16, *"Abraham is the father of us all."* We share with our friends on Old Canton Road, Abraham and Sarah, Solomon and David, Isaiah and Jeremiah, Adam and Eve and the 23rd Psalm. As Paul says in Romans 11:17-24, we Gentiles are the newcomers, the wild branches that have been grafted into a family tree that has Jewish roots.[136]

Poole acknowledged that significant differences exist between Christianity and Judaism; nonetheless, he affirmed the marriage of Joyner and Finkelberg as a union between "two children of God who share a deep rev-

---

[134] Long-Range Planning Committee Report, 2015.
[135] Chuck Poole to the Deacons, October 19, 2008.
[136] Ibid.

erence for the ways of God and a deep love for the people of God" and saw the upcoming wedding as "perhaps a sacred sign of the wide embrace of the love of God."[137]

The wedding ceremony, officiated by Poole and ministerial colleague, Jill Buckley, was a combination of Christian and Jewish elements. The red paraments, given by Beth Israel in the early days of Northminster's history (with the inscription "How good and how pleasant it is for Brothers to dwell together in Unity") were vividly present during the ceremony. One of the Jewish elements, not seen in a Christian ceremony was the "breaking of the glass." The wedding bulletin explained the moment's significance for the couple:

> The breaking of the glass is a custom which is at least fifteen hundred years old. As is true with many sacred gestures and symbols, it has become wrapped in several layers of meaning, one of which is that the broken glass reminds us that even while we are celebrating on this day of joy and gladness, there are others in the world whose hearts are as broken as this shattered glass. Another meaning which is embodied in the breaking of the glass is the solid truth that just as the glass, once broken, is forever changed, so two people, once married, are forever changed and made new.[138]

This unique moment at Northminster brought serious reflection but also laughter. Amy Finkelberg recalled that Arty's best man placed the glass on the floor at the end of the ceremony for Arty to break. But wedding joy erupted, according to Amy, when,

> Arty had practiced the ritual at home (using an extra glass); he was wearing hard-sole shoes, forgetting that his "tuxedo shoes"" had soft soles. So…when Arty stomped on the glass with his "tuxedo shoes" during the ceremony, it did not break! He had to stomp twice, which gave everyone a good laugh, including Arty. We've got a great picture of Arty, me, Chuck (Poole), and Jill (Buckley) "laughing it up" at the front of the sanctuary after Arty finally completed his mission.[139]

---

[137] Ibid.

[138] Amy Finkelberg, email to Barbara Webb, June 21, 2017.

[139] Ibid.

After the wedding (January 17, 2009), Poole said it was one of the "most special spiritual journeys of his life."[140]

To cite ecumenical activity as part of Northminster's identity in the twenty-first century was to state the obvious. From the church's earliest days, interfaith work was done with Beth Israel. Sharing across denominational Christian lines became commonplace in adult, youth and children's ministries and missions. Still, some special, explicit ecumenical activities dotted the church's calendar. Special events at Beth Israel were advertised frequently in the *Northminster News* with invitations for church members to attend. For example, Northminster members were invited to attend a special Jackson Jewish Festival (2011). Youth participated in a worship hour at the synagogue where common biblical texts were examined and participants learned "how we maintain our identity in a pluralistic world" (2015).[141] Northminster also invited the Beth Israel Ensemble to perform at the church.[142]

In 2011, Northminster Baptist Church was invited to join the celebration of the 150th anniversary of Beth Israel. To honor the synagogue's anniversary in the *Northminster News*, Chuck Poole recalled the special relationship between the two communities of faith: "Good and pleasant, right and true, beautiful and holy it is when all the people of God love, honor, celebrate, embrace and welcome one another, as Beth Israel welcomed and embraced us so many years ago; a small act of congregational kindness, but an enormous sign of the true kingdom of God; the one God of Abraham, Isaac, Jacob and Jesus."[143]

The relationship of Beth Israel and Northminster Baptist Church was simply one that Chuck Poole refused to let his congregation forget (not that they would). In August 2014, he preached a sermon titled "Judaism and Christianity," in which he told church members that they must continue to

[140] N News 12 3 08; N Deacons 8 16 09.

[141] N News 1 19 11; N News 11 10 15. Northminster church members were invited to hear Welton Gaddy, progressive Baptist minister from Monroe, Louisiana, and president of the Interfaith Alliance, speak on "Congregations Negotiating the Border Between Religion and Politics" (2009). See N News 3 4 09. See also N News 10 26 11, which advertised a fifteen-week course, Introduction to Judaism, offered by the synagogue.

[142] N Deacons 10 19 14.

[143] N News 9 14 11.

pass along the story of the two churches to their young people. It was that important to their Northminster DNA and it spoke powerfully to the universality of God's hope.

> I know we cannot hang everything on any one single verse of Scripture, but, if that one verse turns out, ultimately, to be true; if Paul's great declaration that God has included all in sin so that God can include all in mercy [Romans 11:32], turns out ultimately and eternally to be true, and if *all* still means what *all* used to mean back home, then you know what that would mean. That would mean that, someday, Beth Israel and Northminster will once again share a room around God; only next time, it won't be temporary.[144]

Adult studies also provided Northminster members continuing education regarding interfaith matters. A four-week study on understanding non-Christian religious traditions included a focus on Judaism (led by Debbie Kassoff, Hebrew Union Congregation, Greenville, Mississippi), Islam (led by Fatih Oscan, Institute for Interfaith Dialogue), and a community interfaith "Panel of American Faiths." The church worked with the Mississippi Religious Leadership Conference, a statewide multiracial organization representing diverse communities, to have the panel.[145]

The congregation participated in a variety of ecumenical mission projects for Habitat for Humanity. In 2010, Amy Joyner Finkelberg reported that the church had contributed in the construction of three "Peace Houses" for Habitat for Humanity and also joined other churches from different faiths in the "Planting Peace Project" where volunteers gathered on four separate workdays to do landscaping for eighteen additional Habitat for Humanity houses. A "festival of faiths" celebrated these cooperative community efforts with a joint observance of the Martin Luther King Jr. national holiday. Youth participated in the day's special parade with youth from Stewpot.[146]

In 2017, the church's financial obligations had many Baptist outlets, especially those of the Metro Baptist Association and the Mississippi Baptist Convention. Since the creation of the Cooperative Baptist Fellowship in

---

[144] Charles Poole, "Judaism and Christianity," August 17, 2014, http://www.northminsterbaptist.org/sermon/judaism-and-christianity/.

[145] N New 3 2 11.

[146] N News 1 5 10.

1990, Baptist church relationships were mostly with Mississippi CBF churches around ministries like Together for Hope in the Delta and the Madison Baptist Fellowship in Jackson, a CBF church start where Poole had preached regularly when Brian Brewer was pastor of Northminster. The congregation's church-to-church relationships (through Wider Net and other local ministries), however, were often with non-Baptist churches and the Jewish synagogue, Beth Israel. Ecumenism was alive and well, front and center.

Baptist Life (and the Mississippi Baptist Convention)

Northminster Baptist Church remained a congregation committed to Baptist principles and Baptist identity. The church was active in Baptist denominational affairs. In 2008, Chuck Poole was a speaker at the national CBF General Assembly in Memphis, Tennessee, and again in 2014 in Atlanta. In 2013, CBF of Mississippi had its annual meeting at Northminster Baptist Church—the church was the largest contributor to the state group. Chuck Poole, Steven Fuller, and Lesley Ratcliff all led sessions at the gathering.[147] The next year Baptist Women in Ministry (an organization that partners with CBF) recognized Northminster for its leadership in affirming both women and men in ministry without restrictions based on gender. Amy Joyner Finkelberg was active in CBF's Spiritual Formation Network Discerning Community. CBF-related activities also dotted the church's calendar.[148] One of the annual winter lecture series (2016), "Religious Liberty in the World Today," was led by Holly Hollman of the Baptist Joint Committee for Religious Liberty. Church member Mark Wiggs, then the liaison officer to the United Nations for the Baptist World Alliance, also led an Adult Series on the state of religious liberty on the international scene.[149]

Northminster had long been active in progressive Baptist life, but at the same time maintained its strong participation in Mississippi Baptist life. While some Baptist state conventions in the South had disfellowshipped churches over issues like women's ordination, the Mississippi Baptist Convention had avoided direct confrontation with churches seemingly out of

---

[147] N Deacons 10 20 13. Northside Baptist Church, Clinton, was the second largest contributor to the Mississippi CBF.

[148] N News 1 20 10; N News 6 27 12; N News 6 11 14.

[149] N News 2 3 16; N Deacons 2 21 16.

step with the larger Southern Baptist rightward direction. Some of Northminster's members had continued to serve as trustees at Baptist colleges (e.g., Jean Williams served on the Board of Trustees of Mississippi College from 1999 to 2015 and the recital hall in the school's Department of Music bears her name, the Jean Pittman Williams Hall).[150]

In 2015–2016, however, rumblings about action against Northminster Baptist Church (as well as Northside Baptist Church in Clinton and University Baptist Church in Hattiesburg) by Mississippi Baptists surfaced. According to deacons' minutes, the accusation was that "Northminster Baptist Church is a church where gay or lesbian people may feel welcome." The charge certainly reflected the current societal and religious culture wars and the angst among Southern Baptists about LGBT inclusion.

In September 2015, Jim Futral, executive director of the MBC Board (MBCB) appeared unannounced at the church, met with Chuck Poole, and expressed concern about information found on some internet websites that indicated that Northminster was a welcoming or inclusive church. Poole noted that he had no knowledge of any information on websites. The congregation had had no role in disseminating information to internet sources, and Futral did not explain how he received his information.[151] Upon hearing the convention's accusation at their October monthly meeting, the deacons discussed the matter and "noted that Northminster was founded as a church that was welcoming to all."[152] The intensity of the situation was real because the MBC Board decided to put a hold on accepting financial contributions from the congregation and were threatening to remove the church from the Mississippi Baptist Convention at its fall meeting in November 2015.[153]

Information listing Northminster Baptist Church as a place friendly to LGBT individuals had evidently been on one church information website since 2013, again unbeknownst to Poole and the congregation until after the saga with MBC leaders was underway. Poole had not preached on the topic of homosexuality, but in November 2014, ten months before Futral visited Poole in September 2015, a pamphlet Poole had written on the topic of homosexuality had been distributed to the congregation and had been post-

---

150 Jean Williams, email to Doug Weaver, November 14, 2016.
151 Chuck Poole, phone interview.
152 N Deacons 10 18 15.
153 N Deacons 10 18 15; N Deacons 4 17 16.

ed on the church's webpage. In November 2015, when Futral returned to the church (two months after his first visit), Poole, in a spirit of transparency, gave him a copy of the pamphlet. According to Poole, neither he nor the church had anything to hide. If Futral was supposed to conduct dialogue with Northminster—the reason given why the congregation was not ousted from the convention in its just completed annual November meeting—then the pamphlet was information that Futral could use.[154] The Mississippi Baptist Convention never indicated it was upset with the church because of the pamphlet, so the pamphlet's actual role in the larger story is unclear (convention officials simply cited websites not connected to the church as the sources for their concerns). Still, the pamphlet offered a window into the careful reflections of Poole's perspective.

In the concise two-page reflection (titled "What Does the Bible Say about Homosexuality?"), Poole noted that he was asked about homosexuality and the Bible four or five times a year. He was a "congenitally conservative" person who was most comfortable not talking about issues of sexuality and had been reluctant to respond to the nudging of the Holy Spirit to speak to the issue. However, he decided to offer a pastoral word. He began,

> Although, if the question is "What does the Bible say about homosexuality?" the answer is not altogether clear; partly because the word "homosexuality" did not exist when the Bible was being written, but, more importantly, because the passages in the Bible which are popularly assumed to be about homosexuality are almost always about something other than an intimate relationship between two people of the same sex.[155]

Poole reminded his readers that the biblical text has to be interpreted and put in historical context. He added,

> There is our own undeniable human experience to be taken into account, and, most importantly, there is the Holy Spirit; the Spirit Jesus said would lead us into all truth. I cannot speak for you, but, as for me,

[154] Chuck Poole, phone interview. In 2017, Poole said that he had only seen material from one of the websites. The website provided a list of LGBT-friendly churches in particular locations and Northminster was listed for Jackson, Mississippi.

[155] Charles Poole, "What Does the Bible Say about Homosexuality," Northminster Baptist Church, n.d.

> when it comes to the subject of homosexuality, I do not know all the truth.... One important truth I have come to believe is that no one chooses their sexual orientation. Rather, all persons, heterosexual and homosexual, discover their sexual orientation. And, one other truth I have come to see is that a person who discovers that they are gay or lesbian is no more or less likely to be a prayerful, spiritual Christian than a person who discovers that they are heterosexual.[156]

Poole concluded his essay by suggesting that the most important biblical verse in the discussion was one that did not even mention sexuality: "Clothe yourselves with compassion, kindness, humility, meekness and patience" (Col 3:12). He asked his congregation to make the verse their "guiding light and governing principle." If convention leaders read the essay, they likely would have dismissed its careful reflections as ambiguous at best, unbiblical at worst.

With no motion made at the 2015 annual fall meeting of the Mississippi Baptist Convention to exclude Northminster Baptist Church from membership, conversation with convention officials continued in subsequent months. The MBCB still refused to accept Northminster financial contributions.[157] The deacons were not aware that the church's contributions were going to continue to be declined after the convention meeting. Unsurprisingly, the deacons were upset by the actions of the convention board and discussed related negative consequences. The convention's financial report, published in February 2016 in Mississippi Baptists' state newspaper, the *Baptist Record*, showed $0.00 contributions from Northminster Baptist Church. To the typical reader, this meant that the congregation had not sent any money to Mississippi Baptists and was not invested in the life of Mississippi Baptists. Northminster, however, clearly considered itself, as the convention's constitution required for member churches, to be "in friendly cooperation with the MBCB," which meant a church that contributed financial resources. A second negative consequence resulted when the local Metro Baptist Association failed to receive their expected financial donations from Northminster because it had not been channeled from the MBCB as it normally was.[158]

---

[156] Ibid.

[157] N Deacons 11 15 15; N Deacons 4 17 16.

[158] N Deacons 4 17 16.

On March 30, 2016, Chuck Poole and Doug Boone, Northminster's chair of the Board of Deacons, met with Jim Futral and the associate director of business services for the MBCB, Barri Shirley. Convention officials said they were unaware of the situation with the association and agreed to send the church's funds immediately. Other contributions, however, were still refused. Futral recommended that Northminster put the contributions in escrow and asked the church to begin sending funds directly to the Metro Baptist Association so that the state convention would not be involved. Poole and Boone kept the chairs of the Denominational Relations Committee, Anne Guidry and Leland Speed, as well as the deacons, in the loop. As the deacons discussed the ongoing tension, they expressed dismay that their donations were not being used for ministry and frustration at the actions of the MBCB: "Why were they holding our money yet taking no further action? What do they want us to do?"[159]

At the April 2016 deacons meeting, while updating deacons about the state convention, Poole affirmed that his and Boone's approach, despite the actions of the MBCB, would remain characteristic of the church's identity: "quick to listen and slow to speak—using careful speech that is reflective of Northminster and listening *for* Northminster." Poole announced to the deacons that he was almost finished writing a reflection piece on the issues of LGBT for the church to read—not to antagonize the convention, but to respond to the Holy Spirit's direction.[160] Poole decided not to release the document, however.

Options regarding the rejected donations to the Mississippi Baptist Convention became clearer in May 2016. The Denominational Relations Committee, with approval from the Finance Committee, recommended, in line with the suggestions of the MBCB, to send contributions directly to the Metro Baptist Association each month and to escrow the remaining money budgeted for the Mississippi Baptist Convention. Consequently, $37,321 was put in escrow.[161] At the June deacons' meeting, the question of the church's status in Mississippi Baptist life dominated the agenda. Poole thought that a resolution might occur during summer 2016 when the execu-

---

[159] Ibid.

[160] Ibid. The brief discussion of Poole's preaching references his focus on careful speech.

[161] N Deacons 5 15 16.

tive board of the MBCB met in August—since Futral and the MBCB did not want to have a crisis at their annual fall meeting. Deacons were concerned that convention officials wanted the church voluntarily to "take a step back from the convention without officially leaving the convention." Such a response might satisfy convention officials and avoid a public crisis, but it would also mean the church ceased to be active in Mississippi Baptist life, something the deacons (or the congregation) had never expressed a desire to do. Deacon Ann Lauman logically asked—given recent Southern Baptist history and actions in other states—if the church could not simply be excluded because of its affirmation of women's ordination (clergy). Poole responded that he had already asked Futral about the church's stance on women in ministry, and the convention leader had said the convention had no intention of enforcing any kind of restriction. The issue was clearly the church's alleged stance on LGBT matters.[162]

The deacons discussed whether to take the initiative to press the MBCB for a resolution, but they decided to wait since it was convention officials that had questioned the church's role in Mississippi Baptist life, not vice versa. Poole and the deacons also discussed the timing of discussing the issue with the entire congregation. Should the congregation be informed of an impending crisis that might not occur? On the other hand, should they be informed so they would not be blindsided if the church was excluded from the convention? Deacons had mixed responses. In subsequent conversations, the Denominational Relations Committee decided to wait to communicate with the congregation until there was specific information to give rather than speculation, but there was ongoing concern about the best time to include the congregation.[163]

In August, Poole wrote a letter to Futral that outlined the church's long involvement in Mississippi Baptist life, traced the recent conversations between the two, and included "a reminder to the convention that Northminster has taken no action to distance itself from Mississippi Baptist life and that we still would be sending our monthly contribution were it not for the MBCB refusing to accept our money—a very important point."[164] The MBCB took no official action to exclude Northminster at its August meet-

[162] N Deacons 6 26 16.

[163] N Deacons 6 26 16; N Deacons 8 21 16.

[164] N Deacons 8 21 16.

ing, but the church learned that it would no longer receive "messenger cards," which was the convention's method of inviting churches to register and participate at convention meetings. Convention officials justified the withdrawal of the cards because Northminster "has been deemed to be presently disengaged with the work of the Convention."[165]

At the September 2016 deacons' meeting, Poole presented a letter to the deacons that he planned to send to the congregation regarding the MBCB crisis. The Denominational Relations Committee had approved the letter, and the deacons then "blessed" the letter. Further delay in communication with the congregation was not feasible since the upcoming 2017 budget was soon to be given to the church—and the escrowed contributions (plus 2017 monies for Baptist causes) were part of the budget configuration.[166] The letter, sent on September 21, 2016, was signed by Chuck Poole, Doug Boone, Anne Guidry, and Leland Speed, and it cautiously explained that the convention had stopped accepting financial contributions from the church because of perceived "theological differences," "details of which we will be glad to share, for those who might wish to know more."[167]

What to do with the escrowed contributions continued to be a matter of great concern to the deacons. The 2016 budget had included $44,000 allotted for the MBCB, and the escrow fund had grown to $53,800. Several deacons voiced the opinion that it was irresponsible to escrow such a substantive amount of money. At the same time, if no future funding was allocated for the convention, the question was asked if that was grounds for exclusion by the MBCB.[168] Subsequently, the Denominational Relations Committee recommended changes to the Baptist contribution component of the 2017 budget. Intended contributions to the Mississippi Baptist Convention were maintained but reduced to $22,000 with the other $22,000 designated for "other Baptist causes."[169] Doug Boone reported to the Board of Deacons at their October meeting that at least two dozen people in the

---

[165] N News 9 18 16.
[166] Ibid.
[167] Charles Poole to Northminster Congregation, September 21, 2016.
[168] N News 9 18 16; N Minutes 11 13 16.
[169] N Deacons 10 16 16; N Minutes 11 13 16.

congregation asked questions about the ongoing saga after receipt of the September 21 letter from the pastor.[170]

It was impossible not to wonder about the future of the relationship between church and convention. To further complicate the issue, the church staff was notified in November 2016 that they were no longer eligible to participate in the retirement program of the Annuity Board (an SBC agency). Annuity Board officials, when questioned, said that the accounting department of the MBCB had told them that Northminster was no longer part of the Mississippi Baptist Convention and thus ineligible. Poole called Futral for clarification and was told that the church was "technically out." Such was not the case, however, since the convention had never officially excluded the church, and Northminster continued its attempt to fully cooperate.[171]

In January 2017, Northminster Baptist Church remarkably again attempted to send its budgeted allotment to Mississippi Baptists; the check was again refused and returned.[172] At the March deacons' meeting, the board voted to keep sending checks to the MBCB (keeping the budgeted allotments of the 2016 budget, not the halved amount earlier recommended for 2017). If the money continued to be rejected, the Denominational Relations Committee recommended that it be given to three Mississippi Baptist-related colleges (Mississippi College, 40 percent; William Carey College, 30 percent; Blue Mountain College, 30 percent). The reallocation idea was not implemented, and the status of contributions remained in limbo. Dudley Wooley suggested that the congregation was not insistent that the relationship with the convention be maintained in such circumstances, and he questioned the deacons as to why the church would continue to send money that was clearly going to be rejected. Poole's response revealed the reason for the church's willingness to be rebuffed again and again: Northminster had a fifty-year relationship with Mississippi Baptists, and they were trying their best to maintain it. The relationship was very important to some members as a "defining relationship."[173]

---

[170] N Deacons 10 16 16.
[171] N Deacons 1 14 17.
[172] N Deacons 2 19 17.
[173] N Deacons 3 19 17.

Mississippi Baptists had clearly been distancing themselves from Northminster without formally excluding the church and making national headlines in Baptist (and other) news outlets. It was the "quiet" Mississippi way, rather than the "go-for-the-jugular" attack approach seen in the 1980s Southern Baptist conflict at the national level (then adopted by various state conservative groups in, for example, North Carolina and Georgia).[174] The church wanted—even begged for—clarity and reconciliation. Chuck Poole wanted to go to a meeting of the MBC Board and simply ask the convention leaders, "Are we in, or are we out?" Deacons hesitated, and preferred, as they understood lay leadership, that if anyone went, a group of laity should go with Poole. On May 1, 2017, the church attempted again to push for action. A letter sent to Futral and MBC Executive Board representative Randy Turner, pastor of First Baptist Church, Laurel, requested that the status of Northminster Baptist Church be put on the board's summer meeting agenda on July 7. When no response came from the convention, Poole called Futral and was told that the church's letter would be read to the executive committee. More occurred, however, than simply having the letter read.

The MBC finally made their position official. A letter received July 24, 2017, from convention officials declared that Northminster Baptist Church was, by unanimous vote of the executive committee of the MBC Board, no longer a member of the Mississippi Baptist Convention.[175] To historians of Baptist life, or close even observers of recent Baptist history, the decision was inevitable; the only surprise was how long it took.

How would the congregation respond? Would it shift more financial allegiances to the Cooperative Baptist Fellowship? Would it attempt to fund isolated Mississippi Baptist agencies or colleges, as some moderate Baptist churches attempted to do (but found too hard to maintain) in the larger SBC conflict of recent decades? Northminster's Baptist identity was secure; its fifty-year relationship with the Mississippi Baptist Convention had finally ended. Year fifty-one at Northminster would reveal new challenges and opportunities for Baptist faith and practice.

---

[174] Paul Pressler, known as one of the architects of the "conservative resurgence" in the SBC, employed the jugular imagery.

[175] Chuck Poole, phone interview.

Conclusion

Poole Two, as the ministry of Chuck Poole might endearingly be called, was not concluding in 2017. With the recent loss of two staff members (Jill Buckley, January 2017; Steven Fuller, December 2016), and search committees underway, the immediate future would have a different look. The church's fiftieth anniversary celebration in May 2017 revealed a church willing to look at its past with reverence, but willing to look forward in hope.

Chapter 10

Northminster at 50
The Fiftieth Anniversary Celebration

Northminster Baptist Church thoroughly planned the celebration of its fiftieth anniversary with numerous events spanning the months preceding the climatic weekend of May 6–7, 2017. Church members were pleased that a bit of "icing on the cake" was the fact that the anniversary would be celebrated—Sunday, May 7—exactly fifty years to the day and date of the congregation's first worship service in 1967.[1]

During the deacons' meeting of May 2016, Chuck Poole addressed the upcoming year-long celebration and offered a few suggestions. "There will be beautiful and joyful remembrances, but it won't just be a stroll down memory lane," Poole said. "We will be thinking about who Northminster is, what the DNA of this place is, what the founding vision was, and how we continue to embody it and live it out in a world that *50* years later is very different—same gospel, same Spirit, same New Testament, same church, but a new and different world. What does that look like today and moving forward?"[2]

With Poole's vision in mind, the congregation had a series of events to remember their heritage while also focusing on the future. The Adult Studies Committee coordinated several evening sessions during October–November 2016 that reviewed the Northminster covenant and specific (favorite) sermons from previous pastors.[3] These sermons included Dudley Wilson's "Crisis at Christmas," led by Kelley Williams Sr.; John Claypool's "Copers, Choosers, and Changers," led by Suzanne Boone; John Thomason's "What Mean These Stones?" led by Mike Peters; Roger Paynter's "What on Earth Should We Do Now?" led by Cathy Davis; Brian Brewer's "A Note of Praise," led by Tim Coker; and Chuck Poole's "A Summing Up," led by Eddie Mahaffey.

---

[1] N Deacons 5 15 16.

[2] N Deacons 5 15 16.

[3] N Deacons 8 17 16; N Deacons 9 28 16.

During the winter months, the Women's Retreat featured Suzii Paynter, executive coordinator of the Cooperative Baptist Fellowship and a former church member and minister's spouse. The retreat topic was "Northminster HERstory," which explored the church's identity through the eyes of women leaders of Northminster's past. The Winter Lecture Series brought back Walter "Buddy" Shurden, favorite son of Mississippi and well-known to the congregation. Shurden's lectures focused on "Five Hundred and Fifty: The Reformation and Northminster." Adult studies continued to provide reflective sessions in spring 2017, which included topics such as "Laying the Foundation," featuring charter members; "Growing Up at Northminster," featuring legacy members, and "Lessons from the Deacons," by former deacon chairs.[4]

At the "Laying the Foundations" session, Jo Ann Ratliff, moderator and co-chair of the Adult Studies Committee, read a letter from Donna (Kennedy) Barksdale who was unable to attend. Barksdale was a Mississippi College student at the time of the church's founding in 1967. Barksdale's letter encapsulated not only her memories of the church, but also much of the narrative of the church that had been preserved over the years:

> I was a college student at the time, and there were powerful forces at work in society. My college years were bracketed by the assassinations of John F. and Robert Kennedy. I had been to Tougaloo to hear Julian Bond and there was powerful resistance in our state to civil rights. None of the Baptist churches in my experience were dealing with these issues. This place dealt with reality head on. It was a big part of the fabric of my belief in Northminster. The core issues of civil liberties and civil rights for all were built in to our church, and in the 60s that was not an assumed or given right.
>
> The lives and work of Mary Hendrick, Jan Purvis, Dot Kitchings and others made indelible imprints on my life in the church. The early influencers at Northminster were women. They played a critical part in vision and leadership. As a young mother, a youth group leader, and a deacon, I found that the underlying principles of justice and responsibility stayed true in every platform of service for every age group.
>
> Moving from the Blind School to our current building caused many of us to worry and speculate that church would become a building and not

[4] N News 1 4 17; N News 2 1 17; N Deacons 2 19 17.

> a community. The community of Northminster was the church. We were somehow pilgrims together when we did not have a place. *Priests to Each Other* by Carlyle Marney was a pivotal book study that influenced us during those days.
>
> The future holds the same issues that were there in the beginning. Supporting a just society and meeting the needs of our community in Jackson, always looking outward, have been continual threads. Thankfully, we continue to be challenged and to make a priority the core values that were there in the 60s.[5]

With only a month to go before the Northminster's golden anniversary celebration, Poole wrote the congregation in the *Northminster News*, summarizing the significance of the upcoming festivities for remembering the past and for being a vehicle to move forward into the future. He explained that the fiftieth year in Scripture was called a year of Jubilee. "Fiftieth is the meaning behind the word 'Pentecost,' making this what one might call the Pentecostal Jubilee Anniversary of our family of faith," Poole said. "Fifty years of seeking to become, more and more, a house and home of hope and grace; the work of the church, never finished or complete; ever seeking, always reaching, for a deeper, wider way. But hopefully, also, always true to the founding vision which first gathered us, and birthed us, on Sunday, May 7, 1967."[6]

The Saturday prior to the weekend celebration of the church's anniversary, *The Clarion-Ledger*, the Jackson newspaper with a statewide circulation, published an essay from its faith columnist Randy Weeks, a longtime Northminster member. In a column titled "Not all those who wander are lost," Weeks wrote about finding Northminster in 1989 while "wandering in a spiritual wilderness." After fifteen years as a full-time church musician, Weeks was looking for a new trajectory for his life, and at Northminster he found a "safe place to heal and to, as Paul wrote in his letter to the Philippians, 'work out my own salvation with fear and trembling.'"

> My journey was just that—my journey. No one could walk that road for me. But I needed the companionship of others who were also on a spiritual quest. I became a part of a nearby fellowship of like-minded peo-

---

[5] Donna Barksdale, Letter Read at "Laying the Foundation" (Charter Members)," church service, March 26, 2017.

[6] N Deacons 4 26 17.

> ple who were known for their honesty, integrity and commitment to living the teachings of Jesus even when the cost was high. They embraced me and gave me the space to do my spiritual work in the ways I needed to. They provided safety, nurture and opportunity for me as I went about the business of seeking truth and meaning again.
>
> Within that fellowship I experienced the freedom to, for the first time in my adult life, be my authentic self. I was given license to explore, question and even fall flat on my face without fear of judgment and desertion. I formed connections with fellow strugglers and we supported each other as we traveled along our unique spiritual paths, unified as a living organism committed to being Jesus' hands and feet in this world. In the context of this gathering of pilgrims, I found my North Star. My focus shifted from looking behind to looking forward. I knew that I would come out of the wilderness and be a better man for having been there.

"These faithful friends were conduits of the divine grace that would not let me sell myself short, but rather challenged me to *risk something big for something good*," concluded Weeks, echoing pastor Roger Paynter's popular benediction which, Sunday after Sunday, offered a grace-filled challenge to the gathered community at the corner of Ridgewood Road and Eastover Drive to not sell themselves short, to take risks to do good and to "remember that the world is now too dangerous for anything but truth."[7] Weeks's testimonial certainly captured the sentiments of many members on the eve of the church's anniversary celebration.

To kick off the anniversary celebration weekend, a panel discussion featuring past pastors was held Saturday afternoon on May 6 in the church sanctuary. With Kelley Williams Sr. as moderator, all living former pastors—Dudley Wilson, John Thomason, Roger Paynter, Brian Brewer—took part in a panel discussion. Wilson was the only pastor not physically present due to health concerns. However, he took part in the conversation via phone. Chuck Poole also attended the session.

The afternoon conversation opened with a moment of silence to remember John Claypool, Northminster's beloved former pastor who passed away in 2005. Jason Coker, coordinator of CBF of Mississippi, read a letter

[7] Randy Weeks, "Not all those who wander are lost," *The Clarion Ledger*, April 29, 2017.

of greetings and gratitude on behalf of the fellowship. "The Cooperative Baptist Fellowship of Mississippi celebrates your consistent, Christ-powered presence in the Jackson metro area and throughout Mississippi," the letter read. "For half a century you've been a prophetic voice in our state, calling all of us to a more just society, structured around the principles of Jesus Christ." The letter continued,

> You've not only been a voice, but you've been a real presence, embodying the best of our Christian faith and living that out from year to year. Through your past and present ministries and missions, you have spread the good news and been the good news to all that truthfully seek a path of promise.
>
> It was some of your members who first gathered to explore the beginnings of what would become the Cooperative Baptist Fellowship. You continue to support through volunteers and generosity to sustain the mission and ministry of CBF in Mississippi, which is in many ways an extension of your voice and presence throughout the state. For all your spiritual gifts in the congregation and for all the ways God uses you in Jackson and across the state and around the world, CBF of Mississippi gives thanks to God for your 50 years of service and presence. We are grateful to be one of your ministry and mission partners, and we look forward to all of the faithful working together for the next 50 years. May the peace of Christ be yours in your celebration.[8]

Dudley Wilson reminisced about his time serving during the founding years of Northminster Baptist Church, noting that the congregation had been "tremendous and virtuous in every way." "I have nothing but praise for them and for the life of the church," he said. When asked to offer advice for Northminster for next fifty years, Wilson urged the church to "keep on." "I'm pleased and amazed what all takes place in the life of the church, in terms of the worship, the service and fellowship—my advice would be to stay on track and keep chugging on."[9]

John Thomason, who succeeded John Claypool as Northminster's third pastor, reflected on the patience and grace the congregation offered him as a

[8] Authors attended the service on May 6, 2017, and have transcripts of the day's activities. Jason Coker to Northminster Baptist Church, May 6, 2017.

[9] Transcription notes, Saturday celebration (May 6, 2017) 4.

young pastor still finding his way. "The plain fact is that both my predecessors and my successors were more experienced than I was," Thomason said.

> One of my great memories of this church is that you accepted me for who I was and did not expect me to be someone else. You were extremely patient. I was uninformed in so many ways as a pastor and as a preacher, as a congregational leader, and as a person. You allowed my formation to continue through your affirmation and encouragement. You may have compared me to other pastors, but you didn't throw that in my face.

"I have felt so supported by this congregation," Thomason continued, who, after leaving Northminster, became a Methodist minister serving appointments in the Northeast. "I will never be able to thank you enough for the love and compassion you showed me, especially at the end of my tenure when I was going through such a difficult time in my personal life, and Northminster once again showed its true colors with your love and compassion."[10] Roger Paynter echoed the words of his predecessor, emphasizing the congregation's desire to be "a different kind of Baptist church." "The thought that I might be a part of that was just an extraordinary privilege," he said.[11]

Paynter added that during his tenure in the early 1990s Northminster had begun to "feel confident and feel good about itself" even in the midst of the Baptist battles raging within the Southern Baptist Convention. Paynter said that the church had largely bucked the trend of other churches in defining its identity in a reactionary way. Instead, Northminster aimed to define itself in terms of who it was and what it was for, rather than what it was against (fundamentalism) and what it was not (fundamentalist).

"The church began to just feel like, this is who we are, and this is the kind of worship we do, we don't apologize for that," Paynter said. "This is how we select our deacons. We don't apologize for that. This is how we honor and respect women's leadership. This is the way we reach out to the poor and needy, we don't apologize for that. There was kind of a very deeply meaningful energy that went on, it seems to me. It was a great time to be here."[12]

---

[10] Ibid., 5.
[11] Ibid., 6.
[12] Ibid., 9.

Brian Brewer, who became Northminster's sixth pastor at the age of thirty-four, shared memories about moving to Jackson just two days after Hurricane Katrina had struck the coasts of Mississippi and Louisiana. Brewer recalled receiving a phone call from a member who advised him to fill his car's tank with gas before crossing into Mississippi. Brewer took the advice and waited an hour in line to get gas. "When we pulled up in the evening, of course there was no power in the city," Brewer remembered.

> Homes were split by trees—this is not new to you. So what I find powerful is that while you all had so many emergency things in your lives, people came to our house to welcome us, to put food in the refrigerator, and make us feel at home during this very difficult time for you. It was strange to start a ministry with an emergency meeting of what to do about Katrina. An Oklahoma boy was of no help along those lines. This was where I got to see what a lay-led church was. The kind of hospitality even from the first day has always stayed with me.[13]

Brewer shared his appreciation for the church's liturgical nature, noting that he wondered while a doctoral student if he would ever find a Baptist church that "appreciated worship and had a liturgical bent to it" where he "could feel at home." "I think I'll be a Baptist but whatever church I go to pastor, it's going to be a very unusual church," Brewer recalled telling his wife, Amy. "I'm just thrilled to have been able to walk along life's way with you for a period because there are very few liturgical Baptist churches like Northminster. There is none where I have felt more at home in."[14]

The afternoon discussion of the four former pastors concluded with a discussion about the much-loved benedictions of each former pastor. Anne Guidry and Amy Williams, talented and artistic church members, designed bronze plaques of the benedictions of all six pastors. The plaques were mounted on the wall at the entrance to the chapel. Emily Benzenhafer presented red stoles, featuring the Northminster logo, to the pastors. The stoles, embroidered and sewn by Benzenhafer and Kay Sullivan, were worn by the pastors during the worship service the following day.[15]

May 7, 2017, marked the fiftieth anniversary of the founding of Northminster Baptist Church. The occasion fell on the fourth Sunday of

---

[13] Ibid., 6.
[14] Ibid., 10.
[15] Ibid., 13.

Eastertide. In the worship bulletin for the historic day, the liturgical significance of this Sunday was explained, offering an informational prelude to the hour of worship:

> The Easter Banner leads us into worship each Sunday during Eastertide; the six Sundays following Easter. The banner bears in gold-color silk the essential symbol of Christianity, the cross in its rays of glory, appropriate to the Easter season. Formerly a symbol of shame, the cross has been transformed into the ultimate symbol of hope and salvation for all mankind. The seasonable color for Easter is white, and the background color of our banner can be interpreted as white fractured into many of pure white's components. The background pattern is the rays of glory of the cross. The banner's pale colors represent the purity and divinity of Christ. The rays leading from the cross remind us of a power that rises above defeat, a power that radiates forth affecting the lives it touches.

Cavett Taff, a Northminster member, designed the Easter banner. While the liturgical color for Eastertide is white, red paraments were used during the May 7 service—the liturgical color for ecclesiastical celebrations. The red paraments were given to Northminster in 1975 by the Beth Israel Congregation. The worship bulletin also featured a reprint of a hymn titled "Now Is the Time of Celebration," written by member Randy Weeks to commemorate Northminster's twenty-fifth anniversary in 1992:

> Now is the time of celebration;
> This is the day of jubilee!
> Let us weave our myriad voices
> In a holy tapestry.
>
> Honor we the sacred memory
> Of the saints who've gone before,
> Laud the gifts of those around us,
> Spirit on us richly poured!
>
> Pilgrims on a great adventure
> More than wanderers are we;
> Fellow strugglers on a journey,
> Seeking truth and liberty.

Praise to God who brought us forward,
Praise to God who makes us free.
Praise to God who now indwells us,
Praise the Holy Trinity!

Following a time of meditation and the prelude—"Fugue in E-Flat (St. Anne)" by Bach—the fiftieth-anniversary worship service of Northminster Baptist Church began with the congregation joyfully singing "This Is the Day the Lord Has Made" as the call to worship. The service continued with the processional Easter Banner to celebrate the Easter season and signify the triumph of Christ's resurrection and power over death. The processional hymn followed with singing of "A Mighty Fortress Is Our God"—one of the best-known hymns of Protestant Reformation leader Martin Luther—with only the choir singing verse three.

Kelley Williams Jr. led the congregation in the litany of praise, which was an adaptation of the Northminster covenant:

> The Lord be with you; And also with you. We covenant with Christ, and with one another: To live together in love, To bear one another's burdens, To remain ever alert to the voice of human need, wherever the cry may be heard. Help us, O Lord to live deeply into our covenant with you and with one another. Help us, O God, to walk in the Spirit and embody your love, within these walls and beyond these walls. Amen.

Williams Jr. offered the invocation:

> Gracious God, as our distant ancestors have for thousands of years and our recent ones have for fifty, we invoke your presence. Be among us. God, we are excited to be here this morning. We are awed by the cloud of witnesses both past and present who surround us. We are humbled by the knowledge that today and every day you are redeeming us, and we are keenly aware, especially today, that the gathered community is of great meaning. So bless our coming, this morning, to this place, in this hour, to worship you.

Following the litany and invocation, Chuck Poole extended greetings to the congregation on this momentous day in the life of Northminster. "Welcome to the worship of God at Northminster," Poole said. "On this beautiful Lord's Day, which is, for the church throughout the world, the fourth Sunday in the sacred season of Eastertide, and which is, for the church at the corner of Ridgewood and Eastover, our fiftieth anniversary—a red-letter day in the life of our church birthed fifty years ago to the day on Sunday, May 7, 1967."

Poole gave thanks to the many visitors in attendance, former members and longtime church friends who traveled from locations near and far to join in the anniversary celebration. "We offer a special word of welcome to our charter members who are with us today," Poole said.

> Those visionary charter members, who launched us all those years ago, some of whom since have moved away, but happily for us, have come back home today. Welcome all from near and far on this Sunday, which in some ways is a special day, but which in other ways is a Sunday like every other because our highest hope for this Lord's Day is also our deepest hope for every Lord's day. That all of us gathered here will find within these walls some of the comfort and courage we need to live the life, which is ours to live, beyond these walls. Welcome all to the worship of God.

The Scripture lessons for the anniversary service were Psalm 23 and Acts 2:42-47, which Poole read to the congregation as they listened intently and reflected in a spirit of reverence. A time of confession and assurance followed. The worship bulletin highlighted that in Leviticus, every fiftieth year was designated as "The year of jubilee"—a year which began every fifty years on the Day of Atonement, a day of confession and repentance. "Let us embrace our Northminster jubilee year, now as the people of God embraced theirs, then; with confession and repentance."

Lesley Ratcliff, associate pastor for children, offered a prayer she had written, which included phrases from the popular benedictions and prayers of all six Northminster pastors and five associate pastors (Nancy Hollomon Peede, Stan Wilson, Tripp Martin, Amy Joyner Finkelberg, and Jill Barnes Buckley). The prayer concluded with Ratcliff leading the congregation in the Lord's Prayer.

"For 50 years you have blessed our coming in, into homes which have hosted worship and Bible study, fellowships and farewells, into the synagogue, into the school for the blind, and into this sanctuary where we have gathered each week to remember your calling on our lives," Ratcliff prayed.

> For fifty years, you have taught us to love and be loved, to be your redemptive people in the world, to care for one another, and to care for others all across our city and our world. As we enter our next fifty years teach us to walk confidently into your future, give us the grace to risk something big for something good, and the strength to rest ourselves in your love. Help our bonds of fellowship to be strengthened in ways that are good for the world.[16]

During the time of intercession and dedication, the congregation sang "Joined Together as One Body" and recited the Doxology. Ratcliff led the congregation in a reading of John 10:1-10 during the time of proclamation of the word, which also included the choral anthem "God of Past, Who by Your Spirit."

This led to the central focus of the anniversary service—the celebration of Holy Communion. "Making our way together to the table of our Lord, waiting on and leaning on one another, bringing our many broken places and promises to the one broken body of Lord, and resting it all one more time in the grace of God, watching the aisle fill with all of these dear and good sisters and brothers from whom we draw so much strength and whom we find so much joy," Poole told the congregation prior to leading the communion litany. He continued,

> Thus, we come again today on this very special first Sunday of the month, as we do on every first Sunday of the month to fill the aisle and watch the line, remembering tenderly all of those who are no longer with us and imagining joyfully all of those who are yet to come. Deeply grateful for a less than perfect but more than wonderful family of faith where every time the table is set, everyone in the room is welcomed and invited to the table of our Lord.[17]

The fiftieth anniversary worship service came to an end with a recessional hymn written for the special occasion by Chuck Poole. The first verse of the hymn titled "Northminster Jubilee" read, "Birthed with hearts and doors wide open; Called to love, serve, think and pray. Birthed with distinctive witness. Which we still embrace today. Birthed by Baptists of hope and

---

[16] Fiftieth anniversary prayer. See appendix.

[17] The authors attended the fiftieth anniversary service. Description of the service is based on their attendance, and use of the day's worship bulletin and a transcript of the service.

courage now we come to jubilee; Still who we were the day we were founded. Still becoming what yet we'll be."[18] After the service, the congregation exited for a dinner on the grounds. Kelley Williams Sr. led a time of remembrance in the packed Great Hall, which was decorated with displays of pictures and newspaper articles from the church's founding. Each former pastor shared memories as did charter members such as John Palmer and Leland Speed. Rousing applause greeted Barbara Webb and the Jeffersons. An open microphone allowed others to share what Northminster Baptist Church meant to them.

[18] The full hymn is in the appendix.

Epilogue

Fifty years ago, when what would become Northminster Baptist Church was being formed, the "Founding Five"—Bob Guyton, Atley Kitchings, John Palmer, Rubel Phillips, and Leland Speed—envisioned a Baptist church unlike the Baptist churches they knew. They wanted something unique. They desired a church, as Phillips later recalled, that was "distinctive, but orthodox; different, but nevertheless Baptist." Over the past half-century, Northminster vigorously embraced three of those four descriptors. The founding congregation declared, accurately, their orthodoxy of basic Christian concepts in order to gain sponsorship from local Baptists, but concentrating on doctrinal statements or equating faithfulness with a creed or confessional statement has never characterized the church.

The Northeast Jackson Baptist Mission was, without a doubt, birthed as a different kind of Baptist church. After all, how many Baptist churches trace their beginnings to an old Jewish synagogue? As a church that welcomed all—people of very diverse viewpoints—and as a church that offered an inclusive space for difficult discussions during the height of a tumultuous and conflict-ridden time in the history of the state of Mississippi, Northminster immediately established itself as unique among Southern Baptist churches in the late 1960s.

Northminster evolved over time from being different to being distinctive. Northminster was not just different from other Baptist churches. Rather, Northminster came to embody and exemplify characteristics that made it truly unique:

> thoroughly liturgical in worship with a focus on reverence for God and characterized by powerful organ-based music and lectionary-based services
>
> connection to the larger Christian church tradition through use of and appreciation for the historic symbols and practices of the Christian faith
>
> strong ecumenical identity, particularly interfaith relationships with Jews and Muslims

inclusive membership that welcomes all attendees to the communion table and recognizes multiple methods of baptismal expression

extensive commitment to mutuality and innovation in social ministry, especially seen in the asset-based community development approach of Wider Net Ministries

excellence in pulpit preaching, a progressive biblical outlook, and adventuresome in theological study

thoroughly egalitarian in ministry with significant ongoing contributions from women and men, adults and youth

particularly strong lay leadership—living out the motto "every member a minister" and visibly exercised in a meticulous committee structure and persistent long-range planning

a deep love for the history and heritage of Northminster—they all become a "child of the church"

Nevertheless, Northminster Baptist Church is and has been Baptist. Being Baptist is in the church's DNA as a former mission sponsored by the local Baptist association and as a longtime generous supporter of countless local, state, national, and global Baptist organizations and mission efforts. While always regarded, as John Thomason described Northminster, as "a melting pot of many Christian traditions," for fifty years Northminster has been deeply rooted in the Baptist tradition.

The Northminster covenant talks about Baptist DNA markers like soul competency and the autonomy of the local church. Even when the Mississippi Baptist Convention no longer wanted them, the congregation desired to maintain the relationship despite its challenges. Northminster has not been "incidentally or accidentally or nominally" Baptist. Northminster has been a Baptist church *and* a distinctively Baptist church.

In an article in the *Northside Sun Magazine* featuring the fiftieth anniversary of Northminster Baptist Church, Chuck Poole reflected on the church's identity as a different kind of Baptist church. "Different does not mean smarter, and different does not mean better. Different just means distinctive.... You see that in the way we worship, in the way we interpret Scripture, in our theology. That's kind of a hallmark of our life together."[1]

What lies ahead for the distinctive Baptist church at the corner of Ridgewood Road and Eastover Drive? For Poole, being the "deepest and best version of who they are" is the hope. "My hope is the church will be its deepest and truest self theologically and liturgically, knowing that being a distinctive church means we are not going to be the place for everyone," he says. Poole sees this as a hope and challenge. Northminster "welcomes all," he said, adding that "not everyone will be attracted to who we are." The challenge is to be "content with that."[2] It is a distinctive vision of incurable hope.

Northminster Baptist Church: Different and distinctive but nevertheless Baptist.

---

[1] "Northminster Baptist Church," *The Northside Sun Magazine* 12/4 (June 2017): 25.

[2] Chuck Poole, phone interview by Doug Weaver, July 31, 2017.

Appendix

Charter Members

William & Annette Banks
Robert Ford Bass
Ross & Betty Bass
Rick Bass
Robert Bass
Elizabeth Bass
Homer & Jane Best
Jimmy Best
Camp Best
Julie Best
Carmen Besterman
Meredith & Liz Bradford
J. W. & Mable Butler
Lynn Camper
Donna Lynn Camper
Trip Camper
Lynton & Peggy Cooper
Kathleen Cooper
Dewitt & Nancy Day
George & Mary Anne Day
Jack & Elizabeth Dean
Linda Dean
Cynthia Dean
Kenneth & Mary Dean
Thomas & Gail Fanning
J. W. & Lynn Fielder
Charles & Rubye Guest
T. E. & Maxine Guillot
Robert & Kathy Guyton
Jim & Mary Hendrick
Rebecca Hendrick
Ann Hendrick
Cynthia Ann Hewitt
Jack & Hilda Holmes
Atley & Betty Jane Kitchings
Marlea Kitchings
John & Dot Kitchings
Taylor Kitchings
Ken Kitchings
W. P. McMullan Jr.
James C. McNees
Fred & Gwen Marshall
Fred Marshall Jr.
Albert & Jackie Meena
Jaime & Mary Ann Miller
Betsy Miller
Ann Miller
Ann Louise Moore
John & Tine Palmer
Robert & Martha Perry
Rubel & Margaret Phillips
Hal Phillips
Bill & Jeannine Pope
James & Leatrica Pridgen
George & Jan Purvis
Julius & Joan Ratliff
Bobbie Jean Sanders
Grady & Marilyn Sandidge
Bill & Sylvia Scott
Hal Scott
Gayden Scott
Trenton & Linda Shelton

Byron & Jamie Speed
Sandra Jane Speed
Leland and Katherine Speed
Lake Chambers Speed
Leland & Bessie Speed
Bobby & Barbara Spell
Guy & Irene Story
Guy Story Jr.
O. B. and Elizabeth Taylor
Kelly & Helen Turner
Hugh & Joe Ann Ward
Henry & Barbara Webb
Ed & Sue Williams
Eddie Williams
Mike Williams
Kelley & Jean Williams
Dudley & Inez Wilson
Cynthia Wilson
O. B. & Easie Wooley
Bo Wooley
John Wooley
Susie Ellen Yates
Lina Yates
Mary Elizabeth Yates
Wirt & Mary Yerger

Church Covenant

The charter members of Northminster Baptist adopted a church covenant on December 10, 1967. Over the past 50 years, this covenant has shaped Northminster's identity and mission and continues to serve as a reminder of the responsibilities of church membership. The church covenant received minor updates over the years. The current version featured below was last revised on July 7, 2008.

Believing that it is in response to the call of Jesus Christ that we have given ourselves to Him as the Lord and Savior of our lives, we publicly acknowledge Him as the Head of the Church and as the true pattern for life and all of life's relationships.

So it is now that we covenant with Him and with one another to live together in love as He has commanded, to feel and to demonstrate genuine concern for one another, to exercise a watchcare over each other as He does with all of us.

Understanding that it is a shared life to which we have been called, and knowing that to live involves happiness and disappointment, success and failure, fulfillment and emptiness, pleasure and suffering, we covenant to share the joys and the sorrows, to bear together the burdens, to pray sensitively for one another, to affirm in the spirit of Christ that we are our brother's and sister's keeper.

Believing that the gathered community is of great meaning, we commit ourselves to participation in the regular assemblies of the church, in its ministries of worship, instruction and service. We intend by the corporate sharing of our lives with God through His Son to build a witness of faith, love, understanding and strength that shall be an eloquent testimony of His presence in the world.

Realizing that it was to the world of human need that our Lord came, that it was for the world of people that He gave Himself and that it is in the world that we find ourselves called to be His servants, we dedicate our lives to ministering in the world, ever alert to the voice of human need wherever the cry may be heard.

Aware that as bearers of His name we personally embrace His Lordship, we shall strive in all of our ways and relationships, in our families, the church and the wider community, to honor and serve Him. We believe in the autonomy of the local church, the soul competency of the individual, the priesthood of all believers, the authority of the Scriptures, religious liberty, and the practice of believer's baptism. Committed to serving, we gladly enter into relationships for mission and ministry with other Baptist churches that share these beliefs and into the larger fellowship of the Christian community as we seek cooperatively to serve Christ in our world.

Sharing a personal commitment to Jesus Christ and a deep concern for the world, and bound by the bonds of love and understanding, we seek to allow the church to be instrumental in accomplishing God's purpose in the world.

Pastor Benedictions

L. Dudley Wilson (1967–1975)
Loving Father,
Thou hast blessed our coming in.
Bless Thou now, we pray Thee,
Our going out. Amen.

John R. Claypool (1976–1981)
Depart now in the fellowship of God the Father
and as you go, remember —
In the Goodness of God
you were born into this world.
By the Grace of God
you have been kept all the day long,
even until this hour;
And by the Love of God,
fully revealed in the face of Jesus,
you are being Redeemed. Amen.

John A. Thomason (1983–1988)
Therefore, since we are surrounded
by so great a cloud of witnesses,
Let us lay aside every weight,
and the sin that does so easily beset us,
And let us run with perseverance
the race that is set before us,
Looking unto Jesus,
the Author and Finisher of our Faith,
Who for the joy that was set before Him,
endured the cross, despising the shame,
And is now seated at the right hand
of the throne of God. Amen

Roger A. Paynter (1989–1996)
May the Lord bless you and keep you.
May the Lord make His face
to shine upon you
and be gracious unto you.
May God give you
Grace not to sell yourself short,
Grace to risk something big
for something good;
Grace to remember that the world is now
too dangerous for anything but truth,
and too small for anything but love.
So may God take your minds
and think through them.
May God take your lips
and speak through them.
May God take your hands
and work through them.
May God take your hearts and set them on fire. Amen.

Brian C. Brewer (2005–2007)
And now unto Him
that is able to keep you from falling
and to present you faultless
Before the presence of His glory
with exceeding joy,
To the only wise God our Savior,
Be glory and majesty,
dominion and power,
Both now and evermore. Amen.

Charles E. Poole (1997–2003; 2007–)
Now go from this place
to all your other places,
Resting yourselves
in the love of God,
Casting your cares

upon the grace of God,
Placing your lives
in the hands of God,
The hands that will hold you
And never let you go. Amen.

Ordinations

Morris K. "Bubba" Thompson Jr.	November 29, 1981
Eugene "Gene" Alonzo Corbin	October 14, 1990
Glenda Jo Smith Hollman	January 5, 1997
Amy Carol Joyner	January 12, 2003
Jill Barnes Buckley	October 14, 2007
Holly Benzenhafer Redford	May 31, 2009
Courtney Elizabeth Allen	July 31, 2011
Kristen Redford Hydinger	October 30, 2016

Fiftieth-Anniversary Prayer

The following is a prayer written by Rev. Lesley Ratcliff, associate pastor for children. Ratcliff offered the prayer during the fiftieth-anniversary celebration worship service on May 7, 2017. The Fiftieth-Anniversary Prayer includes a phrase from the benedictions and prayers of all six Northminster pastors as well as five associate pastors.

Gracious and loving God,

On this day, with these people, we rejoice in Your forgiveness and Your faithfulness, forgiveness of our sin and faithfulness to each of us, and faithfulness for 50 years to this family of faith called Northminster.

Knowing that *we are surrounded by so great a cloud of witnesses,*[1] we remember with gratitude so many who have gone ahead of us to the Other Side, witnesses that are a part of this family of faith, witnesses who have helped to *form us by the deep love of God*[2] and taught us to *practice the presence of Christ.*[3]

For fifty years You *have blessed our coming in,*[4] into homes who have hosted worship and Bible study, fellowships and farewells, into the synagogue, and into the school for the blind, and into this sanctuary where we have gathered each week to remember Your calling on our lives.

For fifty years you have taught us *to love and be loved,*[5] to be your redemptive people in the world, to care for one another, and to care for others all across our city and our world.

As we enter our next fifty years teach us *to walk confidently into your future,*[6] give us the *grace to risk something big for something good,*[7] and the

---

[1] John A. Thomason
[2] Tripp Martin
[3] Stan Wilson
[4] Dudley Wilson
[5] Amy Joyner Finkelberg
[6] Nancy Hollomon-Peede
[7] Roger A. Paynter

strength to *rest ourselves in your love.*[8] Help our *bonds of fellowship to be strengthened in ways that are good for the world.*[9]

And as we come to the table of remembrance prepared here before us, renew our spirits so that we might remember in the breaking of bread and prayer that *we are being redeemed,*[10] redeemed by the *only wise God, our Savior,*[11] and our friend, who taught his friends to pray, saying,

Our father…

[8] Charles E. Poole
[9] Jill Barnes Buckley
[10] John Claypool
[11] Brian Brewer

Northminster Jubilee

Hymn written for the 50th Anniversary
Northminster Baptist Church Jackson, MS

WORDS: Charles Poole, 2016
MUSIC: Rowland H. Prichard, c. 1830

HYFRYDOL
8.7.8.7. D.

Deacon Chairs

1967	Bob Guyton (Steering Committee Chair)
1968	Rubel Phillips
1968–1969	Bob Guyton
1969–1970	Dr. George Purvis
1970–1971	Jack Dean
1971–1972	J. Kelley Williams Sr.
1972–1973	Dr. O. B. Wooley Jr.
1973–1974	Dr. John Kitchings
1974–1975	Lucian Harvey Jr.
1975–1976	Dr. S. H. McDonnieal Jr.
1976–1977	Leland R. Speed
1977–1978	Bill Boone
1978–1979	Dr. George Purvis
1979–1980	Ed Wall
1980–1981	Lucian Harvey Jr.
1981–1982	Bill Boone
1982–1983	Alan Perry
1983–1984	Dick Barnes Sr.
1984–1985	Jan Purvis
1985–1986	Ed Wall
1987	Dr. John Purvis
1988	Dr. Jim Martin
1989	Kane Ditto
1990	John Clark
1991	Ken Toler
1992	Jim Anderson
1993	Lucian Harvey Jr.
1994	Mark Wiggs
1995	David Jones
1996	Bill Lee
1997	Bill Lee
1998	Jim Warren
1999	Bill Boone

2000	Gloria Martin
2001	Kelley Williams Jr.
2002	David Allen
2003	Dudley Wooley
2004	Charles Parrott
2005	Dr. Jim Martin
2006	Stewart Boone
2007	Stewart Boone
2008	Wilson Stribling
2009	J. Kelley Williams Sr.
2010	Paul Smith
2011	Dudley Wooley
2012	Dr. John Purvis
2013	Thomas Elfert
2014	Mike Peters
2015	Jeff Wilson
2016	Doug Boone
2017	Jason Greener

Deacons

These individuals have served as deacons at Northminster Baptist Church (1967–2017)

Cheryl Allen
David Allen
Jim Anderson
Max Arinder,
Donna Barksdale
Barbara Barnes
Dick Barnes Jr.
Dick Barnes Sr.
Barry Barr
Emily Benzenhafer
Homer Best, Jr.
Judy Bigham
Carrie Blount
Philip Blount
Bill Boone
Doug Boone
Stewart Boone
Suzanne Boone
Bob Boteler
Jim Bowles
Smith Boykin
Gregg Caraway
John Clark
Barry Click
Lisa Cobb
Jeanne Wells Cook
Steve Cook
Donna Cox
Bob Crisler
Cathy Davis
Jeff Davis
Jack Dean
Merle Dean
Betsy Ditto
Kane Ditto
Earl Eddins
Bill Edgar
Neva Eklund
Thomas Elfert
Ken Foose
Mary Foose
Shirley Foster
David Foy
Jason Greener
Tom Gregory
Cindy Griffin
Charles Guest
Anne Guidry
Bob Guyton
Jerri Harvey
Lucian Harvey Jr.
Jim Hendrick
Sam Hensley
Annette Hitt
Jo Smith Hollman
David James
Cliff Johnson
Elta Johnston
Richard Joiner
David Jones
Dana Kelly
Marty Kelly
Bob Kirkland
Atley Kitchings
John Kitchings
Ann Lauman
Bill Lee
Donette Lee
Valerie Linn
Eddie Mahaffey
Mike Maples
Gloria Martin
Jim Martin
Jack McDaniel
Nancy McDaniel
S. H. McDonnieal
Howard McMillan
Kurt Metzner
Richard Montague
Bill Nicholas
Katrina Pace
John Palmer Sr.
Guy Parker Jr.
Wayne Parker
Charles Parrott
Alan Perry
Mike Peters
Beth Peterson
Dave Peterson
Margaret Phillips
Rubel Phillips
Josh Poole
Hunter Pratt
Susan Pratt
Jann Puckett
Gayla Purvis

George Purvis
Jan Purvis
John Purvis
Percy Quinn
Julius Ratliff
Ken Redford
Kitty Rushing
Beverly Schaffer
Gorman Schaffer
Linda Shelton
Trenton Shelton
Joe Sims
Dennis Smith
George Smith
J. George Smith
Paul Smith
Suzanne Smith
Victor Smith
Jim Sones
Leland R. Speed
Sue Spitchley
Roger Stribling Jr.
Wilson Stribling
Nancy Studdard
Jonathan Sweat
Cavett Taff
Philip Taff
Dot Taylor
Zach Taylor Jr.
Suzan Thames
Bill Thompson
John Tingle
Ken Toler
Woody Toler
Tom Turner
Harry Vickery
Will Walker
Ed Wall
Jim Warren
Steve Watson
John Weems
Lisa White
Christopher Wiggs
Holly Wiggs
Mark Wiggs
Rebecca Wiggs
Amy Williams
Jean Williams
Kelley Williams Jr.
Kelley Williams Sr.
M'lee Williams
Jan McDonnieal
Wilson
Jeff Wilson
Becky Wooley
Dudley Wooley
John Wooley
O. B. Wooley Jr.
Wirt Yerger

Standing Committees

Adopt-A-School
Adult Ministries
Baptism/Communion
Barbara Oliver Funds
Building Maintenance Supervision
Building Utilization
Caregiving
Children's Ministries
Columbarium
Deacon Nominating
Denominational Relations
Fellowship
Finance/Stewardship
Flower
Greeter
History
Insurance
Landscaping and Grounds
Library
Long-range Planning
Missions
Nominating
Personnel
Pulpit Supply
Senior Adult Ministries
Special Gifts
Technology
Usher
Vacation Bible School
Weddings/Funerals/Special Ceremonies
Wider Net Ministries
Worship and Music
Youth Ministries

Other Lay Leadership

Board of Deacons

Committee on Committees is responsible for annually designating the chairs and members of the standing committees.

Education Leaders

The following members have served the congregation in education leadership roles in the first fifty years of Northminster Baptist Church (1967–2017). Barbara Webb, who compiled the list, notes that more than 250 additional members (not named below) have served Northminster on a limited basis in education roles during these years.

Adult Sunday School

Diann Arinder, Emily Benzenhafer, Gregg Caraway, Lida Caraway, Wilbur Carpenter, Doug Caver, Larry Clark, Steve Cook, Luke Dove, Mary Foose, Tommy James, Elta Johnston, Marty Kelly, Dot Kitchings, Donette Lee, Jud Lee, David McNair, Gloria Martin, Mary Mitchell, Bill Nichols, Guy Parker, Judy Parker, Mike Peters, Margaret Phillips, Rubel Phillips, Jan Purvis, David Raddan, Joan Ratliff, J. George Smith, Mary Elizabeth Smith, Leland R. Speed, Victor Smith, Lynda Street, Dot Taylor, Bill Thompson, Ray Thompson, Woody Toler, Tom Turner, Henry Tyler, Harry Victery, Kelley Williams, Jr., Kelley Williams, Sr.

Youth Sunday School

Jane Best, Sam Cox, Monica Daniels, Neva Eklund, Anne Guidry, Cathy Jones, Eddie Mahaffey, Karen Overstreet, Charlotte Robinson, Linda Shelton, Roger Stribling, Wilson Stribling, Suzan Thames, Steve Watson, Rebecca Wiggs, Kelley Williams, Jr., Jeff Wilson.

Elementary Sunday School

Jane Best, Lee Boyd, Mable Butler, Nena Carmody, Don Clark, Patty Clark, Jeanne Cook, Betsy Ditto, Betty Brown Edgar, Naomi Freeman, Jerri Harvey, Jann James, Cathy Jones, Richard Montague, Katrina Pace, Bill Scott, Sylvia Scott, Virginia Shackelford, Julia Sherwood, Joe Sims, Becky Starling, Barbara Stribling, Jennifer Stribling, Wilson Stribling, Nancy Studdard, Sandra Toler, Mark Wiggs, Jean Williams, Cindy Wilson, Becky Wooley, Easie Wooley.

Preschool and Nursery

Mary Jo Bickerstaff, Suzanne Boone, Cathy Bowles, Robin Browning, Hilda Calhoun, Blakely Fender, Ruth Ellen Harris, Annette Hitt, James Hitt, Jann James, Elta Johnston, Lisa Kelly, Lisa Lloyd, Patricia McClure, Lawana McLennan, Dan Ellen Maples, Megan Mayhan, Noni Montague, Tine Palmer, Marcia Poole, Jeannine Pope, Bessie Speed, Deanie Stogner, Carol Taff, Sally Thompson, Jeanie Welch, Ron Welch, Mark Wiggs, Susie Ellen Yates.

Sunday Evening and Wednesday Evening Leaders

Jim Barfield, Justin Beard, Rebecca Black, Carrie Blount, Philip Blount, Crisler Boone, Smith Boykin, Bryan Bridges, Christine Bridges, Gregg Caraway, Nena Carmody, Buck Cox, Bob Crisler, Misti Crisler, Brooks Elfert, Ron Fender, Shirley Foster, Robin Harvey, Andrew Lake, Meg Lake, Mary McCall McArthur, Will McArthur, Maria Madden, Barrie Mahaffey, Eddie Mahaffey, Dan Ellen Maples, Dabbs Massey, Megan Mayhan, Caroline Sims, Joe Sims, Kandy Sims, Dennis Smith, Sally Thompson, Woody Toler, Maret Watson, Christopher Wiggs, Holly Wiggs, Jean Williams, M'lee Williams, Becky Wooley, Julie Wooley, Hart Wylie.

**Northminster members included in this list are those individuals most frequently listed in the church's annual Education Leadership document*

About the Authors

Dr. Doug Weaver has been at Baylor University since 2003 and is a tenured full professor in the Department of Religion. He is a member of the department's Historical Studies area, and his current research and teaching focus on Baptist history and Pentecostalism. He also serves as the director of the J. M. Dawson Institute of Church-State Studies at Baylor. In recent publications, Dr. Weaver offered a survey of Baptist history as a search for the New Testament church, examined the work of twentieth-century Baptist leader E. Y. Mullins, and studied the importance of freedom of conscience and ecclesiology in Baptist life. He is working on a book about Baptists and the Holy Spirit (and interactions with the Holiness-Pentecostal tradition).

Dr. Weaver and his wife, Pat, are native Virginians. The Weavers have two children (Aaron and Andrea, both Baylor graduates) and four grandchildren (Camden James, James Oliver, Maci Brooke, and Miriam Grace). Dr. Weaver is a lifelong fan of the New York Yankees. His Baylor office is known for its collection of New York Yankees and Christian history bobblehead figures. The Weavers are members of Calvary Baptist Church, Waco, Texas.

Dr. Aaron Weaver has served as communications director of the Cooperative Baptist Fellowship in Atlanta, Georgia, since 2013, where he is the editor of *fellowship!* magazine and oversees media strategies and digital and print communications. He received his PhD in Religion and Politics and MA in Church-State Studies from Baylor University, where he focused on faith-based advocacy and religion and the First Amendment. His dissertation examined the environmental ethics and political advocacy of Southern Baptists and American Baptists over the past fifty years.

Dr. Weaver is the author of *James M. Dunn and Soul Freedom* (Smyth & Helwys Publishing, 2011) and the editor of *CBF at 25: Stories of the Cooperative Baptist Fellowship* (Nurturing Faith Publishing, 2016) and *A Baptist Vision of Religious Liberty and Faithful Politics: The Writings of James M. Dunn* (Smyth & Helwys Publishing, 2018). He is also the author of numerous journal articles as well as a regular contributor to popular digital publications and news outlets including Baptist News Global, Patheos, EthicsDaily.com, and Christian Ethics Today among others. He is a past board member of the Baptist History & Heritage Society and serves on the Commission on Creation Care and the Commission on Baptist Heritage and Identity of the Baptist World Alliance. Dr. Weaver and his wife, Alexis, have two children, Oliver (age 6) and Miriam (age 3). They reside in Tucker, Georgia, where they are members of Smoke Rise Baptist Church.

Index